Andrew V. McLaglen

ALSO BY STEPHEN B. ARMSTRONG

*Pictures About Extremes: The Films of
John Frankenheimer* (McFarland, 2008)

Andrew V. McLaglen

The Life and Hollywood Career

Stephen B. Armstrong

McFarland & Company, Inc., Publishers
Jefferson, North Carolina, and London

LIBRARY OF CONGRESS CATALOGUING-IN-PUBLICATION DATA

Armstrong, Stephen B.
Andrew V. McLaglen : the life and
Hollywood career / Stephen B. Armstrong.
    p.   cm.

Includes bibliographical references and index.

ISBN 978-0-7864-4977-4
softcover : 50# alkaline paper

1. McLaglen, Andrew V. (Andrew Victor), 1920–
2. Motion picture producers and directors — United States — Biography.
3. Television producers and directors — United States — Biography.
4. Theatrical producers and directors — United States — Biography.
I. Title.
PN1998.3.M39775A86   2011   791.4302'32092 — dc23   [B]   2011021771

BRITISH LIBRARY CATALOGUING DATA ARE AVAILABLE

© 2011 Stephen B. Armstrong. All rights reserved

*No part of this book may be reproduced or transmitted in any form
or by any means, electronic or mechanical, including photocopying
or recording, or by any information storage and retrieval system,
without permission in writing from the publisher.*

Front cover: Andrew V. McLaglen, 1967 (Harold Hecht/United
Artists/Kobal Collection); background © 2011 Shutterstock

Manufactured in the United States of America

*McFarland & Company, Inc., Publishers
Box 611, Jefferson, North Carolina 28640
www.mcfarlandpub.com*

For Katie

Acknowledgments

Thanks to the following people for their support and counsel: Andrew V. McLaglen, Brian Garfield, Joseph McBride, James D'Arc, Wheeler Winston Dixon, Ed Faulkner, Harry Carey, Jr., Merritt Olsen, Dorian Oliver, Susan Williams, Cynthia Church, Ellen Wilcox, Dianne Hirning, Sue Bennett, Janeene Cowley, Robert Powell, Adam Walderman, Doug Fowler, Jane and Jay Hudiburg, Janet and Mike Oliveri, Katie Armstrong, Dean and Mimi Armstrong.

Contents

Acknowledgments	vi
Preface	1
Chronology	3
ONE: A Biography	5
TWO: Early Motion Picture Production Experience	29
THREE: The Fifties	69
FOUR: The Sixties	128
FIVE: The Seventies	193
SIX: The Eighties	224
Appendix I: Appearances in Documentaries	245
Appendix II: Stage Productions	248
Chapter Notes	251
Bibliography	261
Index	265

Preface

Standing 6'7", Andrew V. McLaglen may be one of the tallest people ever to have worked in motion picture production, and his list of credits, like his height, is prodigious. As an assistant director during the forties and fifties, McLaglen learned the craft of filmmaking on the sets of pictures like Allan Dwan's *Sands of Iwo Jima* (1950), John Ford's *The Quiet Man* (1952) and William A. Wellman's *The High and the Mighty* (1954). In 1955, he became a director himself and went on to helm 29 features before retiring in 1989.

Among the best known of McLaglen's movies, arguably, are the Westerns he made with John Wayne: *McLintock!* (1963), *The Undefeated* (1969), *Chisum* (1970) and *Cahill, United States Marshal* (1973). "Big A," as friends call him, directed several well-remembered non–Westerns, too, including *Shenandoah* (1965), with James Stewart, *The Devil's Brigade* (1968), with William Holden and *The Wild Geese* (1978), with Richard Harris, Roger Moore and Richard Burton.[1] McLaglen enjoyed tremendous success in television, too. Under contract at CBS from the mid-fifties to the mid-sixties, he directed for hit shows like *Perry Mason*, *Rawhide* and *The Lineup*, and holds the distinction for having helmed the most episodes of both *Gunsmoke* (95) and *Have Gun, Will Travel* (116), perhaps the best of the TV Westerns.

Surprisingly, the academic establishment has largely overlooked this popular and prolific director's work and his undeniable contribution to the history of the Western. Aside from a 32-page monograph titled *John Ford and Andrew V. McLaglen*, which British scholar Michael Burrows published in 1970, no substantive analysis of McLaglen's output as a director has been written. Thus *Andrew V. McLaglen: The Life and Hollywood Career* is the first book of its sort.

The book opens with a biographical section that surveys the events and circumstances that contributed to McLaglen's development as a filmmaker, in particular his relationships with figures like Wayne, Ford, Wellman and McLaglen's father, the actor Victor McLaglen. This section also considers McLaglen's years in television, his experience working in Hollywood during the final years of the studio system and his subsequent experience as a director of independent, multinational productions.

The next section, an extensively annotated filmography, examines every feature film McLaglen directed. Citations include information about running times, alternate titles, production companies, production crews, casts, excerpts from previously published reviews, theatrical release dates, ratings and availability. (Unless noted otherwise, I've provided the dates of the films' releases in the United States.) Every listing also includes a plot summary and additional commentary about each film's production history and its technical, thematic and stylistic characteristics. Readers will also find citations for every television production McLaglen directed, as well as the numerous features he worked on prior to becoming a director. All names are spelled as they appear in credits.

In the appendices, I have included another filmography, albeit a brief one, that surveys the numerous documentaries in which McLaglen has appeared and a list of the stage plays McLaglen has directed since his retirement from filmmaking in 1989.

Chronology

1920: Andrew Victor McLaglen is born to Victor and Enid McLaglen on July 28 in the Wandsworth Common section of London.

1924: An emerging movie actor, Victor McLaglen relocates to Los Angeles, leaving his family behind in London.

1926: Enid McLaglen sets sail for the United States with Andrew and his younger sister, Sheila. The reunited family takes up residence in West Los Angeles.

1931: The McLaglens move to Fairhaven, an estate in La Cañada, California.

1936: Victor McLaglen wins Academy Award for his role in John Ford's *The Informer*.

1938: Andrew graduates from high school.

1939–1940: Andrew attends The University of Virginia for two semesters before dropping out. After returning to his parents' home, he is summoned by the local draft board for a physical. Because of his great height he is given a 4-F classification, which prevents him from serving in the military.

1940–1945: Andrew works for the Lockheed Corporation, a defense contractor.

1941: Andrew becomes an American citizen.

1942: Enid McLaglen dies from cancer.

1943: Andrew appears in David O. Selznick's production of *Since You Went Away*. Marries first wife, Peggy Harrison. First child, Sharon, born in 1944.

1945: Appears in *Paris-Underground*. Quits job at Lockheed. Is hired by Republic Pictures as a company clerk, a job he keeps over the next two years. Works with John Wayne for the first time on a picture called *Dakota*. Other productions include *Love, Honor and Goodbye*, *Apache Rose* and *Angel and the Badman*.

1946: Marries his second wife, Veda Ann Borg. The pair will have a son together, Andrew, in 1954.

1947–1948: Becomes a second assistant director at Republic, but is laid off a short time later and returns to Lockheed.

1949: Called back by Republic to work on *Sands of Iwo Jima* as a second assistant.

1949–1953: As a freelancing assistant director, works on productions for Monogram, Allied Artists and Republic, most notably John Ford's *The Quiet Man*.

1953–1956: Signs on as a contract employee with John Wayne's independent production company Wayne-Fellows, which subsequently has its name changed to Batjac. Among his credits in this period are John Farrow's *Hondo* and William A. Wellman's *The High and the Mighty*.

1955: Directs his first feature film, *Man in the Vault*, which is released a year later.

1956: Directs his second feature, *Gun the Man Down*. Signs a five-year contract with CBS Television.

1956–1965: Directs more than 200 television programs for shows that include *Gunsmoke, Have Gun, Will Travel, Perry Mason* and *Rawhide*.

1957: Directs *The Abductors,* in which his father Victor McLaglen has a starring part. Marries third wife, Sally Pierce.

1959: Victor McLaglen dies. Andrew's third child, Josh, is born.

1960: Andrew's fourth child, Mary, is born. Directs *Freckles*.

1961: *The Little Shepherd of Kingdom Come*.

1963: *McLintock!*

1965: *Shenandoah*.

1966: *The Rare Breed*.

1967: *Monkeys, Go Home! The Way West*.

1968: *The Ballad of Josie. The Devil's Brigade. Bandolero! Hellfighters*.

1969: *The Undefeated*.

1970: *Chisum*.

1971: *One More Train to Rob. Fools' Parade. something big*.

1973: *Cahill, United States Marshal*.

1973–1974: Returns to television, contributing episodes to *The NBC Mystery Movie* series.

1975: *Log of the Black Pearl. Stowaway to the Moon. Mitchell*.

1976: *The Last Hard Men. Banjo Hackett*.

1977: *Murder at the World Series*. Moves to Friday Harbor, Washington.

1978: *The Wild Geese*.

1980: *ffolkes*.

1981: *Breakthrough. The Sea Wolves*.

1982: *The Blue & the Gray. The Shadow Riders*.

1984: *Sahara*.

1985: *The Dirty Dozen: Next Mission*.

1986: *On Wings of Eagles*.

1987: Marries Sheila Greenan.

1989: *Return from the River Kwai*.

1991: *Eye of the Widow*.

1992–present: Stage director for the San Juan Community Theatre in Friday Harbor, Washington; productions include *Shenandoah, Death of a Salesman* and *Rumors*.

ONE

A Biography

Andrew V. McLaglen lives in Friday Harbor, a tiny port town on San Juan Island, an hour's ferry ride off the coast of Washington State.[1] His house sits away from the island's shoreline amidst pastures and forest, with a view of a small lake and trees where bald eagles can often be seen perching. Inside McLaglen's house, his home since 1977, visitors will find dozens of trophies and artifacts the director has collected over the course of his career.[2] Photographs of McLaglen at work with actors like John Wayne, James Stewart and Clint Eastwood hang from every wall. Posters from some of his best remembered films—*Shenandoah, The Undefeated* and *The Wild Geese*—decorate a guest room. A den is stuffed with DVD and VHS copies of movies and TV shows he's worked on, and bound copies of old scripts fill the bookshelves in his living room. A gold statuette occupies a shelf in a corner of the living room, as well—the Oscar his screen actor father Victor McLaglen won in 1936 for playing the lead in John Ford's *The Informer* (1935).

Though McLaglen has spent most of his life in the United States, he was born July 28, 1920 in Wandsworth Common, London. His parents, Enid and Victor, had married the previous year, after Victor returned to England following the end of the Great War.[3] Over the course of the twenties, Victor would establish himself as a major motion picture star and move his family to Los Angeles, but at the time of Andrew's birth, he was not yet an actor. Rather, Victor was a heavyweight prizefighter, an occupation he'd pursued with some success for over a decade. In 1920, however, at the age of 33, Victor no longer enjoyed fighting as he had, and after a match in October that year, when he was badly beaten by an opponent, he decided to retire. "I was vividly conscious of my changed attitude to the fighting game," he recalled in his 1933 memoir *Express to Hollywood*. "There was a decided dizziness in my head and a catch in my voice and I realised that I had taken off the gloves for the last time."

That same October night, fortuitously, the boxer was approached by I.B. Davidson, "one of the leading men in the British film industry." Davidson asked Victor if he might be interested in appearing in a movie that was about to go into production, *The Call of the Road* (1920). Though he had no experience as an actor, Victor accepted the offer. He subsequently impressed Davidson with his performance and the producer presented him with a contract. More pictures followed and by 1924 Victor had appeared "in about twenty British films." But a downturn in the production of movies made in London later that year forced the actor to take a job in the United States, and he left Enid, Andrew and a second child, a daughter named Sheila, behind in Britain.[4] The family would not be reunited until 1926. "[My father] got called over to Hollywood, and a year and a half later my mother brought my sister and me to this country. I was about five and a half years old," Andrew told C. Cortney Joyner.[5]

McLaglen on the set of his third feature film, *The Abductors* (Twentieth Century–Fox, 1957), with his father Victor McLaglen.

Victor McLaglen became a popular star in the States, thanks to starring roles in pictures like Tod Browning's *The Unholy Three* (1925), Raoul Walsh's *What Price Glory?* (1927) and John Ford's *The Black Watch* (1929).[6] At first, the McLaglens lived in rented bungalows in Hollywood and Santa Monica, but thanks to Victor's rising fortunes, they were able to buy a home in Beverly Hills, and then, in 1931, a mansion in La Cañada, twenty miles to the north of Los Angeles.[7] Victor named the house in La Cañada "Fairhaven" and stocked the forest that surrounded it with kangaroos, deer and peacocks. The property, which sat on 200,000 acres of land, also "featured a built-in show ring [for horses] and marble gymnasium," where the actor exercised.[8] Victor pushed his young son to be athletic during these years, as well, teaching him, in particular, how to play tennis and box.[9]

At the age of 14, Victor McLaglen had dropped out of school to fight in the Boer War in South Africa.[10] He nevertheless wanted his own children to be formally educated and sent them to elite private schools in southern California. During grade school and junior high, Andrew attended Black Fox Military Institute and Carl Curtis School in Los Angeles, and for high school, he attended Cates School in Carpinteria, a coastal town an hour-and-a-half north of Los Angeles.[11] It was during his years as a student at Cates that Andrew became interested in motion picture production. On weekends and over school breaks, he would return to his parents' home and accompany his father to the sets of films when Victor was working, an opportunity that allowed the teenager to talk to, watch and study the actors and technicians who made these pictures. One of these people, importantly, was John Ford, the director of three features Victor starred in during this period, *The Lost Patrol* (1934), *The Informer* and *Wee Willie Winkie* (1937).[12]

Watching professional filmmakers at work eventually prompted Andrew to write and shoot his own pictures when he found himself back at school. "I never wanted to act," he told Hollywood columnist Hazel Flynn in 1963. "I've always wanted to direct. When I was 15 I [started] directing sixteen mm movies with pals as performers at Cate."[13] Victor McLaglen regarded his son's interest in filmmaking with some ambivalence, however. "Dad never encouraged me to go into the picture business," Andrew told entertainment writer Bob Thomas in 1967. "He didn't discourage me, either. He told me, 'It's up to you: get into movies or don't. But you're on your own if you do.'"[14]

Andrew finished high school in the spring of 1938. Because his grades were not the best, he decided to attend the Cumnock School, a preparatory school in Los Angeles, to re-take some courses in order to improve his chances of getting into college.[15] Prior to the start of the fall term, he again spent his free time visiting motion picture sets. On the day Andrew graduated from Cates, for instance, he drove up from Carpinteria to Lone Pine, California, to watch his father, along with Cary Grant and Douglas Fairbanks, Jr., appear in George Stevens's *Gunga Din* (1939).[16]

Following his year at Cumnock, Andrew was admitted to The University of Virginia, which he chose in part because of the excellence of its boxing team.[17] He tried out successfully for the team and went on to fight in the heavyweight class.[18] One of the people with whom McLaglen became friends at the university was Robert Aldrich, who, like McLaglen, would become a successful Hollywood director, scoring several hits in the sixties with pictures like *What Ever Happened to Baby Jane?* (1962) and *The Dirty Dozen* (1967). Aldrich asked McLaglen to pledge his fraternity, but the freshman didn't follow up on the invitation. He wasn't happy living on the East Coast. "I was only there one year. The truth of it is, I was sort of in love with a girl from Stanford and I asked my parents if I had to stay in college. They said I didn't, so I came home."[19]

Upon his return to California in the summer of 1940, McLaglen began to look for a job. His situation came to the attention of Robert Gross, the chairman of the board at the Lockheed Corporation, a defense contractor that manufactured military aircraft. Gross was a friend of McLaglen's parents. "When I quit

Andrew V. McLaglen (left), his father Victor (center) and sister Sheila (right) at their home in La Cañada, California, in 1939 (International News).

college, Mr. Gross said to my mother, 'Do you think Andrew would like to go to work at Lockheed?'"[20] McLaglen was interested, but before he could start, he was called up for his physical by the United States's Selective Service System, which had been created that year to oversee a national draft.[21] To his surprise and chagrin, McLaglen was told that he wouldn't be able to serve in the military because he was too tall. He recalled to Wheeler Winston Dixon: "I stood on a scale during the induction physical and the little guy who was taking my height had a stool he had to stand on.... I was six feet seven. That's where I got my nickname, Big A, which stuck from that point on.... [T]he little guy didn't know what to do. I'll always remember that he didn't say a word. He just got down and took a little yellow pad, and he wrote '4F.'" [22] Though he and his father appealed the decision, Andrew was unable to cut through the bureaucratic obstacles that faced him. He then went to work at Lockheed as an expeditor, a job that entailed "overseeing the production of corrugated wings of P38s in the plant's production department."[23]

The hours were long at Lockheed, especially after the United States entered World War II in 1941, but McLaglen still managed to have a social life. Among the friends he had during the war were John Ford's children, Patrick and Barbara. Sometimes when McLaglen was visiting the Fords at their home, he would see their famous father. "I remember one of the rules [Ford] had.... [W]hen you enter his house, you don't talk about the film business."[24] During this period, McLaglen married a woman named Peggy Harrison. In March 1943, the two announced their engagement and two months later they married. A year after that, McLaglen's first child, a daughter named Sharon, was born. The couple's marriage was unsuccessful, however, and Peggy and McLaglen divorced in the summer of 1945.[25]

McLaglen kept his job at Lockheed throughout the war, but on two occasions he took time off to appear in motion pictures. The first of these was *Since You Went Away* (1944), a David O. Selznick production starring Claudette Colbert, Joseph Cotten, Jennifer Jones and Shirley Temple. For his one and only scene in this movie, McLaglen played a hulking soldier who dances briefly with Jennifer Jones. "I did it as a favor for someone who wanted a man my size," McLaglen explained to a publicist in 1966. For his second screen role, he played a stranded aviator in Gregory Ratoff's wartime thriller *Paris-Underground* (1945).[26]

These experiences on the set revived McLaglen's desire to work in pictures, which had been largely dormant since high school. Hankering to be a director rather than an actor, he wrote a letter to Herbert J. Yates, the president of Republic Pictures, and asked for a job.[27] Yates agreed to hire McLaglen, giving him a position as a production clerk on *Love, Honor and Goodbye* (1945), a domestic comedy starring Virginia Bruce, Edward Ashley, Veda Ann Borg and his father Victor. McLaglen's duties on the film were menial, but he liked them. "I had to make the call-sheet and check up on the weather to see if it was okay to ... shoot."[28] During shooting, Andrew and Veda Ann Borg became acquainted and in the spring of 1946, they married. The two would eventually have a child together in 1954, a son named Andrew, before divorcing in 1958.[29]

Once filming on *Love, Honor and Goodbye* was complete, McLaglen was assigned to another movie, *Dakota* (1945), a Western starring John Wayne. Shot in the summer of 1945, *Dakota* marked the first of more than a dozen pictures he and Wayne would work on together over the next three decades.[30] Following *Dakota,* McLaglen remained at Republic for two more years as a clerk. Among the productions he contributed to were several "singing cowboy" pictures, which provided him with the opportunity to work with stars like Roy Rogers and Gene Autry. "Gene Autry was my friend," McLaglen recalled in 2009." "I'd help him when he was singing a song. He'd be singing a verse and then, while he was singing ... I was telling him what the words were."[31]

The stars of *Since You Went Away* (1944). From left to right: Joseph Cotten, Jennifer Jones, Shirley Temple, Claudette Colbert.

In the spring of 1946, McLaglen was assigned to another Western with John Wayne, serving as a clerk on *Angel and the Badman* (1947), which was written and directed by James Edward Grant. He only worked on the production for a couple of days, however, becoming involved when the picture's cast and crew returned to Republic's studio to shoot some interior scenes, following several weeks of filming in Monument Valley.[32] Toward the end of that year, McLaglen felt confident enough to approach Republic's president Herb Yates about moving up from production clerk to second assistant director, a job that entailed greater responsibility and more pay. "Every morning, Herbert Yates would drive in his big limousine, get out and walk along this long path to go into his office. I hid in the bushes one morning and met him halfway.... I said, 'Mr. Yates, I really feel like I'm ready to become a second assistant.' [H]e said, 'Oh, I remember you, son. I'll look into it.' And that was it, believe it or not. I became a second assistant."[33]

As a second assistant, McLaglen continued to prepare call sheets and monitor shooting schedules, as well as make sure principals and extras were on the set when and where they needed to be. Shortly after landing this position, though, he was laid off from Republic, the result of a studio policy that gave preference to employees who had served in World War II, especially those who had been with the studio before they enlisted or were drafted. Forced to find new employment, McLaglen returned briefly to Lockheed and resumed his position as an expeditor. But then in the spring of 1949, a contact in Republic's production office called him about a job as a second assistant director on *Sands of Iwo Jima* (1950), a big-budget war film which Allan Dwan had agreed to direct and in which John Wayne was to star. McLaglen decided to take the job and resign from Lockheed, a risky decision, given that he could not count on Republic to give him more work later.[34]

Shooting on *Sands of Iwo Jima* commenced that July and finished in August.[35] Fortunately for McLaglen, he managed afterward to secure a follow-up assignment at Republic, landing a job as a first assistant director on a picture called *Rock Island Trail* (1950). He didn't wait around for Republic to offer him another assignment once *Rock Island Trail* wrapped. Instead, he went over to Monogram Pictures and signed on as first assistant for a low-budget feature called *Killer Shark* (1950), which Oscar "Budd" Boetticher had been signed to direct. During the production of *Killer Shark,* Boetticher showed McLaglen a script he'd written about some experiences he'd had as a bullfighter in Mexico years earlier. McLaglen subsequently passed the script onto James Edward Grant, with whom he'd worked on *Angel and the Badman* in 1946. Grant, in turn, showed it to John Wayne. Herb Fagen explains that "Grant liked the script and set up a meeting with Wayne. Wayne then arranged for Herb Yates at Republic to finance the film."[36] Wayne went on to produce *Bullfighter and the Lady* (1951), as the movie came to be titled, and Boetticher directed, with McLaglen serving as his assistant director.[37]

The next picture McLaglen worked on, John Ford's comic drama *The Quiet Man,* was produced for Republic, as well. McLaglen had received a call from the studio's production office about the opportunity in the spring of 1951. Ford's brother-in-law, Wingate Smith, was

John Wayne leads the charge in *Sands of Iwo Jima* (Republic, 1950).

scheduled to be the picture's first assistant director, but if McLaglen wanted to come on as a second assistant, the job was his. The chance to work under Ford made the decision an easy one. "I didn't think twice about it," McLaglen recalled.[38] Production on *The Quiet Man* commenced in June 1951, with John Wayne, Maureen O'Hara and Victor McLaglen cast as the picture's principals.[39] Much of the picture was shot on location in Ireland, in and around a village called Cong. The cast and crew stayed in the nearby Ashford Castle Hotel, "a concrete tower with no heat, no windows, no elevators, and no telephones," where McLaglen roomed with Wingate Smith.[40] Smith liked McLaglen and recognized that the younger man was eager to gain as much experience on the production as he could. "[He] just sat back and let me take over all the duties on the set, as if I were actually the first assistant," McLaglen recalled.[41]

McLaglen's responsibilities on *The Quiet Man* included helping the leads prepare for their scenes, which entailed frequent consultation with Ford. In 2009, he recalled, "There's a funny story I remember about *The Quiet Man*. For one of the first scenes that we shot, the scene when Wayne pulls Maureen through the fields, we were using a golf course that was just outside the hotel where we were staying. It looked like we had a bunch of sheep out there. I went over to Ford and said, 'Do you think we ought to clean up that sheep dung before Duke pulls Maureen through it?' 'No,' he says, 'leave it!'"[42]

McLaglen continued to freelance after *The Quiet Man*, heading back to Monogram to be an assistant director on two low budget pictures, *Wild Stallion* (1952) and *Here Come the Marines* (1952). Following this, he landed another job as an assistant director on an independent production called *Hellgate* (1952). Written and directed by Charles Marquis Warren, *Hellgate* featured Sterling Hayden as a veterinarian who is sentenced to a federal prison after he provides medical assistance to a terrorist. James Arness also appeared in the movie, playing one of Hayden's cellmates. A rising actor at that point in his career, Arness would achieve fame later in the decade playing the role of Marshal Matt Dillon on CBS Television's hit series *Gunsmoke*, a show on which McLaglen would eventually work as a director.[43]

Following *Hellgate*, Arness and McLaglen paired up again on *Big Jim McLain* (1952), a political thriller starring John Wayne about federal investigators who break up a Communist spy ring in Hawaii. The film was the first feature made by Wayne-Fellows, an independent production company Wayne had created with his friend Robert Fellows in the spring of 1952.[44] McLaglen worked on the picture as an assistant director. When *Big Jim McLain* was released in September of that year, it opened to hostile reviews from critics who regarded the film as jingoistic and simpleminded. *Big Jim McLain* nevertheless "was a solid hit" and yielded a profit.[45] Pleased with his contributions to the film, as well as his earlier work on *The Quiet Man* and *Bullfighter and the Lady*, Wayne subsequently offered McLaglen a permanent job with Wayne-Fellows, which the younger man accepted.[46]

McLaglen was then assigned to work as an assistant director on Wayne-Fellows's next production, a crime thriller called *Plunder of the Sun* (1953), which was shot in Mexico, with John Farrow directing.[47] Wayne co-produced the picture, but he didn't appear in it. Instead, Glenn Ford played the lead, a suave adventurer who searches through Aztec ruins for treasure. On Wayne-Fellows's next production, *Island in the Sky* (1953), McLaglen took up the role of first assistant director again. An action-adventure picture with Wayne in the lead, *Island in the Sky* follows a group of airmen who crash their plane in a snowy stretch of northern Canada. The film was helmed by veteran director William A. Wellman. A pilot himself who'd flown for the U.S. Army in World War I, Wellman was obsessed with aviation, and it was a subject he'd taken on in many of his previous films, including *Young Eagles* (1930), *Central Airport* (1933), *Thunderbirds* (1942) and, most notably, *Wings* (1927), the first movie to ever win an Academy Award in the Best Picture category.[48]

***The Quiet Man*'s three principals, John Wayne, Victor McLaglen and Maureen O'Hara (Republic, 1952). Andrew V. McLaglen worked on the picture as John Ford's second assistant director.**

The next picture produced for Wayne-Fellows was *Hondo* (1954). Directed by John Farrow, *Hondo* was filmed in Camargo, Mexico.⁴⁹ McLaglen served as *Hondo*'s unit production manager, overseeing the picture's budget throughout its month-long shoot in the summer of 1953.⁵⁰ Scripted by James Edward Grant from a Louis L'Amour story, *Hondo* follows an Army scout who falls in love with a female rancher. Wayne starred as the titular hero. Other players included Geraldine Page, Ward Bond, Michael Pate and James Arness.

Following *Hondo*, McLaglen worked beside William A. Wellman as an assistant director on four pictures over the next two years. The first of these was *The High and the Mighty* (1954), another air disaster film starring Wayne, which follows the efforts of pilots and crewmembers who try to keep a passenger plane in flight over the ocean after one of its engines blows. The film proved to be an enormous hit upon its release in January 1954. Wayne's biographers Randy Roberts and James Stuart Olson report that *The High and the Mighty* "earned more than $8.5 million in domestic and foreign rentals, and Wayne-Fellows ... put only $1.456 million into the production."⁵¹

McLaglen next helped Wellman on *Ring of Fear* (1954), a mystery picture set in a circus. Wellman took over the film's direction midway through shooting, replacing the picture's original director, James Edward Grant. In his memoir *A Short Time for Insanity,* Wellman explains that "[Grant's work] was not good so Duke and his then-partner, Bob Fellows, asked me to help them out and do a little doctoring on it. I didn't get paid and didn't get credit. That was agreeable to all, so I got me a couple of writers and went to work."[52] McLaglen, who served as Wellman's first assistant, worked on the film without credit, as well.[53]

Following this, McLaglen was assigned to Wellman's *Track of the Cat* (1954), an adaptation of a Walter van Tilburg Clark novel about three brothers—played in the film by Robert Mitchum, William Hopper and Tab Hunter—who hunt for a panther in the forest that surrounds their cattle ranch. In 1943, Wellman had brought another Clark novel, *The Ox-Bow Incident*, to the screen with some success—the film was nominated for an Academy Award in the Best Picture category.[54] But *Track of the Cat* failed to generate interest when it was released. As *Variety* noted, "The performances are very good in realizing on the demands of direction and the story characters. Had these people been less unpleasant characters audiences would warm up more to the show, but as it is, there's little to keep them engrossed."[55]

Track of the Cat was the last picture to be produced and released under the Wayne-Fellows banner. Early in 1954, Fellows had announced to Wayne that he needed to sell off his share in the company. Wellman explained to Michael Munn, "Robert Fellows got involved with one of his secretaries and he told his wife Eleanor that he wanted to leave her.... Fellows decided he need to liquidate his assets because of the impending divorce, and he asked Duke to buy him out, and Duke obliged."[56] Wayne liked being a producer, though, and after promising "a payout to Fellows that would evolve over a period of several years ... [he] lost no time in reforming his production company after Fellows left." Wayne christened the new company Batjac Productions, a reference to a trading company that figures in the plot of *Wake of the Red Witch*, a 1948 Republic production in which Wayne had played the lead.[57] Though Wayne and Fellows were no longer partners, the two remained friends, and Fellows served as an uncredited producer on the first picture made for Batjac, William A. Wellman's *Blood Alley* (1955).[58] He also worked briefly on the subsequent *Seven Men from Now* (1956), which Budd Boetticher directed, before severing professional ties with Wayne permanently.[59]

Blood Alley—a story about an American merchant marine who ferries a band of refugees from Red China to Hong Kong—marked the final time McLaglen worked on a picture as an assistant director and his final outing with Wellman.[60] Eager to become a director himself, McLaglen had begun to look in earnest for a picture to develop while he was still working on *Blood Alley*. His friend Robert Morrison, John Wayne's younger brother, wanted to make a picture, too, and they decided to work together as partners. "[Bob] and I found a script we both liked. Duke knew that I wanted to direct, so he said, 'Listen, if you can put this together I'll guarantee the loan from the bank.'"[61] The screenplay McLaglen and Morrison picked was called *Man in the Vault*, a crime thriller scripted by Burt Kennedy.

Though Wayne signed for the loan, *Man in the Vault* was not a Batjac release. Rather, it was an independent production, with Morrison and McLaglen sharing producing duties. The picture was shot in April 1955 over ten days on locations throughout Los Angeles. Among its cast were several people McLaglen had worked with previously, including actors Anita Ekberg, Mike Mazurki and Paul Fix from *Blood Alley* and William Campbell and Karen Sharpe, who had had big roles in *The High and the Mighty*. McLaglen and Morrison secured a deal with RKO to distribute their film and when it was released in December 1956, it turned a profit. As McLaglen told Joyner, "Duke got all his money back, and then some."[62]

McLaglen was eager to follow up on *Man in the Vault*. Pairing up again with Bob Morrison, he found another script from Burt Kennedy that he liked, a Western called *Seven Men from Now*. As McLaglen told Wheeler Winston Dixon, "I thought to myself, 'That's one that I'm going to direct, too.' Well, for some reason, Bob Fellows got Budd Boetticher to direct, with Morrison and I as the producers.... This was a script that Bob Morrison and I developed with Burt, and not being able to direct it was really a blow. So, we ended up producing it."[63]

McLaglen's frustration over losing *Seven Men from Now* to Boetticher prompted him to think about leaving Batjac.[64] But the disappointment was somewhat mitigated when he and Bob Morrison were able to arrange a financing deal through the company for another cowboy picture they wanted to make called *Gun the Man Down* (1956). For the lead in this picture, McLaglen signed his friend Jim Arness, who had just completed his first year as Marshal Dillon on *Gunsmoke*. *Gun the Man Down* was shot in late spring 1956, in fact, while *Gunsmoke* was on hiatus.[65] Arness enjoyed working with McLaglen and when he returned to CBS to resume work on *Gunsmoke* later that summer, he convinced the show's producers to give McLaglen a chance to direct a pair of episodes for the series.[66]

In 1956, episodes of *Gunsmoke* had 30-minute running times and the shooting schedule for each program was swift. Arness in his autobiography explains, "Our weekly program was shot in three days after a half day of rehearsal."[67] McLaglen handled himself well and brought the two shows he was given in on time, eventually prompting CBS to offer him a five-year contract.[68] McLaglen went on to shoot 20 episodes of *Gunsmoke* over the course of his first season on the show. There would have been more, perhaps, but in December of that year he was asked to direct the pilot episode for another Western series CBS had developed, *Have Gun, Will Travel*, with Richard Boone in the lead as a genteel gunman who hires himself out to people in need. The network was confident *Have Gun, Will Travel* would be a hit and before the first program was broadcast in September 1957, several additional episodes were shot. McLaglen helmed them all, contributing a total of 26 episodes for the first season.[69]

McLaglen's ability to turn in high quality programs on time and within budget made him a favorite at CBS and he worked constantly. "They kept me pretty busy; I was doing about thirty-nine shows a year. That's a lot, especially when you have to prepare them and cast them."[70] Among the other TV Westerns he made during these years were *Rawhide* and *Hotel de Paree;* he also shot episodes of *Perry Mason,* the popular courtroom drama series, and *The Lineup,* a police show. "It was a great training ground for me. We kept a very strict schedule. Nothing was left out. We always had total coverage of every scene — close ups, cross shoulders and so forth. You weren't able to leave those out, otherwise they wouldn't hire you."[71]

Despite his commitments to CBS, McLaglen continued to direct motion pictures whenever he found time in his schedule, among them *The Abductors* (1957), *Freckles* (1960) and *The Little Shepherd of Kingdom Come* (1961). *The Abductors* was significant for McLaglen because one of the picture's leads was his father Victor McLaglen. Based on a true story, the film follows a criminal gang that attempts to exhume the corpse of Abraham Lincoln and hold it for ransom. McLaglen's father played one of the film's leads. The experience was positive for both men. "When I was a second assistant," McLaglen recalled "my father used to kid me about making first assistant director before he died. It was a great pleasure to be fortunate enough to direct him before he died."[72] Victor McLaglen passed away in November 1959.[73] After completing *The Abductors,* incidentally, McLaglen married his third wife, Sally Pierce. She and Andrew would have two children together, Josh (born in 1959) and Mary (born in 1960).[74]

During his years at CBS, McLaglen helmed more than 200 television productions, directing hundreds of actors, including such notables as Angie Dickinson, Charles Bronson, Burt Reynolds and Clint Eastwood. He worked repeatedly with several popular supporting actors, too, whom he later cast in his own films, including Denver Pyle, Roy Barcroft, Rayford Barnes, Strother Martin, George Kennedy, Ed Faulkner, and Harry Carey, Jr.

1. Biography 15

William Campbell, the lead in *Man in the Vault* (RKO, 1956), McLaglen's first feature film.

Impressed by McLaglen's TV work, John Wayne approached the director in 1962 about shooting a Western comedy called *McLintock!* (1963) for his Batjac company. The film was to be produced by Wayne's son, Michael, with a cast that included Maureen O'Hara, Wayne's co-star in *The Quiet Man*. "Duke thought it was about time that I be able to direct him," McLaglen recalled, "and that's how I got my first big movie."[75] Scripted by James Edward Grant, *McLintock!* depicts a wealthy rancher's efforts to subdue his estranged and headstrong wife. Among the picture's cast were Wayne's friends—Bruce Cabot, Chuck Roberson and Hank Worden—as well as several actors McLaglen had been working with at CBS—Hal Needham, Strother Martin and Ed Faulkner. The movie commenced shooting in Arizona in November 1962, making use of locations in Nogales, Tucson, Old Tucson and Tombstone. Despite cold temperatures, filming on *McLintock!* proceeded without much trouble, though an unexpected visit to the shoot from John Ford briefly caused a stir.[76]

Ford's motives for crashing the production are not particularly clear. It seems, perhaps, that he may have been interested in encroaching on McLaglen's role as the picture's director. Cinematographer William H. Clothier explained to Michael Munn, "Andy McLaglen was directing and doing a fine job.... [T]here was Chill Wills and Bruce Cabot, and even Duke's old friend from college, Bob Steele, had a small role—it was like a Ford-family film. Maybe that's why he decided to turn up. Maybe he felt left out. He pushed Andy out of the way, walked up to me, and said, 'Okay Bill, let's go to work.'" Wayne stood up to the bullying director, though. "This was Duke's production, and ... he wasn't going to let Ford take over."[77]

McLintock! went on to do well at the box office when Warner Bros. released it in November 1963, earning $10 million.[78]

Once his work on *McLintock!* was done, McLaglen returned to CBS to shoot new episodes for *Gunsmoke* and *Have Gun, Will Travel.* He was eager to make another feature, but no new projects materialized at first. Then McLaglen received a call from the actor James Stewart. "I was still riding out the last year of my contract with CBS in '63, and ... right out of the blue, Jimmy Stewart called me.... He said, 'Listen, the script that I've got here from Universal called 'Seals of Honor' by a fellow named James Lee Barrett ... I'd really like you to direct it.'"[79] Stewart and McLaglen were casual acquaintances. Both belonged to the Bel Air Country Club and had played golf together, but they'd never talked about collaborating on a picture.[80] "I couldn't believe what I was hearing. I said to Jimmy, 'What made you think of me? Did you see *McLintock!?*" Stewart was not aware of *McLintock!* Rather, he'd been impressed — much as Wayne had been — by Big A's work on *Gunsmoke.*[81]

Production on the film — which eventually had its title changed to *Shenandoah* (1965) — started in the summer of 1964, in Oregon's Mohawk Valley, outside Eugene.[82] Set in the final months of the Civil War, the movie relates the story of a Virginian planter named Charlie Anderson (Stewart) who opposes slavery on moral grounds and refuses to let his sons fight for the Confederate army. After Anderson's youngest son is mistakenly captured by Union soldiers and sent to a prison camp, the farmer and his family are forced to take up arms. When *Shenandoah* premiered in July 1965, the picture enjoyed critical and commercial success, yielding $14 million at the box office, making it Universal's highest grossing picture that year.[83]

Chester Goode (Dennis Weaver) and Marshal Dillon (James Arness) protecting Dodge City in the popular *Gunsmoke* television series (CBS).

Understandably pleased with McLaglen's work on *Shenandoah,* Universal offered him the opportunity to shoot a follow-up picture with Stewart called *The Rare Breed* (1966), a Western about a cattle drover and a British businesswoman who fall in love as they transport a Hereford bull across the United States. Joining Stewart in the film was Maureen O'Hara, the female lead from *McLintock!* In addition to star power, *The Rare Breed* was visually impressive, thanks to cinematographer William H. Clothier's footage of some of California's most scenic landscapes, areas like Indio and Sonora, where much of the picture was filmed.[84] The film's beauty and the strength of its narrative drew favorable notices and generated decent returns at the box office upon its release in July 1966, giving McLaglen his third hit picture in a row. Altogether, *McLintock!, Shenandoah* and *The Rare Breed* "grossed a total of $35 million on a combined budget of $10 million."[85]

McLaglen's success on these films led to more offers to direct other features, allowing him to make a complete break from television in 1965. The first picture he directed following *The Rare Breed* was for Disney, a comedy called *Monkeys, Go Home!* (1967) As the Disney film was shooting, Universal again approached McLaglen and signed him to a multi-picture non-exclusive contract.[86] Before he could do anything for Universal, however, he went to work on *The Way West* (1967) for independent producer Harold Hecht. Financed in part by United Artists, *The Way West* featured three of the entertainment industry's most bankable names—Kirk Douglas, Robert Mitchum and Richard Widmark. Filming commenced in July 1966, again in the Bend, Oregon, area.[87] Among the other actors in the cast were Sally Field and McLoglen's daughter, Sharon, who at the time was engaged to one of Mclaglen's assistant directors, David Zinnemann—the son of director Fred Zinnemann.[88]

The Way West presented McLaglen with numerous challenges. The bulk of the picture was shot on Mount Bachelor outside Bend, with a large, ensemble cast of principals and hundreds of extras.[89] "It was an enormous and complicated production, and for McLaglen and his crew as much a feat of engineering as of cinematic craft. Rivers had to be forded, wagons had to be raised and lowered from the tops of cliffs by antiquated means."[90] The picture also experienced difficulties during post-production, after the chiefs at United Artists told McLaglen, producer Harold Hecht and supervising editor Otho Lovering to remove large chunks of material from the film in order to shorten its running time. In 2009, McLaglen recalled: "The [head] of United Artists [Arthur Krim] called me up and he said, 'I beg of you to cut the first 22 minutes off of *The Way West*.' I said, 'What? I mean, how can you possibly do that? That's where I introduce my characters.' 'Well, we've just released a picture with Heston [*Khartoum*, 1966]. It was too long and we had to recut it and it cost us a lot of money'.... I had to go back and re-cut the picture with Harold Hecht. I went and started chipping away at it. It definitely hurt the bloody picture."[91]

Despite William H. Clothier's sterling photography and strong performances from Mitchum, Douglas and Widmark, *The Way West* floundered at the box office when United Artists released it May 1967, marking McLaglen's first commercial disappointment as a director.[92] The problems he experienced with *The Way West* both before and after the film's release fortunately left him unscathed professionally and he remained busy. In 1967 alone McLaglen directed three major pictures. The first of these was a comic Western for Universal called *The Ballad of Josie* (1968), which featured Doris Day as a sheep rancher. The second was *The Devil's Brigade* (1968), a United Artists release starring William Holden as a World War II–era officer who leads a group of unruly soldiers. And the third was *Bandolero!* (1968), a hardboiled Western for Twentieth Century–Fox in which James Stewart and Dean Martin played the leads.

McLaglen stayed busy in 1968, as well, making two pictures with John Wayne. The first of these was *Hellfighters* (1969) for Universal, with Wayne playing the head of a company that puts out oil well fires around the world. Ostensibly an action film, *Hellfighters* also gives generous screen time to the private lives of its heroes, a tendency that prompted many critics to respond to the movie with scorn. The review that ran in *Time,* for instance, asked, "When he isn't hellfighting, [John Wayne] puzzles out all sorts of complicated personal relationships: Will he get back together with his wife? Will daughter find true happiness with Her Man? Will the womenfolk ever resign themselves to their menfolk's dangerous pursuits?"[93] McLaglen

John Wayne inflicts some pain on Big John Hamilton in McLaglen's comic Western *McLintock!* (United Artists, 1963).

himself was not happy with the film. "I didn't like the movie that much," he said in 2009. "I didn't think the script was that great."[94]

McLaglen's next picture was another actioner with Wayne, a Twentieth Century–Fox production called *The Undefeated* (1969). Set in the months following the Civil War, the film tells the story of a Union officer and a Confederate officer who aid one another when they face a shared enemy in Mexico. For Wayne's co-star, Fox signed Rock Hudson. Roberts and

Olson explain that the studio had "wanted to team up ... Wayne and Rock Hudson for the first time, and to get Duke to sign, they gave him a lucrative contract and complete control of the film." One of the conditions Wayne insisted on was that McLaglen would direct the picture. Filming began early in 1969 in Durango, Mexico, and later the production moved to Baton Rouge, Louisiana, where footage of Rock Hudson's character's plantation home was shot.[95] When Fox released *The Undefeated* in October that year, the pairing of two of the decade's most popular actors helped to bring audiences into the theatres, and the picture was a commercial hit.[96]

McLaglen followed up on *The Undefeated* with *Chisum* (1970), another Batjac Western with Wayne playing the lead. Also shot in Durango, *Chisum* dramatizes the Lincoln County War, a violent land dispute fought by ranchers and their hirelings in New Mexico in the 1870s.[97] When Warner released the picture in June 1970, it received favorable notices. Howard Thompson at *The New York Times*, for example, declared: "A large, sprawling cast, trotting at the heels of Wayne, performs vigorously. And under the direction of Andrew V. McLaglen, it looks as Western as all get-out. It may ramble but it does move."[98] *Chisum* went on to yield in excess of $12 million at the box office.[99]

McLaglen returned to Universal for his next film, *One More Train to Rob* (1971), a comic Western starring George Peppard. Following this, he developed and co-produced a film called *Fools' Parade* (1971) with James Lee Barrett, who'd scripted three earlier pictures for the director: *Shenandoah, Bandolero!* and *The Undefeated*. Adapted from a novel by Davis Grubb, *Fools' Parade* tells the story of three ex-convicts who are menaced by an obsessive prison official during the Great Depression. McLaglen and Barrett signed James Stewart to play the film's lead, an eccentric, one-eyed, reformed murderer, and Strother Martin and Kurt Russell as his ne'er-do-well friends. Shooting commenced in September 1970 in Moundsville, West Virginia, making great use of this coal mining area's scenic mountains and railroad.[100] *Fools' Parade* stalled at the box office, however, when Columbia released the picture in August 1971. As Stewart's biographer Roy Pickard notes, "Many critics liked the picture, but the public didn't. It flopped."[101]

After production wrapped on *Fools' Parade*, McLaglen and James Lee Barrett went to work on another film, a Western comedy called *"something big"* (1971), which featured Dean Martin in the lead. The pair secured a deal with National General Pictures to distribute the picture, and in February 1971, they headed down once again to Durango to start shooting.[102] On the verge of bankruptcy when the film had its release in November 1971, National General Pictures was unable to distribute *"something big"* adequately and the movie did not make an impression at the box office. "They went broke and *'something big'* got lost in the shuffle," McLaglen said in 2010.[103]

McLaglen's next picture, *Cahill, United States Marshal* (1973), was filmed in Durango, too.[104] His fifth — and final — feature with Wayne, *Cahill* was another Batjac production, with Wayne's son Michael again handling producer's duties. Harry Julian Fink, who'd penned several television scripts for McLaglen at CBS, co-wrote the screenplay, which centers on a lawman whose sons participate in a bank robbery. Released in the summer of 1973, *Cahill, United States Marshal* struggled at the box office, yielding "just $4 million in rentals."[105] While lukewarm reviews probably contributed to the picture's disappointing performance, it should also be noted that by the early seventies, the public's appetite for Westerns had begun to wane, a troubling development for a director like McLaglen, who'd spent so much of his career working in the genre.

Whatever the case, following *Cahill* McLaglen found himself without a new film project to pursue for the first time since *McLintock!* Needing work, he decided in the fall of 1973 to

John Wayne chats with Pamela McMyler in *Chisum* (Warner, 1970). Among the film's admirers was Richard Nixon.

return to television to shoot a pair of episodes for *Banacek,* one of the rotating programs featured on NBC's popular "umbrella" series, *Sunday Mystery Movie.*[106] George Peppard, who'd starred in *One More Train to Rob,* played *Banacek*'s titular lead, a Boston private investigator who finds lost items of great value for insurance companies. McLaglen also contributed shows to two other series featured on *Mystery Movie: Amy Prentiss,* a police procedural starring Jessica Walter, and a cowboy-themed program called *Hec Ramsey,* which featured Richard Boone as a lawman in the Old West. Boone and McLaglen had gotten along well when they'd worked together on *Have Gun, Will Travel* more than a decade earlier, but the actor showed little interest in being friendly to McLaglen on the set of *Hec Ramsey.* The director explained to Boone's biographer David Rothel, "As well as I knew him when I did the *Hec Ramsey* show, he was almost like a stranger to me. We just didn't seem to have much to talk about…. I think Richard was pretty well into the bottle by that time. It was just like he was some other guy."[107]

More offers to work in television followed for McLaglen, and over the next two years, he helmed a pilot for NBC, *The Log of the Black Pearl* (1975) and an original telefeature for CBS, *Stowaway to the Moon* (1975). Though he turned out first-rate work on these productions, he still preferred making movies to television, and in November 1974, he signed with an independent group called Essex Enterprises to direct *Mitchell* (1975), a low budget thriller about

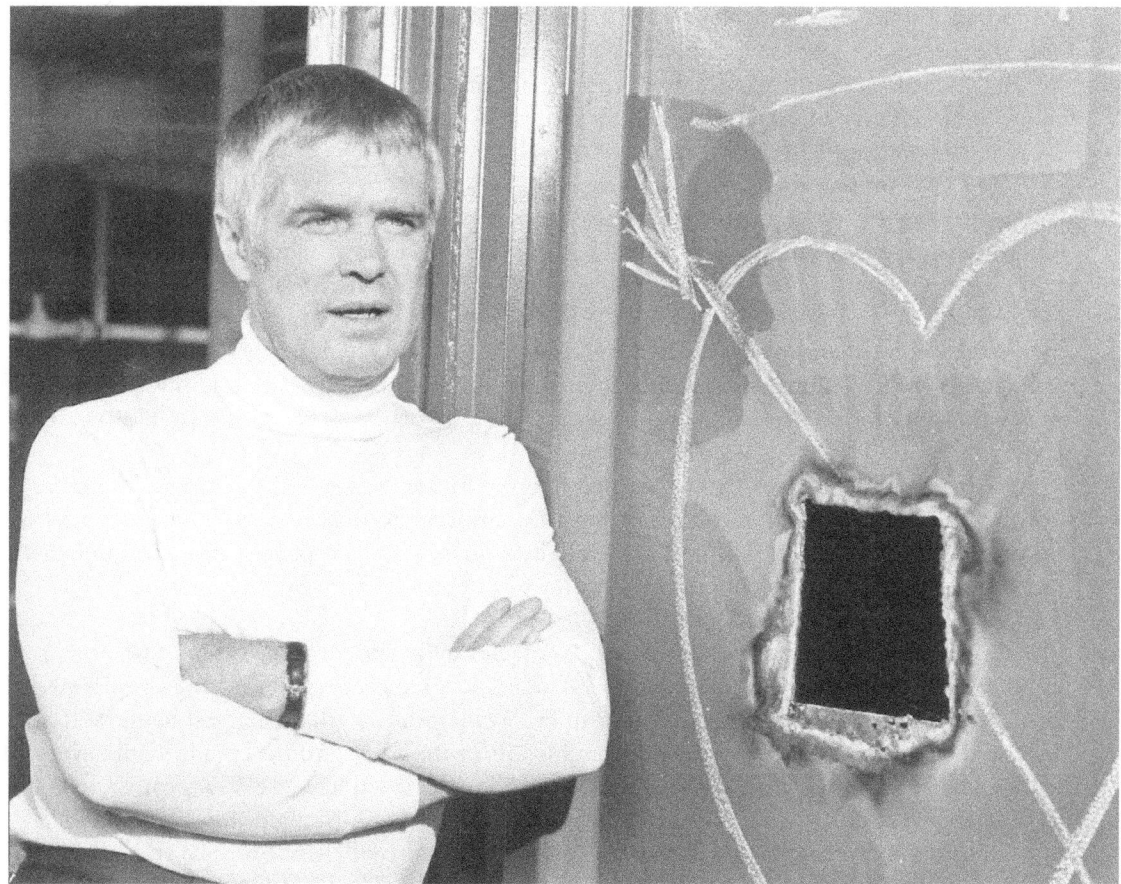

George Peppard turns his attention to a bizarre crime in "The Three Million Dollar Piracy," an episode McLaglen directed for NBC's *Banacek* (Universal Television).

a Los Angeles detective.[108] "I did it for a very small salary," he recalled in 2009. "That was in my real down period."[109] The picture didn't initiate a full-time return to motion picture directing, and McLaglen picked up more television work once shooting was complete, helming a pair of pilots (*Banjo Hackett*, NBC, 1976 and *Royce*, CBS, 1976), neither of which was picked up as a series.

McLaglen was then approached by Twentieth Century–Fox to direct a feature film with Charlton Heston and James Coburn, an adaptation of a novel by Brian Garfield called *Gun Down*, which tells the story of a bandit who kidnaps the daughter of a retired lawman. Released under the title *The Last Hard Men* (1976), the picture was shot in Arizona in the fall of 1975.[110] Though Guerdon Trueblood received sole credit for the screenplay, novelist Brian Garfield was asked to be on the set during filming to handle re-writes. In 2010, Garfield recalled, "[W]hat little I did was mainly help cut dialogue out of the script. The rest of the time I just hung out and made friends and learned as much as I could about the filmmaking process. Andy McLaglen was extremely patient in answering my questions."[111]

The Last Hard Men is one of McLaglen's strongest features. Much like *Shenandoah*, it follows a father's efforts to find a child who has been abducted. Heston's and Coburn's performances as two men who are undone by their hatred for one another, though, imbue this movie with a frightening intensity that *Shenandoah* lacks. As *New York Times* reviewer Richard

Eder noted: "'The Last Hard Men' is not just a horse opera; it's practically Tristan and Isolde. Only the love-death relation isn't between a man and a woman but between a retired lawman and a half-breed Navajo who is obsessed with the notion of killing him."[112] The film's bloodshed and pessimistic point of view prompted several critics to compare *The Last Hard Men* to the "ultraviolent" Westerns of Sam Peckinpah, as well.[113]

The Last Hard Men experienced indifferent returns at the box office unfortunately. Garfield remembers: "[T]he movie opened in Times Square without fanfare. It was neither a winner nor a loser in the box office sweepstakes ... it didn't make a lot of money but then it hadn't cost much to produce." *The Last Hard Men* may have been a victim of the same lack of interest in Westerns that had hurt *Cahill, United States Marshal*. Some blame might be attached to the picture's odd title, as well. As Garfield points out, "[S]omebody at the studio tacked the ... title on at the last minute, prompting complaints from Heston, Coburn and myself—none of us was happy to have our names on a movie the title of which made it look like a porn flick."[114]

Following *The Last Hard Men,* McLaglen found himself again without a motion picture deal and he headed back to television. Among the projects he worked on in 1976 were a television movie for ABC titled *Murder at the World Series* (1977), a pair of children's dramas for NBC's *The Wonderful World of Disney* and pilot episodes for two television series, *The Fantastic Journey* for NBC and *Code R* for CBS.

That same year, he headed up from Los Angeles with a friend to vacation on San Juan Island in northwestern Washington State.[115] The island's remoteness and its beauty charmed the director and he decided to build a home in Friday Harbor, the island's largest town. McLaglen, by the way, had recently separated from his third wife, Sally, and the couple would eventually divorce. "'I found myself five acres ... and thought I would settle down for the good life," he explained to Bob Thompson.[116] In the summer of 1977, though, just as the builders were finishing up on the house, McLaglen was approached by British producer Euan Lloyd to direct a $10 million action film about mercenaries called *The Wild Geese* (1978). "I got a call from Euan Lloyd right out of the blue. He said, 'Andrew, old boy, how are you?' I said, 'I'm fine.' 'Well, I'm doing a film with Richard Burton and Richard Harris and Roger Moore. Would you be interested?' I said, 'Yeah, I'll be interested.'" Though the house in Friday Harbor was not yet finished, McLaglen soon departed for Africa, where the film was to be shot that fall.[117] Joining McLaglen, incidentally, was his daughter, Mary, who assisted on the production with the actors' makeup.[118]

Featuring a script by Reginald Rose, *The Wild Geese* follows a band of professional soldiers who try to rescue a kidnapped African leader. Lloyd originally planned to have the film shot on location in Rhodesia (now Zimbabwe), but a war between the country's government and guerrilla insurgents made this impossible, and the producer settled on "the northern Transvaal of South Africa, only a few miles from the Rhodesian Border." Cast and crew stayed in a resort in the bush. As McLaglen recalled, "It wasn't exactly roughing it. Our headquarters was a very nice hotel with two swimming pools, mineral spa and tennis courts. It was hard to realize that guerrilla warfare was raging across the border only a few miles away."[119] In defiance of South Africa's apartheid policies, Lloyd insisted on having the black members of the cast stay at the resort, as well.[120]

The Wild Geese premiered in South Africa in the summer of 1978 and became a hit, drawing in both black and white audiences. The picture quickly found an international audience, too. An Associated Press story published in September of that year reported: "In London, 'The Wild Geese' has outdistanced all films except 'Star Wars,' and yielded $400,000 in the first week in three Tokyo theaters."[121] The movie was much less successful in the United States,

McLaglen behind the camera during the production of *The Last Hard Men* (Twentieth Century–Fox, 1976).

however, a result of Lloyd's decision to have Allied Artists distribute the film. By the end of 1978, when the picture was scheduled for release on this side of the Atlantic, Allied Artists was experiencing difficulties meeting its operating expenses. As a result, it was unable to promote *The Wild Geese* adequately and managed only to secure limited theatrical bookings in the States, curbing the film's exposure and returns.[122]

Aside from his problems with Allied Artists, Euan Lloyd was delighted with *The Wild Geese,* and he commenced with plans to make a second picture with McLaglen, a re-make of George Stevens's *Gunga Din.* Lloyd went so far as to send out a press release, announcing that Richard Burton, Richard Harris and Roger Moore would take on the roles played by Cary Grant, Douglas Fairbanks, Jr., and Victor McLaglen in the original picture.[123] The project never bore fruit, but thanks to the success of *The Wild Geese,* McLaglen found himself on the receiving end of other offers during this period. Very briefly, for instance, he was attached as a director to a production about the Korean War called *Inchon.* But he quit the project after learning that the film was being financed by Sun Myung Moon, the right-wing, messianic leader of the Unification Church.[124]

McLaglen next turned his attention to a West German picture called *Breakthrough.* Filmed in Germany and Austria in the fall of 1978, *Breakthrough* follows a German soldier who becomes involved in a plot to assassinate Adolf Hitler.[125] Produced by Wolf C. Hartwig, *Breakthrough* was the sequel to *Cross of Iron* (1977), which American director Sam Peckinpah had made two years earlier.[126] Richard Burton, one of the stars of *The Wild Geese,* was cast in the lead, with Robert Mitchum, Rod Steiger, Michael Parks and Curt Jurgens filling out the cast.

McLaglen stayed on in Europe after finishing *Breakthrough* to make another picture, *ffolkes* (1980), a thriller about a gang of criminals who threaten to blow up an oil production platform in the North Sea. The film drew its title from the last name of its central character, a counter-terrorism expert named Rufus Excalibur ffolkes. *The Wild Geese's* Roger Moore played the titular hero, while Anthony Perkins, the star of Alfred Hitchcock's *Psycho* (1960), was cast as his nemesis. Much of *ffolkes* was filmed in the summer of 1979 off the coast of Galway, Ireland, not far from the village of Cong, where McLaglen had worked with John Wayne on *The Quiet Man* 28 years earlier.[127] Wayne actually died of stomach cancer in June of that year, just as principal photography on *ffolkes* got underway. Because of his commitment to the film, though, McLaglen was unable to attend his old friend's funeral in faraway Newport Beach, California.[128]

After *ffolkes,* McLaglen and Moore made a third movie together, *The Sea Wolves* (1981). Like *The Wild Geese, The Sea Wolves* was produced by Euan Lloyd. Lloyd had decided to make this picture, which follows a band of middle-aged British men as they try to sink a German reconnaissance ship during World War II, after the *Gunga Din* remake he'd planned fell through. The producer initially hoped to sign his principals from *The Wild Geese*— Richard Burton, Richard Harris and Roger Moore — but he managed only to secure Moore. He was successful, however, in persuading two other big names — Gregory Peck and David Niven — to join the cast. Shooting on *The Sea Wolves* commenced in the fall of 1979 on location in Goa, India, a port city that lies along the Arabian Sea.[129]

Following *The Sea Wolves,* McLaglen headed back to the States to direct *The Blue & the Gray* (1982), a miniseries about the Civil War for CBS. Budgeted at $17 million, the production was filmed in the fall of 1981, entirely in Arkansas. "We shot two weeks at Ft. Smith and the rest from Fayetteville," McLaglen told the Associated Press. "Within the area we were able to reproduce Virginia, Washington, Gettysburg, Vicksburg, every locale we needed. The logistics were enormous. The wardrobe itself was valued at $18 million to replace."[130] In addition to stars like Gregory Peck, Lloyd Bridges, Geraldine Page, Stacy Keach, Warren Oates and Sterling Hayden, the production featured hundreds of extras. "We took advantage of a lot of re-enactment groups from all over the country. At one time, we had as many as 200 men representing both sides. I was a little leery of them at first, until we staged a fight," McLaglen explained. "These groups have their own uniforms, equipment and weapons and plenty of spirit.... When we had scenes of hand-to-hand combat they really got into it. They had spirit."[131]

In 1982, McLaglen shot two more television productions. The first of these was a pilot for ABC called *Travis McGee* (1983), an adaptation of crime writer John D. Macdonald's novel *The Empty Copper Sea,* with Sam Elliott playing the lead. The series was not picked up, however.[132] McLaglen and Elliott paired up again to make *The Shadow Riders* (1982) for CBS, a feature-length treatment of a story by Western writer Louis L'Amour. Among Elliott's co-stars were Tom Selleck and Katharine Ross, an actress who'd previously worked with McLaglen on *Shenandoah* and *Hellfighters.* Helping McLaglen in the production, by the way, was his youngest son, Josh, who is listed in the closing credits as an assistant to the director.

In 1983, McLaglen worked on just one production, a feature called *Sahara* (1984) for Cannon Films. A $15 million production, the picture starred Brooke Shields as a young woman who enters an automobile race in the North African desert. McLaglen was drafted by producers Menahem Golan and Yoram Globus to replace the picture's original director, John Guillermin.[133] McLaglen came onto the production in January after shooting had already begun, bringing his son Josh along with him again to gain experience as an assistant director. Filmed in Israel, *Sahara* presented McLaglen with several challenges. A story that appeared in *People* magazine noted: "An average day on the set is chaotic. Rain has slowed shooting.... Bedouin performers stop to pray every few hours. All directives are translated into Hebrew over a bullhorn—'Shut up and move your asses' is a frequent command. The production includes a 130-member crew, 32 actors, 120 horsemen, 12 stuntmen and some 3,000 extras."[134]

For his next project, McLaglen teamed up with actor Lee Marvin to make *The Dirty Dozen: Next Mission* (1985), a made-for-television sequel to Robert Aldrich's 1967 box office hit *The Dirty Dozen*. The telefilm was shot in Britain in November 1984, with a cast that included two other actors who'd appeared in the original movie, Richard Jaeckel and Ernest Borgnine.[135] While the picture was filming, an American woman named Sheila Greenan, who was staying in London at the time, contacted McLaglen. Like McLaglen, Sheila was an avid tennis player. She'd wanted a partner to play with and a friend had recommended McLaglen. McLaglen agreed to meet Sheila and was taken by her personality and good looks. The two eventually married in 1987 and stayed together until Sheila's death in April 2005.[136]

Following *The Dirty Dozen* sequel, McLaglen directed actor Burt Lancaster in an NBC miniseries called *On Wings of Eagles* (1986). An adaptation of a bestselling non-fiction book by Ken Follett, the film follows the efforts of Texas businessman (and future presidential candidate) H. Ross Perot as he tries to liberate some of his employees from a Tehran prison during the Iranian Revolution. Richard Crenna was

Though it failed to find a large audience in the United States, *The Wild Geese* (Allied Artists, 1978) was a big hit around the world.

cast as Perot, while Lancaster played Arthur "Bull" Simons, a retired Army officer who leads the rescue effort.

More than two years passed before McLaglen directed his next picture. In the time between, he and Sheila traveled around the world. During one of their trips, a visit to Sheila's family in Hawaii, McLaglen was contacted by a producer named Kurt Unger, who asked the director if he'd like to shoot a film in the Philippines called *Return from the River Kwai* (1989). Despite similarities in their titles, the film Unger wanted to make was not going to be a sequel to David Lean's acclaimed *The Bridge on the River Kwai* (1957). Rather, it was to be an adaptation of a non-fiction book by Joan and Clay Blair, Jr., about a World War II–era maritime disaster in which hundreds of Allied prisoners of war were injured and killed. McLaglen agreed to make the picture and flew out to the Philippines directly from Hawaii, bringing Sheila with him.[137]

McLaglen's next picture, *Eye of the Widow* (1991), was shot overseas, too, this time in Spain, Greece, Austria and France. A spy thriller, *Eye of the Widow* chronicles the adventures of a character named Malko Linge, an Austrian prince who freelances for the CIA. Created by French writer Gerard de Villiers, Linge had appeared in more than a hundred novels since the sixties, and *Eye of the Widow*'s producer Daniel Carillo hoped the film might be the first of a series of movies featuring the character. Carillo wanted a vigorous action adventure picture

Tom Selleck (left), Sam Elliot (center) and Jeff Osterhage (right) play three brothers in **The Shadow Riders** (Columbia Pictures Television, 1982), McLaglen's final Western.

McLaglen at his home in Friday Harbor, Washington, March 2009 (Stephen B. Armstrong).

and felt that McLaglen would give him one, having admired the director's work on *The Wild Geese* and *ffolkes*. But once production got underway in June 1989, Carillo proved to be an intrusive presence on the set, continuously undermining the director. Then, after principal photography was completed in September of that year, Carillo had additional footage shot and subsequently edited the film without McLaglen's consultation. The producer's efforts seem to have hurt the picture, rather than helped it, however, and two years would pass before the film had a limited released in Europe, never making its way to the United States. To this day, McLaglen refers to *Eye of the Widow* as "the movie we don't talk about."[138]

The frustration McLaglen experienced on *Eye of the Widow* prompted him to think about retiring. And though in 1993 he was briefly attached to a picture called *The Sextant*, which was never realized, he has not directed a film or television program since 1989.[139] McLaglen has remained active as a director, however. Since 1992, he has been helming stage productions for the San Juan Community Theatre, which is located in Friday Harbor, Washington, a few miles from his home. He directed his first play for the theatre in 1992, a musical adaptation of his 1965 film *Shenandoah*. In the years since, he has directed another 16 productions. He explained in 2009, "I've done every kind of play you can think of, from Chekhov to you name it, I've done it here.... It's something I probably never would have been asked to do in the movies."[140]

Now in his nineties, McLaglen spends much of his time in Friday Harbor, frequently hosting dinners and parties for friends, among them the actors he's come to know through his work at the San Juan Community Theatre. Every year, for instance, he invites friends over to his home to watch the televised Academy Awards ceremony in the same room where he keeps his father's Oscar on display.[141] Despite his age, he continues to travel, as well, enjoying occasional trips down to Seattle during the NFL season to watch professional football games.[142] He also takes pleasure these days in following the careers of his two youngest children, Josh and Mary, who, like their father, have both enjoyed a great deal of success in filmmaking. While Josh is a busy assistant director, with credits that include *Titanic* (1997) and *Avatar* (2009), Mary is a producer, who has worked on hit pictures like *Divine Secrets of the Ya-Ya Sisterhood* (2002) and *Dodgeball* (2004). In the summer of 2010, McLaglen flew out to Detroit to watch his son and daughter work together on the set of a science fiction thriller called *Real Steel*. When asked about the experience of watching his children at work and being near actors, movie cameras and lights again, he replied simply, "It was terrific, terrific."[143]

TWO

Early Motion Picture Production Experience

From an early age, Andrew V. McLaglen wanted to work in the movies. His first opportunity came in 1943, when he was asked to play a small scene as a soldier in the David O. Selznick production *Since You Went Away*.[1] McLaglen was always more interested in making movies than appearing in them, however, and in 1945 he took a job at Republic Pictures as a production company clerk. He later became an assistant director and landed jobs on several noteworthy films over the next decade, among them John Ford's *The Quiet Man*.

Since You Went Away—1944 (172 mins)

Presented by: David O. Selznick, Selznick International Pictures, Vanguard Films, Inc.
Director: John Cromwell
Script: David O. Selznick, based on Margaret Buell Wilder's *Since You Went Away: Letters to a Soldier from His Wife*
Photography: Stanley Cortez, Lee Garmes (B & W)
Editor: John D. Faure, Arthur Fellows and Wayland M. Hendry
Music: Max Steiner
Cast: Claudette Colbert (Anne Hilton), Jennifer Jones (Jane Hilton), Joseph Cotten (Tony Willett), Robert Walker (Bill Smollet), Shirley Temple (Bridget "Brig" Hilton), Monty Woolley (Col. Smollet), Lionel Barrymore (Clergyman), Hattie McDaniel (Fidelia), Agnes Moorehead (Emily Hawkins), Albert Basserman (Dr. Golden), Craig Stevens (Danny Williams), Keenan Wynn (Solomon), Guy Madison (Harold)
Summary: Anne Hilton is the mother of two teenage daughters, Jane and Brig. In January 1943, as World War II wears on, Anne's husband Tim leaves his job as an advertising executive to serve overseas. Forced to live on reduced means, the Hiltons let their beloved maid Fidelia go. They also lease out a room in their home to a retired army officer, Col. William Smollett. Shortly after this, another tenant moves in with the Hiltons, Tony Willett, an officer in the Navy and a family friend. Fidelia soon comes to live with the Hiltons, as well, trading housekeeping duties for rent.

As the weeks pass, Anne struggles to accept the loneliness and sadness she feels now that her husband Tim is gone. Wanting to contribute to the war effort, Brig collects discarded cans for scrap drives. Jane becomes involved, too, agreeing to attend a dance for enlisted men.

There, Jane socializes with a nervous young corporal, Bill Smollet, the grandson of Col. Smollet. Bill and the colonel are at odds because Bill was once a cadet at West Point, but he failed out, bringing dishonor to the Smollet family.

Eventually Tony Willett is summoned for duty and leaves the Hiltons' home. His departure upsets Jane, who has fallen in love with him. As the family comes to terms with Tony's departure, they receive a telegram informing them that Tim Hilton has been reported "missing in action." Despite these developments, Jane finds some happiness, spending time with Bill Smollet. A courtship begins, the two fall in love and they eventually become engaged. During this time, Jane also serves as a nurse's aide at a rehabilitation ward for injured soldiers.

Bill is soon summoned for duty, however, and later dies in battle in Salerno not long after his deployment. The news devastates Jane, prompting her to devote more of her time to the injured soldiers she works with in the hospital. Bill's death also affects Anne, inspiring her to become more involved in the war effort and take a job as a welder at a shipyard.

Several months pass and Tony Willett comes back from the war a decorated hero. Tony's return provides little comfort to Anne, who continues to wonder if her husband is dead or alive. Then on Christmas Eve, she receives a phone call and learns that Tim is not only safe, but will soon be coming home. The happy mother rushes to tell her daughters the good news.

Comment: Production on *Since You Went Away* spanned from September 1943 to February

A promotional still from Republic Pictures's *Love, Honor and Goodbye* (1945), the first film on which McLaglen worked as a production clerk. From left to right: Edward Ashley, Virginia Bruce and Victor McLaglen.

1944. The film's narrative is based on a series of letters Margaret Buell Wilder sent her husband after he volunteered for service in World War II. The letters were collected and published by Whittlesey House in 1943 under the title *Since You Went Away: Letters to a Soldier from His Wife*. Producer David O. Selznick adapted Wilder's book himself and is listed in the opening credits as the film's writer.[2]

McLaglen has a small onscreen part in the film. He appears briefly with Robert Walker (Bill) and Jones during a sequence in which Jones's character, Jane, attends a dance that is being held for enlisted soldiers. McLaglen can be seen standing at the end of a conga line behind Jones, holding her waist. McLaglen's character, a soldier, is not the best dancer and he scares her, lurching her hips back and forth with his hands. The following exchange transpires:

> JANE: What do you think you're doing anyway?
> SOLDIER: I ain't used to dancing. I'm used to pushing a plow.
> JANE: You're not kidding.

McLaglen is not listed in the film's screen credits. *Since You Went Away* received nine Academy Award nominations, including Best Film, Best Editing and Best Cinematography. It won for Best Music, earning composer Max Steiner his third (and final) Oscar.[3]

Reviews: "It's a box-office mop-up, an audience heart-tug and, in no small measure, a human document of World War II as it affects all of us." *Variety,* July 19, 1944; "[The film's] humors are frequent and cheerful; its spirit is hopeful and brave. But it does come off, altogether, as a rather large dose of choking sentiment." *New York Times,* July 21, 1944; "Viewers should have at least one box of tissues at their side while watching this. If not sincerely moved by *Since You Went Away,* they should have their pulse rate taken." *Motion Picture Guide,* 2932; "One of the signal 'home front' movies of World War II, it brings the best out of Hollywood in technique and style." *War Films,* 170.
Release: July, United Artists
Availability: VHS, LD, DVD

Love, Honor and Goodbye—1945 (87 mins)

Associate Producer: Harry Grey, Republic Pictures
Director: Albert S. Rogell
Script: Arthur Phillips, Lee Loeb and Dick Irving Hyland, story by Art Arthur and Albert S. Rogell
Photography: John Alton (B & W)
Editor: Richard L. Van Enger
Music: Roy Webb
Cast: Virginia Bruce (Roberta Baxter), Edward Ashley (William Baxter), Victor McLaglen (Terry O'Farrell), Jacqueline Moore (Sally), Nils Asther (Tony), Helen Broderick (Mary Riley), Veda Ann Borg (Marge), Victoria Horne (Miss Whipple), Therese Lyon (Miss Hopkins), Robert Greig (Charles), Ralph Dunn (Detective)
Summary: Roberta Baxter and her husband Bill, a lawyer, live in an apartment in New York. Their marriage has begun to suffer because Roberta, a stage actress, has been spending the bulk of her time rehearsing scenes for a new play with her co-star Tony, making Bill jealous. Unknown to Roberta, Bill is one of the play's primary backers, having invested more than $30,000 into the production.

When the show opens, however, it fails and Bill orders it to be closed. The play's failure is a boon for Bill at first, as Roberta is now free to give her time and attention to him. But then Tony shows up, presenting the actress with the opportunity to appear in a new production.

The offer upsets Bill and he discourages Roberta from pursuing it. Tony then reveals to Roberta that Bill made the decision to close the play they'd appeared in together previously, a revelation that angers Roberta, prompting her to leave her husband.

Distraught, Bill takes to drink. He also opens the Baxter's apartment to a group of paupers: Terry O'Neill, a cranky tattoo artist, Terry's female friend, Marge, and a gamine named Sally. When Roberta learns about this development, she begins to wonder if Bill has fallen in love with Marge. She then decides to divorce Bill, but in order to make the case that her husband has adulterous tendencies, she must collect evidence. To do this, Roberta poses as a governess named Fleurette and convinces Bill to hire her on to take care of little Sally.

Bill is aware, however, that Fleurette is actually his wife and he allows the governess to flirt with him. Later, when Terry O'Neill stumbles on to the two kissing, he is appalled by their apparent lack of morality and rushes off from the apartment with Sally. Soon after, Roberta and Bill reconcile and resume their old life in the apartment.

Comment: *Love, Honor and Goodbye* is the first picture McLaglen was assigned to after he took a job at Republic as a production clerk. His duties included relaying information between the film's crew and the studio's administrative offices. The film was produced in the spring of 1945, following McLaglen's on-screen appearance in *Paris-Underground*, but *Love, Honor and Goodbye* had the earlier release.[4] *Love, Honor and Goodbye* is also the first picture on which McLaglen worked with his father Victor McLaglen; the father and son paired up again on *The Quiet Man* and *The Abductors*, as well as episodes of *Have Gun, Will Travel* and *Rawhide*. McLaglen would marry Veda Ann Borg (Madge) in 1946.[5]

Reviews: "Gay comedy.... [E]xcellent bill of entertainment highlighted by sparkling gems of wit." *Hartford Courant*, September 29, 1945.

Release: September, Republic Pictures

Paris-Underground — 1945 (98 mins)

Alternate Titles: *Madame Pimpernel, Guerillas of the Underground*
Producer: Constance Bennett, Constance Bennett Productions, Inc.
Director: Gregory Ratoff
Script: Boris Ingster and Gertrude Purcell, based on a story by Etta Shiber, with Anne and Paul Dupre & Oscar Ray.
Photography: Lee Garmes (B & W)
Editor: Hanson Fritch
Music: Alexandre Tansman
Cast: Constance Bennett (Kitty de Mornay), Gracie Fields (Emmyline Quayle), George Rigaud (Andre de Mornay), Kurt Kreuger (Capt. von Weber), Charles Andre (Father Dominique), Vladimir Sokoloff (Undertaker), Gregory Gaye (Tissier)
Summary: The film opens in the spring of 1940. Kitty de Mornay, an American woman living in Paris, is having marital difficulties with her husband André. The couple decides to separate and Kitty goes to her friend Emmy, a British antiques merchant, who also lives in the city. From Emmy, Kitty learns that France has lost its fight against Germany and Paris will soon be occupied by the Nazis. The two friends then decide to flee. Because the main road out of the city is choked with refugees, the women veer off, looking for a shortcut. They are soon stopped at a checkpoint and told to return to Paris.

After they start back, Kitty decides to pull over at a nearby lodge. The innkeeper there, a friend of Kitty, explains that he has been hiding a stranded British pilot. Wanting to help, Kitty and Emmy take the pilot with them into Paris, concealing him behind a pile of luggage.

Kitty then asks for help from her estranged husband André, an officer in the French Army. André directs Kitty and Emmy to a baker with a rowboat who smuggles refugees out of the occupied territory for a fee.

After the women turn the pilot over to the smuggler, they return to Paris and direct their attention to helping others. Eventually the pair makes contact with a priest who is providing cover to a band of stranded aviators in the basement of his church. Kitty and Emmy leave with two of the men concealed in their car. When they learn that the smuggler they used previously has been executed, the women are forced to pursue other means for getting their charges out of the country. They find a patriotic undertaker who agrees to transport the pilots out of Occupied France in a funeral carriage.

Kitty and Emmy then return to Paris, where they become active members of the French Resistance and successfully transport hundreds of men to safety. In 1943, though, they are captured by the Gestapo and sent to a concentration camp. Following the Germans' retreat from France in the summer of 1944, the two friends are freed. They are subsequently recognized by Gen. Charles De Gaulle's Free French Forces for their bravery.

Constance Bennett, star and producer of *Paris-Underground* (United Artists, 1945).

Comment: Production on *Paris-Underground* ran from January to March 1945.[6] McLaglen took time off from his job at the Lockheed Corporation to appear in the picture, playing a character named McNair, one of several servicemen who hide in the basement of a French church.[7] McLaglen was cast in the part because of his towering height. After Kitty and Emmy come to the church and explain to a priest that they can deliver one of the men to safety, lots are drawn to determine who will go with them. With a thick Scottish burr, McNair says, "The chap who draws the short one goes." McNair then draws the shortest stick, but tells Kitty and Emmy to take two smaller men, rather than him: "I say, ma'am, couldn't you take two little chaps instead? We gotta couple of regular shrimps here.... The way things are, two guns are better than one."

Reviews: "[P]ic has good, solid story content once it gets going, enough suspense, and is produced, directed and acted with a fine appreciation of the action involved." *Variety*, September 22, 1945; "[The film] turns out to be just another adventure with a glamour girl—a glamour girl in occupied Paris, which is not a very tasteful place for same." *New York Times*, October 20, 1945; "[A] tense tale of the battle of the French underground against the Gestapo." *Chicago Daily Tribune*, January 17, 1946.

Release: October, United Artists
Availability: DVD

Dakota—1945 (82 mins)

Associate Producer: Joseph Kane, Republic Pictures
Director: Joseph Kane
Script: Lawrence Hazard, adaptation by Howard Estabrook, from an original story by Carl Foreman
Photography: Jack Marta (B & W)
Editor: Fred Allen
Music: Walter Scharf
Cast: John Wayne (Devlin), Vera Hruba Ralston (Sandy), Walter Brennan (Sandy), Ward Bond (Bender), Mike Mazurki (Bigtree Collins), Ona Munson (Jersey), Olive Blakeney (Mrs. Stowe), Hugo Hass (Poli), Nicodemus Stewart (Nicodemus), Paul Fix (Carp), Grant Withers (Slagin), Robert Livingston (Lieutenant), Pierre Watkin (Wexton), Robert H. Barrat (Stowe), Jonathan Hale (Col. Wordin), Bobby Blake (Little Boy), Roy Barcroft (Poli's Driver)
Summary: John Devlin, a drifter with a fondness for guns and cards, elopes with Sandy Poli, the daughter of Chicago tycoon Marko Poli. The news infuriates Mr. Poli and the newlyweds decide to run away. At the train station in downtown Chicago, Sandy reveals to John that she has stolen a painting that belongs to her father and sold it for $20,000. Though John

Vera Hruba Ralston and John Wayne as a pair of newlyweds in *Dakota* (Republic, 1945).

would like to use the money to purchase a home in the gold fields of California, Sandy persuades him to take her to Fargo in the Dakota Territory. Her father is planning to run his railroad through this part of the country, she explains, and she and John can use the money to purchase land owned by local wheat farmers, which they can then sell to her father at a dear price.

John concedes and the newlyweds make their way north. Along the way, they meet two travelers, Jim Bender and Bigtree Collins, who are also bound for Dakota. Like the Devlins, Bender plans to buy up land around Fargo and sell it to Sandy's father. Sensing that John and Sandy pose a potential threat to his interests, Bender hires a pair of thugs to rob the couple of their $20,000. Suspecting Bender is behind the theft, John searches for the businessman when he and Sandy arrive in Fargo. Once John finds Bender, the two men fight, a gun goes off and Sandy is wounded in the shoulder. As Sandy recovers, Bender explains to John that he will return the stolen money if and only if the Devlins agree to leave Fargo. John refuses this offer and instead resolves to drive Bender out of Dakota himself.

Comment: Produced for Republic, *Dakota* was shot in the summer of 1945.[8] McLaglen served on the movie as a production clerk; his duties included preparing call sheets for the actors and rehearsing lines with them.[9] Among the film's cast were several actors who regularly appeared in movies with leading man John Wayne: Ward Bond, Paul Fix and Mike Mazurki. Fix and Mazurki would both have prominent roles in the first film McLaglen directed, *Man in the Vault*. Cast members Roy Barcroft, Bobby Blake and Grant Withers would work with McLaglen again, too. Barcroft had roles in the features *Freckles* and *Bandolero!*, and Blake and Withers both appeared in episodes of *Have Gun, Will Travel* that McLaglen directed.

At the time of the film's production, Wayne's co-star, Vera Hruba Ralston, was the girlfriend of Herbert J. Yates, the president of Republic Pictures. *In Pappy: The Life of John Ford*, Dan Ford explains that Yates "was madly in love with a Czechoslovakian ice skater forty years his junior named Vera Hruba Ralston. She was stiff, awkward, and spoke with a heavy, almost unintelligible accent. But Yates thought she was the greatest thing ever to hit Hollywood, and he was determined to make her a star. He made picture after picture with her, and they were all financial disasters."[10]

Reviews: "Republic has dressed up a familiar land-grab story with sufficient production to give this outdoor epic more than formula values.... Action isn't always robust, but there are a number of knock-down fights to help carry it along." *Variety*, November 11, 1945; "Foreman's story is a brisk, no-nonsense Western in which Wayne plays gambler John Devlin, an unlikely champion of small farmers." *Time Out Film Guide*, 235.

Release: December, Republic Pictures
Availability: VHS, LD, DVD

Sioux City Sue—1946 (69 mins)

Associate Producer: Armand Schaefer, Republic Pictures
Director: Fred McDonald
Script: Olive Cooper
Photography: Reggie Lanning (B & W)
Editor: Fred Allen
Music: Dale Butts
Cast: Gene Autry (Himself), Lynne Roberts (Sue), Sterling Holloway (Nellie Bly), Richard Lane (Lang), Ralph Sanford (Big Gulliver), Ken Lundy (Jody), Helen Wallace (Miss Price), Pierre Watkin (Rhodes), Cass County Boys

Summary: Paragon Pictures, a Hollywood movie studio, is looking for someone to provide the voice for a new cartoon character it has created, a singing donkey named Ding Dong. While in Arizona, one of the studio's employees, Sue Warner, hears cattle rancher Gene Autry singing. Sue becomes certain that Autry is the man Paragon needs, but when she approaches him about appearing in the movies, she inadvertently triggers a stampede and many of Autry's animals run off. Needing money to replace his lost cattle, Autry agrees to come with Sue to Los Angeles, thinking he and his horse Champion will appear together in an actual movie. Once there, he learns he will merely be doing some voice work for a cartoon and becomes angry. To placate him, the chief at Paragon decides to film Autry and Champion performing tricks, though he has no intention of ever using this material in a picture. When Autry realizes he's been snookered again, he heads back to his ranch. The studio chief later reviews the footage that's been shot and realizes that Autry is star material. A director from the studio is then sent to Arizona to bring the singing cowboy back to Hollywood to appear in a live-action feature.

Comment: Gene Autry was the most popular of the numerous "singing cowboys" who worked on the Republic studio lot in the thirties and forties. From 1942 to 1946, however, he appeared in no movies. During this period, he was a combat pilot in the Army Air Corps, flying missions in Asia. Autry made *Sioux City Sue* following his return from service in the summer of 1946.[11] McLaglen worked on this picture as an uncredited clerk—handling the duties a production assistant performs today. In particular, he helped the film's actors practice their lines and rehearse the numerous songs that were performed.[12]

Reviews: "It's standard Autry fare slated for his regular fans who have been fed on almost two dozen Autry reissues since his induction into the Army in 1942. Following the fixed formula, pic combines a dash of action seasoned with romance, with the story acting as a peg for an armlong musical score of pleasant oatunes." *Variety,* November 27, 1946.

Release: December, Republic Pictures
Availability: VHS, DVD

Publicity photograph of Gene Autry and his horse, Champion.

Out California Way—1946 (67 mins)

Associate Producer: Louis Gray, Republic Pictures
Director: Lesley Selander

Script: Betty Burbridge, story by Barry Shipman
Photography: Bud Thackery (Color)
Editor: Charles Craft
Music: Nathan G. Scott
Cast: Monte Hale (Monte), Adrian Booth (Gloria), Bobby Blake (Danny), John Dehner (Mason), Nolan Leary (Sheridan), Fred Graham (Ace), Tom London (Ace), Foy Willing & The Riders of the Purple Sage
Summary: Little Danny McCoy wants to get his trained horse Pardner into the movies. He goes to Globe Pictures in Hollywood, hoping to arrange an audition. Monte Hale, a singing cowboy, wants to break into the movies, too. Monte and Danny agree to pair up and put on a routine outside the studio. As Monte sings a song, Danny has Pardner perform tricks. The little show impresses a director who is passing by and Monte and Pardner are cast in a picture called *Out California Way*. However, one of the film's other stars, Rod Mason, takes a dislike to Monte, worried that the newcomer may be more talented than he. Mason then orders one of his friends to hurl dynamite at Monte as he rides Pardner during a scene. The explosion leaves the horse skittish and Monte takes Parder to a ranch to recover. To spare Danny from worrying, Monte doesn't tell him what's happened to Pardner. Monte's well-meaning plan comes undone when Mason approaches Danny and tells him that his horse has been stolen.

Comment: *Out California Way* is another of the "singing cowboy" features McLaglen worked on as a production clerk. McLaglen later directed Bobby Blake (Danny) and John Dehner (Rod) in episodes of *Have Gun, Will Travel*.

Reviews: "Hale registers as a likeable cowchanter, handling the vocals in easy, if not exceptional style. Backing up nicely are young Blake, his big sister, Adrian Booth, the menace, John Dehner, and the hoss." *Variety*, December 11, 1946.
Release: December, Republic Pictures
Availability: VHS, DVD

Angel and the Badman—1947 (100 mins)

Producer: John Wayne, Patnel Productions
Director: James Edward Grant
Script: James Edward Grant
Photography: Archie J. Stout (B & W)
Editor: Harry Keller
Music: Richard Hageman; song "A Little Bit Different" by Kim Gannon and Walter Kent
Cast: John Wayne (Quirt), Gail Russell (Penelope), Harry Carey (McClintock), Bruce Cabot (Laredo), Louis Faust (Hondo), John Halloran (Worth), Irene Rich (Mrs. Worth), Lee Dixon (Randy), Paul Fix (Mouse), Hank Worden (Townsman), Stephen Grant (Johnny), Tom Powers (Dr. Mangram), Paul Hurst (Carson), Joan Barton (Lila), Craig Woods (Withers), Marshall Reed (Nelson)
Summary: After getting himself shot in a gunfight, Quirt Evans is nursed back to health by a family of Quakers named the Worths. A onetime lawman who now rustles cattle, Quirt enjoys his life with the Worths and stays on at their home in the desert after he recovers, helping them work the land. The one condition for living there is that he must leave his gun hanging on the porch outside.

As the weeks pass, Quirt falls in love with the Worths' daughter, Penny. The life of virtue embraced by his new friends appeals to him and he agrees to attend one of their religious

Republic's chief, Herbert J. Yates, meets with Gail Russell and John Wayne during the production of *Angel and the Badman* (Republic, 1947).

services. Along the road to this meeting, Quirt and the Worths are approached by Quirt's old outlaw buddy McCall, who manages to persuade the gunfighter to leave the Worths and rustle some cattle. The subsequent raid is successful and the men trade the animals they've stolen for money and spend an evening drinking and fighting, as well as carousing with prostitutes. Quirt quickly realizes that he no longer has the appetite for activity like this and returns to the Worths' home. A short time later, a U.S. Marshal named McClintock shows up, trying to determine what role, if any, Quirt played in the cattle raid a few days earlier. Because he has no evidence, McClintock refrains from arresting Quirt, but he warns Penny to stay away from the man she now loves.

Following this, Quirt asks Penny to marry him. Penny doesn't answer at first. Rather, she takes him to a nearby canyon where they pick berries. During a pause, Quirt explains that he was "half-raised" by a kindly, but crooked rancher for whom stealing cattle was not a serious crime. As the two start back to Penny's farm, Hondo and Laredo, a couple of bandits who hate Quirt, fire at the couple, sending them and their wagon into a river. The bandits then head off, leaving Quirt and Penny for dead.

The pair survives, but Penny is badly hurt. Quirt then takes her home and soon learns from a doctor that she is likely to die. Craving revenge, Quirt heads to town to hunt down

Hondo and Laredo. Shortly after he sets out, however, Penny recovers consciousness. Because killing is forbidden by the Quaker faith, Penny and her parents rush after Quirt, hoping to stop him. They find Quirt in town and Penny convinces him to turn his gun over to her. Right at that moment, though, Hondo and Laredo step out of a saloon, with their six-irons aimed at Quirt and the Worth family.

Before the outlaws can act, shots are fired and the two drop to the ground dead. The man who pulled the trigger is Marshal McClintock. The marshal then approaches Quirt and explains that a similar fate lies before him if he continues to live outside the law. Quirt scoffs at this, explaining to McClintock that he has given up crime and will now be a farmer. Carried away from town on the Worths' wagon, Quirt tosses his gun to the ground, signaling to everyone watching that his days as a bad man are behind him.

Comment: Republic released *Angel and the Badman,* but the picture was produced by Patnel, a company owned by John Wayne. The picture is in fact the first film on which Wayne received a producer's credit. Wayne became a film producer in part because it allowed him to have greater creative control over the movies he appeared in; producing also provided him with the ability to generate more income for himself. He would receive a producer's credit on two more movies for Republic, *The Fighting Kentuckian* (1949) and *Bullfighter and the Lady.* After severing ties with Republic in 1952, Wayne and his friend Robert Fellows launched an independent production company called Wayne-Fellows, which subsequently became Batjac in 1955.[13] McLaglen worked on *Angel and the Badman* as an uncredited clerk.[14] McLaglen, by the way, felt that Wayne was a superior film producer: "I would say that Duke is one of the best of the actors that ever became a producer. First of all, he knew a lot about movies — how you make them, why you make them, who's going to be in them. Duke knew what he was doing."[15]

Angel and the Badman was scripted and directed by James Edward Grant. Grant's execution of the film pleased Wayne, and Grant would work again with the actor on several occasions, primarily as a screenwriter, until Grant's death in 1966.[16] Among the films Grant scripted for Wayne are several McLaglen worked on, including *Sands of Iwo Jima, Bullfighter and the Lady, Big Jim McLain, Hondo* and *Ring of Fear.* Grant penned *McLintock!,* too, the 1963 Western comedy that McLaglen directed for Wayne's Batjac company and in which Wayne starred.

Reviews: "Big-time western drama has resulted from John Wayne's first production effort. "Angel and the Badman" is solid entertainment way above what might be expected on its western locale and characters. It's loaded with sharp performances, honest writing and direction." *Variety,* February 12, 1947; "Mr. Wayne and company have sacrificed ... roaring action to fashion a leisurely Western, which is different from and notch or two superior to the normal sagebrush saga." *New York Times,* March 3, 1947; "Great performances from a top-notch cast make this gentle western well worth seeing. Though the film didn't do well at the box office at the time, it stands up better today than most of Wayne's other, more action-packed westerns." *Motion Picture Guide,* 68.

Release: February, Republic Pictures
Availability: VHS, LD, DVD

Apache Rose—1947 (75 mins)

Associate Producer: Edward J. White, Republic Pictures
Director: William Witney
Script: Gerald Geraghty

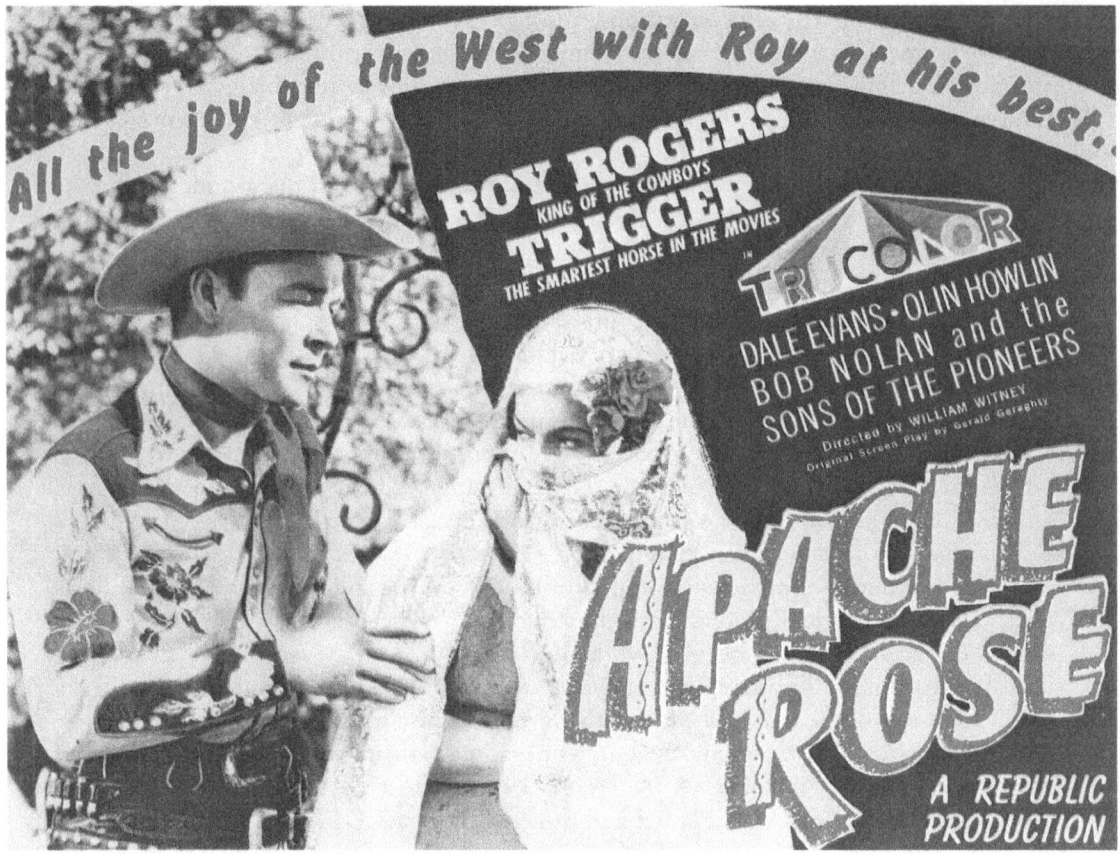

A lobby card for *Apache Rose* (Republic, 1947), one of several "singing cowboy" pictures McLaglen was assigned to at the start of his career.

Photography: Jack Marta (Color)
Editor: Les Orlebeck
Music: Morton Scott, songs by Jack Elliott and Tim and Glenn Spencer
Cast: Roy Rogers (Himself), Dale Evans (Billie Colby), Olin Howlin (Alkalai Elkins), John Laurenz (Pete), Russ Vincent (Vegas), Minerva Urecal (Felicia), LeRoy Mason (Hilliard), Donna DeMario (Rosa), Terry Frost (Sheriff), Conchita Lemus (Dancer), Tex Terry (Likens), Bob Nolan and the Sons of the Pioneers
Summary: Carlos Vegas belongs to an aristocratic family that traces its roots to California's Spanish past. The Vegas family owns land along the ocean that is rich with oil, but Carlos, a compulsive gambler, has dissipated the family fortune. He also owes a crooked casino owner named Calhoun more than $100 thousand. When Carlos fails to pay him the money he owes, Calhoun tries to kill Carlos's sister, Rosa, and when this fails, he kidnaps Carlos. Roy Rogers and his singer friend, Billie, come to the aid of Rosa and Carlos, eventually apprehending Calhoun and bringing the villain to justice.
Comment: A mixture of action and song, *Apache Rose* was produced in the summer of 1946.[17] McLaglen worked as an uncredited clerk on the picture, helping its cast members practice their lines and rehearse songs.[18] Roy Rogers was one of Republic's busiest leading men during the forties, performing in a string of "singing cowboy" features like *Apache Rose*.

Rogers and his wife and co-star Dale Evans left Republic in 1951 and moved onto television to star in *The Roy Rogers Show* for NBC.[19] With its good samaritan characters and animal actors (Trigger the horse, Bullet the dog), the program primarily targeted young audiences, offering them a wholesome portrait of cowboy life. These sanitized depictions of the West would be upended later in the decade with the emergence of a new wave of television Westerns that featured morally ambiguous heroes who strove to maintain order and deliver justice in a violent world. These "adult" Westerns — the best of which were perhaps *Gunsmoke* and *Have Gun, Will Travel*— enjoyed great popularity until the mid-sixties.[20] McLaglen would become one of the directors most closely associated with the adult Western style, contributing episodes to not only *Gunsmoke* and *Have Gun, Will Travel*, but similar shows like *Rawhide*, *The Virginian*, *Wagon Train*, *Gunslinger* and *Hotel de Paree*.

Reviews: "William Witney's direction of the Gerald Geraghty original script spots some good action moments." *Variety*, March 26, 1947.
Release: February, Republic Pictures
Availability: VHS, DVD

Sands of Iwo Jima—1950 (110 mins)

Associate Producer: Edmund Grainger, Republic Pictures
Director: Allan Dwan
Script: Harry Brown and James Edward Grant, story by Harry Brown
Photography: Reggie Lanning (B & W)
Editor: Richard L. Van Enger
Music: Victor Young
Cast: John Wayne (Stryker), John Agar (Conway), Forrest Tuck (Thomas), Wally Cassell (Ragazzi), James Brown (Bass), Richard Webb (Shipley), Arthur Franz (Dunne), Richard Jaeckel (Pfc. F. Flynn), Bill Murphy (Pfc. E. Flynn), Adele Mara (Allison), Peter Coe (Hellenopolis), Julie Bishop (Mary), James Holden (Soames), Hal Fieberling (Choynski), John McGuire (Joyce), William Self (Fowler)
Summary: John Stryker is a sergeant in the United States Marine Corps whose commitment to his job has left him estranged from his family. As the film opens, he is assigned to train and lead an unruly group of grunts for combat. At first, many of the men he works with dislike and resist the abrasive Stryker, in particular a private named Al Thomas, who Stryker once beat in a boxing match. Another man, Pete Conway, also hates the sergeant, having been taunted all his life by his father, a Marine Corps colonel — and a good friend of Stryker.

Nevertheless, the marines in Stryker's unit eventually develop a fondness for their sergeant. Following training, they are dispatched to an atoll in the south Pacific called Tarawa, where they fight a long and bloody battle with the Japanese. The men who survive recuperate briefly in Hawaii, before being sent on to Iwo Jima, another island controlled by Japan. Upon their arrival, Stryker's marines find themselves in peril as they fight the enemy, many of them dying. Their efforts eventually yield success as they rush up and take Iwo Jima's highest point, Mount Suribachi. With victory near, they raise the American flag. A moment later, however, Stryker is shot and killed by enemy fire.

Comment: *Sands of Iwo Jima* was produced in the summer of 1949. Much of the picture was shot at Camp Pendleton, a Unites States Marines Corps base that sits along the Pacific coast in southern California. Additional footage was filmed at El Toro Marine Air Station in Orange County.[21] McLaglen worked on the picture as an uncredited second assistant to director Allan Dwan.[22]

Given a $1 million budget, the film featured a large ensemble cast as well as thousands of extras.²³ Upon its general release in March 1950, *Sands of Iwo Jima* enjoyed tremendous popularity at the box office. It also received four Academy Award nominations, including Best Actor (John Wayne), Best Writing, Best Sound and Best Editing.²⁴ While the film's dramatic portions were scripted, many of the battle sequences make use of real combat footage shot during World War II. McLaglen would subsequently direct two films that depict the efforts of the U.S. military to train a unit of angry young men for dangerous combat missions, *The Devil's Brigade* and *The Dirty Dozen: Next Mission*. Four cast members from *Sands of Iwo Jima*—John Wayne (Stryker), Forrest Tucker (Thomas), John Agar (Conway) and Richard Jaeckel (Flynn)—had parts in McLaglen's *Chisum*. Jaeckel also had parts in both *The Devil's Brigade* and *The Dirty Dozen: Next Mission*.

Reviews: "Although far from rating as the best film to be inspired by the recent conflict, 'Sands of Iwo Jima' wraps up all the familiar war pix formulas into a star-spangled ear-shattering entertainment package." *Variety*, December 14, 1949; "John Wayne and the other actors hired by Republic to represent a rifle squad that is bloodied on Tarawa and helps clear the way for the historic raising of the Stars and Stripes atop Mt. Suribachi are a credit to the uniform. Wayne is especially honest and convincing, for he manages to dominate a screen play which is crowded with exciting, sweeping battle scenes, some real and some simulated. His performance holds the picture together, lessening to some extent the hackneyed devices employed by the authors in their poverty-stricken personal fiction about the men." *New York Times,* December 31, 1949; "Wayne is in his element as the tough sergeant sternly molding a group of recruits, from training camp to beachhead, into an efficient fighting force." *Time Out Film Guide*, 917; "Unlike many of Wayne's superman films of World War II where he single-handedly destroys whole Japanese armies, *Sands of Iwo Jima* provides an intelligent look at warfare and at Wayne, though he is no less heroic than in his other films." *Motion Picture Guide*, 2731.

Release: March, Republic Pictures
Availability: VHS, DVD, LD

Killer Shark—1950 (76 mins)

Producer: Lindsley Parsons, Monogram Productions, Inc.
Director: Oscar Boetticher
Script: Charles Lang
Photography: William Sickner (B & W)
Editor: Leonard W. Herman
Music: Edward J. Kay
Cast: Roddy McDowall (Ted), Roland Winters (White), Laurette Luez (Maria), Edward Norris (Ramon), Rick Vallin (Agapito), Douglas Fowley (Bracado), Nacho Galindo (Maestro), Ralf Harold (Slattery), Dick Moore (Jonesy), Ted Hecht (Gano), Charles Lang (McCann), Robert Espinoza (Pinon), Julio Sebastian (Tony), Julian Rivero (Doctor), Frank Sully (Pat), George Slocum (Capt. Hansen)
Summary: Ted White, an American college student, has come to the Mexican coast to visit his father Jeff, a fishing boat captain. The two have not seen each other in many years, and Jeff, eager to renew their relationship, gives Ted a job on his boat.

One day when Ted is working on the boat, he falls overboard into shark-filled water. He is rescued by Jeff and one of Jeff's crew, who are both injured during the effort. Because Jeff is nearly bankrupt and cannot afford medical care, Ted commences to look for ways to raise money. Eventually he is hired by a businessman named McCann who needs a fresh supply of shark livers. The young man puts together a crew, which includes a shady individual named Bracado. The expedition goes well, at first, and several sharks are caught. But after the animals' livers are harvested, Bracado and some cronies attack Ted and make off with the haul. Once Ted's back on land, he solicits help from some friends and soon recovers the stolen livers.

Comment: *Killer Shark* was filmed in November 1949 in Ensenada, Mexico.[25] McLaglen worked beside director Oscar "Budd" Boetticher as a second assistant director on *Killer Shark*. He would team up with Boetticher two more times, first as an assistant director on *Bullfighter and the Lady* and later as a co-producer on *Seven Men from Now*.

Reviews: "[T]he story is a weak one that unfolds leisurely with the exception of several shark-fishing scenes at sea." *Variety,* April 19, 1950; "About the only thing exciting here is the film's title." *Motion Picture Guide,* 1525.

Release: March, Monogram Distributing Corp.

Availability: VHS

Rock Island Trail—1950 (76 mins)

Associate Producer: Paul Malvern, Republic Pictures
Director: Joseph Kane
Script: James Edward Grant
Photography: Jack Marta (Color)
Editor: Arthur Roberts
Music: William Roy
Cast: Forrest Tucker (Loomis), Adele Mara (Constance), Adrian Booth (Aleeta), Bruce Cabot (Morrow), Chill Wills (Hogger), Barbra Fuller (Annabelle), Grant Withers (Strong), Jeff Corey (Abe Lincoln), Roy Barcroft (Barnes), Jimmy Hunt (Stinky)
Summary: Civil engineer Reed Loomis is overseeing the construction of a railroad bridge that will cross the Mississippi River. His efforts are confounded by Kirby Morrow, the owner of a steamboat company, who regards the railroad as a direct threat to his maritime business. After Morrow's fiancée, Constance, falls in love with Loomis and breaks off her engagement to him, Morrow decides to destroy his rival. He attacks Loomis with a mop that has been plunged into hot soup. He blows up one of Loomis's trains. He sends out thugs to menace the men who work for Loomis, descending on them as they lay railroad track. A successful counterattack against Morrow results in the shipping mogul's death, freeing Loomis to complete his bridge and pursue his relationship with Constance.
Comment: *Rock Island Trail* is the first film on which McLaglen worked as a first assistant director. The exteriors for the picture were shot in McAlester, Oklahoma, in the state's rural, southeastern corner.[26] James Edward Grant's script is an adaptation of a 1933 novel by Frank J. Nevins titled *A Yankee Dared: A Romance of our Railroads*. The picture's cast includes several actors McLaglen later directed in his own movies: Chill Wills (*The Little Shepherd of Kingdom Come, McLintock!*), Roy Barcroft (*Freckles, Bandolero!*), Bruce Cabot (*McLintock!, Hellfighters*), Forrest Tucker (*Chisum*) and Jeff Corey (*The Wild Geese, Banjo Hackett*).
Reviews: "When James Edward Grant's screenplay is mixing it up in physical brawls it's good, but he has spent too much time dilly-dallying with a hokey romance and accompanying corny dialogue." *Variety,* May 3, 1950; "Forrest Tucker as Loomis and Bruce Cabot as Morrow are typical strong, quick-tempered men. They are a good match. As far as we are concerned, 'Rock Island Trail' is a good, very old-fashioned Western." *New York Times,* June 5, 1950.
Release: May, Republic Pictures

Bullfighter and the Lady—1951 (87/124 mins)

Producer: John Wayne, Republic Pictures
Director: Budd Boetticher
Script: James Edward Grant, story by Budd Boetticher and Ray Nazarro
Photography: Jack Draper (B & W)
Editor: Richard L. Van Enger
Music: Victor Young
Cast: Robert Stack (Regan), Joy Page (Anita), Gilbert Roland (Manolo), Virginia Grey (Lisbeth), John Hubbard (Barney), Katy Jurado (Chelo), Antonio Gómez (Antonio), Ismael Perez (Panchito), Rodolfo Acosta (Juan), Ruben Padilla (Dr. Sierra), Dario Ramirez (Pepe Mora)
Summary: Johnny Regan, an American theatrical producer, attends a bullfight in Mexico. One of the featured matadors, Manolo Estrada, impresses Regan with his gracefulness in the *corrida*. When Regan later spots Manolo in a nightclub, he sends a bottle of champagne to the matador's table. Manolo in turn invites the American to join him. After complimenting Manolo on his earlier performance, Regan says that he would like to become a bullfighter himself. Manolo agrees to mentor Regan, if the American, a world-class marksman, will teach him how to shoot. Also seated at Manolo's table is a young woman named Anita.

Regan proves to be a quick study under Manolo's tutelage and a strong friendship develops between the two. Regan's skills in the bullring impress Anita, too, and she soon falls in love with the gringo. Weeks pass and Manolo decides that Regan is ready to fight his first bull before a paying crowd. Jeered at first for being a novice, Regan nonetheless does well. A burst of exuberance, however, prompts Regan to turn his back on the animal — a macho gesture he's adopted from Manolo. As Manolo looks on, the bull prepares to attack Regan, and the matador jumps in to save his friend. He succeeds, but the bull gores him, and later that day Manolo dies.

Filled with self-loathing, Regan asks a bullfighting official to allow him to fight a bull in Manolo's honor. The official reluctantly grants him permission and the following Sunday Regan shows up at Plaza Mexico, Mexico City's most popular bullring. He fights the animal with great finesse and afterward addresses the crowd, telling them, "I am no *torero*. The man you saw with my bull today was Manolo Estrada. His hands made every pass." As Regan leaves the bullring, Anita rushes to meet him and the couple kisses.

Comment: Produced for Republic by John Wayne, *Bullfighter and the Lady* was filmed in Mexico from May to July 1950.[27] The picture features extensive footage of actual bullfighting shot in the Plaza Mexico. Director Budd Boetticher experienced many frustrations as he made the picture. In his autobiography, *When in Disgrace,* he explains that he crafted the original treatment for the film's narrative, drawing upon his own earlier experiences as a bullfighter in Mexico. But then Wayne had screenwriter James Edward Grant rework the story, forcing changes that Boetticher did not like.

When shooting began, the director adhered to his own ideas for the film. His defiance in turn strained his relationship with Wayne; during post-production, the two frequently argued and Boetticher became worried that his picture would never be screened. He approached John Ford about assisting with the editing, and to his dismay, Ford trimmed the picture's running time from 124 minutes to 87 minutes. Boetticher recalled in his autobiography that after screening the film, Ford told him, "The only problem with your show, Budd ... is that it's got about 40 minutes of chi-chi shit that's just gotta go."[28] The film was later restored to its original length by the UCLA Film and Television Archive with support from Boetticher and actor Robert Stack.[29]

McLaglen worked on *Bullfighter and the Lady* as Boetticher's first assistant. In his memoir, Boetticher describes McLaglen as "my loyal assistant director — who really cared." Boetticher credits McLaglen with helping him handle actor Gilbert Roland (Manolo), whose "unbelievable ego" led to problems on the set:

> I had cast [him] because he certainly looked the part of a successful matador de toros.... I'm happy that I did because Roland gave a splendid performance. But his personality on the screen didn't keep him from being a major pain in everybody's ass, most especially mine.... He became so obnoxious that Andy McLaglen kept him on call most of the time so he could strut around in his bullfight suit and sign autographs, which placed him at a fair distance from me and my camera.[30]

Reviews: "Film's topnotch action-drama values are sharpened by authenticity of atmosphere and scene captured by the lensing of Mexico's bull arenas, cities and ranches." *Variety,* May 2, 1951; "Dire continuity and shifts in point of view, endless didactic sequences extolling the bullfighter's grace, and generally wooden performances result in a surprising fiasco of almost unbearable tedium." *Time Out Film Guide,* 146; "Good performances, lush visuals and a genuine love and feel for the country in which it was filmed." *Motion Picture Guide,* 316.
Release: May, Republic Pictures
Availability: VHS, LD

The Quiet Man — 1952 (129 mins)

Producer: John Ford, Merian C. Cooper, Argosy Pictures
Director: John Ford
Script: Frank S. Nugent, from story by Maurice Walsh
Photography: Winton C. Hoch (Color)
Editor: Jack Murray
Music: Victor Young
Cast: John Wayne (Sean Thornton), Maureen O'Hara (Mary Kate Danaher), Victor McLaglen ("Red" Will Danaher), Ward Bond (Father Lonergan), Mildred Natwick (Mrs. Tillane), Francis Ford (Tobin), Eileen Crowe (Mrs. Playfair), May Craig (The Woman), Arthur Shields (Rev. Playfair), Charles fitzSimons (Forbes), James Lilburn (Father Paul), Sean McClory (Owen Glynn), Jack MacGowran (Feeney), Joseph O'Dea (Guard), Eric Gorman (Engine Driver), Kevin Lawless (Fireman), Paddy O'Donnell (Porter), Web Overlander (Station Master)
Summary: Sean Thornton, a professional boxer, decides to retire after he unintentionally kills an opponent in the ring. Wanting to start his life over, he sets out for Innisfree, Ireland, where he lived as a young boy before his parents brought him to America. Upon his return to the village, Sean tries to buy his family's old home. He soon finds himself at odds with Red Danaher, a local who also wants to purchase the property. The tension between the two men only escalates when Thornton falls in love with Danaher's sister, Mary Kate.

The former boxer commences to court the maid and they eventually marry. But Red refuses to give Mary Kate her dowry. Though Thornton is indifferent to money, Mary Kate is outraged by her brother's greed. Thornton at first refuses to take action, remembering the man he killed in the ring, but to appease his new wife, he goes to Red and tells him to turn over the dowry. Sean's courage pleases Mary Kate, but the anger between Thornton and Red is now so great, they begin to brawl. The fight is spectacular, lasting for hours and carrying the two through Innisfree, until Red finally submits. The men become friends after this and drink to one another in a pub. Thornton then returns home, where Mary Kate, filled with love and pride, greets him.

Comment: *The Quiet Man* was filmed on location in Ireland from June to July 1951, with interiors completed in Burbank at Republic's studio facilities.[31] McLaglen is listed in the credits as the movie's second assistant. The film was the second picture on which McLaglen had a chance to pair up with his father Victor (Red Danaher). The two had worked together previously on *Love, Honor and Goodbye*. Victor McLaglen was nominated for an Academy Award in the Best Supporting Actor category for his performance in *The Quiet Man*. He did not win, but the picture took home awards in the Best Director and Best Cinematography categories.[32]

The source for Frank Nugent's script was a short story by Maurice Walsh titled "The Quiet Man," which first appeared in *The Saturday Evening Post* in 1933.[33] Otho Lovering cut the film; he would subsequently work as an editor on McLaglen's *McLintock!*, *Shenandoah*, *The Ballad of Josie* and *The Way West*. Although vastly different from one another in tone and theme, the narratives of *The Quiet Man* and McLaglen's *Monkeys, Go Home!* share a noteworthy parallel. In Ford's film, a boxer comes to Ireland from America to purchase a farmhouse once owned by his family. In McLaglen's film, an American Air Force officer arrives in France to claim the farmhouse his deceased mother has left him in her will.

Reviews: "It is a robust romantic drama of a native-born's return to Ireland, filmed in Technicolor." *Variety*, May 14, 1952; "Mr. Ford is in love with Ireland, as is his cast, and they give us a fine, gay time while they're about it." *New York Times*, August 22, 1952; "Because of its novelty and the beauty of its scenery, not to speak of its laughs and humanness, 'The Quiet Man' will probably find a larger audience than even the usual Ford feature." *Los Angeles Times*, October 3, 1952.

Release: September, Republic Pictures
Availability: VHS, LD, DVD

Wild Stallion—1952 (71 mins)

Producer: Walter Mirisch, Monogram Pictures Corp.
Director: Lewis D. Collins
Script: Dan Ullman
Photography: Harry Neumann (Color)
Editor: William Austin
Music: Martin Skiles
Cast: Ben Johnson (Dan Light), Edgar Buchanan (Wintergreen), Martha Hyer (Caroline), Hayden Rorke (Callan), Hugh Beaumont (Wilmurt), Orley Lindgren (Young Dan), Don Haggerty (Keach), Susan Odin (Young Caroline), I. Stanford Jolley (Bill Cole), Barbara Woodell (Mrs. Light), John Holloran (Mr. Light)
Summary: A young boy named Dan Light lives with his mother and father on a ranch. The bright spot of Dan's life is the colt he owns, Top Kick. When Dan's parents are killed by Indians, however, Top Kick runs off. The orphaned boy is soon found by a man named Wintergreen, who makes his living rounding up wild horses and selling them to the U.S. Cavalry. Wintergreen proceeds to take the boy to an army fort and turns him over to the care of Maj. Callan.

As Dan grows up, he never forgets Top Kick, and he searches for the animal whenever he can. On a couple of occasions, he comes close to capturing the horse, but the animal always escapes. When Dan eventually manages to trap the great horse, he is told by his friends at the fort that the animal belongs to the army, and that he must turn the stallion over to them. Exasperated by this claim, Dan rushes off from the fort with Top Kick.

During his flight, Dan learns that an Indian war party is planning an attack on the cavalry and he turns around, warning his pursuers about the threat. He even briefly joins the soldiers to fight against the Indians. He and Top Kick then start back to alert Callan and the others. As they make their way, they are shot at by braves and attacked by wolves. Dan nevertheless manages to return and alert the command, and the Indians are subsequently turned away. Afterward, Dan is told that he is forgiven for having run off with Top Kick and the animal is now his. Dan responds to this good news by deciding to join the cavalry.

Comment: McLaglen is listed in *Wild Stallion*'s credits as an assistant director. The film is notable because it features extensive coverage of Ben Johnson (Dan), a world champion rodeo rider, displaying his skills as a horseman.[34] Prior to *Wild Stallion,* Johnson had prominent roles in John Ford's *She Wore a Yellow Ribbon* (1949), *Wagon Master* (1950) and *Rio Grande* (1950). The actor would subsequently appear in several pictures McLaglen directed, including *The Undefeated, Chisum* and *"something big."* Edgar Buchanan (Wintergreen) also worked with McLaglen again, appearing as Bunny in *McLintock!*

Reviews: "Okay outdoor program actioner dealing with wild horses, the cavalry and Indians." *Variety,* May 15, 1952; "Standard stuff made watchable by a solid cast." *Motion Picture Guide,* 3862; "[Johnson's] skill with horses makes this mundane story somewhat appealing." *Encyclopedia of Westerns,* 491.

Release: April, Monogram Distributing Corp.

Here Come the Marines—1952 (67 mins)

Alternate Title: *Bowery Leathernecks*
Producer: Jerry Thomas, Monogram Productions Corp.
Director: William Beaudine
Script: Tim Ryan, Charles R. Marion, Jack Crutcher
Photography: Marcel LePicard (B & W)
Editor: William Austin
Music: Jacques Offenbach
Cast: Leo Gorcey (Slip), Huntz Hall (Sach), Hanley Stafford (Col. Brown), Paul Maxey (Jolly Joe Johnson), Myrna Dell (Lulu Mae), Bernard Gorcey (Louie), Arthur Space (Capt. Miller), Tim Ryan (Sheriff Benson), David Condon (Chuck), Gil Stratton, Jr. (Junior), Bennie Bartlett (Butch)
Summary: The Bowery Boys, an amiable but not especially intelligent street gang from New York, join the United States Marine Corps. The Boys are assigned to mess duty, where one of them, Sach, concocts a horrific-tasting soup. The soup is so awful that Sach's superior officers decide it can be used against the enemy in battle. Sach is then rewarded with a promotion from private to sergeant, to the consternation of Slip, the gang's leader.

While on leave, Sach and his friends lose all their money at a gambling house owned by a crook named Jolly Joe Johnson. Later, after a marine is beaten up and killed, Sach wonders if the same shady characters who got his money at the gambling house are connected to the murder. He then contacts the local sheriff. The sheriff happens to be a friend of Jolly Joe and tells him about Sach's hunches. Jolly Joe responds by sending out some goons to silence Sach.

Comment: McLaglen is listed in *Here Come the Marines*'s opening credits as an assistant director. The Bowery Boys was a comedy team comprised of Leo Gorcey, Huntz Hall, Gil Stratton, Jr.,

The Bowery Boys go out for a night of gambling in *Here Come the Marines* (Monogram, 1952). McLaglen worked on the picture as a first assistant director. From left to right: Bennie Bartlett, Gil Stratton, Jr., Leo Gorcey, Huntz Hall, David Condon, Myrna Dell, Paul Maxey.

Bennie Bartlett, David Condon and others that appeared in several pictures produced by Monogram in the forties and fifties.[35]

Reviews: "A mildly diverting programmer in Monogram's low budget Bowery Boys series." *Variety,* May 28, 1952; "The Bowery Boys with their long-running series seem to be running out of gas in this one." *Motion Picture Guide,* 1209.

Release: June, Monogram Distributing Corp.

Hellgate—1952 (87 mins)

Producer: John C. Champion, Commander Films Corporation
Director: Charles Marquis Warren
Script: Charles Marquis Warren, story by Charles Marquis Warren and John C. Champion
Photography: Ernest W. Miller (B & W)
Editor: Elmo Williams
Music: Paul Dunlap
Cast: Sterling Hayden (Gil Hanley), Joan Leslie (Elly), Ward Bond (Lt. Vorhees), James Arness (Redfield), Peter Coe (Jumper), John Pickard (Gundy), Robert Wilke (Kearn), Kyle James (Brechene), Richard Emory (Mott), Richard Paxton (Nye), William R. Hamel (Woods), Marshall Bradford, Sheb Wooley (Price), Rory Mallinson (Banta)
Summary: Two years have passed since the Civil War ended. Gil Hanley fought in the war

for the Confederacy, but now he lives peacefully in Kansas with his wife, Elly, trying to make a living as a veterinarian. Late one night, as he tends to a pregnant mare, Hanley is visited by Vern Brechene, a member of a group of anti–Union guerrillas who have been terrorizing Kansas. Injured, Brechene needs medical attention, and the veterinarian does his best to help him, unaware of who Brechene is and what he's been doing. Brechene and some cronies subsequently steal Hanley's horses, leaving their own exhausted animals behind on his property. The guerrillas inadvertently drop a saddlebag with stolen money near the veterinarian's front door, as well. When federal soldiers come by Hanley's home, searching for Brechene, they find the saddlebag and the worn out horses and conclude that Hanley is one of the guerrillas himself. A quick trial follows and the innocent man is convicted. He is then sent to Hellgate, a federal prison in the New Mexico desert.

The prison's commandant, Lt. Vorhees, is a bitter and vicious person, whose wife and daughter were burned to death during the war by Confederate rebels. Vorhees takes pleasure in badgering the new prisoner and assigns Hanley to an underground cell filled with killers and thieves. One of these men, a psychopath named Redfield, has found a cleft in the cell's ceiling, which he thinks he and his cellmates can turn into a passageway to freedom. Redfield asks for Hanley's assistance as he tries to dig his way into the cleft. Hanley refuses at first, but as Vorhees continues to abuse him, he changes his mind. Redfield, Hanley and the others soon tunnel their way out of their cell, but all of them — with the exception of Hanley — are shot and killed by sentries as they run from the prison through the open air. Quickly captured by some sentries, Hanley is turned over to Vorhees, who confines him in the ground beneath a metal door that heats up under the desert sun.

An outbreak of typhus soon besets the prison. The need for water is critical for treating the sick, but no one will sell water to Vorhees's men or deliver a shipment to the prison. Vorhees then decides to send one of his prisoners out to get water — Hanley. The veterinarian now has a chance to escape his tormentors. Instead, he persuades a group of nearby merchants to give him water, explaining that water is necessary to prevent the typhus from spreading. When Hanley returns to the prison with the water, Vorhees realizes that the man he has so horribly treated must be innocent, and arranges for him to be released. Hanley then heads home to his wife in Kansas.

Comment: McLaglen served on *Hellgate* as a first assistant. The film's director, Charles Marquis Warren, had first come to Hollywood in the forties to work as a writer. In the fifties, Warren moved into movie direction, turning out several Westerns in addition to *Hellgate: Little Big Horn* (1951), *Arrowhead* (1953), *Seven Angry Men* (1955). In 1955, CBS asked Warren to help adapt the popular *Gunsmoke* radio program for television, superseding the program's original creators, John Meston and Norman Macdonnell. It was Warren's decision to cast James Arness — one of the inmates in *Hellgate*— as the show's lead character, Marshal Matt Dillon. McLaglen started directing episodes for *Gunsmoke* in 1956, during the show's second season (1956–1957).[36]

Warren can be credited with getting *Gunsmoke* off to a good start, serving as a producer and a director on most of the shows filmed for the series' first season (1955–1956). Despite this, Warren left the show midway through the second season to produce several feature films, including *Copper Sky* (1957) and *Ride a Violent Mile* (1957). Later in the decade, he returned to CBS and developed two more Western-themed shows, *Rawhide* and *Gunslinger*. McLaglen contributed episodes to these programs, as well.[37]

Reviews: "Picture, a first for the indie Commander Films unit, is a lesson in production economics, achieving creditable values within a tight budget without costly locations treks or expensive stage settings." *Variety,* August 15, 1952.

Release: September, R.L. Lippert Pictures
Availability: DVD

Big Jim McLain—1952 (90 mins)

Producer: Robert Fellows, Wayne-Fellows Productions
Director: Edward Ludwig
Script: James Edward Grant, Richard English and Eric Taylor, from a story by Richard English
Photography: Archie Stout (B & W)
Editor: Jack Murray
Music: Emil Newman, Arthur Lange, Paul Dunlap
Cast: John Wayne (McLain), Nancy Olson (Nancy), James Arness (Baxter), Alan Napier (Sturak), Veda Ann Borg (Madge), Hans Conreid (Henreid), Hal Baylor (Poke), Gayne Whitman (Dr. Gelsteri), Gordon Jones (Olaf), Robert Keys (White), John Hubbard (Lt. Comm. Grey), Madame Soo Yong (Mrs. Nomaka), Dan Liu (Himself), Red McQueen (Briggs)
Summary: Jim McLain and his partner Mal Baxter are federal investigators who work for the House Un-American Activities Committee; their job is to expose and break up Communist spy rings. For an assignment called "Operation Pineapple," the pair is sent to Hawaii. Through contacts, they discover that the leader of a cell operating in the islands is an Englishman named Sturak. McLain and Baxter conduct a vigorous search as they try to collect information on Sturak, at one point even visiting a leper colony. But then Baxter is murdered. Working with local police, McLain continues the investigation, eventually tracking

James Arness and John Wayne play a pair of federal investigators in *Big Jim McLain* (Warner, 1952).

Sturak to a palatial home, where the spy is scheming with a scientist to release a bacteriological agent that will sicken and kill people. The meeting is broken up and Sturak and his associates are apprehended. At their trial, the spies invoke the Fifth Amendment and refuse to provide self-incriminating testimony. Disgusted by this, McLain leaves the courtroom. He finds some comfort, however, by walking along a nearby wharf, where he and his wife wave at a U.S. battleship as it sets out to sea.

Comment: *Big Jim McLain* is the first film made for Wayne-Fellows, John Wayne's independent motion picture production company. The movie was shot in May 1952 on location in Hawaii, with McLaglen serving as director Edward Ludwig's first assistant.[38] McLaglen's second wife, Veda Ann Borg, has a small part in the film, playing an alcoholic landlady named Madge. The film's script is based loosely on an article by Richard English titled "We Almost Lost Hawaii to the Reds," which appeared in February 1952 in the *Saturday Evening Post*. *Big Jim McLain* was just one of many anti–Communist films produced by Hollywood in the decade following the end of World War II. Others included: Robert Stevenson's *I Married a Communist* (1949), Leo McCarey's *My Son John* (1952) and Sam Fuller's *Pickup on South Street* (1953).[39]

Reviews: "Continuity is choppy, the script sketchy and lacking in clarity. But these critical flaws become almost submerged in forceful scenes, a number of good action spots and the excellent dialog." *Variety*, August 27, 1952; "It is hard to tell precisely whether the Warners' 'Big Jim McLain' is to be taken seriously as a documentation of the sort of work that is done by the House Un-American Activities Committee in its investigations of the Communist peril or whether it is merely intended to arouse and entertain." *New York Times*, September 18, 1952.

Release: August, Warner Bros.
Availability: VHS, DVD

Kansas Pacific—1953 (73 mins)

Producer: Walter Wanger, Allied Artists Productions, Inc.
Associate Producer: Edward Morey, Jr.
Director: Ray Nazarro
Script: Dan Ullman
Photography: Harry Neumann (Color)
Editor: William Austin, Walter Hannemann
Music: Albert Sendrey
Cast: Sterling Hayden (John Nelson), Eve Miller (Barbara Bruce), Barton MacLane (Calvin Bruce), Harry Shannon (Smokestack), Tom Fadden (Gustavson), Reed Hadley (Quantrill), Douglas Fowley (Janus), Bob Keys (Lt. Sam Stanton), Irving Bacon (Casey), Myron Healey (Morey), James Griffith (Farley), Clayton Moore (Stone), Jonathan Hale (Johnson)
Summary: In the months preceding the outbreak of the Civil War, a band of anti–Union guerrillas turns its attention to a railway line that the federal government and the Kansas Pacific railroad company are building in Kansas. Led by Bill Quantrill, the guerrillas tear up tracks and shoot at Kansas Pacific's workers. In response, the U.S. Army sends one of its officers, an engineer named John Nelson, to see the job through to completion.

Nelson proceeds to hire several new workers, including armed guards, and the project resumes. Quantrill and his men, in turn, use increasingly dangerous methods to frustrate the railroad company's efforts, at one point blowing up a shipment of blasting dynamite. A garrison of U.S. soldiers is then sent from Washington to Kansas. A bloody battle commences and Quantrill's men are undone, enabling Nelson and the others to return to their work.

Comment: *Kansas Pacific* was shot in the summer of 1952 for Allied Artists, a unit of Monogram Pictures. While Monogram specialized in low budget movies, Allied Artists produced higher end offerings.[40] McLaglen is credited as *Kansas Pacific*'s assistant director. Among the picture's cast of supporting actors is Clayton Moore, who plays one of Quantrill's saboteurs; Moore would become famous later in the decade for playing the Lone Ranger in films and television.[41]

Although Walter Wanger received a producer's credit on *Kansas Pacific,* he was serving a prison sentence at the time of the film's production. In *Walter Wanger, Hollywood Independent,* Matthew Bernstein explains that Wanger had come to work for Monogram-Allied Artists in June 1951. In December of that year, Wanger shot a man named Jennings Lang in the groin, after finding Lang with his wife, the actress Joan Bennett. Wanger was subsequently convicted and served a jail sentence from June 1952 to September 1952. According to Bernstein, the studio gave Wanger the producer's credit in part to help him out of the financial difficulties he was experiencing after his release from prison. The decision to give Wanger the credit was spearheaded by Walter Mirisch, an executive at Monogram during this period. Actual producer duties were handled by the picture's associate producer, Edward Morey, Jr. Mirisch also gave Wanger a fabricated producer's credit for *Fort Vengeance,* another Allied Artists release on which McLaglen served as assistant director.[42]

Though "'Kansas Pacific' is fictitious, William Quantrill was a real figure who led raids against Union sympathizers throughout the Civil War, before being killed in 1865.[43] In McLaglen's own *Bandolero!,* Dean Martin plays a character named Pike Bishop who served as one of Quantrill's Raiders.

Reviews: "'Kansas Pacific' shapes as one of the better pix to emerge under the Allied Artists banner. A carefully executed production by Walter Wanger." *Variety,* March 17, 1953.

Release: February, Associated Artists
Availability: VHS, LD, DVD

Fort Vengeance—1953 (75 mins)

Producer: Walter Wanger, Allied Artists Pictures
Associate Producer: William Calihan, Jr.
Director: Lesley Selander
Script: Dan Ullman
Photography: Harry Neumann (Color)
Editor: Walter Hannemann
Music: Paul Dunlap
Cast: James Craig (Dick), Rita Moreno (Bridget), Keith Larsen (Carey), Reginald Denny (Trevett), Charles Irwin (Saxon), Morris Ankrum (Crowfoot), Guy Kingsford (MacRea), Michael Granger (Sitting Bull), Patrick Whyte (Harrington), Paul Marion (Eagle Heart), Emory Parnell (Fitzgibbon)
Summary: In the summer of 1876, Carey Ross and his brother, Dick, flee to Canada after Carey shoots a man in a gunfight. The two wander across Saskatchewan, eventually finding a military outpost called Fort Vengeance, which quarters a unit of the North-West Mounted Police. Needing work, the brothers meet with one of the fort's commanding officers, Maj. Trevett, who gives them jobs as constables. Trevett needs men because Sitting Bull, chief of the Lakota Sioux, has come to Canada to wage war on white settlers and escape persecution from the U.S. Cavalry, having decimated Custer and his men at Little Big Horn earlier in the year.

Though he now works for the Mounted Police, Carey Ross is a scoundrel. With a trapper named Luboc, Carey steals a collection of pelts that belongs to the Sioux. When the Mounties announce that Luboc is a prime suspect in this crime, Carey decides to track down and kill his partner, in order to silence him forever. After Carey finds Luboc in a remote cabin, a fight breaks out between the two, during which Luboc is killed and Carey flees. Some Mounties who investigate the killing mistakenly attribute Luboc's death to a Blackfoot Indian named Eagle Heart. The Indian is then charged with the murder and taken into custody, a development that has the potential for prompting the Blackfoot tribe to side with the Sioux and trigger a war with Canadian forces.

Dick Ross suspects that his brother Carey is the actual killer and heads off to find him. When Dick locates Carey, he asks him to tell the other constables the truth about Luboc's death. Unwilling to do this, Carey attacks Dick instead. One of Sitting Bull's sons, Blue Cloud, comes to Dick's aid and Carey is killed. Dick then proceeds to tell his superiors at Fort Vengeance that Eagle Heart had nothing to do with the death of Luboc. The disclosure leads to the Indian's release, a development that pleases both the Blackfoot and the Sioux, and war is averted.

Comment: Lesley Selander, a prolific director of "B" Westerns, directed *Fort Vengeance*; McLaglen served as the picture's first assistant. McLaglen had previously worked with Selander on *Apache Rose* when he was a production clerk at Republic. Just as he had for *Kansas Pacific*, on which McLaglen also worked, Walter Wanger received a producer's credit for *Fort Vengeance*, though he was serving time in prison during the film's production. Associate producer William Calihan, Jr., actually oversaw the film's production.[44]

Reviews: "Picture isn't equipped with as much excitement as desirable in this type of yarn and, as a consequence, the footage is inclined to walk more often than it runs." *Variety*, April 1, 1953.

Release: March, Allied Artists Pictures

Island in the Sky—1953 (109 mins)

Producer: Robert Fellows, Wayne-Fellows Productions
Director: William A. Wellman
Script: Ernest Gann, from his novel *Island in the Sky*
Photography: Archie Stout; aerial photography directed by William H. Clothier (B & W)
Editor: Ralph Dawson
Music: Emil Newman
Cast: John Wayne (Dooley), Lloyd Nolan (Stutz), Walter Abel (Col. Fuller), James Arness (McMullen), Andy Devine (Moon), Allyn Joslyn (Handy), James Lydon (Murray), Harry Carey, Jr. (Hunt), Hal Baylor (Stankowski), Sean McClory (Lovatt), Wally Cassell (D'Annunzia), Gordon Jones (Walrus), Frank Fenton (Capt. Turner), Robert Keys (Dotson), Sumner Getchell (Cord), Regis Toomey (Harper), Paul Fix (Miller), Jim Dugan (Gidley), George Chandler (Rene), Bob Steele (Wilson), Darryl Hickman (Swanson), Touch Connors (Gainer), Carl Switzer (Hopper), Cass Gidley (Stanish), Guy Anderson (Breezy), Tony De Mario (Ogden)
Summary: Capt. Dooley, a civilian pilot in the U.S. Army's Air Transport Command, is flying through northern Canada when a violent storm sets in, forcing him and his crew to crash land their DC-3 near an icy lake. Although the men are unhurt, their supply of food, protective clothing and electricity is low. When Col. Fuller, chief of the Air Transport Command's North Atlantic Wing, realizes that Dooley's aircraft is down, he sends out every

Produced for Wayne-Fellows, *Island in the Sky* marked the first time McLaglen worked beside director William A. Wellman (Warner, 1953).

available plane to search the vast landscape. Finding the men proves to be difficult because the section of land where they've crashed is uncharted, and covered with mountains, trees and snow.

As pilots from the Air Transport Command continue their search, the stranded men experience hardships in the snow below. Hungry, frightened and cold, they can't find dry wood to light fires or animals to hunt and eat. One of the men, Dooley's co-pilot Lovatt, even dies in a snowstorm. Days pass and the search continues unsuccessfully. But then, thanks to a hand-cranked sound transmitter, Dooley and the others manage to deliver a signal to their airborne friends, and finally they are rescued.

Comment: McLaglen is listed in the opening credits as *Island in the Sky*'s assistant director. The film marks the first time McLaglen collaborated with both William A. Wellman and cameraman William H. Clothier, who shot the picture's aerial footage. Frank Thompson notes that "[b]ecause the film takes place in a snow-covered environment, Wellman chose Donner Lake, near Truckee, California for the location work."[45] Ernest Gann penned the script for *Island in the Sky,* working from his 1944 novel of the same name. Gann also served as the picture's technical advisor, having flown for the Air Transport Command during World War II. Gann in fact piloted the plane that carried Clothier as the cameraman shot footage of actual DC-3 bombers in flight.[46]

Reviews: "Wayne and the cast of male co-stars and featured players are perfectly at home in their characters, each giving the picture a little something extra to make it entirely satisfactory entertainment." *Variety,* August 12, 1953; "John Wayne is the star, and it's a strangely non-active role for this usually rambunctious fellow. But there is suspense in this tale of a Military Air Transport crew downed in a snowstorm." *Washington Post,* September 5, 1953; "While sometimes talky, the script does a fine job of showing men battling nature. Exceptional performances, especially from the rescue team, are a plus." *Motion Picture Guide,* 1412.

Release: September, Warner Bros.
Availability: DVD

Plunder of the Sun — 1953 (81 mins)

Producer: Robert Fellows, Wayne-Fellows Productions
Director: John Farrow
Script: Jonathan Latimer, based on the novel by David Dodge
Photography: Jack Draper (B & W)
Editor: Harry Marker
Music: Antonio Diaz Conde; song "Sin Ella" composed by Enrique Fabregat
Cast: Glenn Ford (Al Colby), Diana Lynn (Julie Barnes), Patricia Medina (Anna Luz), Francis L. Sullivan (Thomas Berrien), Sean McClory (Jefferson), *Eduardo Noriega* (Raul Cornego), Julio Villareal (Navarro), Charles Roomer (Capt. Bergman), Douglas Dumbrille (Consul)
Summary: Al Colby, an American insurance man, finds himself broke in Havana. When an art collector named Thomas Berrien offers him $1,000 if he will smuggle a package into Mexico, Colby accepts and he and Berrien, along with Berrrien's nurse, Anna Luz, soon set off by ship. Before they arrive in Mexico, Colby is approached by an inquisitive Irishman named Jefferson, who asks the American repeatedly about his reasons for travelling to Mexico. A short time later, Berrien is found dead in his cabin.

Colby and Anna Luz make it into Mexico safely, and Colby finds lodging in the city of Oaxaca. In his hotel room, he unwraps the package Berrien gave him, finding some fragments

Leading man Glenn Ford and his co-star Patricia Medina in *Plunder of the Sun* (Warner, 1953).

of an ancient manuscript and a jade disc. He later searches through Oaxaca, hoping to find someone who can help him translate the manuscript. A museum curator directs Colby to an art collector named Navarro, a patriot who wants to protect Mexico's cultural heritage from being plundered. Recognizing that Colby's fragmentary manuscript provides directions to a secret stash of Zapotecan loot, Navarro steals the document.

Having anticipated trouble of this sort, Colby has prepared a backup copy of the manuscript for himself. He proceeds to contact Jefferson — a "disbarred" archaeologist, we learn — and the Irishman translates Colby's copy of the manuscript. The treasure, Jefferson determines, is located on an archeological site called Mitla, which is covered with magnificent ruins. Sneaking into the site at night, the two men break into a crypt that is filled with priceless artifacts. They load up a burro with the relics, but as they prepare to depart, Jefferson shoots Colby, leaving him to die.

The insurance man wakes up days later in the home of Navarro, where he's received care from Anna Luz, who, it turns out, is Navarro's ward. An American woman named Julie has been helping him, too. Colby explains to Navarro that he never actually intended to keep the Zapotechan treasure for himself; instead, he planned to turn it over to Mexican authorities for a reward.

Once he is strong enough, Colby sets out to find Jefferson, tracing him to a storage space behind a museum. A fight ensues and Jefferson dies when a large statue falls and crushes him.

Colby is then apprehended by the police. When Navarro explains that the American has been very helpful about recovering the lost artifacts, Colby is let go. He and Anna Luz, with whom he has fallen in love, then fly back to Havana.

Comment: *Plunder of the Sun* was shot in the fall of 1952.[47] A title card appearing at the end of the picture explains that it was "filmed entirely in Mexico, in the Zapotecan ruins of Mitla and Monte Alban. We wish to express our gratitude to the wonderful people of Oaxaca, Veracruz and the Churubusco-Azteca Studios in Mexico City for their help and cooperation." This was the second picture to be produced for Wayne-Fellows, with McLaglen handling assistant director duties, as he had on the company's first picture, *Big Jim McLain*. McLaglen would work with director John Farrow again on Wayne-Fellows's *Hondo,* which was also shot in Mexico. *Plunder of the Sun* was adapted from a 1949 crime novel by David Dodge, also titled *Plunder of the Sun*. The film's script was penned by Jonathan Latimer, who'd written Farrow's well-regarded *film noir, The Big Clock* (1948).[48] Like McLaglen, Latimer would work on the *Perry Mason* television show later in the decade, but there's no record he contributed to any of the episodes McLaglen directed.

Reviews: "This Mexican-locale and filmed adventure melodrama delivers only a fair amount of entertainment. The production by the Wayne-Fellows unit for Warner Bros. release has atmosphere and mood aplenty, highly interesting settings and an okay plot. But misses out on needed suspense because of a flashback presentation that fails to maintain audience pull." *Variety,* August 21, 1953; "[T]he independent production team of John Wayne and Robert Fellows has given [film] a truly impressive patina by journeying down to Oaxaca, Mexico, and the nearby Zapotecan temples, palaces and pyramids. The towering remnants of a civilization that once was great not only provides atmosphere but also adds some suspense to a yarn that very often can use it." *New York Times,* August 27, 1953; "Performances are adequate, with the photography of the ruined temples providing the proper atmosphere." *Motion Picture Guide,* 2422.

Release: August, Warner Bros.
Availability: DVD

Hondo—1954 (84 mins)

Producer: Robert Fellows, Wayne-Fellows Productions
Director: John Farrow
Script: James Edward Grant, based on Louis L'Amour's short story "The Gift of Cochise"
Photography: Robert Burke, Archie Stout (Color)
Editor: Ralph Dawson
Music: Emil Newman, Hugo Friedhofer
Cast: John Wayne (Hondo Lane), Geraldine Page (Angie Lowe), Ward Bond (Buffalo), Michael Pate (Vittorio), James Arness (Lennie), Rodolfo Acosta (Silva), Leo Gordon (Ed Lowe), Tom Irish (Lt. McKay), Lee Aaker (Johnny Lowe), Paul Fix (Maj. Sherry), Rayford Barnes (Pete)
Summary: In 1870, the U.S. Cavalry is at war with the Apache nation. One of the army's best scouts and dispatch riders is Hondo Lane, who roves the desert with a dog named Sam. When his horse dies, Hondo is forced to cross the arid landscape on foot. He eventually finds a ranch, where a woman named Angie Lowe and her son, Pete, live. Mrs. Lowe explains that she is married, but her husband has gone into the nearby hills to find missing cattle. Hondo suspects differently. After unsuccessfully trying to persuade the woman to leave her ranch, warning her that the Apaches are killing white settlers, Hondo sets off for an army outpost to meet with his employers; to get there, he uses one of Mrs. Lowe's horses.

After making his report, Hondo is approached by Mrs. Lowe's husband, who, it turns out, has long ago abandoned his wife and son. Lowe recognizes the horse Hondo has been riding as one of his own and demands to have it returned to him. Instead, Hondo starts for the Lowe ranch to give the horse back to Mrs. Lowe. Aggrieved and ornery, Lowe follows Hondo. He even tries to kill him, but Hondo is faster with the gun and Lowe dies. Hondo then returns to Mrs. Lowe, planning to tell her what he has done. Before he can, the widow professes her love to him. Then a band of scouts and cavalry officers shows up, telling Mrs. Lowe that she and Pete must leave their ranch if they hope to stay alive.

Around the same time, a young scout named Lennie confronts Hondo, telling the older man that he knows who killed Lowe, a disclosure Mrs. Lowe overhears. The news fails to upset her because her husband, she reveals, was an awful person. As the threat from the Apaches becomes more acute, the cavalry officers, the scouts, the Lowes and other settler families start for safer territory. A terrific battle ensues, ending when the leader of the Apaches is killed. As the wagon train resumes its course, Hondo and Mrs. Lowe make plans to move to his ranch in California, where they will live as husband and wife.

Comment: *Hondo* was filmed on location in Camargo, Mexico, during the summer of 1953.[49]

The picture was originally shot in 3-D, but when it was released in January 1954, the appetite for 3-D films had faded, and exhibitors were no longer interested in screening

John Wayne addresses James Arness in a scene from *Hondo* (Warner, 1954), with Ward Bond standing in the background. McLaglen was assigned to the film as a unit production manager.

films in this format. Randy Robert and James Stuart Olson explain: "When *Hondo* was released, angry theater owners were threatening to boycott 3-D films, and ticket buyers had already tired of the cumbersome novelty. Only a week into *Hondo*'s release, Wayne-Fellows replaced it with a regular, flat-projection version."[50]

James Lee Grant based his script for *Hondo* on a short story by Louis L'Amour titled "The Gift of Cochise," which had appeared in July 1952 in *Collier's*. L'Amour would subsequently expand the story into a novel, which Fawcett Books published in 1953 under the title *Hondo*.[51] McLaglen served as the film's unit production manager. He would later shoot his own adaptation of a L'Amour story, *The Shadow Riders*, a 1982 television movie starring Tom Selleck and Sam Elliott.

In his autobiography, James Arness (Lennie) reports that John Ford worked without credit on *Hondo*, shooting parts of the climactic battle scene between the Apaches, the settlers and the army.[52] Ronald L. Davis adds: "Ford himself decided to pay a visit to the set, showing up on the Mexican location dressed in army fatigues and a wide-brim hat cocked over one eye. Wayne arranged for him to supervise some of the second-unit work."[53] Geraldine Page received a Best Actress nomination from the Motion Picture Academy for her performance as Mrs. Lowe.[54] In addition to Arness, the future star of *Gunsmoke*, *Hondo* features two actors — Michael Pate (Vittorio) and Rayford Barnes (Pete) — who would work frequently with McLaglen during his tenure at CBS Television in the late-fifties and early-sixties.

Reviews: "'Hondo,' like 'Shane,' gives the western an aura of maturity. It depicts a conflict of interests rather than an individual battle of good versus evil." *Variety*, 25 November 1953; "The film is partly inspired by *Shane*, accentuating the close relationship of hero-worshipping youngster to virtuous gunfighter, and its exterior shooting has the look of a John Ford work, but *Hondo* stands tall on its own." *Motion Picture Guide*, 1262.
Release: January, Warner Bros.
Availability: VHS, DVD

The High and the Mighty—1954 (147 mins)

Producer: Robert M. Fellows, Wayne-Fellows Productions
Director: William A. Wellman
Script: Ernest K. Gann, from his novel *The High and the Mighty*
Photography: Archie Stout; aerial photography by William H. Clothier (Color)
Editor: Ralph Dawson
Music: Dimitri Tiomkin
Cast: John Wayne (Dan Roman), Claire Trevor (May Hoist), Laraine Day (Lydia Rice), Robert Stack (Sullivan), Jan Sterling (Sally McKee), Phil Harris (Ed Joseph), Robert Newton (Gustave Pardee), David Brian (Ken Childs), Paul Kelly (Flaherty), Sidney Blackmer (Agnew), Julie Bishop (Lillian Pardee), Gonzales Gonzalez (Gonzalez), John Howard (Howard Rice), William Campbell (Hobie Wheeler), Ann Doran (Mrs. Joseph), John Qualen (José Locota), Paul Fix (Frank Briscoe), George Chandler (Sneed), Joy Kim (Dorothy Chen), Michael Wellman (Toby Field), Douglas Fowley (Alsop), Carl Switzer (Keim), Robert Keys (Mobray), William Dewolf Hopper (Roy), William Schallert (Dispatcher), Julie Mitchum (Susie), Karen Sharpe (Nell Buck), Doe Avedon (Miss Spalding), John Smith (Milo Buck)
Summary: Veteran pilot Dan Roman once crashed a plane into the side of a hill in South America, killing everyone on board except himself. Among the victims were his wife and son. The tragedy damaged his career and he now works for Trans-Orient-Pacific as a co-pilot

John Wayne, Robert Stack and William Campbell, the stars of *The High and the Mighty* (Warner, 1954), contemplate a damaged aircraft engine.

on a DC-4, taking orders from men who are several years his junior. On a flight from Honolulu to San Francisco, Roman finds himself sharing the cockpit with Capt. John Sullivan, a neurotic who has developed a fear for flying. Other members of the crew include a second officer, Hobie Wheeler, a navigator, Lenny Wilby and a flight attendant, Miss Spalding.

The DC-4 takes off without incident, loaded with commercial cargo and several passengers. Once the craft is over the ocean, an engine begins to act erratically, causing the plane to shake, but Sullivan and the crew proceed with the flight. Several hours later, the engine bursts into flame, causing a propeller to snap loose, strike the wing, and damage a fuel line. The incident terrifies the passengers. Some weep, some drink, some try to console one another. Members of the flight crew grow upset, too, including Sullivan, who suffers an emotional breakdown, certain the plane will descend into the ocean long before they reach land. Roman, in contrast, remains calm, offering reassurance to the passengers and the other crew. He settles Sullivan down, too, slapping him across the face. With new resolve, the pilots fly the plane successfully to shore. Once they're on the ground, the crew and the passengers exit the plane onto the tarmac, where they are greeted by families, co-workers and journalists.

Comment: Andrew V. McLaglen served on *The High and the Mighty* as director Wellman's first assistant. The film was shot in Cinemascope, using a soundstage leased from the Samuel Goldwyn Studio.[55] Archie Stout received credit as the picture's director of photography; he worked primarily in the studio, however. William H. Clothier was responsible for the film's extensive aerial footage, as he had been for Wellman's previous picture *Island in the Sky*, which similarly focuses on the efforts of an air crew facing duress. Ernest Gann, a former "trans-oceanic airline pilot" wrote both films, as well, basing his scripts upon his own novels.[56]

John Wayne did not initially intend to play the role of Dan Roman, but after Wellman's first choice for the role, Spencer Tracy, dropped out of the project, the actor took the part. McLaglen told Wayne's biographer Michael Munn: "Bill Wellman was the best-prepared director I'd ever met, but he also had a reputation for browbeating his actors. He got Tracy to read the script, and they had lunch and shook hands on a deal. But then Tracy's friends who'd worked with Wellman told him that he was in for an ego-bruising ride, so Tracy pulled out, telling Wellman that the script was lousy."[57] *The High and the Mighty* received good reviews and performed well at the box office upon its release in July 1954. Dimitri Tiomkin's score for the film went on to win an Academy Award.[58]

Reviews: "CinemaScope goes airborne, and in the bright, beautiful hues of color, for visual emphasis." *Variety*, May 25, 1954; "Loaded with touches of lumpy humor and assorted heavy sentiments, it rocks and buffets and bounces across the wide screen for more than two hours, spitting fire, tossing propellers and strewing emotional wreckage all over the place." *New York Times*, July 1, 1954; "A stirring and often frightening production, this is a landmark Cinema-Scope film that takes full advantage of the wide-screen process as well as providing a socko story and wonderful characters." *Motion Picture Guide*, 1222.

Release: July, Warner Bros.
Availability: DVD

Ring of Fear—1954 (93 mins)

Producer: Robert M. Fellows, Wayne-Fellows Productions
Director: James Edward Grant, William A. Wellman (uncredited)
Script: Paul Fix, Phillip MacDonald and James Edward Grant
Photography: Edwin Dupar (Color)
Editor: Fred MacDowell
Music: Emil Newman, Arthur Lange; credits also cite Stan Purdy for composing "Mickey Spillane's 'Velda'" and "The Mike Hammer Theme"
Cast: Clyde Beatty (Himself), Mickey Spillane (Himself), Pat O'Brien (Frank Wallace), Sean McClory (O'Malley), Marian Carr (Valerie St. Dennis), John Bromfield (Armand St. Dennis), Gonzalez Gonzalez (Pedro), Emmett Lynn (Twitchy), Jack Stang (Himself), Kenneth Tobey (Shreveport), Kathy Cline (Suzette)
Summary: Following an injury he sustained at Iwo Jima, Dublin O'Malley, a one-time circus ringmaster, has gone insane and now lives in a state hospital. After he's told by doctors that he is too unstable to ever leave the institution, O'Malley attacks one of the orderlies who watches over him and escapes. In a nearby town, the fugitive kills a man, dresses the victim in his hospital clothes and throws the body under a train; when authorities find the dead man, they misidentify him as O'Malley.

The killer then lands a job as a ringmaster with the Clyde Beatty Circus. Years earlier, prior to the onset of his mental illness, O'Malley had also worked for this outfit; but he quit after Clyde Beatty himself laughed at him for being scared of one of the circus's big cats. His resentment over this long ago incident has transformed into homicidal rage and O'Malley commences on a campaign to destroy Beatty and his circus, setting free dangerous animals and booby trapping the performers' equipment. Helping O'Malley is an alcoholic clown named Twitchy.

To find out who the saboteurs are, the manager of the circus, Frank Wallace, seeks advice from Mickey Spillane, the popular crime writer. Spillane is joined by his friend Jack Stang, an undercover police detective. The investigators soon suspect O'Malley is the culprit, but establishing the madman is guilty, as well as apprehending him, proves to be difficult and dangerous.

Comment: The original director assigned to *Ring of Fear* was James Edward Grant, who'd earlier directed *Angel and the Badman* (1947) for Patnel, John Wayne's first production company; Melvin A. Dellar worked on *Ring of Fear* as the picture's original first assistant. Wayne and his partner Robert Fellows were not pleased with Grant's work, however, and director William A. Wellman was brought on to shoot new material. McLaglen was assigned to the film to be Wellman's first assistant. Neither he nor Wellman received screen credit for their contributions.[59]

Ring of Fear was one of many circus-themed films produced in the mid-fifties, a trend prompted in part by C.B. DeMille's *The Greatest Show on Earth* (1952), which won the 1952 Academy Award for Best Picture. The period also saw the release of Carol Reed's *Trapeze*

Sean McClory in a scene from *Ring of Fear* (Warner, 1954).

(1956), as well as Fellini's *La Strada* (1954) and Ophuls's *Lola Montes* (1955). The script for *Ring of Fear* featured contributions from James Edward Grant, actor Paul Fix and Phillip MacDonald. MacDonald wrote the original story upon which John Ford's *The Lost Patrol* was based, the 1934 war drama in which Victor McLaglen played the lead.[60] MacDonald would subsequently write for *Perry Mason* in the 1950s; one of the scripts he penned, "The Case of the Terrified Typist," was directed by McLaglen during the show's first season.

Reviews: "Exploitable melodrama with circus background. Marred by mediocre scripting." *Variety*, July 2, 1954; "Both a fine title and a reputable circus have been wasted in 'Ring of Fear.' ... Produced in CinemaScope and Color by Robert M. Fellows, this Warners melodrama half-heartedly projects some colorful glimpses of the Clyde Beatty Circus in action and repose. On the whole, however, the slow, contrived and often absurd incidents of the plot elbow the authenticity aside and stir up only a modicum of suspense." *New York Times*, July 30, 1954;

"McClory gives a stunning performance as the half-crazed man, making himself likeable despite his ruthlessness." *Motion Picture Guide*, 2623.
Release: July, Warner Bros.
Availability: DVD

Track of the Cat—1954 (103 mins)

Producer: No producer credit, Wayne-Fellows Productions
Director: William A. Wellman
Script: A.I. Bezzerides, from the novel by Walter Van Tilburg Clark
Photography: William H. Clothier (Color)
Editor: Fred MacDowell
Music: Roy Webb
Cast: Robert Mitchum (Curt), Teresa Wright (Grace), Diana Lynn (Gwen), Tab Hunter (Hal), Beulah Bondi (Ma), Philip Tonge (Pa), William Hopper (Arthur), Carl Switzer (Joe Sam)
Summary: Curt Bridges is an embittered rancher who lives on a mountain ranch with his parents and his siblings. For years, a panther has been killing the Bridges's cattle during the winter months and Curt desperately wants to destroy it. An ancient Indian named Joe Sam, who lives with the Bridges, wants to see the animal dead, too, because the creature once killed his wife and daughter. As the film opens, Joe Sam wakes up Curt and his two brothers, Arthur and Hal, certain the panther has returned to prey on the Bridges's herd.

Curt and Art soon head out into the deep snow to find the creature, while Hal remains behind with the family and his girlfriend, Gwen, who is visiting the Bridges's ranch. Gwen would like to marry Hal, but the young man is too poor to start out on his own and move away from home, thanks largely to Curt, who has prevented him from being able to share in and access the family's wealth. As the day wears on, Gwen prods Hal, telling him to assert himself more forcefully.

After failing to find the cat, Curt briefly leaves Art in the woods and returns to the family ranch to replenish their supplies. During Curt's absence, the panther kills Art. Curt returns to the mountain and proceeds to hunt for the animal on his own. Soon overcome by hunger and exhaustion, he wanders off the edge of a cliff and dies. Several days later, Hal and Joe Sam start up the mountain to find Curt. During their search, Hal spots the cat and kills it. He and the old man then head home.

Comment: *Track of the Cat* is based on Walter Van Tilburg Clark's 1949 novel *The Track of the Cat*. In his memoir *A Short Time for Insanity*, Wellman explains that for *Track of the*

William Hopper and Robert Mitchum, two of the leads in Wellman's *Track of the Cat* (Warner, 1954). Hopper subsequently worked with McLaglen on the *Perry Mason* television show.

Cat he and director of photography William H. Clothier decided "to make a black and white picture in color." Wellman at the time was frustrated by the garish appearance of many color films. "Most color pictures remind me of scrambled eggs," he wrote, "only they don't use eggs—just paints." To create the effect he wanted, Wellman had the Bridges's ranch house "painted off-white, the snow was white, the cattle and horse black and white or a combination of the two. The big pine trees I shot from the shady side so they photographed black. The characters were all clothed in black and white. The only splash of color was the red mackinaw that Mitchum [Curt] wore and a little flimsy yellow silk scarf that Diana Lynn [Gwen] wore." The results pleased the filmmakers: "Never have I seen such beauty, a naked kind of beauty. Bill and I saw the first print back from the lab. We sat there together, drooling."[61]

McLaglen was Wellman's first assistant on *Track of the Cat*. The movie's outdoor sequences were shot on Mt. Rainier in Washington from June to July in 1954.[62] *Track of the Cat* marks the first time McLaglen worked with Robert Mitchum. Mitchum appeared in two pictures McLaglen directed, *The Way West* and *Breakthrough*. William Hopper (Art) went on to play the role of Paul Drake on the *Perry Mason* television show and appeared in all seven of the episodes McLaglen directed for the program.[63]

Reviews: "Mr. Wellman's big-screen picture seems a heavy and clumsy travesty of a deep matriarchal melodrama or a Western with Greek overtones," *New York Times,* December 2, 1954;

"A bleak, moody, slow, somewhat pretentious, but nonetheless fascinating filmic experiment in style from director Wellman and cinematographer Clothier." *Motion Picture Guide,* 3517
Release: November, Warner Bros.
Availability: VHS, DVD

Blood Alley—1955 (115 mins)

Producer: No producer credit, Batjac Productions
Director: William A. Wellman
Script: A.B. Fleischman, from his novel
Photography: William H. Clothier (Color)
Editor: Fred MacDowell
Music: Roy Web
Cast: John Wayne (Wilder), Lauren Bacall (Cathy), Paul Fix (Mr. Tso), Joy Kim (Susu), Berry Kroeger (Old Feng), Mike Mazurki (Big Han), Anita Ekberg (Wek Long), Henry Nakamura (Tack), W.T. Chang (Mr. Han), George Chan (Mr. Sing)
Summary: Tom Wilder, an American merchant marine, has been confined in a Red Chinese prison cell for two years. To keep sane and to thwart his captors' efforts at brainwashing him, Wilder has created an imaginary female friend named "Baby." Much of his time is spent talking to Baby and staring out the window at a nearby bay and the dilapidated ferryboat that crosses it each day.

One afternoon, a guard gives Wilder a new mattress to replace the one the prisoner has recently set on fire. Inside it, Wilder finds a gun and a Russian officer's uniform. He proceeds to escape from the jail and is met by a boatman named Big Han, who carries him to a fishing village called Chiku Shan. One of the elders in the village, Mr. Tao, reveals that he has facilitated Wilder's escape, having bribed some guards at the prison. Unwilling to live under Communist rule, Tao explains, the residents of Chiku Shan are planning to flee to Hong Kong, which lies 300 miles away.

To get there, they will use the ferryboat that Wilder has seen so often from his cell. To captain the ship, the villagers need someone with an expert's knowledge of Blood Alley, their name for the long and dangerous waterway that will get them to Hong Kong. Wilder recognizes the tremendous challenge a trip of this sort presents, but the idea of undermining the Red Chinese appeals to him, and he agrees to help. After elaborate preparations, Wilder and the villagers set off on their journey. Joining them is an American woman, Cathy Grainger, whose father has been murdered by the Communists. Tao also insists upon bringing the Fengs, the one family in the village that supports Chairman Mao, out of fear these people will be mistakenly credited with — and killed for — helping the others escape.

Comment: *Blood Alley* was the first picture made for John Wayne's Batjac Productions. The picture was shot from January to March 1955 in Marin County, California around, the San Francisco Bay.[64] Robert Mitchum was originally cast to play the role of Tom Wilder. The actor had successfully worked with Wellman on two earlier pictures, *The Story of G.I. Joe* (1945) and *Track of the Cat.* But Wellman fired his star shortly after production for *Blood Alley* got underway, annoyed with the actor's obnoxious (and drunken) behavior.

John Wayne was subsequently persuaded to play the film's lead. Aissa Wayne in her memoir *John Wayne, My Father* recalls: "The third day of shooting, Wellman called my dad in a snit. He said Mitchum was drinking all night, sleeping through morning wakeup calls, making location life miserable for cast and crew. As producer, my father urged conciliation, but one day Mitchum stormed off the set and said he could not work for Wellman. Wellman insisted my father move into the starring role. Although my dad had once passed on the script, feeling the role needed Mitchum's devil-may-care, he finally relented and took over the part."[65]

Reviews: "On an entertainment count, 'Blood Alley' holds up rather well in a pulp fiction vein, mixing action, romance and suspense to about equal measure to draw and hold viewer interest, even over the lengthy running time of 115 minutes." *Variety,* September 21, 1955; "A viewer may get the uneasy feeling that Mr. Wayne has been through this sort of trial before and that 'Blood Alley,' despite its exotic, oriental setting, is a standard chase melodrama patterned on a familiar blueprint. But our tough hero, abetted by Lauren Bacall, whose cool, statuesque charms he obviously cannot ignore, and director William A. Wellman, a known stickler for brisk action, have made 'Blood Alley' the scene of a lively, if not top-flight, adventure." *New York Times,* October 6, 1955; "An ace director, top performers, an imaginative cameraman and a strong supporting cast get together in a whopping story of adventure and suspense." *Los Angeles Examiner,* September 29, 1955.

Release: October, Warner Bros.
Availability: VHS, LD, DVD

John Wayne and Lauren Bacall, the stars of William A. Wellman's *Blood Alley* (Warner, 1955).

Seven Men from Now — 1956 (78 mins)

Producers: Andrew V. McLaglen and Robert E. Morrison, Batjac Productions
Director: Budd Boetticher
Script: Burt Kennedy
Photography: William H. Clothier (Color)
Editor: Everett Sutherland
Music: Henry Vars; songs "Seven Men from Now" and "Good Love" by By Dunham and Henry Vars
Cast: Randolph Scott (Ben Stride), Gail Russell (Annie Greer), Lee Marvin (Bill Masters), Walter Reed (John Greer), John Larch (Bodeen), Donald Barry (Clete), John Beradino (Clint), John Phillips (Jed), Chuck Roberson (Jed), Stuart Whitman (Cavalry Lieutenant), Pamela Duncan (Señorita), Steve Mitchell (Fowler)
Summary: A seven-man gang robs the Wells Fargo office in Silver Springs, Arizona. During the robbery, a clerk is killed, a woman who's married to Ben Stride, the town's former sheriff. Following the crime, Stride sets out on his own to find the bandits and reclaim the money they've taken. He tracks down two of the men and shoots them dead. Then he heads west toward California to find the other five.

In a valley, Stride meets and helps a married couple, John and Annie Greer, who've gotten stuck trying to cross a muddy stream in their wagon. The ex-lawman decides to stay on with the Greers, in part to protect them should Indians attack. The party soon stops at an abandoned rest station, where they are met by a drifter named Bill Masters and his partner Clete. Like Stride, Masters is looking for the Wells Fargo robbers, hoping to find the cashbox they took. If he finds the money, however, he will keep it for himself.

Masters, Clete, Stride and the Greers eventually leave the station. In the desert, they rescue a man who's being attacked by a band of Chiricahua braves. After the Indians retreat, the man turns his gun on Stride — he's one of the Wells Fargo outlaws — and Masters shoots him dead. Despite this, Stride regards Masters with little more than contempt, and that night, when Masters makes a pass at Annie Greer — in front of Stride and her husband — Stride tells him and Clete to leave. Masters then heads into a town called Flora Vista and there he meets up with Payte Bodeen, the man who organized the Wells Fargo robbery. In exchange for a share of the stolen money, Masters tells Bodeen where he can find Stride. Bodeen then sends two of his men into the desert to kill Stride. But Stride is too fast for them with his gun.

Following this, Greer confesses to Stride that he has been hired by Bodeen to transport the cashbox that was stolen from the Wells Fargo in Silver Springs to Flora Vista. Stride, in response, tells Greer to hand the box over to him. The Greers then leave, headed again for California. Stricken by his conscience, Greer elects to go on to Flora Vista, to tell the sheriff there about the deal he made with Bodeen. Before he can do this, Greer is shot and killed by Bodeen. Bodeen and his gang then ride out to the desert, looking for Stride, with Masters and Clete following them. Once they are all out of town, Masters proceeds to kill off Bodeen and the others. He then goes after Stride to get the Wells Fargo box, but the ex-lawman is once again too fast with the gun and shoots Masters dead.

Later in Flora Vista, Stride meets up with Annie Greer, who tells him that she is taking a stage to California. Stride explains to her that he will be returning to Silver Springs to take a job as a deputy. After he leaves Flora Vista, Annie changes her mind about California and decides to follow Stride back to Silver Springs.

Comment: *Seven Men from Now* was produced for John Wayne's Batjac Productions by McLaglen and Wayne's brother Bob Morrison. The film was shot in Lone Pine, California, where

McLaglen would subsequently direct several episodes of *Have Gun, Will Travel*.[66] *Seven Men from Now* largely disappeared from circulation after its first theatrical run in the summer of 1956. The film was restored by the University of California at Los Angeles's Film and Television Archive in the late-nineties and was subsequently screened at film festivals throughout the U.S., including the New York Film Festival in 2000.[67]

Seven Men from Now has long been a favorite of critics. Writing in *Cahiers du Cinema* in 1957, André Bazin described the picture as "perhaps the best Western I have seen since the war."[68] Boetticher would subsequently direct Randolph Scott in five more Westerns that have come to be regarded as classics: *The Tall T* (1957), *Decision at Sundown* (1957), *Buchanan Rides Alone* (1958), *Ride Lonesome* (1959), and *Comanche Station* (1960).

Reviews: "Listed as a Batjac presentation for Warner Bros., pic rates excellent production helming from Andrew V. McLaglen and Robert E. Morrison." *Variety,* July 11, 1956; "Kennedy's script is characteristically terse and witty, William H. Clothier's camerawork sharp and direct, and Boetticher's direction a model of inventive economy," *Time Out Film Guide,* 941; "A strong Scott western with a typical revenge theme that is worked well by director Boetticher and screenwriter Kennedy." *Motion Picture Guide,* 2838; "The dandy screenplay keeps taking surprising turns and disclosing new layers of complexity in the journeys and interrelationships of its characters.... Boetticher's setups are never fancy or pretentious, but there's always something tensile about the point of view — the disposition of people within the frame and within the spare, mostly desert-rock landscape." *The B List,* 138.

Release: August, Warner Bros.
Availability: DVD

THREE

The Fifties

After spending the first decade of his career in motion picture production working for other directors, McLaglen became a director himself in 1955 with *Man in the Vault*, a low budget crime melodrama. He followed this in 1956 with another low budget programmer, a Western called *Gun the Man Down*, which featured James Arness in the lead. In 1956, McLaglen also signed a long term contract with CBS Television and quickly became one of the network's busiest directors. Before the end of the decade, he helmed more than a hundred television programs, working on shows like *Gunsmoke, Have Gun, Will Travel, Rawhide* and *Perry Mason*. McLaglen directed one more motion picture in the fifties, as well, a thriller called *The Abductors* in which his father Victor McLaglen had a lead role.

Feature Films

Gun the Man Down — 1956 (74 mins)

Alternate Title: *Arizona Mission*
Producer: Robert E. Morrison, Batjac Productions
Script: Burt Kennedy, from a story by Sam C. Freedle
Photography: William H. Clothier (B & W)
Editor: A. Edward Sutherland
Music: Henry Vars
Cast: James Arness (Rem Anderson), Angie Dickinson (Janice), Robert Wilke (Matt Rankin), Emile Meyer (Sheriff Morton), Don Megowan (Ralph Farley), Michael Emmet (Billy Deal), Harry Carey, Jr. (Deputy Lee), Pedro Gonzalez Gonzales (Hotel Man)
Summary: Three bandits — Matt Rankin, Ralph Farley and Rem Anderson — hold up the Palace City bank for $40,000. As they make their escape, Rem is shot in the chest. When the robbers reach their mountain cabin hideout, Rankin and Farley decide to abandon Rem, certain he will slow them down in the future. Rankin and Farley persuade Rem's girlfriend, Jan, to join them and they flee.

A posse soon arrives at the hideout and arrests Rem. Once in custody, the injured robber refuses to share information about his accomplices and is sentenced to a year in jail. Following his release, Rem sets out to find Rankin, Farley and Jan, wanting revenge and his share of the money from the bank job. He learns from a friend, a gunslinger named Billy Deal, that the trio has set itself up in a nearby mining community.

Harry Carey, Jr., Emile Meyer and James Arness in a scene from *Gun the Man Down* (United Artists, 1956).

Rem soon appears in town, where he learns that Rankin and Farley have purchased a saloon. His arrival draws the attention of Morton, the town sheriff, as well as Rankin and Farley, who proceed to contact the gunslinger Billy Deal, ready to give him $5,000 if he will kill Rem. Though Jan is now Rankin's lover, she still cares about Rem and sets out to find and warn him about the danger he's in. Rem proceeds to find Billy and warns his friend to leave him alone. Billy reaches for his gun instead and Rem, with the quicker draw, shoots Billy dead. Rem is then locked up by Sheriff Morton and his slow-witted deputy, Lee, who warn the ex-convict to abide by the law and put aside his desires for revenge.

Billy's death frightens Rankin, Farley and Jen, and they take flight. After questioning Rem about the circumstances of Billy's death, Morton concludes that the gunfighter's death was justified, and he allows Rem to walk free. Rem then heads out after Rankin and the others, tracking them through the woods. Once again, he is approached by Jen, who tells him where Rankin and Farley are hiding. After this, Jan returns to Rankin. When he realizes that she's betrayed him, he kills her. Later, Rankin mistakes Farley for Rem and kills him, too.

Flustered, Rankin runs through the woods, followed closely by Rem. The two wind up in a box canyon, where Rem springs on his enemy. Instead of killing Rankin, though, he merely beats him up. Rem then turns Rankin over to the custody of Morton and Lee. The lawmen respond by praising the young man for being a good citizen.

Comment: Though *Gun the Man Down* ends on a positive note, with Rem deciding to spare Rankin's life, the picture otherwise presents a bleak, almost noirish view of human existence.

Throughout this picture, we find several instances in which characters are tempted by ambition and greed to abandon and hurt people they like and love. For example, when Rankin and Farley realize that the bullet wound in Rem's chest might jeopardize them, they decide to leave their comrade. As Rankin explains, "We got our hands on a lot of money and I'm not going to spend it hanging from the end of a rope." Rem's girlfriend, Jan, leaves, as well, without even bothering to hide Rem from the approaching posse or nurse his injuries. Billy Deal also likes Rem, but his affection fails to deter him when Rankin approaches him about gunning Rem down. In one of the film's few comic moments, Billy actually tells Rankin, after he accepts the job: "You better see [Rem's] buried real good. He's a friend of mine."

Nor is Rem particularly attractive himself. He may refrain from killing Rankin in the film's final moments, but this doesn't stop him from using excessive force to subdue his former partner, pummeling him with his fists until he collapses. When Rem turns Rankin over to the custody of Morton and Lee, in fact, Rankin is still unconscious. And while Rem's killing of Billy earlier in the picture is an act of self-defense, it has to be noted at the same time that Rem undoes his friend with a bullet in the back.

Though *Gun the Man Down* was released a month prior to *Man in the Vault,* it is actually the second film McLaglen directed. Shot in March 1956, *Gun the Man Down* features a number of actors McLaglen would work with again once he became a contract director at CBS Television.[1] James Arness, most notably, appeared in every one of the 95 *Gunsmoke* episodes McLaglen directed. Harry Carey, Jr., Robert Wilke, Pedro Gonzales Gonzales, Don Megowan and Angie Dickinson all appeared in episodes McLaglen helmed for *Gunsmoke,* too.

Reviews: "*Gun the Man Down* packs enough action and suspense to rate okay for the Western market. Film generally is ingrained with the type of ingredients to keep spectator interested." *Variety,* March 6, 1957; "This is a good little Western with an intelligent script that never stoops to cliché or easy outs. Instead the characters are well-drawn and the acting is impressive." *Motion Picture Guide,* 1126. "Dickinson and Wilke give solid performances ... as do Meyer and Carey as representatives of the law. This is an enjoyable and significant Western." *The Western,* 247–248; "Average mid–1950s theatrical oater aided by a good plot and nice cast." *Western Movies,* 165.

Release: November, 1956, United Artists
Availability: DVD

Man in the Vault—1956 (73 mins)

Producer: Robert E. Morrison, Batjac Productions
Script: Burt Kennedy, from Frank Gruber's novel *The Lock and the Key*
Photography: William H. Clothier (B & W)
Editor: Everett Sutherland
Music: Henry Vars; song "Let the Chips Fall Where They May" by Henry Vars and By Dunham
Cast: William Campbell (Tommy Dancer), Karen Sharpe (Betty Turner), Anita Ekberg (Flo Randall), Berry Kroeger (Willis Trent), Paul Fix (Herbie), James E. Seay (Paul De Camp), Mike Mazurki (Louie), Robert Keys (Earl Farraday), Gonzales Gonzales (Pedro), John Mitchum (Andy)
Summary: A mobster named Willis Trent approaches Tommy Dancer, a locksmith who works in Hollywood, about springing a bank safe deposit box for him that contains $200,000. The money belongs to Paul De Camp, Trent's former partner. Dancer declines at first. Though he's poor, he has no desire to consort with criminals. The locksmith is nevertheless

interested in one of the Trent's acquaintances, Betty Turner, a Beverly Hills debutante he meets at Trent's house during a party. After just a couple of dates, Dancer and Betty fall in love.

Convinced that Dancer is the only man who can get into De Camp's deposit box, Trent concocts a scheme, telling him that he's kidnapped Betty. If Dancer won't steal De Camp's money for him, Trent warns, he will have Betty's pretty face smashed up and ruined. Believing that the threat is real, Dancer creates a key that allows him to access the bank box, which he then plunders. But just as he arrives at Trent's house to deliver the stolen cash, Dancer spots Betty leaving the gangster's house with her old boyfriend, a crooked lawyer named Farraday. Seeing this, Dancer concludes that Betty has been feigning her love for him. Unknown to him, Betty has broken up with Farraday for good—and she's in the dark about the threats Trent has been making.

The locksmith then decides to keep the cash for himself, hiding it in a locker at a bowling alley. Around the same time, De Camp discovers that his money in the deposit box has disappeared. Suspecting Trent, he starts for his former partner's home. Simultaneously, Trent kidnaps Betty and again threatens Dancer with ruining her looks unless the locksmith turns over the money. Understanding that the danger for Betty this time is real, Dancer heads back to the bowling alley. Yet another man who wants De Camp's money, a hoodlum named Herbie, is waiting for him there.

A prolonged chase through the bowling alley follows. Eventually the police arrive and Herbie is picked up, while Dancer escapes and rushes off to Trent's house with De Camp's cash. Once he arrives, he learns that De Camp, Farraday and Trent have all been killed. Betty, fortunately, is safe. Dancer then finds a policeman and tells him about the role he's played in the preceding events and turns Trent's money over to his custody.

Comment: Scripted by Burt Kennedy, *Man in the Vault* is an adaptation of a 1948 crime novel by Frank Gruber called *The Lock and the Key*. By turns sympathetic and repellant, Tommy Dancer is the first of several crooked protagonists who appear in McLaglen's films. But unlike the bank robber anti-heroes we find in pictures like *One More Train to Rob* and *"something big,"* Dancer is not a fulltime, professional criminal. Rather, he is a hardworking laborer who turns to crime only when opportunity presents itself. Though he may be forced at first by Trent to take the cash out of De Camp's deposit box, Dancer decides on his own to keep the money for himself later—a result of the resentment he feels toward Betty after he sees her walking with Farraday and the envy he has for her wealth. Even the most ordinary of men, the film intimates, are capable of ignoring their moral instincts and committing serious crimes.

McLaglen's first film, *Man in the Vault* features several people with whom he'd worked previously when he was an employee under contract for John Wayne's Wayne-Fellows and Batjac production companies in the fifties. Actors William Campbell (Dancer), Karen Sharpe (Betty), Paul Fix (Herbie) and Gonzales (Pedro) each had parts in *The High and the Mighty*, for instance, while Mike Mazurki (Louie) and Anita Ekberg (Flo) appeared in *Blood Alley*. Cinematographer William H. Clothier had worked with McLaglen on *The High and the Mighty* and *Blood Alley*, too, as well as *Island in the Sky*, *Track of the Cat* and *Seven Men from Now*. Clothier would serve as McLaglen's director of photography on 11 more pictures over the next two decades.

Reviews: "McLaglen's direction works up a fair amount of tension in a couple of sequences but otherwise doesn't rise above the script." *Variety* December 26, 1956.

Release: December, RKO Radio Pictures

Availability: DVD

George Macready and Victor McLaglen try to steal the corpse of Abraham Lincoln in *The Abductors* (Twentieth Century–Fox, 1957).

The Abductors—1957 (80 mins)

Alternate Title: *Secret Service*
Producer: Ray Wander, Regal Films, Inc.
Script: Ray Wander
Photography: Joseph LaShelle (B & W)
Editor: Betty Steinberg
Music: Paul Glass
Cast: Victor McLaglen (Tom Muldoon), George Macready (Jack Langley), Fay Spain (Sue Ellen), Gavin Muir (Herbert Evans), Carl Thayler (Jed), John Morley (Fred Winters), Carlyle Mitchell (Becker)
Summary: Surly and violent Tom Muldoon is freed after serving a long prison sentence in Joliet, Illinois. He heads to Springfield, the state capital, where he reunites with an old friend, John Langley, who works in a mortuary. Muldoon explains to Langley that he shared a cell in prison with a master counterfeiter, a man named Boyd. After showing Langley some of Boyd's work — an authentic-looking $50 note — Muldoon convinces his friend that if they can get the counterfeiter released, they will enjoy wealth for the rest of their lives. To make this come about, Muldoon asks Langley to help him abduct Sue Ellen, the daughter of the Joliet penitentiary's warden, and use her to secure Boyd's freedom.

Assisted by a pair of grafters named Evans and Jed, Muldoon proceeds to kidnap Sue Ellen, rushing her off with a hearse taken from Langley's mortuary. The hearse tips over before they can get far, however, spilling Sue Ellen onto the street. The abductors flee, leaving the warden's daughter behind. She then goes to the authorities, providing them with information about her kidnappers. An investigation is opened, with a Secret Service agent named Winters assigned to the case.

Unwilling to abandon their ambitions, Langley and Muldoon hatch a new plot for winning Boyd's release. Instead of ransoming a living person, they will snatch the body of Abraham Lincoln from its tomb in Springfield. They again ask their crooked friend Evans to help them. A veteran of the Civil War, Evans is appalled by the idea of stealing the president's corpse. To ease his discomfort, he gets drunk in a bar, where he begins to talk about the plan with a stranger. The stranger happens to be Agent Winters, who passes on what he learns to Chief Becker of the Springfield police.

Unaware that their scheme has been exposed, Muldoon and Langley depart for the cemetery where Lincoln is resting. They break into the president's mausoleum and find his coffin, which proves to be much harder for them to open than they expected. As the men struggle to lift the heavy lid that covers the coffin, Langley's hand becomes stuck. Before he can get it free, Winters and Becker arrive, firing a gun into the tomb. Fearing apprehension, Muldoon rushes off, leaving Langley behind.

Muldoon is subsequently killed and Langley is captured. In police custody, the undertaker learns that the $50 bill that Boyd passed on to Muldoon in the Joliet penitentiary was not a fake at all. Rather, it was an actual note that Boyd used to trick his cellmate into believing that he was not only a superior counterfeiter, but someone to spring from prison, as well.

Comment: *The Abductors* was filmed in early 1957.[2] It is the only feature McLaglen directed in which his actor father Victor McLaglen appeared, though the actor also had roles in two television shows Andrew directed, "The O'Hare Story" for *Have Gun, Will Travel* and "Incident of the Shambling Man" for *Rawhide*. *The Abductors* is the first picture McLaglen directed after severing ties (albeit temporarily) with John Wayne's Batjac Productions in 1956. The picture was shot by veteran cameraman Joseph LaShelle, whose previous credits included Otto Preminger's *Laura* (1944) and Delbert Mann's *Marty* (1955).[3]

Like *Man in the Vault*, *The Abductors* chronicles the botched efforts of criminals as they try to pull off a heist. While the earlier picture is bereft of humor, *The Abductors* is frequently comic, thanks primarily to Victor McLaglen's blustering performance as Tom Muldoon. The plot for *The Abductors* draws in part on actual events. According to historian Thomas Craughwell, in the summer of 1876, a Chicago criminal named James Kennally recruited a pair of grave robbers to exhume President Lincoln from the Oak Ridge Cemetery in Springfield and deliver him to a hiding place along the shores of Lake Michigan. Kennally hoped to both ransom the corpse for $200,000 and use it to force the governor of Illinois to release his counterfeiter associate Benjamin Boyd from the penitentiary in Joliet. A police informant named Lewis Swegles learned about the plan and alerted the Secret Service. Agents were subsequently sent to the tomb where Lincoln's body was kept and the crooks' efforts were stymied.[4]

Reviews: "The film comes off—even if the plot does not—in spite of, or more probably because of, a curious clumsiness on the parts of the miscreants. You would have to see it to begin to comprehend their motives—and there's a surprise twist at the finish that wraps it up neatly." *Los Angeles Times*, June 2, 1957; "Though this film is based upon a real incident, it fails to hold interest." *Motion Picture Guide*, 3.

Release: July, Twentieth Century–Fox

Series Television

Gunsmoke

Gunsmoke had a 20-year run on CBS, making it one of the longest running series in television history. Originally developed in 1952 as a radio program by writer John Meston and producer Norman Macdonnell, the show followed U.S. Marshal Matt Dillon and his efforts to uphold the law and preserve the peace in Dodge City, Kansas. Meston and Macdonnell adapted *Gunsmoke* for television in 1955, but Charles Marquis Warren, rather than Macdonnell, served as the show's first producer; when Warren stepped down midway through the second season, Macdonnell took his place.[5] Starring James Arness as Dillon and Dennis Weaver as the marshal's sidekick, Chester, *Gunsmoke* frequently addressed weighty topics, such as racism, women's rights, vigilantism and alcoholism, contributing to the program's popularity with adult viewers. Actors Milburn Stone and Amanda Blake, who played the roles of Doc Adams and Miss Kitty, appeared regularly on the show, as well.

SEASON TWO, 1956–1957

"Cow Doctor"

First Broadcast: September 8, 1956
Producer: Charles Marquis Warren
Script: John Dunkel, story by John Meston
Photography: Fleet Southcott
Editor: Leslie Vidor
Guest Stars: Robert H. Harris (Ben Pitcher), Dorothy Adams (Mrs. Pitcher), Tommy Kirk (Jerry Pitcher)
Summary: Ben Pitcher despises doctors. But after one of his cows gets sick, he summons Doc Adams out to his farm. When Doc arrives and learns that he has made a house call for an animal rather than a person, he expresses his annoyance, yet nevertheless treats the cow. Soon after Doc finishes, Pitcher's son, Jerry, shows up, having just come back from Dodge City. The boy explains that earlier in the day a woman cut her arm and bled to death because no one in town knew how to help her. Doc responds to this news by slugging Pitcher and blaming him for the tragedy. Pitcher, in turn, lunges at Doc with a knife and cuts him badly. Back in Dodge, the doctor recuperates in bed, aided by Kitty and Dillon. But then he learns that Pitcher himself has become ill. Committed to helping the sick man, Doc returns to Pitcher's home. He succeeds in saving the farmer's life, but Pitcher, mean-spirited to the end, refuses to pay him for his services.

"Legal Revenge"

First Broadcast: November 17, 1956
Producer: Charles Marquis Warren
Script: Sam Peckinpah, story by John Meston
Photography: Fleet Southcott
Editor: Leslie Vidor
Guest Stars: Cloris Leachman (Flory Tibbs), Philip Bourneuf (George Bassett), Robert Strong (Clerk)
Summary: After delivering a baby to a couple of farmers in the countryside, Doc Adams heads back for Dodge. Along the trail, he stops at a shack that some new tenants now occupy.

A beautiful woman with a hard manner meets him out front. Her name is Flory and she tells the doctor to move on. As Doc prepares to leave, a voice calls from inside the cabin. Doc enters and finds a man lying in a bed with a badly injured leg. The man says his name is George Bassett and that he hurt his leg with an ax. As Doc examines the wound, he sees that George is holding a gun, which he aims at Flory. Once Doc finishes treating George, he departs for Dodge, where he reports what he's seen to Dillon and Chester. The two lawmen start for the shack to find out more about Flory and George's strange relationship.

Comment: This is the first of 11 episodes Sam Peckinpah wrote for the *Gunsmoke* series. Peckinpah moved on to motion picture direction in 1961 with *The Deadly Companions,* a Western starring Maureen O'Hara and Brian Keith. With Burt Kennedy and McLaglen, Peckinpah was one of the few American directors in the sixties who distinguished himself in the Western genre, thanks to films like *Ride the High Country* (1962) and *The Wild Bunch* (1969).[6] Peckinpah also directed the 1977 war picture *Cross of Iron. Breakthrough,* the sequel to *Cross of Iron,* was directed by McLaglen.

"The Mistake"

First Broadcast: November 24, 1956
Producer: Charles Marquis Warren
Script: Gil Doud, story by John Meston
Photography: Fleet Southcott
Editor: Leslie Vidor
Guest Stars: Touch Connors (Bostick), Gene O'Donnell (Haney), Cyril Delevanti (Driver), Robert Hinkle (Rider), Bert Rumsey (Bartender)
Summary: A card dealer named Haney is beaten over the head and robbed behind the Long Branch Saloon in Dodge. As he lies dying, Haney tells Dillon that a man with a moustache and a red shirt attacked him. The marshal presumes the robber is Jim Bostick, a roustabout with a moustache and a red shirt who's had previous trouble with Haney. Bostick claims he's innocent, and when Dillon tells Chester to lock him up in jail, the suspect flees. A manhunt follows, with Dillon eventually shooting Bostick in the shoulder. When Dillon, Chester and Bostick return to Dodge, they learn from Doc Adams that another card dealer has been fatally beaten over the head behind the Long Branch. The injured man was able to fire a couple of shots at his attacker and kill him. The dead man, Doc says, had a moustache and was wearing a red shirt. Bostick appears to be innocent after all.

"Poor Pearl"

First Broadcast: December 22, 1956
Producer: Charles Marquis Warren
Script: Sam Peckinpah, story by John Meston
Photography: Fleet Southcott
Editor: Leslie Vidor
Guest Stars: Constance Ford (Pearl Bender), Denver Pyle (Willie Calhoun), Michael Emmett (Webb Thorne), Jess Kirkpatrick (Frank Teeters), Bert Rumsey (Bartender), John Hamilton (Big John), Johnny McGough (Jimmie)
Summary: Willie Calhoun, an uncouth but gentle-hearted farmer, loves Pearl Bender, a saloon girl at the Long Branch. Certain that she loves him, too, Willie proposes to Pearl. But to his disappointment, Pearl declines his offer. Willie subsequently concludes that she

has been coerced by an old boyfriend, a gambler named Webb Thorne, to turn him down. To correct the situation, the farmer comes to town with his gun, looking for his rival.

Comment: Denver Pyle (Willie) auditioned for the role of Matt Dillon when John Meston and Norman Macdonnell were preparing the *Gunsmoke* radio program for television. The series' original producer, Charles Marquis Warren, ultimately decided on giving the lead to James Arness.[7] Pyle would later appear in McLaglen's *Shenandoah, Bandolero!, "something big"* and *Cahill, United States Marshal.*

"Cholera"

First Broadcast: December 29, 1956
Producer: Norman Macdonnell
Script: Les Crutchfield, story by John Meston
Photography: Fleet Southcott
Editor: Leslie Vidor
Guest Stars: Peg Hillias (Jenny), Paul Fix (Macready), Bartlett Robinson (Gabriel), Stuart Whitman (Bart), Gordon Gebert (Billy), John Smith (David)
Summary: Thanks to a summer drought, water is scarce in Kansas. A homesteader named Gabriel has a spring on his land, and his neighbor, a cattleman named Macready, wants access to it. To make this come about, Macready has been terrorizing Gabriel and his wife, Jenny, trying to drive them off of their farm, but his efforts have all failed. Then the Gabriels's son, David, becomes sick with cholera. Macready sees an opportunity in this: should the boy die, his heartbroken parents will be more likely to give up on their dream of owning a farm in Kansas and abandon their land—and their water. Macready then kidnaps Doc Adams, preventing the doctor from being able to treat the Gabriels's ailing child.
Comment: Paul Fix (Macready) was a friend of John Wayne and appeared in several pictures with the actor, including many on which McLaglen worked before he became a director, among them *Dakota, Hondo, Island in the Sky, The High and the Mighty* and *Blood Alley.*[8] Fix also had roles in several movies McLaglen directed: *Man in the Vault, Shenandoah, The Ballad of Josie, The Undefeated, "something big"* and *Cahill, United States Marshal.* Fix was the father-in-law of another actor who collaborated with McLaglen frequently, Harry Carey, Jr.[9]

"Pucket's New Year"

First Broadcast: January 5, 1957
Producer: Norman Macdonnell
Script: John Meston
Photography: Fleet Southcott
Editor: Leslie Vidor
Guest Stars: Edgar Stehli (Ira Pucket), Grant Withers (Jed Larner), Richard Deacon (Botkin), Rocky Shahan (Jim), Bert Rumsey (Bartender)
Summary: A bitter cold has settled over the Kansas prairie. As Dillon and Chester make their way home to Dodge, they spot a rundown wagon and a team of horses. Inside the wagon, they find an ornery buffalo hunter, Ira Pucket, who explains that he has an injured, gangrenous foot, and that his partner has left him to die. The lawmen take the old man to Doc Adams, who is forced to cut off most of Pucket's foot, bringing an end to his days as a hunter. Unable to earn money for himself, Pucket turns to crime, robbing the town bank.

"Sins of the Father"

First Broadcast: January 19, 1957
Producer: Norman Macdonnell
Script: John Dunkel, story by John Meston
Photography: Fleet Southcott
Editor: Leslie Vidor
Guest Stars: Angie Dickinson (Rose Daggitt), Peter Whitney (Big Dan Daggitt), Gage Clarke (Dobie), Paul Wexler (Rodin)
Summary: Mountain man Dan Daggitt and his beautiful wife, Rose, an Arapaho Indian, are headed for Colorado. As they pass through Kansas, they decide to spend a few nights in Dodge, at the Dodge House, in particular. Remembering an earlier incident when some Kansas settlers were massacred by Arapaho Indians, the Dodge House's manager, Dobie, is less than willing to provide the visitors with lodging. After Dillon steps in and forces him to give the couple a room, Dobie stands out front of the inn and complains to anybody who will listen that he has an Arapaho staying in his hotel. The old man's remarks prompt a pair of bad characters to kidnap Rose and torture her.
Comment: Angie Dickinson (Rose) played the female lead in McLaglen's *Gun the Man Down*.

"Kick Me"

First Broadcast: January 26, 1957
Producer: Charles Marquis Warren
Script: Endre Bohem and Lou Vittes, story by John Meston
Photography: Fleet Southcott
Editor: Leslie Vidor
Guest Stars: Robert H. Harris (Fred Meyers), Julie Van Zandt (Jennifer Myers), Paul Lambert (Harry Bent), Frank DeKova (Tobeel)
Summary: Following a robbery in Wichita, outlaw Fred Meyers makes for Dodge with his wife, Jennifer. Once there, the two pretend to be law-abiding merchants and open a dress store. But Jennifer does not love her husband—she actually hates him—and when she threatens to tell the authorities about his participation in the robbery, Meyers murders her. To deflect suspicion from himself, Meyers accuses an impoverished Indian named Tobeel of the crime.

"Executioner"

First Broadcast: February 2, 1957
Producer: Norman Macdonnell
Script: Gil Doud, story by John Meston
Photography: Fleet Southcott
Editor: Leslie Vidor
Guest Stars: Robert Keys (Abe Curry), Michael Hinn (Morgan Curry), Liam Sullivan (Tom Clegg)
Summary: The Curry brothers, Abe and Morgan, own a ranch outside Dodge. After they find a drifter named Tom Clegg helping himself to some of their hay, a fight breaks out, and Abe is shot dead by Clegg. Morgan then goes to Dillon and asks the marshal to execute Clegg. When the marshal refuses, Morgan begins to follow Clegg around town, harassing him. If he can get his brother's murderer to shoot him, Morgan reasons, Dillon will be forced to confront, and hopefully kill, Clegg.

"Bloody Hands"

First Broadcast: February 16, 1957
Producer: Norman Macdonnell
Script: John Meston
Photography: Fleet Southcott
Editor: Leslie Vidor
Guest Stars: Russell Johnson (Stanger), Lawrence Dobkin (Brand), Gloria Marshall (Linda), Harvey Grant (Billy), David Saber (Tom)
Summary: Dillon comes up on some bank robbers and shoots three of them dead. Brand, the gang's lone survivor, is surprised by the cool manner in which Dillon responds to the shooting, and says that although the lawman wears a badge, he's no different than a murderer. Unsettled by the rebuke, Dillon starts to wonder if he might be happier if he put his gun down. He then quits his job and proceeds to enjoy himself, teaching children to track animals, picnicking with Miss Kitty and the like. He is interrupted during one of these outings when he learns from Chester that a bandit named Stanger has shot and killed a young saloon girl in Dodge. Upon hearing this, Dillon realizes that he must return to his job, that it is duty to protect the city and its residents, whether he likes the work or not.

"What the Whiskey Drummer Heard"

First Broadcast: April 27, 1957
Producer: Norman Macdonnell
Script: Gil Doud, story by John Meston
Photography: Fleet Southcott
Editor: Michael Luciano
Guest Stars: Vic Perrin (Wilbur Hawkins), Robert Burton (Sheriff), Robert Karnes (Roberts), Bert Rumsey (Sam)
Summary: Wilbur Hawkins is a whiskey vendor whose circuit includes Dodge City. When he arrives in town, Wilbur approaches Dillon and gives the lawman some cryptic news. While riding a stage the previous day, the drummer overheard a pair of men discussing plans to kill the marshal. A short time later, someone shoots at Dillon in the alley behind his office. Dillon and Chester then set out to find and capture the gunman.

"Cheap Labor"

First Broadcast: May 4, 1957
Producer: Norman Macdonnell
Script: John Meston
Photography: Fleet Southcott
Editor: Leslie Vidor
Guest Stars: Andrew Duggan (Fos Capper), Peggy Webber (Flora Stancil), Robert F. Simon (Ben Stancil), Susan Morrow (Melanie), James Nusser (Bum)
Summary: Ben Stancil forces his sister Flora to work on his farm. Not only does he refuse to pay Flora, but if she defies him, he beats her. Ben likes to use his fists on Flora's suitors, as well, preventing her from finding someone to marry. Then Fos Capper, a chivalrous veteran of the Civil War, develops a fondness for Flora. Ben thinks at first that he can intimidate Fos, but it soon becomes apparent that the soft-spoken Fos is in fact a gunfighter, a revelation that forces the malicious farmer to let go of his hold on Flora.

"Who Lives by the Sword"

First Broadcast: May 18, 1957
Producer: Norman Macdonnell
Script: John Meston
Photography: Fleet Southcott
Editor: Michael Luciano
Guest Stars: Harold J. Stone (Joe Delk), Steven Terrell (Billy Baxter), Robert C. Ross (Lew Baxter), Harry Woods (Snyder), Sheila Noonan (Mrs. Baxter), Hal Baylor (Mike)
Summary: An arrogant and cruel gunslinger named Joe Delk arrives in Dodge and prompts a fight with two young brothers, killing them both with his gun. Infuriated by these wasteful deaths, Dillon brutally beats Delk and keeps him locked up for a week in a cell. Once Delk regains his freedom, he finds that he's lost his confidence. Fearing other gunmen may be looking to kill him, Delk asks Dillon for protection. The marshal declines, explaining that any man "who lives by the sword" must die the same way.

"Uncle Oliver"

First Broadcast: May 25, 1957
Producer: Norman Macdonnell
Script: John Meston
Photography: Fleet Southcott
Editor: Sam Gold
Guest Stars: Earle Hodgins (Uncle Oliver), Paul Wexler (Viney)
Summary: Two drifters, Oliver Stang and his nephew, Viney, come into Dodge. Oliver decides that Viney should replace Chester as Dillon's assistant. When Oliver presents this idea to Dillon, the lawman explains that he doesn't need a new assistant. Oliver proceeds to shoot Chester, hoping that killing him will change the marshal's mind.

"Daddy-O"

First Broadcast: June 1, 1957
Producer: Norman Macdonnell
Script: John Meston
Photography: Fleet Southcott
Editor: Leslie Vidor
Guest Stars: John Dehner (Wayne Russell), Judson Pratt (Bill Pence), Cyril Delevanti (Messenger)
Summary: Kitty's father, Wayne Russell, abandoned her and her mother shortly after Kitty's birth. Now Russell wants to become acquainted with his daughter and he stops in Dodge to see her. Almost immediately, he expresses his discontent at Kitty's willingness to work in a saloon. When he learns that Kitty actually owns a part of the establishment, he tries to persuade her to sell her share and invest money in the freight company he owns. Soon Kitty starts to wonder, along with Dillon, if her father may be more of a crook than a businessman.

"Liar from Blackhawk"

First Broadcast: June 22, 1957
Producer: Norman Macdonnell

Script: John Meston
Photography: Fleet Southcott
Editor: Sam Gold
Guest Stars: Denver Pyle (Hank Shinn), Strother Martin (Ed Davey), John Doucette (Al Janes), Fred Graham (Cowboy), Howard Culver (Hotel Clerk), Bert Rumsey (Sam)
Summary: Hank Shinn claims to be a gunman who killed three men one night in a saloon in the Dakotas. In reality, he watched the men kill one another in a shootout. Now in Dodge with a sycophantic companion named Ed Davey, Shinn trades on his reputation as a killer, making exaggerated claims about his acumen with a gun. Though Dillon suspects Shinn may be an impostor, a genuine gunfighter named Al Janes takes Shinn's claims seriously. Shots are soon fired and Shinn is killed.
Comment: Strother Martin (Ed Davey) had parts in McLaglen's *McLintock!*, *Shenandoah* and *Fools' Parade*. He also worked with the director on the *Hotel de Paree* series, playing the shopkeeper Aaron Donager. He appeared in several episodes of *Have Gun, Will Travel* that McLaglen directed, too. Editor Sam Gold worked on *Gunsmoke* and *Have Gun, Will Travel* and was sometimes credited as Samuel.

"Jealousy"

First Broadcast: July 6, 1957
Producer: Norman Macdonnell
Script: Sam Peckinpah, story by John Meston
Photography: Fleet Southcott
Editor: Sam Gold
Guest Stars: Jack Kelly (Cam Durbin), Joan Tetzel (Tilda Durbin), Than Wyenn (Lonnie Pike), Jack Mann (Jack Davis), Kenn Drake (Cowboy), Barbara Dodd (Waitress)
Summary: Cam Durbin, an old friend of Dillon, moves to Dodge with his wife Tilda and takes a job managing a faro table at the Long Branch. For an assistant, Durbin hires an unsavory gambler named Lonnie Pike, who despises Dillon. Like Iago in Shakespeare's *Othello*, Pike goes out of his way to make Durbin suspect that Tilda is guilty of infidelity, telling him that the young woman has fallen in love with Dillon. Exasperated and humiliated, Durbin turns on the marshal, threatening to kill him.

SEASON THREE, 1957–1958

"Kitty's Outlaw"

First Broadcast: October 5, 1957
Producer: Norman Macdonnell
Script: Kathleen Hite, story by John Meston
Photography: Fleet Southcott
Editor: Samuel Gold
Guest Stars: Ainslie Pryor (Cole Yankton), Dabbs Greer (Mr. Jonas), Chris Alcaide (Cowboy), Howard Culver (Hotel Clerk), Jack Mann (First Man)
Summary: A big man with a rough manner, Cole Yankton intimidates the locals in Dodge when he arrives in the city. However, one person in town warms to the stranger — Miss Kitty. As she explains to Dillon, she and Cole had a love affair long ago in New Orleans. After Cole and two cronies attack the Dodge City Bank and make off with $10,000, Dillon, Chester and Doc wonder if Kitty has in any way served as an accomplice.

"Jesse"

First Broadcast: October 19, 1957
Producer: Norman Macdonnell
Script: John Meston
Photography: Fleet Southcott
Editor: Leslie Vidor
Guest Stars: Edward Binns (Bill Stapp), George Brenlin (Jesse Pruett), James Maloney (Karl), Dabbs Greer (Mr. Jonas), George Selk (Moss Grimmick)
Summary: Teenager Jesse Pruett comes into Dodge, looking for the man who killed his father. Shortly after his arrival, Jesse meets Dillon, who reveals that he is the one responsible for the man's death. At first, Jesse wants to pay the marshal back for this by blowing his head off with a shotgun. But when he learns that his father, one of Quantrill's Raiders, regularly murdered people during the Civil War, the youngster changes his mind and starts back for home.

SEASON FOUR, 1958–1959

"Jayhawkers"

First Broadcast: January 31, 1959
Producer: Norman Macdonnell
Script: John Meston
Photography: Fleet Southcott
Editor: Leslie Vidor
Guest Stars: Jack Elam (Dolph Quince), Ken Curtis (Phil Jacks), Lane Bradford (Jay), Chuck Hayward (Studer), Earl Parker (Snyder), Cliff Ketchum (Cowboy), Brad Payne (Cook)
Summary: Trail boss Dolph Quince is moving a herd up from Texas into Kansas. Five days out from Dodge City, he sends one of his men ahead to find Dillon, concerned that a group of outlaws are preparing to lay siege to his cattle. The marshal rides out to help to Quince, but his presence can't stop the bandits from attacking.
Comment: This episode marks the first time McLaglen directed Ken Curtis (Jacks). The two would work together frequently over the next decade in television, especially after Curtis joined *Gunsmoke*'s permanent cast in 1964. Curtis also played the part of Wessner in McLaglen's *Freckles*. Jack Elam (Steed) appeared in two features McLaglen directed, *The Rare Breed* and *The Way West*. Lane Bradford (Jay) played a character named Tinkham in McLaglen's *Shenandoah*.

"The F.U."

First Broadcast: March 14, 1959
Producer: Norman Macdonnell
Script: John Meston
Photography: Fleet Southcott
Editor: Al Joseph
Guest Stars: Bert Freed (Al Clovis), Fay Roope (Botkin), Joe Flynn (Onie Becker), Steve Raines (1st Cowboy), Ed Faulkner (2nd Cowboy)
Summary: Mild-mannered Onie Becker is shot to death in Dodge. Dillon suspects that Al Clovis, a gambler, is the killer. When Clovis boards a train bound for St. Louis, Chester and Dillon follow and apprehend him. After the lawmen return to town with their prisoner,

they learn that bandits have struck the Dodge City bank during their absence, prompting Dillon to wonder if Clovis may have had something to do with this crime, too.

"Fawn"

First Broadcast: April 4, 1959
Producer: Norman Macdonnell
Script: John Meston
Photography: Fleet Southcott
Editor: Leslie Vidor
Guest Stars: Peggy Stewart (Mrs. Phillips), Wendy Stuart (Fawn), Robert Karnes (Jep Hunter), Robert Rockwell (Roger Phillips)
Summary: For ten years, a white woman named Mrs. Phillips has been held captive by a band of Cheyenne Indians. Though she's been basically treated well, Mrs. Phillips longs to return to her family, especially her husband. The Cheyenne permit her to leave, allowing her to take a young Indian girl named Fawn along, too. Almost immediately, the two are captured by some buffalo hunters, who use them like slaves. A passing cowboy witnesses this mistreatment and rides into Dodge to tell Dillon. Dillon and Chester then head out to help the women, freeing them and bringing them into town. Once there, Mrs. Phillips reveals that Fawn is her daughter.
Comment: Peggy Stewart (Mrs. Phillips) played the role of Mrs. Turley in *The Way West*.

"Renegade White"

First Broadcast: April 11, 1959
Producer: Norman Macdonnell
Script: Les Crutchfield, story by John Meston
Photography: Fleet Southcott
Editor: Leslie Vidor
Guest Stars: Michael Pate (Wild Hog), Barney Phillips (Ord), Robert Brubaker (Jim Buck), Hank Patterson (Jake)
Summary: Ord Spencer has no fear of the law. After shooting a man dead in the Long Branch, he purchases some rifles from a merchant in Dodge. He proceeds to sell the guns to a band of Cheyenne Indians who have fled their reservation. He also bushwhacks a pair of cowboys, killing them and stealing their horses. Once Dillon becomes aware of these crimes, he sets out for the prairie to find the outlaw, but he is knocked unconscious after he is thrown from his horse. When he awakens, the marshal finds himself surrounded by the vicious Spencer and some of his Cheyenne clients.
Comment: Michael Pate (Wild Hog) played the role of Puma in *McLintock!*

"Murder Warrant"

First Broadcast: April 18, 1959
Producer: Norman Macdonnell
Script: John Meston
Photography: Fleet Southcott
Editor: Leslie Vidor
Guest Stars: Ed Nelson (Prentice), Mort Mills (Harbin), Onslow Stevens (Sheriff), Fay Roope (Botkin), George Selk (Moss)
Summary: Lee Prentice has lived on a ranch twenty miles outside Dodge for the last year.

One night he is shot in the shoulder by an unknown assailant. He then makes the long ride to Dodge, where Doc treats him for his injury. As Prentice recovers, Doc tells Dillon about the attack and the marshal initiates a search in Dodge, hoping the shooter has come to town. While visiting the Long Branch, Dillon learns from Miss Kitty that a man named Jake Harbin had been asking about Prentice the previous night. Harbin happens to be in the bar at that moment and Dillon confronts him. Harbin then explains that a few years earlier, Prentice murdered a businessman's son in the town where he once lived, and Harbin has been sent to bring Prentice back, dead or alive.

"Change of Heart"

First Broadcast: April 25, 1959
Producer: Norman Macdonnell
Script: John Meston
Photography: Fleet Southcott
Editor: Samuel Gold
Guest Stars: Lucy Marlowe (Bella Grant), James Drury (Jerry Cass), Ken Curtis (Brisco)
Summary: Bella Grant has been working in the Long Branch as a saloon girl for a week. On a visit to town, rancher Jerry Cass sees Bella and falls in love with her. Soon the pair is talking marriage. But Jerry's brother, Brisco, disapproves of the affair, disgusted by the idea of having his brother consort with a woman of low repute. In reality, Bella and Brisco are scheming together, trying to dupe Jerry in order to steal his ranch.

"There Was Never a Horse"

First Broadcast: May 16, 1959
Producer: Norman Macdonnell
Script: John Meston
Photography: Fleet Southcott
Editor: Leslie Vidor
Guest Stars: Jack Lambert (Kin Creed), Joe Sargent (Drunk), Larry Blake (Budge), Bill Wellman, Jr. (Roy), Perry Ivins (Clerk)
Summary: Kin Creed is a gunfighter who takes pride in his work. When he stops in Dodge for a drink at the Long Branch, he learns that the town has its own U.S. marshal. Creed then decides to add Dillon to the list of men he's killed.
Comment: Jack Lambert (Creed) would later play the role of Duncan in McLaglen's *Freckles*. Bill Wellman, Jr. (Roy), the son of director William A. Wellman, appeared in several episodes of *Gunsmoke* and *Have Gun, Will Travel* that McLaglen directed; he also had a role in McLaglen's 1983 television miniseries *The Blue & the Gray*.

"Blue Horse"

First Broadcast: June 6, 1959
Producer: Norman Macdonnell
Script: John Meston, story by Marian Clark
Photography: Fleet Southcott
Editor: Fred Berger
Guest Stars: Gene Nelson (Hob Cannon), Michael Pate (Blue Horse), William Murphy (Lt. Eldridge), Monte Hale (Sergeant)
Summary: Dillon and Chester are bringing Hob Cannon in from the prairie to stand trial for

murder. On the trail to Dodge, they meet a cavalry outfit. The leader of this group, Lt. Eldridge, explains to Dillon that he is looking for Blue Horse, a Cheyenne chief who has run off the reservation where he's been sent by the government. Following this exchange, Dillon and Chester resume the trek to Dodge. But as they descend a hill, Dillon falls from his horse, breaking his leg. Dillon then tells Chester to continue on to Dodge to get help, leaving him behind with Cannon. As the hours pass, the marshal's health worsens. When he loses consciousness, Cannon frees himself and takes Dillon's gun. As the criminal prepares to flee, the fugitive chief Blue Horse appears. An old friend of Dillon, Blue Horse stops Cannon and tends to the marshal's leg. In return for this kindness, Dillon sets aside his obligations as a lawman and warns the chief about the cavalry outfit that is searching for him.

Comment: McLaglen had worked with Monte Hale (Sergeant) previously on the Republic picture *Out California Way*, when he was a production clerk at the studio in the mid-forties.

SEASON FIVE, 1959–1960

"Target"

First Broadcast: September 5, 1959
Producer: Norman Macdonnell
Script: John Meston, story by Les Crutchfield
Photography: Fleet Southcott
Editor: Otto Meyer
Guest Stars: John Carradine (Kader), Suzanne Lloyd (Nayomi), Frank de Kova (Leader), Darryl Hickman (Danny)
Summary: Kader owns a ranch outside Dodge. When a band of gypsies sets up camp on a remote spot of his land, Kader tells his son Danny to scare the strangers off by firing pot shots in their direction. Danny refuses because he's in love with a young woman named Nayomi who lives in the camp. Deciding that he wants nothing further to do with his father, Danny decides to depart for good, taking Nayomi with him. The young woman's kinfolk have no interest in seeing her leave with Danny, however, and they head after the pair, ready to use their fists and even their guns to prevent the two from eloping.
Comment: John Carradine (Kader) may be best remembered for having been a member of John Ford's "stock company" of movie actors, with appearances in *Stagecoach* (1939), *The Grapes of Wrath* (1940), *The Man Who Shot Liberty Valance* (1962) and *Cheyenne Autumn* (1964).[10] Carradine worked again with McLaglen in 1974, playing the role of Jacob Avril in the television movie *Stowaway to the Moon*.

"Horse Deal"

First Broadcast: September 26, 1959
Producer: Norman Macdonnell
Script: John Meston
Photography: Fleet Southcott
Editor: Al Joseph
Guest Stars: Harry Carey, Jr. (Deesha), Bartlett Robinson (Bowers), Trevor Bardette (Slim), Michael Minn (Wirth), Fred Grossinger (Harper)
Summary: Several merchants in Dodge have been tricked into buying stolen horses. When Deesha, the horses' owner, shows up in town to reclaim the animals, the aggrieved businessmen ask Dillon to find the con man who sold them the horses in the first place, not realizing that Deesha is in on the scam.

Comment: Harry Carey, Jr. (Deesha) and McLaglen were close friends. In his autobiography *Company of Heroes,* Carey describes the experience of working with McLaglen: "Andy stands on your feet and gets you bruised up some, all that good stuff, but I love him — all six-foot-seven, 230 pounds of him."[11] The pair first worked together on William A. Wellman's *Island in the Sky,* in which Carey, Jr. played one of the pilots who searches for lost men in the Canadian wilderness. Carey, Jr. was the son of Harry Carey, an actor who John Ford worked with regularly in the twenties and thirties.[12] Carey, Jr. himself had prominent roles in several Ford films, including *3 Godfathers* (1948), *Wagon Master* (1950) and *The Searchers* (1956). Carey, Jr. appeared in several television productions McLaglen shot for CBS Television during the fifties and sixties. He also had parts in McLaglen's *Gun the Man Down, Shenandoah, The Way West, The Ballad of Josie, The Devil's Brigade, Bandolero!, The Undefeated, "something big"* and *One More Train to Rob.* The final production the pair worked on together was the 1982 television movie *The Shadow Riders.*

"Kangaroo"

First Broadcast: September 26, 1959
Producer: Norman Macdonnell
Script: John Meston
Photography: Fleet Southcott
Editor: Otto Meyer
Guest Stars: Peter Whitney (Ira), Richard Rust (Dal), John Crawford (Hod), Lew Brown (Jim McBride)
Summary: Ira Scurlock, a religious extremist, takes pride in punishing people who defy the Bible's teachings. A tyrannical father, he has raised his sons to fear him and help him deliver justice to sinners. When Ira's youngest son, Dal, begins to resist his father's fanatical decrees, Ira responds with great cruelty, flogging the boy before a crowd in downtown Dodge. Rather than breaking Dal's spirit, the beating prompts the boy to doubt the legitimacy of his father's beliefs. The conflict between the father and son only increases as the episode progresses, eventually ending when Dal shoots Ira dead with his rifle.

"Saludos"

First Broadcast: October 31, 1959
Producer: Norman Macdonnell
Script: John Meston, story by Les Crutchfield
Photography: Fleet Southcott
Editor: Al Joseph
Guest Stars: Gene Nelson (Foss), Robert J. Wilke (Pegger), Jack Elam (Steed), Connie Buck (Sochi)
Summary: Sochi, a Pawnee woman, has been shot in the back. After Dillon and Chester find the injured woman on the prairie, they bring her to Doc's office in Dodge. Drifting in and out of consciousness, Sochi explains that a white man shot her and also murdered her husband. The lawmen then set out to find the killer.

"Odd Man Out"

First Broadcast: November 11, 1959
Producer: Norman Macdonnell
Script: John Meston, story by Les Crutchfield
Photography: Fleet Southcott

Editor: Otto Meyer
Music: Rene Garriguenc
Guest Stars: Elisha Cook, Jr. (Cyrus Tucker), William Phipps (Hody Peel), Dabs Greer (Jonas), Elizabeth York (Mrs. Peel), George Selk (Moss Grimmick), Dallas Mitchell (Cowboy), Clem Fuller (Clem)
Summary: After 32 years of marriage, Cy Tucker's wife walks out on her husband without an explanation. When a pauper shows up in Dodge trying to sell the missing woman's clothes, Dillon wonders if Mrs. Tucker has been murdered. The marshal then visits Cy Tucker's house, seeking an answer.

"Miguel's Daughter"

First Broadcast: November 28, 1959
Producer: Norman Macdonnell
Script: John Meston, story by Marian Clark
Photography: Fleet Southcott
Editor: Al Joseph
Guest Stars: Simon Oakland (Miguel), Fintan Meyler (Chavela), Wesley Lau (Ab), Ed Nelson (Rusk)
Summary: Chicken farmer Miguel Ramírez lives outside Dodge with his daughter Chavela. One day Chavela comes into town to sell eggs. Her beauty attracts the unwanted attention of two drunken cowboys, Ab and Rusk, who follow her out to her home. After knocking Miguel unconscious, Ab and Rusk chase Chavela into the forest, where she runs into a tree, severely injuring her head. Later, after Miguel is back on his feet, he finds one of the cowboys and kills him. When he brings the dead man's body to Dillon, the marshal has no choice but to arrest the old farmer for murder.

"Groat's Grudge"

First Broadcast: January 2, 1960
Producer: Norman Macdonnell
Script: John Meston, story by Marian Clark
Photography: Fleet Southcott
Editor: Otto Meyer
Music: Rene Garriguenc
Guest Stars: Ross Elliot (Lee), Thomas Coley (Tom), Ben Wright (Walt), Dabs Greer (Jonas), Clegg Hoyt (Cook), Howard Culver (Dobie), Clem Fuller (Clem)
Summary: During the Civil War, Lee Grayson fought for the South. At the Battle of Manassas, he found a Union soldier named Tom Haskett lying on the ground injured, and spared Haskett's life. Upon his return home to Georgia after the War, Grayson discovered that Union soldiers burned his house and killed his wife during Sherman's march to the sea. One of the men serving under Sherman, he learned, was Haskett. The realization has unleashed tremendous hatred in Grayson, and in the years since the war, the former Confederate has been searching obsessively for the man he allowed to live on the battlefield. When he finds out that Haskett is leading a herd of cattle into Dodge, Grayson heads for the city to find the man he hates and kill him.

"Big Tom"

First Broadcast: January 9, 1960
Producer: Norman Macdonnell

Script: John Meston, story by Marian Clark
Photography: Fleet Southcott
Editor: Otto Meyer
Music: Leith Stevens
Guest Stars: Robert Wilke (Tom), Harry Lauter (Clay), Don Megowan (Creel), Howard Caine (Brady), Gregg Palmer (Harry), Rand Harper (Jim), Clem Fuller (Clem)
Summary: Tom Burr once enjoyed a career as a successful prize fighter. But now his body is worn out and he lives in a shack outside Dodge, supporting himself as a laborer. He is persuaded to return to boxing, however, when an old opponent, Hob Creel, arrives in town. On the morning of the re-match, Tom stops in at Doc Adams's office, complaining about dizzy spells he's been having. Doc soon determines that the broken-down boxer has a heart problem, and that he must not spar with Creel. Fearing he will be regarded as a coward, Tom refuses to follow Doc's advice and commences with his plans to fight Creel. Dillon then steps in, locks up Tom in a cell and spars with Creel himself.
Comment: Robert Wilke (Pegger) and Don Megowan (Creel) played the roles of Rank and Farley in McLaglen's *Gun the Man Down*.

"Hinka Do"

First Broadcast: January 30, 1960
Producer: Norman Macdonnell
Script: Les Crutchfield
Photography: Fleet Southcott
Editor: Al Joseph
Music: Fred Steiner
Guest Stars: Nina Varela (Mamie), Walter Burke (Herman), Mike Green (Cowboy), Richard Reeves (Drunk), Ric Roman (Manuel), Bob Hopkins (Pete)
Summary: Herman Bleeker, owner of the Lady Gay saloon in Dodge City, disappears one night and the next morning a sign appears on the establishment's front door announcing that the saloon has a new owner. Concerned that something sinister may have happened to Bleeker, Dillon and Chester closely watch the establishment's new proprietress, a stout woman named Mamie, who is speedy with a gun. Their suspicions only increase when they discover that Mamie has buried Bleeker's clothes and shoes in a root cellar. Dillon is then forced to separate Mamie from her gun if he hopes to bring her into jail.

"Moo Moo Raid"

First Broadcast: February 13, 1960
Producer: Norman Macdonnell
Script: John Meston, story by Les Crutchfield
Photography: Fleet Southcott
Editor: Al Joseph
Guest Stars: Lane Bradford (Tush), Richard Evans (Pete), John Close (Joe), Raymond Hatton (Onie), Robert Karnes (Bert)
Summary: A cowboy named Tush is leading a herd of cattle toward Dodge. Before he and the animals can enter the city, they need to cross the Arkansas River. Because the cattle are skittish about traversing water, Tush heads out to find Onie Tucker, a farmer who owns a cow that can swim and lead the others safely to shore. When Tush arrives at Onie's house, he finds the old man's furniture turned over and blood on the floor. The trail boss concludes

that Onie and his cow have been murdered and that a rival cattleman, Bert, is guilty of the crime.

"Unwanted Deputy"

First Broadcast: March 5, 1960
Producer: Norman Macdonnell
Script: John Meston, story by Marian Clark
Photography: Fleet Southcott
Editor: Al Joseph
Music: Fred Steiner
Guest Stars: Charles Aidman (Vince), Mary Carver (Maise), Marlowe Jensen (Dave), Dick Rich (Rudd), Ed Faulkner (Harry), Dirk London (Tourney), Craig Fox (Lee), Bob Wiensko (Bob), Joe Haworth (Charlie)
Summary: Dillon apprehends a fugitive murderer named Dave Walsh. After Walsh is hanged, his brother, Vince, develops a grudge against the marshal, blaming him for Walsh's death. Vince then comes to Dodge to pick a fight with Dillon, thinking that if he can get the lawman to draw his gun on him, he can shoot him in self-defense without fear of consequence.

"Crowbait Bob"

First Broadcast: March 26, 1960
Producer: Norman Macdonnell
Script: Les Crutchfield
Photography: Fleet Southcott
Editor: Al Joseph
Guest Stars: Hank Patterson (Crowbait), Ned Glass (Elbin), Shirley O'Hara (Martha), John Apone (Ace)
Summary: Bob "Crowbait" Cutler is an alcoholic pauper who lives on handouts. Sick and close to death, Bob dictates his last will and testament to Dillon, telling the marshal that he wants everything he owns to go to Miss Kitty. When Dillon asks him to explain his decision, Bob reveals that Kitty has been providing him with free meals for the last two years. As Bob's condition worsens, Dillon gives him a warm bed in his jail. A rumor then spreads through town that the old mendicant is actually quite wealthy, that he owns a gold mine. When Bob's niece and her husband hear the rumor, they come to Dodge, insisting that any money Kitty stands to inherit actually belongs to them.
Comment: Shirley O'Hara (Martha) played Mrs. Turner in McLaglen's *The Little Shepherd of Kingdom Come* and Elizabeth in *The Ballad of Josie*.

"The Ex-Urbanites"

First Broadcast: April 9, 1960
Producer: Norman Macdonnell
Script: John Meston
Photography: Fleet Southcott
Editor: Al Joseph
Guest Stars: Robert Wilke (Pitt), Ken Curtis (Jesse), Lew Brown (Nage)
Summary: As they return from a four-day trek around the prairie providing medical care to farmers, Doc and Chester find a trapper named Nage lying in a gulley with a bullet wound in his belly. Once Doc begins to treat the injured man, two more trappers — Jesse and

Pitt — appear, claiming to be Nage's partners. They caution Doc to leave the patient alone, that he shot himself and is thus responsible for taking care of himself. In reality, Jesse and Pitt shot Nage, and now they fear that he will tell his rescuers what happened. The outlaws then attack the camp, shooting Doc in the belly, before fleeing. Chester is then forced to perform surgery on his friend in the open woods.

"The Lady Killer"

First Broadcast: April 23, 1960
Producer: Norman Macdonnell
Script: John Meston
Photography: Fleet Southcott
Editor: Al Joseph
Guest Stars: Jan Harrison (Mae), Harry Lauter (Sy), Ross Elliott (Lucas), George Selk (Moss), Charles Sterrett (Cowboy), Clem Fuller (Clem)
Summary: Sy Welsh has been charged with swindling an old man out of his land and now faces an impending trial. One of Welsh's neighbors, Grant Lucas, arrives in Dodge to appear in court as a witness for the prosecution. When he stops in at the Long Branch for a drink, Lucas meets Mae, a beautiful saloon girl who takes a fancy to him despite his homely looks. Mae then invites Lucas to visit her that night at her rooming house. But after he shows up, Mae fatally shoots him. Mae, it turns out, is an assassin, who's been hired by Sy Welsh to silence everyone who plans to testify against him in the courtroom.

"Speak Me Fair"

First Broadcast: May 7, 1960
Producer: Norman Macdonnell
Script: Les Crutchfield
Photography: Fleet Southcott
Editor: Otto Meyer
Music: Rene Garriguenc
Guest Stars: Douglas Kennedy (Traych), Ken Curtis (Scout), Chuck Roberson (Driver), Perry Cook (Gunner)
Summary: A rancher named Traych has lost several cows to rustlers and he asks for Dillon's help. On the trail to Traych's ranch, the marshal spots a young Indian boy who has been severely beaten. His throat injured, the boy cannot tell Dillon anything about what's happened. The marshal soon becomes convinced that the men who've been stealing cattle from Traych also attacked the boy.
Comment: This episode takes its title from a passage in Shakespeare's *The Merchant of Venice*, in which the title character says to a friend: "'Say how I lov'd you, speak me fair in death" (IV.I.284). Chuck Roberson (Driver) was a stuntman who regularly served as John Wayne's onscreen double. He occasionally had his own roles in films and television, too. Among the movies he appeared in that McLaglen directed are *McLintock!*, *Hellfighters*, *The Undefeated*, *Chisum* and *Cahill, United States Marshal*.[13]

"Cherry Red"

First Broadcast: June 11, 1960
Producer: Norman Macdonnell
Script: Les Crutchfield

Photography: Fleet Southcott
Editor: Otto Meyer
Guest Stars: Joanna Moore (Cherry), Arthur Franz (Red), Douglas Kennedy (Yancey), Cliff Ketchum (Nightshirt)
Summary: Cherry Odell, a seamstress in Dodge, has waited for more than a year for her husband, Slim, to come home from a business trip. While Dillon is certain that the man is dead, Cherry holds to the idea that he will soon return. Her mind changes when a man named Red shows up, claiming that he's seen Slim's corpse. In truth, Slim tried to rob a stage in which Red was riding and Red shot him dead. Smitten with Cherry, Red hopes she will find it in her heart to overlook the fact that he killed her husband.

Have Gun, Will Travel

Created by Sam Rolfe and Herb Meadow, *Have Gun, Will Travel* ran for six seasons on CBS from 1957 to 1963. The show featured Richard Boone as Paladin, a genteel gun-for-hire who lives in the palatial Hotel Carlton in San Francisco. Paladin provides his services to anyone who might need them, as long as the client's needs are just. Actor Kam Tong appeared on the show, as well, playing Hey Boy, an employee at the Hotel Carlton who helps Paladin find new clients. Episodes for *Have Gun, Will Travel* were frequently filmed on location throughout the American West, making use of scenic settings in places like Lone Pine, California, Gallup, New Mexico and Bend, Oregon.[14]

SEASON ONE, 1957–1958

"Three Bells to Perdido"

First Broadcast: September 14, 1957
Producer: Julian Claman
Script: Herb Meadow, Sam Rolfe
Photography: Fleet Southcott
Editor: Fred Berger
Music: Bernard Herrman
Guest Stars: Jack Lord (Dave Enderby), Janice Rule (Nancy), Harry Shannon (Jesse Reed), Francis MacDonald (Gotch), Christian Drake (Dark Youth), Ted Marcuse (Bartender)
Summary: Beautiful Nancy Reed has run off and married Dave Enderby, a dangerous criminal. The couple

Richard Boone as Paladin, the hero for hire in *Have Gun, Will Travel* (CBS).

now lives in Perdido, Mexico. Nancy's father, a rancher named Jesse, hires Paladin to find his daughter and bring her home.

Comment: "Three Bells to Perdido" is *Have Gun, Will Travel*'s premiere episode.

"The Outlaw"

First Broadcast: September 21, 1957
Producer: Julian Claman
Script: Sam Rolfe
Photography: William Margulies
Editor: Leslie Vidor
Guest Stars: Charles Bronson (Manfred Holt), Grant Withers (Sheriff Ludlow), Steve Mitchell (Gage), Barry Cahill (Abe Talltree), Peggy Stewart (Sarah Holt), Warren Parker (Ned Alcorn)
Summary: Manfred Holt, a convicted murderer, has escaped from prison. Ned Alcorn testified against Holt at his trial and now fears for his life; he hires Paladin to find the fugitive and return him to custody. The gunfighter soon captures Holt, but he takes pity on him when he learns that Holt, a new father, has been unable to meet his son. Instead of taking Holt straight to jail, Paladin allows him to visit his home one last time. As the two men ride together, they become friends. After the killer sees his newborn son and wife, however, he refuses to rejoin Paladin and complete the trip back to prison.

"The Great Mojave Chase"

First Broadcast: September 28, 1957
Producer: Julian Claman
Script: Gene Roddenberry
Photography: William Margulies
Editor: Samuel Gold
Guest Stars: Claude Akins (1st Gunman), Lawrence Dobkin (Billy Jo Kane), Earl Hodgins (2nd Gunman), William Fawcett (Jake), Hal Smith (Bartender), Jonathan Hole (Elkins), Walter Reed (Captain)
Summary: Lured by the promise of a large purse, Paladin enters a survival contest that is being held in the Mojave Desert. To win, he needs an animal that can travel a long distance without needing to stop for water. He decides on a camel that was once used by the U.S. Cavalry for missions in the region.
Comment: Claude Akins (1st Gunman) played one of the American soldiers in McLaglen's *The Devil's Brigade*. In the early sixties, scenarist Gene Roddenberry would develop *The Lieutenant* television series for NBC, for which McLaglen directed several episodes. Roddenberry also created the immensely popular *Star Trek* film and television series.[15]

"Winchester Quarantine"

First Broadcast: October 5, 1957
Producer: Julian Claman
Script: Herb Meadow
Photography: William Marguiles
Editor: Samuel Gold
Guest Stars: Anthony Caruso (Joseph Whitehorse), Leo V. Gordon (Clyde McNally), Robert Karnes (Peavey), Don Keefer (Kelso), Vic Perrin (Rheinhart), Carol Thurston (Martha), Jim Parnell (Sheriff)

Summary: Joseph Whitehorse, a Cherokee Indian, has purchased a large spread where he hopes to raise cattle with his wife. Recently his animals have taken ill and begun to die. Certain that the cows carry a contagious disease, Whitehorse's racist neighbor, McNally, forbids the rancher from leaving his land, fearing that Whitehorse may introduce the sickness into neighboring herds. When Paladin learns about this situation, he offers to help Whitehorse. Unconvinced the cattle are diseased, he has the soil on the Whitehorses' property tested, and finds that it is rich with molybdenum, a chemical element that has poisoned the grass. Paladin then tricks McNally into buying the Whitehorse ranch.

"A Matter of Ethics"

First Broadcast: October 12, 1957
Producer: Julian Claman
Script: Sam Rolfe
Photography: William Margulies
Editor: Samuel Gold
Guest Stars: Harold J. Stone (Holgate), Angie Dickinson (Amy Bender), Strother Martin (Fred Coombs), Roy Barcroft (Sheriff Swink), Steven Terrell (Harry Dill), Willis Bouchey (Max Bender), Burt Nelson (Farmer), Ken Mayer (Willy), John Mitchum (McHeath), Theodore Marcuse (Folger), Peter Brocco (Clerk)
Summary: A ruffian named Holgate has been taken into custody, charged with murdering a man named Bender. Fearing he will be killed before he gets his chance to stand trial, Holgate hires on Paladin for extra protection. The arrangement outrages Bender's sister, Amy. She decides to take action, organizing a lynch mob. The vigilantes try to break into the town jail where Holgate is being held, but Paladin, waving a bundle of dynamite, turns them away.
Comment: Roy Barcroft (Sheriff Swink) had roles in three McLaglen features: *Freckles, The Way West* and *Bandolero!* He and McLaglen first worked together on Joseph Kane's *Dakota* in 1945. John Mitchum (McHeath) appeared in *Man in the Vault, Bandolero!, Chisum* and *One More Train to Rain*. John Mitchum was the brother of Robert Mitchum, another actor McLaglen worked with on several occasions.

"The Bride"

First Broadcast: October 19, 1957
Producer: Julian Claman
Script: Steve Fisher
Photography: William Margulies
Editor: Harry Coswick
Guest Stars: Marian Seldes (Christie Smith), Michael Connors (Johnny Dart), Bruce Gordon (Louis Drydan), Barry Cahill (Guard)
Summary: Paladin accompanies a young woman named Christie Smith, a mail-order bride, as she makes her way to her fiancé's ranch in the Texas desert. The man waiting for her at the ranch has an unpleasant personality and Christie wonders if he may be someone other than the person she has come out to marry. Paladin shares the bride's doubts and takes action to protect her.

"Strange Vendetta"

First Broadcast: October 26, 1957
Producer: Julian Claman

Script: Ken Kolb
Photography: William Margulies
Editor: Samuel Gold
Guest Stars: June Vincent (Maria Rojas), Michael Pate (Miguel Rojas), Gerald Milton (Farley), Onslow Stevens (Dr. Mayhew), Ned Glass (Wilkins), Abel Fernandez (Bandit), Roberto Contreras (Hernandez), Rocky Shahan (Stage Driver)
Summary: An assassin stabs Don Miguel Rojas at the opera in San Francisco. Though the wound itself is not fatal, the assassin's knife had been dipped in lethal poison, and now Rojas is dying. He summons Paladin and offers to pay him well if the gunfighter will transport his corpse to his ranch in Mexico. Paladin agrees, and after Rojas dies, he secures a stage, straps Rojas's coffin to the top and starts the trip. Shortly after Paladin crosses into Mexico, he learns that his client is actually alive and that the coffin on top of the stage is filled with stolen money.

"High Wire"

First Broadcast: November 2, 1957
Producer: Julian Claman
Script: Donald Brinkley
Photography: William Margulies
Editor: Harry Coswick
Guest Stars: Strother Martin (Dooley Delaware), John Dehner (Ben Marquette), Fay Spain (Rena), Buddy Baer (Bolo), Jack Albertson (Bookie), Theodore Marcuse (Wally), Duane Grey (Driver)
Summary: Dooley Delaware was once a popular high wire walker. But after a fall, he lost his courage, and now he performs acrobatic tricks in saloons for small change. When he is taunted by a bully named Ben Marquette, Dooley decides to face his fears and cross the Salamander Canyon, a 100-foot span. Paladin bets Marquette $3,000 that Dooley will succeed. To make sure he wins the bet, Marquette tries to sabotage the high wire that will carry Dooley across the canyon.
Comment: John Dehner (Rack) played the role of Paladin on the *Have Gun, Will Travel* radio show, which CBS Radio broadcast from 1958 to 1960.[16] He also played the part of Rod Mason in *Out California Way,* one of the "singing cowboy" pictures McLaglen was assigned to when he was a production clerk at Republic. Fay Spain played Sue Ellen in McLaglen's *The Abductors.*

"Show of Force"

First Broadcast: November 9, 1957
Producer: Julian Claman
Script: Ken Kolb and Lee Erwin
Photography: William Margulies
Editor: Harry Coswick
Guest Stars: Rodolfo Acosta (Pedro Valdez), Russ Conway (Jared Martin), Peter Coe (Carlos Valdez), Joe Bassett (Matt Garson), Vic Perrin (Haskins), Ned Glass (Bernard), Walter Brennan, Jr. (Cowboy)
Summary: Paladin wins a box of antiquated rifles in a poker game. After he reads in the papers about a land dispute that has arisen between two ranchers, he heads out to meet with both men, ready to give his help — and his guns — to the person he thinks deserves it

most. The first rancher he meets is Jared Martin, an American with a bullying personality. The second rancher is a Mexican man named Pedro Valdez. When Valdez tells Paladin that Martin has been trying to cheat him out of land he inherited, the gunslinger offers him the use of his guns. The flimsy weapons cannot fire, however. To deter Martin, Paladin explains, Valdez needs to convince his enemy that the guns are indeed dangerous without ever firing a shot.

"The Long Night"

First Broadcast: November 16, 1957
Producer: Julian Claman
Script: Sam Rolfe
Photography: William Margulies
Editor: Samuel Gold
Guest Stars: Kent Smith (Louis Strome), James Best (Andy Fisher), William Schallert (Clyde Broderick), Michael Granger (Emanual), Kenneth Alton (Jackson)
Summary: Texas rancher Louis Strome comes home to find his wife keeping company with a strange man. The stranger runs off before Strome can see his face, though he notes that the man wears a black shirt. Strome then shoots his wife dead. Instead of reproaching himself for his wife's murder, he directs his anger toward the man in the black shirt, blaming him for sullying his wife and ruining their marriage. With some cowhands, Strome proceeds to string a noose from a tree along the trail that leads out of Texas and detains every rider who wears a black shirt. Among the men he stops is Paladin.
Comment: James Best (Andy Fisher) played the role of Carter in McLaglen's *Shenandoah*.

"The Colonel and the Lady"

First Broadcast: November 23, 1957
Producer: Julian Claman
Script: Michael Fessier
Photography: William Margulies
Editor: Michael Luciano
Guest Stars: Robert F. Simon (Col. Lathrop), June Vincent (Martha Lathrop), Denver Pyle (Clay Sommers), Faye Nuell (Tuolumne O'Toole), Robert Stevenson (Steve), Jess Kirkpatrick (Bartender), Mercedes Shirley (Mazie), Peggy Rea (Lulu), Woodrow Chambliss (Hotel Clerk)
Summary: Col. Lathrop, an elderly amateur historian, hires Paladin to visit Lode Star, a lawless mining town in Nevada, to learn what he can about Gloria Morgan, a notorious saloon girl who once lived there. Upon his arrival, the gunfighter finds himself on the receiving end of hostility from the locals, who resent his inquiries about a person they all hold in the highest regard. Paladin soon learns that Gloria Morgan, far from being a slattern, was a kind person, who rescued many from cholera. As he conducts his research, Paladin comes to realize that Gloria Morgan is also Col. Lathrop's wife.

"No Visitors"

First Broadcast: November 30, 1957
Producer: Julian Claman
Script: Don Brinkley
Photography: William Margulies
Editor: Samuel Gold

Guest Stars: June Lockhart (Dr. Phyllis Thackeray), Grant Withers (Mulrooney), Ruth Storey (Clara Benson), Whit Bissell (Mr. Jonas), Peg Hillias (Mrs. Jonas)

Summary: While passing through the desert, Paladin finds a young mother and her baby stranded and alone. The mother explains that she has been expelled from a wagon train. The train's wagon master, a religious fanatic named Mulrooney, believes that she and her baby were both sick with typhoid and has decided to leave them behind, rather than find medical assistance. Wanting to help, Paladin starts for the nearest town. Once there, he meets Mulrooney, who tells him to leave the mother and child alone. Mulrooney subsequently convinces the local population that any contact with the mother and child will kill them all. Phyllis Thackeray, the community's only doctor, ignores the locals' hysterical response and joins Paladin. When the gunfighter and the doctor bring the mother and child back to town, they are met with jeers, threats and rifles.

"The Englishman"

First Broadcast: December 7, 1957
Producer: Julian Claman
Script: Sam Rolfe
Photography: William Margulies
Editor: Samuel Gold
Guest Stars: Tom Helmore (James Brunswick), Alix Talton (Felicia Carson), Murvyn Vye (N.G. Smith), Ted de Corsia (Chief Harry Blackfoot), Clinton Sundberg (Waddy), Abel Fernandez (Little Horse), Robert Bice (Husband)

Summary: James Brunswick has come from Britain to claim his inheritance, a share in a remote Montana ranch. While in San Francisco, he hires Paladin to lead him safely up to the ranch. Once they arrive, Brunswick finds himself at odds with the locals who live in this section of the west.

"The Yuma Treasure"

First Broadcast: December 14, 1957
Producer: Julian Claman
Script: Gene Roddenberry
Photography: William Margulies
Editor: Michael Luciano
Guest Stars: Warren Stevens (Maj. Wilson), Henry Brandon (Gerada), Harry Landers (Lt. Harvey), Russ Thorsen (Col. Harrison), Barry Cahill (Sgt. Combs)

Summary: Traveling through Arizona, Paladin stops at a U.S. Cavalry outpost where he meets Maj. Wilson, the camp's commander. Wilson tells the gunfighter that he is concerned that the truce that has been struck between the army and a local tribe of Maricopa Indians is coming undone. He then asks Paladin to take him to meet with Gerada, chief of the Maricopas. Wilson is a liar, however. Far from being interested in securing peace, he wants to find out what he can about the location of a rich vein of gold that reputedly exists on Maricopa land. Once Paladin learns about the major's ulterior motives, he steps up to protect the Indians' treasure.

"The Hanging Cross"

First Broadcast: December 21, 1957
Producer: Julian Claman

Script: Gene Roddenberry
Photography: William Margulies
Editor: Samuel Gold
Guest Stars: Edward Binns (Nathaniel Beecher), Abraham Sofaer (Cah-la-te), Don Beddoe (Tater), Johnny Crawford (Robbie), Mary Adams (Maggie), Frances Osborne (Maudie), Nyra Monsour (Tia), Bucky Young (Pete), Mitchell Kowal (Jesse), James Gavin (Cowboy)
Summary: On Christmas Eve, Paladin is summoned by Nathaniel Beecher to find Beecher's son Robbie, who was abducted by Indians six years earlier. Once Paladin arrives at Beecher's ranch, he learns that Robbie has been found, and thus his services are no longer needed. A few days earlier, Beecher explains, the boy was spotted riding with Cah-la-te, a Pawnee chief, and Beecher and his men snatched the boy and brought him back to the ranch. Robbie only speaks Pawnee now, however, and his father cannot communicate with him. Paladin then explains that he speaks Pawnee, too, and Beecher hires him on to translate. Simultaneously, Cah-la-te prepares to attack the Beecher ranch, wanting to reclaim the child he considers his own.

"Helen of Abajinian"

First Broadcast: December 28, 1957
Producer: Julian Claman
Script: Gene Roddenberry
Photography: William Marguiles
Editor: Michael Luciano
Guest Stars: Harold J. Stone (Samuel Abajinian), Wright King (O'Riley), Lisa Gaye (Helen), Vladimir Sokoloff (Gourken), Nick Dennis (Jorgi), Naomi Stevens (Marga)
Summary: Beautiful Helen is the daughter of Samuel Abajinian, a rich Armenian vintner. Helen is infatuated with Jimmy O'Riley, a cowboy, and she follows after him when O'Riley passes by her father's farm. Samuel subsequently hires Paladin to find the couple and return them to him.

"Ella West"

First Broadcast: January 4, 1958
Producer: Julian Claman
Script: Gene Roddenberry
Photography: William Marguiles
Editor: Samuel Gold
Guest Stars: Norma Crane (Ella West), William Swan (Tracey Calvert), Earle Hodgins (Tomahawk Carter), Mike Mazurki (Breed), Mason Curry (Manager)
Summary: A crack shot, Ella West works for a traveling circus show. Angry over the abuse and poverty she experienced as a young girl, she treats everyone she meets in an insolent manner. Concerned that Ella's obnoxious personality is hurting his business, Ella's employer hires Paladin to teach the young woman how to dress, speak and conduct herself more like a lady.
Comment: Mike Mazurki (Breed) appeared in McLaglen's first feature, *Man in the Vault*.

"The Reasonable Man"

First Broadcast: January 11, 1958
Producer: Julian Claman

Script: Joel Kane and Ken Kolb
Photography: William Margulies
Editor: Leslie Vidor
Guest Stars: Geoff Parish (Grady Stewart), Adam Williams (Frank Gault), Norma Moore (Sheila Stewart), Barry Atwater (Gene Morgan), Lennie Geer (Ben)
Summary: Rancher Gene Morgan asks Paladin to help him fix his relationship with a young man named Grady Stewart. An orphan, Grady was raised by Morgan, but the two are now locked in a dispute over land rights, each man claiming ownership of the other's property.

"The High Graders"

First Broadcast: January 18, 1958
Producer: Julian Claman
Script: Ken Kolb, Wilton Schiller and Jack Laird, story by Wilton Schiller & Jack Laird
Photography: William Margulies
Editor: Michael Luciano
Guest Stars: Susan Cabot (Angela), Robert Wilke (Casey Bryan), Robert Steele (Jockey), Nico Minardos (Gino), Carlyle Mitchell (Governor), Chris Alcaide (Morgan)
Summary: Paladin wonders if his late friend, Polo, a tailor who owned a gold mine, has been cheated and murdered by his partner, Casey Bryan. Paladin visits the mine and discovers that his suspicions are valid. Bryan has been allowing the men who work for him at the mine to leave each day with as much high grade ore as they can carry in exchange for a hefty fee.

"The Last Laugh"

First Broadcast: January 25, 1958
Producer: Julian Claman
Script: Don Brinkley
Photography: William Margulies
Editor: Al Joseph
Guest Stars: Peter Whitney (Judd Calhoun), Murray Hamilton (Ed McKay), Stuart Whitman (Gil Borden), Jean Allison (Nora Borden), Frankie Darro (Mickey), Jack Holland (Hank)
Summary: Ed McKay likes to pull pranks on people and tease Judd Calhoun, a slow-witted cowhand. As this episode opens, McKay convinces Judd to place a burr under the saddle of a horse. When a local woman named Nora Borden mounts the horse, the animal begins to buck, throwing her to the ground and breaking both her legs. Nora's hotheaded husband, Gil, mistakenly blames Paladin for playing the trick. He then rounds up a posse to find the gunfighter. Among the posse's members are Ed McKay and Judd Calhoun.

"The Bostonian"

First Broadcast: February 1, 1958
Producer: Julian Claman
Script: Berni Gould, Milton Pascal and Ken Kolb
Photography: William Margulies
Editor: Michael Luciano
Guest Stars: Constance Ford (Gloria Prince), Harry Townes (Henry Prince), Joe De Santis (Clint Bryant), Chris Alcaide (Bill Whitney), Luis Gomez (José), Frederick Ford (Cowboy)
Summary: Henry Prince, a wealthy Easterner, has moved to Nevada with his wife, Gloria.

Unwittingly, Prince purchased a piece of land that a local named Clint Bryant wanted for himself. Bryant now regularly harasses the meek Prince, beating him up, damaging his property, even killing one of his employees. Under Paladin's guidance, Prince learns how to stand up to Bryant, a development that improves his standing in the community and allows him to commence with his new life as a cattleman.

"The Singer"

First Broadcast: February 8, 1958
Producer: Julian Claman
Script: Ken Kolb and Sam Peckinpah
Photography: William Margulies
Editor: Michael Luciano
Guest Stars: Johan Weldon (Faye Hollister), Richard Long (Rod Blakley), Denver Pyle (Pete Hollister), Jay Adler (Bottellini) Gloria Pall (Della), Richard Hartunian (Curley)
Summary: A lovelorn cowboy named Rod Blakley barges into Paladin's suite at the Hotel Carleton. Blakley explains that his former employer, Pete Hollister, has stolen his bride-to-be, a woman named Faye, and forced her into marriage. The cowboy and the gunfighter then rendezvous with Faye on Hollister's isolated ranch. After Faye explains that she would rather be with Blakley than stay with her husband, Blakley and Paladin steal her away to San Francisco. It becomes quickly apparent, though, that the woman is not deeply committed to Blakley. What she really wants is to be an opera singer and living in the city improves her chances for achieving this goal.

"Bitter Wine"

First Broadcast: February 15, 1958
Producer: Julian Claman
Script: Ken Kolb
Photography: William Margulies
Editor: Samuel Gold
Guest Stars: Eduardo Ciannelli (Renato Donatello), Rita Lynn (Teresa Donatello), Richard Shannon (Tim Gorman), Donald Foster (Fair Chairman), James Waters (First Guard), Val Benedict (Second Guard)
Summary: Renato Donatello is a vintner in central California. For 20 years, he has successfully grown grapes, producing a Riesling wine that draws admiration from many connoisseurs, including Paladin. But now Renato faces a potentially catastrophic problem. A neighbor named Tim Gorman has begun to drill for oil on land that lies adjacent to his vineyard and the fumes and run-off from the operation have begun to damage his grapes. Infuriated, Renato leads an armed attack on Gorman's operation; the oilman responds with violence, as well. Paladin fortunately keeps a cool head and strives to negotiate an arrangement that manages to satisfy both men.

"The O'Hare Story"

First Broadcast: March 1, 1958
Producer: Julian Claman
Script: Marvin Wald and Jack Jacobs
Photography: William Margulies
Editor: Michael Luciano

Guest Stars: Victor McLaglen (Mike O'Hare), Herbert Rudley (Henry Ritchie), Christine White (Myra Ritchie), John Doucette (Joe Marsh), Ken Mayer (Elie Gardner), Ric Vallin (Cal), Alex Sharp (First Guard), Paul Hahn (Carson)

Summary: Henry Ritchie is a real estate salesman who lives and works in Ashley, California. When the leaders of neighboring Central City begin to build dams and aqueducts in order to increase their water supply, Ritchie starts to worry, fearing that these efforts will diminish Ashley's water resources and the value of the land. Ritchie then hires Paladin, with the hope of using him to force the leaders of Central City and their chief engineer, Mike O'Hare, to abandon their plans. At first, Paladin is sympathetic to Ritchie and he sabotages O'Hare's supply of cement. But once the gunfighter learns from O'Hare that Ritchie's complaints are overstated and disingenuous, he begins to wonder if he's given his help to the wrong man.

Comment: This episode marks the second time McLaglen directed his father, Victor. The actor had previously appeared in McLaglen's 1957 motion picture *The Abductors*. The two would pair up a final time for the "Incident of the Shambling Man" episode of *Rawhide* in 1959.

"Birds of a Feather"

First Broadcast: March 8, 1958
Producer: Julian Claman
Script: Fred Eggers and Terence Maples, story by Terence Maples
Photography: William Margulies
Editor: Fred W. Berger
Guest Stars: James Craig (Ralph Coe), Robert H. Harris (John Sukey), Harry Bartell (Sheriff Quinn), Joan Marshall (Molly), William Erwin (Citizen), Duane Grey (Garner), John Mitchum (Crabbe), Ric Vallin (Clary), Alexander Lockwood (Foster)

Summary: Two competing railroad companies have moved into Big Spur, Colorado, each wanting to take control of this tiny mining town as they expand their presence in the west. The companies' chiefs have hired legions of gunmen who now patrol Big Spur's streets, killing one another and terrorizing local residents. The sheriff in Big Spur is an old friend of Paladin, and when the gunfighter reads about the conflict in the newspaper, he starts out for Colorado, ready to offer his help.

"Killer's Widow"

First Broadcast: March 22, 1958
Producer: Julian Claman
Script: Albert Aley
Photography: Fleet Southcott
Editor: Samuel Gold
Guest Stars: Barbara Baxley (Lucy Morrow), Roy Barcroft (John Griffin), R.G. Armstrong (Jaffey), Ray Roope (E.J. Randolph), Ben Morris (Clete), Perry Ivins (Proprietor)

Summary: Lucy Morrow lives alone in a shack with her newborn baby. Because Lucy has been unable to pay her property taxes, her house will soon be auctioned and she and her child will be left without a home. Lucy cannot afford her bills because her husband, Steve Morrow, is dead. A professional criminal, Morrow was shot and killed by Paladin following a bank robbery. Feeling somewhat responsible for Lucy's predicament, Paladin tries to help the woman by finding money for her to pay off her debts.

"The Prize Fight Story"

First Broadcast: April 5, 1958
Producer: Julian Claman
Script: Ken Kolb
Photography: Fleet Southcott
Editor: Samuel Gold
Guest Stars: Don Megowan (Oren Gilliam), George E. Stone (Joe Roland), Gage Clarke (Jake Webber), King Calder (Clint Forbes), Hal Baylor (Bryan Sykes), Carl Saxe (Man), Red Morgan (Tom), Jack Perry (Bartender)
Summary: Joe Roland, a boxing promoter, wants to organize a bare-knuckle bout between two boxers, Jake Webber and Clint Forbes. His efforts are being frustrated by a corrupt sheriff, who threatens to shut down the fight if he is denied a share of the gate receipts. Unwilling to give in, Roland asks Paladin for assistance.

"Three Sons"

First Broadcast: May 10, 1958
Producer: Julian Claman
Script: Ken Kolb
Photography: Fleet Southcott
Editor: Leslie Vidor
Guest Stars: Parker Fennelly (Rupe Bosworth), Paul Jasmin (Hank Bosworth), Warren Oates (John Bosworth), Kevin Hagen (Ed Bosworth), Jacqueline Mayo (Janie Bosworth), S. John Launder (Roy Daggett), Jon Lormer (Judge Cates), Olan Soulé (Hotel Clerk), Fred Dale (Sheriff)
Summary: Hank Bosworth and his new wife, Janie, have come to San Francisco for their honeymoon. The Hotel Carlton is fully occupied and Paladin offers the couple his suite for the night. During breakfast the next morning, Janie receives a gift from Hank's two brothers: a mutilated cat. Hank explains to Paladin that his brothers John and Ed hate him because his father Rupe evicted them from the family farm. Hank adds that he is worried that John and Ed are going to kill Rupe. Ready to help, Paladin heads out to the Bosworth farm. A quick friendship arises between him and the old man. Rupe subsequently reveals that John and Ed are not actually planning to kill him; instead, they are trying to prove to the state that he is insane and that his land needs to be turned over to them. A hearing follows in which Paladin defends the old man successfully.
Comment: Warren Oates (John Bosworth) would work again with McLaglen on subsequent episodes of *Have Gun, Will Travel* and *Gunsmoke*; he also played the roles of Billy Parker in McLaglen's *Shenandoah* and the deranged preacher in *The Blue & the Gray*. Kevin Hagen (Ed Bosworth) had a role in *Shenandoah*, as well, playing a murderous Confederate deserter.

"The Return of Dr. Thackeray"

First Broadcast: May 17, 1958
Producer: Julian Claman
Script: Stanley H. Silverman and Sam Rolfe, story by Stanley H. Silverman
Photography: Fleet Southcott
Editor: Samuel Gold
Guest Stars: June Lockhart (Dr. Phyllis Thackeray), Grant Withers (Sam Barton), Charles Aidman (Tom Barton), John Anderson (Fred Cooley), Johnny Western (Steve), Cy Malis (Nate)

Summary: When one of his men becomes sick with small pox, cattleman Sam Barton calls upon Dr. Thackeray, a female doctor, for help. The doctor immediately sends out for vaccines for everybody who's been exposed to the disease on his ranch. Fearing that Barton's ranch hands will scatter before the vaccine arrives, the doctor asks Barton to hold their pay, forcing the men to remain near the ranch. Fearing this action may trigger violence, Dr. Thackeray sends an emergency telegraph to Paladin, requesting his help.

Comment: In this episode, cowboy singer Johnny Western briefly appears on screen as a gunman who is killed by Paladin. Western would later write and record "The Ballad of Paladin," which was subsequently adopted as *Have Gun, Will Travel*'s closing musical theme.[17]

"Twenty-Four Hours at North Fork"

First Broadcast: May 24, 1958
Producer: Julian Claman
Script: Irving Rubine
Photography: Fleet Southcott
Editor: Harry Coswick
Guest Stars: Morris Ankrum (Maxim Bruckner), Jacqueline Scott (Tildy Buchanan), Harry Shannon (Marty Buchanan), Brad Dexter (Jud Polk), Adeline de Walt Reynolds (Baba), Karl Swenson (Milo Culligan), Michael Hinn (Tom Ferris), Wayne Heffley (Johann Schmidt), Dennis Cross (Bill Hode), Sam Gilman (Clerk), Hank Patterson (Stage Driver)
Summary: The Bruckners, a family of Mennonites, have come from Iowa to a town called North Fork to grow wheat. Their religious traditions have made them the butt of jokes in the local community, and they are regularly threatened with physical violence. In an effort to drive them off of their land, a scoundrel named Tom Ferris sets fire to the Bruckners' crops. When he becomes aware of this mistreatment, Paladin offers his protection to the family.

"The Statue of San Sebastian"

First Broadcast: June 14, 1958
Producer: Julian Claman
Script: Albert Aley
Photography: Fleet Southcott
Editor: Samuel Gold
Guest Stars: John Carradine (Father Bartolme), Simon Oakland (Sancho Fernandez), Judson Pratt (Ian Crown), Bart Bradley (Pedro), Fred Graham (Stocker), Than Wyenn (Clerk)
Summary: For two decades, the monks in an old Spanish mission have been trying to recover a statue of St. Sebastian that has fallen into the hands of Ian Crown, a miserly rancher whose land lies adjacent to theirs. Crown has his problems, as well — an outlaw named Sancho Fernandez has been killing his livestock. Paladin comes to Crown, offering his assistance. In exchange for the monks' statue of St. Sebastian, he will drive Fernandez out of the rancher's valley.

Season Two, 1958–1959

"In an Evil Time"

First Broadcast: September 20, 1958
Producer: Sam Rolfe
Script: Shimon Wincelberg
Photography: Howard Schwartz

Editor: Harry Coswick
Guest Stars: Hank Patterson (Pappy French), William Stevens (Morley), Charles Horvath (Bull Swanson)
Music: Pappy French organizes a bank robbery with several young associates. After the heist, Pappy runs off with the $50,000 he and his partners have taken from the bank. He falls from his horse, however, severely breaking his leg. Hired by the bank to recover the money, Paladin finds the injured old man and persuades him to divulge where he's stashed the loot. As the pair starts for the hiding place, they are set upon by two of Pappy's former partners, who still want their share of the money from the bank job. A prolonged shootout follows, with everyone dying except Paladin.
Comment: This episode's title is a reference to Ecclesiastes 9:12: "For man also knoweth not his time: as the fishes that are taken in an evil net, and as the birds that are caught in the snare; so are the sons of men snared in an evil time, when it falleth suddenly upon them."

"The Man Who Wouldn't Talk"

First Broadcast: September 27, 1958
Producer: Sam Rolfe
Script: Fanya Lawrence
Photography: Fleet Southcott
Editor: Samuel Gold
Guest Stars: Charles Bronson (Chris Sorenson), Grace Raynor (Maria de Castro), Celia Lovsky (Aunt Anna), Harry Carey, Jr. (Bud), Edmund Johnston (Jeff Brewer), Junius Matthews (Clem), Bob Tetrick (Wrangler), Diane Cannon (Fifi), Marcia Drake (Mimi)
Summary: Rancher Chris Sorenson is in love with his neighbor Maria de Castro, but he has a difficult time talking to her. Impressed by Paladin's suave manner, Sorenson hires the gunfighter to come out to his ranch and teach him the art of eloquent speech.

"The Hanging of Roy Carter"

First Broadcast: October 4, 1958
Producer: Sam Rolfe
Script: Gene Roddenberry
Photography: Howard Schwartz
Editor: Samuel Gold
Guest Stars: John Larch (Chaplain Robert April), Robert Armstrong (Sidney Carter), Scott Marlowe (Roy Carter), Paul Birch (Warden Bullock), Francis J. McDonald (Jesse), John Duke (Keno Smith), Michael Hinn (Marshal), K.L. Smith (1st Guard), Ed Faulkner (2nd Guard), Rusty Westcoatt (3rd Guard)
Summary: Roy Carter has been mistakenly convicted of murder. Shortly before his scheduled execution date, he is cleared of the crime. Because of a broken telegraph line, news of Carter's innocence does not reach the penitentiary where the young man lives. Fearing that his son will be hanged, Carter's father hires Paladin to head up to the prison and persuade the warden there to postpone the execution. The warden, however, is unwilling to listen. A chaplain at the prison subsequently comes to Paladin's aid and Carter is spared the rope.

"Duel at Florence"

First Broadcast: October 11, 1958
Producer: Samuel Rolfe

Script: Bruce Geller
Photography: Fleet Southcott
Editor: Harry Coswick
Guest Stars: Dean Harens (Ernie Teller), Bonnie Bolding (Belle Hooper), Charles Gray (Jeff), John Alderson (Max), Hank Patterson (Plainsman)
Summary: Ernie Teller, a barber, despises violence and refuses to carry a gun. His unwillingness to hurt others, even in self-defense, has become a problem because his fiancée Belle believes that men should be willing to use force to settle conflicts and she regards his pacifism as an expression of cowardice. In addition, a pair of gunmen both desire Belle and are ready to kill anyone who stands in their way as they try to win her heart. Teller contacts Paladin, asking for guidance.

"The Protégé"

First Broadcast: October 18, 1958
Producer: Sam Rolfe
Script: Frank Gilroy
Photography: Howard Schwartz
Editor: Samuel Gold
Guest Stars: Peter Breck (Kurt Sprague), Ken Mayer (Man), George Mitchell (Joe Sprague), Mel Welles (Red Harper), Cy Malls (Bartender), Charles Tannen (Floyd)
Summary: Kurt Sprague leaves his home in New Mexico after being taunted and shamed by a gunman named Red Harper. Before he can return, Sprague must learn how to use a gun himself. He hires Paladin to teach him. A quick study, the young man heads back to New Mexico, meets Harper and shoots him dead. The incident restores Kurt's pride. But it also uncaps an appetite for killing and Kurt soon becomes a menace.

"The Road to Wickenberg"

First Broadcast: October 25, 1958
Producer: Sam Rolfe
Script: Gene Roddenberry
Photography: Howard Schwartz
Editor: Samuel Gold
Guest Stars: Christine White (Susan), Harry Carey, Jr. (Sheriff Jack Goodfellow), Donald Barry (Tom Goodfellow), Rayford Barnes (Sol Goodfellow), Michael Forest (Peter Keystone), Ed Faulkner (Jim Goodfellow), Mickey Finn (Ed Goodfellow)
Summary: On his way to San Francisco, Paladin stops at a saloon in a town called Bluebell. When he's not looking, someone drugs his drink. The next morning, he wakes up on a floor in a shack and finds that his gun and his money have been taken. A saloon girl named Susan tells him that someone named Sol Goodfellow poisoned his drink. Paladin goes to the local sheriff for help, explaining what Sol Goodfellow has done. But the sheriff takes offense: Sol is his brother. The sheriff then summons Sol and three of his other brothers and they begin to harass Paladin. With Susan's help, the gunfighter flees Bluebell. Hiding in the forest that lies outside town, he waits for the Goodfellows to come after him, ready to strike back and recover his money and his gun.
Comment: Rayford Barnes (Sol) had parts in McLaglen's *Shenandoah, Cahill, United States Marshal* and *Mitchell*.

"The Lady"

First Broadcast: November 15, 1958
Producer: Sam Rolfe
Script: Shimon Wincelberg
Photography: Howard Schwartz
Editor: Harry Coswick
Guest Stars: Patricia Medina (Diana Coulter), Robert Karnes (Rancher), George Richardson (Chief's Son), Earl Parker (Indian)
Summary: Diana Coulter has come from her native Britain to the United States to visit her brother, Richard, on his ranch in Arizona. She hires Paladin to help her make the trip out to Richard's ranch. After they arrive, Diana and Paladin find that Richard and his family have been massacred by Comanche Indians. Sensing they can be killed themselves, Diana and Paladin struggle to get away from the ranch before the Comanches return.
Comment: Patricia Medina (Diana) played the role of Anna Luz in John Farrow's *Plunder of the Sun,* one of the movies on which McLaglen worked when he was a first assistant at Wayne-Fellows Productions.

"The Solid Gold Patrol"

First Broadcast: December 13, 1958
Producer: Sam Rolfe
Script: Irving Wallace
Photography: Stuart Thompson
Editor: Samuel Gold
Guest Stars: Sean McClory (Cpl. Callahan), Mike Kellin (Sgt. Siebert), Perry Cook (Pvt. Krosowski), James Kline (Pvt. Ritter), Robert Cabal (Pvt. Espinosa), Don Keefer (Maj. Barlowe), Eddie Little Sky (White Bull), Michael Hagen (Adjutant)
Summary: A band of U.S. Cavalry soldiers has disappeared in Apache country. When Paladin learns that one of these men, Cpl. Callahan, has won a huge lottery prize, he heads out to tell him, hoping to collect a fee for his service. Though he finds Callahan and the others easily enough, Paladin has to negotiate with an Apache tribe in order to get the soldiers safely out of the territory and back to civilization.
Comment: Irish actor Sean McClory (Callahan) and McLaglen had worked together previously on *The Quiet Man, Island in the Sky, Plunder of the Sun* and *Ring of Fear,* when McLaglen was still an assistant director. McClory would later play the role of Robbie O'Hare in McLaglen's *Bandolero!*

"Something to Live For"

First Broadcast: December 20, 1958
Producer: Sam Rolfe
Script: John Tucker Battle and Don Ingalls, story by John Tucker Battle
Photography: Howard Schwartz
Editor: Harry Coswick
Guest Stars: Rayford Barnes (Harleigh Preston), Nancy Hadley (Elaine Evans), Malcolm Atterbury (Hugh Evans), Tom Brown (Bob Pelley), John Anderson (Martin Wheeler), Don Megowan (Wichita Walker)
Summary: A businessman named Hugh Evans asks for Paladin's help when a gang of crooks tries to drive him off of some land he's purchased. As he rides out from San Francisco to

rendezvous with Evans, Paladin meets Harleigh Preston, an alcoholic ne'er-do-well. Preston joins the gunfighter and follows him all the way to Evans's place, where he meets Evans's daughter, Elaine. The young woman's beauty and kindness deeply affect Preston, prompting him to repudiate the vice and self-pity that have characterized his life for so long.

Comment: A note in the closing credits states that this episode was filmed in the San Bernardino National Forest. McLaglen would return to this wilderness area in 1960 and 1961 to direct *Freckles* and *The Little Shepherd of Kingdom Come*.

"The Moor's Revenge"

First Broadcast: December 27, 1958
Producer: Julian Claman
Script: Melvin Levy
Photography: William Marguiles
Editor: Sam Gold
Guest Stars: Vincent Price (Charles Mathews), Patricia Morison (Victoria Vestris), Morey Amsterdam (Bellingham), Richard Shannon (Ben Jackson)
Summary: Actors Charles Mathews and Victoria Vestris travel from city to city, playing scenes from Shakespeare's *Othello*. While in San Francisco, they impress Paladin with their performances and the gunfighter invites them over to the Hotel Carlton for dinner. As the actors finish their meal, Mathews explains that he and Victoria are scheduled next to perform in San Diego. Paladin warns them that San Diego is a magnet for charlatans and bandits, and that they'd be wise to avoid it. The couple rejects Paladin's advice and proceeds to the southern city. Sensing that they will soon be needing his services, Paladin starts for San Diego himself.

"The Wager"

First Broadcast: January 3, 1959
Producer: Sam Rolfe
Script: Denis and Terry Sanders
Photography: Stuart Thompson
Editor: Harry Coswick
Guest Stars: Denver Pyle (Sid Morgan), Jacqueline Scott (Stacy Neal), Ken Lynch (Shawcross), Steve Gravers (Howard Gorman), William Erwin (Clerk), Bob Hopkins (Bartender)
Summary: Businessman Sid Morgan fears that one of his rivals, a man named Shawcross, wants him dead. For protection, Morgan hires Paladin to accompany him and his wife, Stacy, as they make their way home from San Francisco. When the party stops at a saloon to rest, they are harassed by a belligerent gunman named Gorman, who works for Shawcross. Paladin is forced to kill him. Paladin subsequently learns that Morgan and Shawcross are actually friends. It turns out the two men enjoy playing a sinister game in which they hire on men like Paladin and Gorman and try to trick them into shooting one another.

"The Taffeta Mayor"

First Broadcast: January 10, 1959
Producer: Sam Rolfe
Script: Albert Aley
Photography: Stuart Thompson
Editor: Samuel Gold

Guest Stars: Norma Crane (Lucy Kellaway), Edward Platt (Arnold Oaklin), Robert Karnes (Clay Morrow), Bobby Hall (Ben Trask), Jeanne Bates (Harriet Morrow), Tom Steele (Bailey), William Shaw (Townsman), Paul Hahn (Townsman)

Summary: Paladin travels up to Colton, Wyoming, to provide protection for John Kellaway, a political candidate who is committed to establishing law and order in the tiny town. Once he arrives, Paladin learns that Kellaway has been murdered by Arnold Oaklin, a corrupt saddle maker. The gunfighter then persuades the dead man's wife to run for mayor, a decision that shocks the conservative residents of Colton.

"Juliet"

First Broadcast: January 31, 1959
Producer: Sam Rolfe
Script: Gene Roddenberry
Photography: Stuart Thompson
Editor: Harry Coswick
Guest Stars: Miranda Jones (Juliet Harper), Earle Hodgins (Jeremiah Pike), John Berardino (Nelson Pike), Allen Case (Tad Pike), Ronald Green (Jenkins), Buff Brady (Stage Guard), Tex Terry (Stage Driver)
Summary: Col. Pike and his nephews, Tad and Nelson, are hardened secessionists who have settled in remote Tonopah, Nevada. Unwilling to abide by any law, they murder everybody who interferes with them. Sick of the Pikes and their tyranny, 17-year-old Juliet Harper decides to flee Tonopah, leaving the city on a stagecoach. Enraged, the Pikes set out after the young woman. Fortunately for her, Paladin is riding in the same stage.

"Hunt the Man Down"

First Broadcast: February 7, 1959
Producer: Sam Rolfe
Script: Harry Julian Fink
Photography: Stuart Thompson
Editor: Samuel Gold
Guest Stars: Robert Wilke (Walt DeVries), James Drury (Tony DeVries), Madlyn Rhue (Elizabeth DeVries), Ric Roman (Morales), Ralph Reed (Jesse Starrett), Mark Tapscott (Tom Semper), Ian MacDonald (Homesteader), Robin Riley (The Boy), Chantal Noel (The Woman)
Summary: Tony DeVries, a young rancher, once saved Paladin's life. When the gunfighter reads in the papers that Tony and his older brother Walt — one of Paladin's best friends — are feuding over some land, he heads out to help, to negotiate a peace, if possible. Once Paladin arrives, he learns from Tony that the brothers' dispute involves more than land. Five years earlier, Walt had been engaged to a woman named Elizabeth. Tony fell in love with Elizabeth, too, and successfully wooed her away. Unable to forgive this betrayal, Walt has been seeking opportunities to punish his brother ever since.
Comment: Scenarist Harry Julian Fink with his wife, Rita, co-wrote the screenplay for McLaglen's *Cahill, United States Marshal.*

"The Scorched Feather"

First Broadcast: February 14, 1959
Producer: Sam Rolfe

Script: Bruce Geller
Photography: Stuart Thompson
Editor: Samuel Gold
Guest Stars: Lon Chaney, Jr. (William Ceilbleu), Mario Alcalde (Robert Ceilbleu), Cy Malis (Piggo), Mike Steele (Al)
Summary: Paladin is hired by Robert Ceilbleu, a young gentleman, to protect his father William Ceilbleu from an angry Comanche warrior who plans to kill him. When Paladin finds the old man, he realizes that William Ceilbleu is actually Billy Blue Skies, a retired army scout who has slain hundreds of Indians. Shortly after this, Paladin learns that his client Robert Ceilbleu is in fact half-Comanche and that he is the warrior who plans to kill Billy.

"The Return of the Lady"

First Broadcast: February 21, 1959
Producer: Sam Rolfe
Script: Shimon Wincelberg
Photography: Stuart Thompson
Editor: Harry Coswick
Guest Stars: Patricia Medina (Diana Coulter), Gene Nelson (Vance), Theodore Marcuse (B.G.), Pilar del Ray (Maria)
Summary: Paladin receives a note from an old flame, a British woman named Diana Coulter, letting him know that she is planning to marry a Texas rancher. In the same letter, Diana asks the gunfighter if he'd be interested in giving her away at the wedding. A bit saddened by the news, but still willing to help his friend, Paladin starts for Texas. Once he is reunited with Diana, he learns that she actually has no intention to marry. The groom, an elderly ex–Confederate named B.G., has been keeping her a prisoner on his remote ranch. Paladin then offers to help Diana return with him to San Francisco, but getting away from B.G.— and his armed ranch hands — is anything but easy.

"The Long Hunt"

First Broadcast: March 7, 1959
Producer: Sam Rolfe
Script: Harry Julian Fink
Photography: Stuart Thompson
Editor: Harry Coswick
Guest Stars: Steve Roberts (Dundee), Anthony Caruso (José), Anne Barton (Mrs. Ordey), Lane Bradford (Frank Tanner)
Summary: Dundee, a rich landowner in New Mexico, hires Paladin to help him track down Ordey, a former employee who has murdered a pair of Dundee's friends. To lure the fugitive in from the forest, Dundee kidnaps Ordey's wife, forcing her to accompany him and Paladin as they begin their search. This development does not sit well with the gunfighter and he shifts his loyalty from his client to Mr. and Mrs. Ordey.

"Incident at Borrasca Bend"

First Broadcast: March 21, 1959
Producer: Sam Rolfe
Script: Jay Simms

Photography: Stuart Thompson
Editor: Samuel Gold
Guest Stars: Jacques Aubuchon (Judge Wesson), Perry Cook (Sugie), Ben Wright (Jackson), Ed Faulkner (Curly), Ted Markland (Patterson), Stewart East (Swede)
Summary: As Paladin travels through the mountains on horseback, he sees an Indian brave roasting a bird on a spit. The man abruptly runs off, triggering the gunfighter's curiosity. As he bends over the fire, Paladin spots a bandana and a bag of gold dust lying in the dirt. He then sets out for a nearby mining community, Borrasca Bend, to see if he can find the gold's rightful owner.

"Maggie O'Bannion"

First Broadcast: April 4, 1959
Producer: Sam Rolfe
Script: Gene Roddenberry
Photography: Stuart Thompson
Editor: Harry Coswick
Guest Stars: Marion Marshall (Margaret O'Bannion), Peggy Rea (Cookie), Don Haggerty (Cyrus), Mickey Simpson (Jake), George Cisar (Matt Perk), John Close (Bushwhacker), Paul Sorensen (Pete)
Summary: As he makes his way across some rangeland, Paladin is attacked by a pair of crooked cattlemen, who take his horse, his gun and his clothes. Wanting to recover his possessions, the gunfighter starts for the nearest ranch house. There, he is given a job as a servant by the ranch's owner, Maggie O'Bannion. Paladin comes to realize that the foreman on the ranch is one of the individuals who bushwhacked him earlier.

"Alaska"

First Broadcast: April 18, 1959
Producer: Sam Rolfe
Script: Albert Aley
Photography: Stuart Thompson
Editor: Samuel Gold
Guest Stars: Karl Swenson (Boris Tosheff), Richard Shannon (Carl Grimes), Elizabeth York (Abby Morton), Allen Case (Ralph Morton) Fay Roope (Wade)
Summary: Paladin's old friend Boris Tosheff, a Russian who trades in furs and pelts, asks the gunfighter to visit him in Alaska. Once Paladin arrives, Boris explains that two settlers, Carl Grimes and Ralph Morton, have been trying to drive him away from the valley where he hunts and traps animals. To resolve the conflict, Boris, Paladin and the two settlers decide to have a dog sled race. Whoever wins will take control of the valley.

"Return of Roy Carter"

First Broadcast: May 2, 1959
Producer: Sam Rolfe
Script: Gene Roddenberry
Photography: Stuart Thompson
Editor: Harry Coswick
Guest Stars: Clu Gulager (Roy Carter), Larry Blake (Robert April), Brad von Beltz (Eddie Clinton), Craig Duncan (Sid), Diana Crawford (Margie)

Summary: Rich kid Roy Carter learns that Robert April, a chaplain who once saved his life, has disappeared in some nearby mountains while searching for and trying to help a fugitive killer named Eddie Clinton. Carter contacts Paladin, asking for help. Because the gunfighter regards the chaplain as an exemplary person, he turns up at Carter's ranch immediately. The two men then start for the frigid mountains. When they find April, he is nearly dead, having been attacked and robbed by Clinton. As the trio prepares to return to civilization, Clinton shows up with a rifle and attempts to kill them.

"The Sons of Aaron Murdock"

First Broadcast: May 9, 1959
Producer: Sam Rolfe
Script: Harold Jack Bloom
Photography: Stuart Thompson
Editor: Harry Coswick
Guest Stars: Philip Coolidge (Aaron Murdock), Lee Kinsolving (Jamie Murdock), Wesley Lau (Lew Murdock), Elizabeth York (Mae), Frank Gorshin (Marty), Dale Cummings (Willie), William Shaw (Carl), William Mims (Man)
Summary: Aaron Murdock, a rancher in the Arizona Territory, has two sons, Jamie and Lew. Murdock explains to Paladin that while Jamie is kindhearted and law-abiding, Lew takes pleasure in breaking the law and "hurting what is helpless." Fearing that Lew's influence has begun to poison Jamie, Murdock hires Paladin to do whatever it takes to keep the bad son away from the good one, killing him if necessary.

"Comanche"

First Broadcast: May 16, 1959
Producer: Sam Rolfe
Script: Irving Wallace
Photography: Stuart Thompson
Editor: Harry Coswick
Guest Stars: Susan Cabot (Becky Carver), Larry Pennell (Henry Carver), Roy Barcroft (Sgt. Barsky), Robert Anderson (Sam Dolan), Shirley O'Hara (Mrs. Carver), Stewart East (Lt. Bradley)
Summary: Henry Carveris have been forced by his father, a distinguished general, to enlist and serve in the Indian Wars as a member of the 7th Cavalry. His distaste for the military prompts the young soldier to desert his post and flee to Canada with his new wife, Becky. Concerned that her son will be captured by the army and executed, Henry's mother hires Paladin to ride up to Montana to find the fugitive and turn him over to the custody of military officials.
Comment: As the episode ends, Paladin, Henry and Becky stumble onto a battlefield where hundreds of U.S. soldiers and their horses have been slain by Sioux Indians. Henry, we learn in these final moments, has been serving under Gen. George Armstrong Custer, and his desertion has spared him from having to experience, and probably die in, the Battle of Little Big Horn. The episode takes its title from a U.S. Cavalry horse named Comanche that Paladin and the others find near the massacre site.

"Homecoming"

First Broadcast: May 23, 1959
Producer: Sam Rolfe

Script: Albert Aley
Photography: Stuart Thompson
Editor: Samuel Gold
Guest Stars: Ed Nelson (Ed Stacy), Don Megowan (Ben Stacy), Lewis Martin (Will Stanhope), Dick Rich (Sheriff Clyde), Thom Carney (Dan), Frank Gerstle (Bartender), Jim Hyland (Floyd), Larry Blake (Deputy), Fran Frost (Woman)
Summary: After he is wrongly convicted of a robbery, Ben Stacy returns home from prison. One of the men who insisted that Ben was guilty of the crime and saw to it that he was sent to prison is Will Stanhope. Fearing that Ben will seek revenge against him, Stanhope hires Paladin for protection.

"The Haunted Trees"

First Broadcast: June 13, 1959
Producer: Sam Rolfe
Script: Kay Lenard, Jess Carneol
Photography: Howard Schwartz
Editor: Samuel Gold
Guest Stars: Doris Dowling (Sara Howard), Roy Barcroft (Flannigan), Jane Chang (Birdie), Brad Trumbull (Brad), Duane Grey (Egert), Burt Metcalfe (Ben Howard)
Summary: Sara Howard is the sole inheritor of her late husband's lucrative timber concern. Mrs. Howard suspects that her stepson, Ben, wants to steal the company from her, and she asks for Paladin's assistance. The gunfighter proceeds to pay a visit to some forest land that Mrs. Howard owns. Once he's there, several accidents occur that convince him that Ben is dangerous. The lumberjacks in the camp, however, think Mrs. Howard may actually be the one behind the accidents.
Comment: In this episode, stuntman Hal Needham made his first appearance on *Have Gun, Will Travel,* doubling for Richard Boone. McLaglen told C. Courtney Joyner, "In 1957 in Big Bear, California, when I was doing a *Have Gun* about logging and tree climbers, Boone's stand-in said, 'Oh yeah, I can climb a tree.' And he didn't know how to climb a tree! I mean, it was ridiculous. And I got this tap on my shoulder, and this fellow standing there said, 'Pardon me, sir, my name's Hal Needham. Do you want me to show you how to go up that tree?' He said, 'I'm a tree-topper.'"[18] McLaglen had Needham appear in the scene. Afterward, he regularly used him as a stuntman and stunt supervisor in television productions and several features he directed, among them *McLintock!, Shenandoah, Bandolero!, Hellfighters, The Undefeated* and *Chisum*. In the late seventies, Needham took up directing himself. His most successful picture was *Smokey and the Bandit* (1977), a "trucker" comedy starring Burt Reynolds, who'd played Quint Asper on *Gunsmoke*. This film was scripted by another McLaglen associate, James Lee Barrett, whose collaborations with McLaglen included *Shenandoah, Bandolero!, The Undefeated, Fools' Parade* and *"something big."*[19]

SEASON THREE, 1959–1960

"Les Girls"

First Broadcast: September 26, 1959
Producer: Sam Rolfe
Script: Gene Roddenberry
Photography: Stuart Thompson
Editor: Samuel Gold

Guest Stars: Mabel Albertson (Madame Chalon), Helene Stanley (Yvonne), Roxanne Berard (Cecile), Danielle De Metz (Annette), Lane Chandler (J. Brodie), Dallas Mitchell (Tom), Hal Needham (Mac), Carol Henry (Alfred), Bob Hopkins (Lyman)

Summary: An anxious businessman named Lyman approaches Paladin about safely transporting a group of mail order brides to Bend O' The River, Oregon. Previous attempts to get the women to this part of the country have been thwarted by "wife poachers," who have taken the brides for themselves. Paladin soon finds himself escorting three, young French women and their mistress, Madame Chalon, through the forests of the Pacific Northwest.

"The Posse"

First Broadcast: October 3, 1959
Producer: Sam Rolfe
Script: Gene Roddenberry
Photography: Fleet Southcott
Editor: Samuel Gold
Guest Stars: Perry Cook (Dobie O'Brien), Denver Pyle (McKay), Harry Carey, Jr. (Sheriff), Ken Curtis (Curley), Paul Sorenson (1st Posseman), Bill Wellman, Jr. (2nd Posseman), Hal Needham (3rd Posseman)

Summary: After a farmer and his wife are murdered, a rancher named McKay puts together a posse and tries to find the killer. The group soon comes upon Paladin, who has stopped to eat and talk to Dobie O'Brien, a friendly drifter. Dobie is actually the murderer, but once the posse arrives, Dobie persuades McKay and the others that Paladin is guilty of the crime. Unwilling to bring the suspect into town for trial, the men prepare for a lynching.

"Pancho"

First Broadcast: October 24, 1959
Producer: Frank Pierson
Script: Shimon Wincelberg
Photography: Stuart Thompson
Editor: Everett Sutherland
Guest Stars: Rafael Campos (Doroteo), Rico Alaniz (Paul Rancher), Lisa Montell (Soledad), Edward Colmans (Don Luis)

Summary: As Paladin crosses the Mexican desert to meet a client, he stops to help a teenager he finds who's been buried up to his neck in the dirt. Once he is safe, Doroteo, as the boy is called, shows his gratitude to Paladin by stealing his gun and horse. Paladin is then forced to continue his trek on foot. When he meets the man who has sent for him, a rich land owner named Don Luis, Paladin learns that Doroteo is in fact a revolutionary who plans to exact revenge on the Mexican gentry for mistreating the poor. Fearing for his daughter Soledad's security, Don Luis asks the gunfighter to convey her safely to the United States. As Paladin and his charge head out, they are attacked by Doroteo and his gang, who take them prisoner. At first, Soledad is attracted to the young bandit. But when she learns that he plans to murder her father, her desires cool. Paladin manages to free himself and subdues Doroteo. He listens with bemusement as Doroteo explains that someday he will lead a revolution in Mexico. The gunfighter eventually decides to free the young boy, and as he and Soledad resume their journey to America, she explains that Doroteo is so certain about his future military success that he has given himself a nom de guerre. When Paladin asks her what this name is, she replies, "Pancho Villa."

"Fragile"

First Broadcast: October 31, 1959
Producer: Frank Pierson
Script: Shimon Wincelberg
Photography: Stuart Thompson
Editor: Everett Sutherland
Guest Stars: Werner Klemperer (Ledoux), Jacqueline Scott (Clair Ledoux), Alan Caillou (Roy Cooney), Gregg Palmer (Drunk), William Boyett (Rancher), Douglas Bank (Duck)
Summary: Etienne Ledoux owns a restaurant in a mining town in eastern California. Eager to install a window in his restaurant, he comes to San Francisco to purchase a sheet of glass. He then hires Paladin to help him transport the fragile object through the wilderness.
Comment: McLaglen and Werner Klemperer (Ledoux) were classmates in the thirties at Cates School in Carpinteria, California.[20]

"The Unforgiven"

First Broadcast: November 7, 1959
Producer: Frank Pierson
Script: Jay Simms
Photography: Stuart Thompson
Editor: Everett Sutherland
Guest Stars: David White (Crommer), Hampton Fancher (Beauregard Crommer), Joel Ashley (Caterall), Hank Patterson (Ronson)
Summary: Gen. Crommer, a war time acquaintance of Paladin, summons the gunfighter to his bedside. He explains to Paladin that he needs a message sent to an old enemy, a man named Caterall. The gunfighter takes the job and soon discovers that Caterall is an elusive and dangerous character who is more interested in killing him than in receiving the general's message.

"The Black Handkerchief"

First Broadcast: November 14, 1959
Producer: Sam Rolfe
Script: Jay Simms
Photography: Stuart Thompson
Editor: Sam Gold
Guest Stars: Ed Nelson (Pierre Deverall), Joe Perry (Sheriff), Terrence De Marney (Fitzgerald), Svea Grunfeld (Michelle), Gordon Polk (Luss), Ed Faulkner (Dink)
Summary: Pierre "Pete" Deverall falls in with a trio of murderous buffalo hunters. When these dangerous men rob a stagecoach and kill some passengers, Pete is apprehended and charged with the murder, though he didn't himself participate in the crime. The young man's aunt hires Paladin to help Pete escape the gallows.

"The Golden Toad"

First Broadcast: November 21, 1959
Producer: Sam Rolfe
Script: Gene Roddenberry
Photography: Stuart Thompson
Editor: Everett Sutherland

Guest Stars: David White (Webster), Lorna Thayer (Doris), Kevin Hagen (Everette), Bill Wellman, Jr. (Bob), Stewart East (Simms), Paul Sorenson (Herb), Dorothy Dells (Jacqueline), Jan Burrell (Caroline), Eileen Wilk (Willodean), Nancy Valentine (Beverly)

Summary: David Webster owns a spread of land in the Arizona desert, which he wants to farm with his children. The region's arid conditions have ruined him financially, and he needs money to dig a well deep enough to irrigate his crops. His neighbors, the Golemons, find themselves in the same predicament. Instead of helping one another, though, the families are feuding. Paladin decides to assist the two groups by looking for a supply of water.

"Champagne Safari"

First Broadcast: December 5, 1959
Producer: Sam Rolfe
Script: Frank R. Pierson and Whitfield Cook, story by Whitfield Cook
Photography: Stuart Thompson
Editor: Samuel Gold
Music: Lucien Moraweck
Guest Stars: Valerie French (Charity), Patric Knowles (Trevington), Lou Krugman (Antoine), Gil Rankin (Chief), Bill Mims (Gravely), Carole Evern (Girl)

Summary: Paladin's friend Gravely leads expeditions into buffalo country for rich clients. After one of his clients, a British aristocrat named Trevington, is struck by an arrow and dies, Gravely contacts Paladin, worried that he and the others will soon be killed by Indians. When the gunfighter arrives, he conducts an investigation, much like a detective, trying to determine who actually shot the slain man with the arrow. Evidence soon points to one of the surviving members of the hunting party, a beautiful woman named Charity.

Comment: Patric Knowles (Trevington) appeared in McLaglen's *The Way West*, *The Devil's Brigade* and *Chisum*.

"The Naked Gun"

First Broadcast: December 19, 1959
Producer: Sam Rolfe
Script: Jay Simms
Photography: Stuart Thompson
Editor: Everett Sutherland
Guest Stars: Ken Curtis (Monk), Robert Wilke (Rook), Lane Chandler (Lace), Dallas Mitchell (Kew), Hal Needham (Mabry), Stewart East (Rex)

Summary: Monk is a drifter who supports himself by killing and skinning cows that wander off from herds. His enemy is a trail boss named Rook. When Monk meets Paladin along the trail to Portland, he tells him that Rook recently murdered his uncle. Monk and Paladin then build a camp together. Once Paladin falls asleep, Monk steals his gun and sets out to find and kill Rook.

"The Prophet"

First Broadcast: January 2, 1960
Producer: Sam Rolfe
Script: Shimon Wincelberg
Photography: Stuart Thompson
Editor: Samuel Gold

Guest Stars: Shepherd Strudwick (Col. Nunez), Lorna Thayer (Serafina), Barney Phillips (Maj. Ferber), Florence Marly (Madam L), Brad von Beltz (Brother), Eddie Little Sky (Indian Scout)

Summary: Col. Nunez has spent his career in the army routing out and destroying renegade Indians. Despite this record, he has married Serafina, an Apache woman. After some American soldiers rape Serafina, Nunez demands revenge. He joins up with his wife's tribe and teaches its members how to fight the cavalry effectively. Paladin is then hired by the U.S. government to track down Nunez and persuade him to stop helping the Apaches.

"The Pledge"

First Broadcast: January 16, 1960
Producer: Sam Rolfe
Script: Shimon Wincelberg
Photography: Stuart Thompson
Editor: Samuel Gold
Guest Stars: Robert Gist (Ike Brennan), Brad Weston (Esteban), Charles Gray (Lieutenant), Joseph Hamilton (Father), Susan Davis (Maureen), Cyril Delevanti (Speedy)

Summary: Ike Brennan and his wife head for the Kaibab forest in southern Utah to purchase lumber for their furniture company. Shortly after they arrive, a band of renegade Indians takes Mrs. Brennan hostage. If Ike wants his wife alive again, he must provide the tribe with a Gatling gun. Once Ike manages to find one of these weapons, he contacts Paladin, asking the gunfighter to accompany him as he makes his way back to the forest and his wife's abductors.

"Jenny"

First Broadcast: January 23, 1960
Producer: Sam Rolfe
Script: Jack Jacobs
Photography: Stuart Thompson
Editor: Everett Sutherland
Music: Rene Garriguenc
Guest Stars: Trevor Bardette (Carruthers), Ellen Clark (Jenny), Peter Leeds (Wilson), Phil Chambers (Matlock), Quentin Sondergaard (Billy), Ron Brogan (Sheriff), Bud Osborne (Driver), Olan Soulé (Cashier), Hal Needham (Gunman #1)

Summary: Jenny Lake, a guest in the Hotel Carlton, has secured a seat on the next stage out of San Francisco. As she prepares to leave, she tells Paladin that a man named Wilson has been bothering her. The gunfighter warns Wilson to leave the young woman alone. Paladin subsequently learns that Jenny, far from being a harassed woman, is a master criminal and Wilson is a member of the Secret Service.

"Return to Fort Benjamin"

First Broadcast: January 30, 1960
Producer: Sam Rolfe
Script: Robert E. Thompson
Photography: Stuart Thompson
Editor: Samuel Gold
Guest Stars: Anthony Caruso (Yellow Star/Gimp), Charles Aidman (Lt. Graham), Robert

Wilke (Maj. Blake), Herbert Patterson (Sgt. Kern), Frank Sentry (Nephew), Chief White Horse (Dark Leaf), Stewart East (Soldier), Harold Needham (Soldier)

Summary: Chief Dark Leaf's son, Yellow Star, has been sentenced to hang for murdering a soldier. Dark Leaf hires Paladin to meet with army officials and arrange for Yellow Star to be transferred back to his father's custody following the execution. The gunfighter departs for the fort where Yellow Star is being held. Once there, he is appalled by the cruel manner in which the condemned man is treated. He soon discovers that Yellow Star is not even guilty of the crime for which he's been charged. Paladin attempts to save Yellow Star, but his effort is hindered because the prisoner, a hopeless alcoholic, has little interest in staying alive.

"The Ledge"

First Broadcast: February 13, 1960
Producer: Ben Brady
Script: Robert Gottlieb, story by Joel Kane and Robert Gottlieb
Photography: Stuart Thompson
Editor: Samuel Gold
Guest Stars: Richard Shannon (Cass), Don Beddoe (Stebbins), John Hoyt (Dr. Stark), Richard Rust (Corey)
Summary: Paladin is crossing through a mountain pass. Just as he spots some travelers ahead, rocks start to slide and one of the men in the group is buried. The gunfighter offers his help, but quickly realizes that he may be the only person who is willing to do something to save the stricken man.

"The Misguided Father"

First Broadcast: February 27, 1960
Producer: Ben Brady
Script: Don Mullally
Photography: Stuart Thompson
Editor: Samuel Gold
Music: William Lava
Guest Stars: Douglas Kennedy (Loring), Hampton Fancher (Keith Loring), Harry Carey, Jr. (Sheriff Stander), Gregg Palmer (Brogan), Lee Sands (Sims)
Summary: Charlie Blackburn, one of Paladin's friends, is murdered in San Francisco. The gunfighter suspects that Whit Loring, a malicious businessman in California's redwood country, is the culprit. Paladin sets out for Loring's home, where he meets the businessman's son, Keith. The boy, Paladin discovers, is just as mean and dangerous as his father.

"The Hatchet Man"

First Broadcast: March 5, 1960
Producer: Ben Brady
Script: Shimon Wincelberg
Photography: Stuart Thompson
Editor: Samuel Gold
Guest Stars: Benson Fong (Joe Tsin), Philip Ahn (Hoo Yee), Nolan Leary (Magruder), Allen Jung (Loo Sam), Fuji (Bodyguard), Lisa Lu (Li Hwa)
Summary: San Francisco's Chinatown is controlled by gangsters and the one man brave enough to stand up to them is Joe Tsin, a police detective. Wanting to be rid of Tsin, the

criminals put a price on his head, offering anyone who kills him a $1,000 reward. Fearing that it will lose its best man in Chinatown, the San Francisco Police Department hires Paladin to protect Tsin until the threat passes.

Comment: Actress Lisa Lu appears in this episode as Tsin's wife Li Hwa. During the fourth season of *Have Gun, Will Travel* (1960–1961), Lu played the role of a character named Hey Girl, after Kam Tong, the actor who played Hey Boy, temporarily left the show's cast. Hey Girl, like Hey Boy, would help Paladin find customers.[21]

"Love of a Bad Woman"

First Broadcast: March 26, 1960
Producer: Ben Brady
Script: Robert Dozier
Photography: Stuart Thompson
Editor: Samuel Gold
Music: Nathan Scott
Guest Stars: Geraldine Brooks (Tamsen Somers), Lawrence Dobkins (Haskell Sommers), Ed Faulkner (Gunman), Harry Landers (1st Cowboy), Franz Roehn (Opponent), Lillian Adams (Servant), Bob Hopkins (1st Dandy), Sherwood Keith (2nd Dandy), Edwin Mills (3rd Dandy), Mitchell Kowal (2nd Cowboy)
Summary: Haskell Somers collects beautiful statues and paintings, which he keeps on display in his home. Somers has married his wife Tamsen, in fact, because she is beautiful, not because he loves her. Bored and resentful, Tamsen posts an advertisement in the newspaper, calling for single men who may be interested in marriage to visit her. Once people start to arrive she explains that she is still married, and anyone who hopes to gain access to her and her fortune must eliminate her husband first. When Somers becomes aware of this scheme, he goes to Paladin in the Hotel Carlton and hires the gunfighter to transport him safely to his home — and kill as many of his wife's murderous suitors along the way as he can.

"Never Help the Devil"

First Broadcast: April 16, 1960
Producer: Ben Brady
Script: Archie L. Tegland
Photography: Stuart Thompson
Editor: Everett Sutherland
Guest Stars: Jack Lambert (Doggie Kramer), Dick Rich (Toby), Lewis Martin (Doctor), Bill Wellman, Jr. (Terry Gallagher)
Summary: Paladin comes into a town called Junction City. One of the locals there is Doggie Kramer, a psychopath who takes pleasure in picking fights with men and killing them whenever he can with his gun. After Kramer is injured in one of these incidents, he decides to leave town. But his neighbors, eager for revenge and retribution, would prefer to see him lynched or shot. Unwilling to allow this to happen, Paladin decides to help Kramer and safely convey him out of Junction City.

"The Twins"

First Broadcast: May 21, 1960
Producer: Ben Brady

Script: Robert James
Photography: Stuart Thompson
Editor: Everett Sutherland
Guest Stars: Brian Hutton (Adam/Sam), Jenifer Lea (Wife), Lane Chandler (Sheriff), Sonia Warren (Young Lady), Tony Reagan (Desk Clerk)
Summary: Adam Mirakian and his twin brother, Sam, have contrasting personalities. While Sam is wild and violent, Adam is congenial and mild. After Sam murders a man, authorities mistakenly charge Adam with the crime. The only person who can distinguish the two brothers from one another is Adam's wife. Unfortunately for him, she has fallen in love with Sam and she, in turn, tells the police that they've got the right man. The situation comes to the attention of Paladin and the gunfighter decides to do what he can to help Adam.

The Lineup

The Lineup was a police procedural series produced by Desilu for CBS Television. Starring Warner Anderson and Tom Tully as Lt. Guthrie and Lt. Grebb, a pair of San Francisco detectives, the show ran for six seasons from 1954 to 1959. Much like Jack Webb's *Dragnet*, *The Lineup* dramatized actual criminal investigations. To enhance the show's believability, episodes were adapted from actual investigations conducted by the San Francisco Police Department.[22] The six episodes McLaglen directed for *The Lineup* were all shot on location in San Francisco in the spring of 1957.[23]

SEASON FOUR, 1957–1958

"The Fleet Queen Case"

First Broadcast: September 27, 1957
Producer: Jaime del Valle
Script: James Calvelli
Photography: Nick Musuraca
Editor: Bud Sheets
Guest Stars: James Bell (Captain Ferguson), Ed Stevlingson (Purser), Harry Carey, Jr. (Jack Sansbury), Claire Carleton (Terry Orr), Paul Sorenson (Sam Adams), Nora Marlowe (Landlady), Pat Goldin (Chief), Tom Landon (Chips)
Summary: A freighter in the San Francisco Bay becomes a crime scene when one of its crew is murdered and the corpse clogs the ship's bilges. Everyone on board, excluding the dead man, is regarded by the police as a likely suspect.

"The Missing Crime Case"

First Broadcast: October 25, 1957
Producer: Jaime del Valle
Script: Arthur Orloff
Photography: Nick Musuraca
Editor: Bud Sheets
Guest Stars: Harry Lauter (Haefly), Carla Balinda (Ruth Haefly), Jil Jarmyn (Lisa Farrier), John Goddard (Leroy Spangler), Marjorie Bennett (Janitress), Jack Mulhall (Old Man), Ken Christy (Caller)
Summary: A man named Haefly is brutalized and robbed in his home. Despite his wife's petitions, he refuses to ask for the police's help.

"The #17643 Case"

First Broadcast: November 7, 1957
Producer: Jaime del Valle
Script: Fred Eggers
Photography: Nick Musuraca
Editor: Bud Sheets
Guest Stars: William Forrest (Charles Forden), Pat Coleman (Jennings Wilson), Jack Carol (Lab Man), Frances Morris (Mrs. Wilson), Billy Nelson (David Hurachi), Ken Lynch (Doctor), Hallene Hill (Doris Weston)
Summary: An event from Charles Forden's past leads to mayhem in his present, including a vicious attack by a thug and the near murder of Forden's wife.

"The Happy Janitor Case"

First Broadcast: December 20, 1957
Producer: Jaime del Valle
Script: Lawrence Resner
Photography: Nick Musuraca
Editor: Bud Sheets
Guest Stars: John Day (Steve Henderson), Ann Lee (Teddy Fontaine), Jil Jarmyn (Cheri Jackson), Wally Brown (Happy Sherman), Jim Nolan (Art Brierly)
Summary: Teddy Fontaine is a lounge singer with criminal ties. When Lt. Guthrie and Lt. Grebb investigate a murder of a maintenance man, Fontaine becomes a person of high interest for them.

"The Missing Russian Hill Matron"

First Broadcast: December 6, 1957
Producer: Jaime del Valle
Script: Lawrence Resner
Photography: Nick Musuraca
Editor: Bud Sheets
Guest Stars: Lennie Sherman (Eddie Boyle), Kathleen Mulqueen (Maud), Mary Newton (Olive Nelson), Jack Carol (Len Conover), Damian O'Flynn (Lewis Cavanaugh), Raymond Greenleaf (Austin Lancaster), Kathy Nolan (Colleen Thompson), Doug Odney (Larry Daniels), John Sorrentino (Ralph Vincent), Gil Rankin (Williams)
Summary: A scandal develops in San Francisco high society when an affluent woman is murdered. As Lt. Guthrie and Lt. Grebb conduct their investigation, unflattering secrets from the victim's past start to surface.

"The Little Hero Case"

First Broadcast: March 28, 1958
Producer: Jaime del Valle
Script: Joseph Calvelli
Photography: Nick Musuraca
Editor: Bud Sheet
Guest Stars: Hal Baylor (Tubby Larkin), Ed Parker (Charles Fromkas), Jim Canino (Flip Phillips), Victor Sen Yung (Houseboy), Jil Jarmyn (Connie Lynn)

Summary: After kidnappers abduct a professional gambler, a young boxer, eager to be a hero, tries to find the missing man. He manages to recover a $50,000 ransom that has been paid to the crooks, but winds up getting stabbed during the effort.

Perry Mason

Based upon characters created by crime novelist Earle Stanley Gardner, *Perry Mason* ran for nine seasons on CBS (1957–1966).[24] Raymond Burr played the show's eponymous hero, a defense lawyer who practices in Los Angeles. Mason regularly won his cases, thanks in part to the people he worked with: his secretary Della Street (Barbara Hale) and Paul Drake (William Hopper), a private investigator. Other regulars on the program included Lt. Arthur Tragg (Ray Collins) and Mason's nemesis, District Attorney Hamilton Burger (William Tallman).

SEASON ONE, 1957–1958

"The Case of the Deadly Double"

First Broadcast: March 1, 1958
Producer: Ben Brady
Script: Sam Neuman
Photography: Frank Redman
Editor: Richard W. Farrell
Guest Stars: Constance Ford (Helen Reed), Denver Pyle (Robert Crane), Carole Mathews (Cora Dunbar), Paul Langton (Harry Vance), Murray Hamilton (Johnny Hale), Abraham Sofaer (Dr. Maitland), Louise Truax (Sarah), Carleton G. Young (David Reed), Pierre Watkin (Judge), Frank Jenks (Cab Driver), Clark Howat (Sgt. Grant), Carlyle Mitchell (Dr. Desmond), Jack Gargan (Court Clerk), George E. Stone (George), Peter Opp (Johnson), Josef Elman (Tony), Kellogg Junge, Jr. (Tommy Reed)

Raymond Burr as the unbeatable defense attorney Perry Mason (CBS).

Summary: Helen Reed wants to divorce her husband, David, and retain custody of their son, Tommy. Helen's unhappy marriage is not her only problem; she's also a schizophrenic with multiple personalities. In the evening, for instance, she often transforms into Joyce Martel, an ill-mannered tramp with an appetite for seedy men. Helen's life becomes even more complicated when someone shoots David to death and her brother, Robert, is charged with the murder. After agreeing to defend Robert, Mason learns about a witness who was present at the shooting; if he can get this person to testify, he can prove Robert's innocence. Unfortunately, the witness is none other than Joyce Martel.

Comment: Abraham Sofaer (Dr. Maitland) played Chief White Buffalo in *Chisum*.

"The Case of the Empty Tin"

First Broadcast: March 8, 1958
Producer: Ben Brady
Script: Seeleg Lester
Photography: Frank Redman
Editor: Richard Cahoon
Guest Stars: Warren Stevens (Alan Neil), Benson Fong (Gow Loong), Olive Deering (Rebecca Gentrie), Toni Gerry (Doris Hocksley), Mary Shipp (Miriam Hocksley), Anthony Jochim (Elston Carr), Frank Wilcox (Judge), Otto Waldis (John Lowell), Bert Holland (Dr. Morton)
Summary: Doris Hocksley reads a want ad in the newspaper that asks for "Information concerning the daughter of a man named Hocksley who was a partner in certain adventures in China during the years 1931 through 1956. Daughter is approximately thirty years old. To claim estate in excess of two million two hundred thousand dollars." Doris is certain she is the person described in the ad, though she lacks documented proof of her kinship to Hocksley. For help, she retains Perry Mason. When the lawyer who is overseeing the Hocksley estate is murdered, Doris is named a suspect. Mason subsequently directs his attention to proving her innocence.

"The Case of the Screaming Woman"

First Broadcast: April 26, 1958
Producer: Ben Brady
Script: Dick Stenger and Gene Wang, story by Dick Stenger
Photography: Frank Redman
Editor: Otto W. Meyer
Guest Stars: Ruta Lee (Connie Cooper), Berry Kroeger (Eugene Jarech), Josephine Hutchinson (Leona Walsh), Arthur Shields (Dr. George Barnes), Marian Seldes (Mary K. Davis), Philip Ober (Ralph Davis), Karin Booth (Susan Marshall), Don Gardner (Bob Shroeder), Morris Ankrum (Judge Cameron), Phil Arnold (Apartment Manager), Richard Ryan (Mr. Hill), Jeanne Bates (Miss Clay), Marian Collier (Attendant), Jack Gargan (Court Clerk)
Summary: Gossip columnist Mary Kate Davis has told her estranged husband that she is expecting a child, hoping this will discourage him from divorcing her. But she is not pregnant. Instead, she has sought the services of Dr. Barnes, an obstetrician who arranges clandestine adoptions for infertile women, supplying them with illegitimate babies who are born in his clinic. After the columnist's secretary alerts Dr. Barnes that her employer would not be a suitable mother, the doctor refuses to give Mrs. Davis a baby. Mrs. Davis retaliates by taking a book from the doctor's office, which contains the names of his clients, and threatens to print them in her column unless he gives her what she wants. Hoping to stop this from happening, Dr. Barnes's secretary, a woman named Leona Walsh, comes to Perry Mason, asking for his help. Before Mrs. Davis can publish the damaging article, however, someone murders her. The police suspect that Leona Walsh is the killer and their hunches seem to be confirmed when the secretary admits that she is guilty. Mason suspects differently.
Comment: Cast regular William Hopper was the son of Hedda Hopper, who, like the Mrs. Davis character, was a popular, powerful — and frequently vindictive — gossip columnist.[25] Berry Kroeger, one of the heavies in McLaglen's *Man in the Vault*, plays an unsavory lawyer named Jarech in this episode.

"The Case of the Gilded Lily"

First Broadcast: May 24, 1958
Producer: Ben Brady
Script: Richard Grey and Gene Wang
Photography: Frank Redman
Editor: Otto W. Meyer
Guest Stars: Peggy Knudsen (Sheila Bowers), Barbara Baxley (Enid Griffin), Mari Aldon (Anne Brent), Grant Withers (Charles Stewart Brent), Richard Erdman (Arthur Binney), Wally Brown (Harry Mitchell), Fay Roope (Judge Kyle), Alan Dexter (Dr. Cortley), Carleton Young (Dr. Parsons), Jack Gargan (Court Clerk), Cy Malis (Garage Attendant), Max Wagner (Janitor)
Summary: Charles Stewart Brent owns the building where Mason keeps his office. Following a two week courtship, Brent marries a pretty blonde named Anne in Las Vegas. After the announcement of the wedding appears in the newspaper, Arthur Binney, a blackmailer, approaches Brent. Binney has learned that Mrs. Brent once served a year in prison for fraud; if Brent wants to keep him from going public with this information, he'll need to pay Binney $30,000. The businessman agrees and makes plans to pay off the crook in a room at a squalid motel, bringing along a gun for protection. After Brent enters this room, however, he is struck from behind by Binney with a sap. When Brent wakes, he finds that his money is gone and Binney is lying dead on the floor, apparently shot by Brent's gun. Once the police arrive, Brent admits to the crime, fearing the police might otherwise suspect and charge his new wife. After Mason interviews Brent, he concludes that Brent has been framed and sets out to determine who the actual killer might be.

"The Case of the Terrified Typist"

First Broadcast: June 21, 1958
Producer: Ben Brady
Script: Robert C. Dennis, Phillip Macdonald, Ben Brady
Photography: Frank Redman
Editor: Otto W. Meyer
Guest Stars: Alan Marshall (James Kincaid alias Duane Jefferson), Joanna Moore (Patricia Taylor), Joan Elan (Mrs. Lumis), Ben Wright (Walter Lumis), Connie Cezon (Gertie), Jack Raine (George Baxter), Kenneth R. MacDonald (Judge), Harold Dyrenforth (Henrich), Hank Patterson (Jack Gilly), Jack Gargan (Court Clerk), James Stone (Jury Foreman), Frankie Darro (Elevator Operator), Red Morgan (Muscleman), Steve Carruthers (Duane Jefferson)
Summary: Diamond merchant Duane Jefferson has come into the possession of some embarrassing letters written by Patricia Taylor, the wife of Ralph Taylor, a U.S. senator. Mrs. Taylor sneaks into Jefferson's office, hoping to recover the documents. While sorting through a filing cabinet, she is surprised by George Baxter, a diamond supplier who has come to meet with Jefferson. Mrs. Taylor soon flees, running into Mason's office, which is located in the same building. There she meets Mason's secretary, Della, who assumes that Mrs. Taylor has been sent over by a temp agency to type up some documents for Mason. Mrs. Taylor gets to work and proves to be excellent at typing, but then she abruptly disappears. Later that day, Baxter's body is found dead, floating in the ocean. The police accuse Jefferson, the diamond merchant, of committing the crime. After Mason agrees to defend Jefferson, he wonders if the enigmatic Mrs. Taylor might have information that can exonerate his client. Jefferson tells Mason not to pursue this strategy, however, explaining that he has been threatening to blackmail Mrs. Taylor with the embarrassing letters he has in his possession. His

refusal prevents Mason from successfully defending him, and Jefferson is convicted of murder, a development that delights Hamilton Burger. The D.A.'s victory is short-lived, though, after Mason discovers that the man he's been defending is not in fact Duane Jefferson.

Season Two, 1958–1959

"The Case of the Shattered Dream"

First Broadcast: January 3, 1959
Producer: Ben Brady
Script: Robert Bloomfield and Seeleg Lester
Photography: Frank Redman
Editor: Art Seid
Guest Stars: Osa Massen (Sarah Werner), Marion Marshall (Irene Bedford), Virginia Vincent (Virginia Trent), Kurt Krueger (Hans Breel), Chris Alcaide (Jerry Morrow), Ludwig Stossel (Adolph Van Beers), Ivan Triesault (Fred Schoenbeck), Theodore Marcuse (William Walker), Lilian Bronson (Judge), Robert Carson (Lawrence David), Gil W. Rankin (Autopsy Surgeon), Cy Malis (Hilton), Barry Brooks (Dealer), Brandy Bryan (Doris)
Summary: A compulsive gambler, Hans Breel owes money to several people, including a loan shark named William Walker. If he wants to stay healthy, Breel must deliver $15,000 to Walker in the next 48 hours. To get himself out of this situation, Breel visits a lady friend named Irene Bedord who owns the Pundit Dream, an enormous diamond. He convinces Irene to sign the rock over to him, promising to provide her with a big return if and when he finds a buyer for it. He then visits Virginia Trent, a Los Angeles jeweler, and persuades her to buy the diamond, taking a $15,000 down payment from her, which he immediately loses at a poker game. Breel later returns to Miss Trent's store and attempts to cleave the diamond, telling her that the smaller stones will bring her an enormous return, some of which he will share. He is unsuccessful, however, and the rock shatters. Breel subsequently heads out to muster any money he can with the diamond fragments. That afternoon his body is found in his apartment, a 9mm bullet in his chest. The police suspect Breel's wife, whom he abandoned years earlier in Chicago, is the killer. Mason agrees to help the woman, certain of her innocence, though all evidence suggests to the contrary.

Rawhide

Rawhide was a fixture on CBS from 1959 to 1966. The show starred Eric Fleming and Clint Eastwood as Gil Favor and Rowdy Yates, a pair of drovers who make their living moving cattle herds along the Sedalia Trail from Texas to Missouri. The show's other regular cast members included Sheb Wooley (Pete Nolan), Jim Murdock (Mushy), Paul Brinegar (Wishbone), Jim Murdock (Mushy), Steve Raines (Jim Quince), and Rocky Shahan (Joe Scarlet).[26] Charles Marquis Warren developed the series and served as *Rawhide*'s producer until 1961, when he was replaced by the show's head writer Endre Bohem.[27] McLaglen first worked with Warren in 1952 as assistant director on *Hellgate,* which Marquis produced and directed.

Season One, 1958–1959

"Incident on the Edge of Madness"

First Broadcast: February 6, 1959
Producer: Charles Marquis Warren
Script: Herbert Little, Jr., and David Victor

Photography: Philip Lathrop
Editor: Roland Gross
Guest Stars: Lon Chaney, Jr. (Jesse Childress), Marie Windsor (Narcie), Alan Marshall (Warren Millett), Ralph Reed (Boston), Duane Grey (Brad), Fay Roope (Mayor Haslip), Jester Hairston (Zachariah), George Hickman (The Professor)
Summary: Col. Warren Millett, who fought for the Confederacy during the Civil War, wants to form his own army and create a new country within Panama, where he and his supporters will be free to own plantations and slaves. When Millett approaches Favor and his men looking for recruits, the trail boss warns him away; Favor also threatens to forcefully subdue anyone in his group who thinks about signing on with Millett. A drover named Childress rejects Favor's orders, however, and joins the colonel. Charged with training the other enlistees,

Cattle drovers Rowdy Yates (Clint Eastwood) and Gil Favor (Eric Fleming) in CBS's *Rawhide*.

Childress quickly transforms into a martinet and deludes himself into thinking that Millett's little army is really his. To prove this, he kills the colonel and kidnaps the dead man's wife.
Comment: Marie Windsor (Narcie) played the roles of Louella in McLaglen's *One More Train to Rob* and Hetty in *Cahill, United States Marshal*.

"Incident of the Power and the Plow"

First Broadcast: February 13, 1959
Producer: Charles Marquis Warren
Script: Fred Freiberger
Photography: Philip Lathrop
Editor: Roland Gross
Guest Stars: Brian Donlevy (Jed Reston), Rodolfo Acosta (Chisera), Dick Van Patten (Matt Reston), Malcolm Atterbury (Will Morton), Michael Pate (Taslatch), Jeanne Bates (Henny Morton), Carol Thurston (Waneea), Robert Gist (Sheriff)
Summary: Cattleman Jed Reston hates Comanche Indians, particularly those who live on the reservation that lies adjacent to his ranch. Intent on driving these people away and taking over their land, Reston regularly accuses his neighbors of committing crimes. The Comanche he hates the most is Taslatch, who wants to be a farmer. After watching Reston's son, Matt, horsewhip Taslatch, Favor and Rowdy decide to help the beleaguered Indian, giving him a plow. When Reston and his men object to this, Rowdy and Favor draw their guns.

"Incident of Fear in the Streets"

First Broadcast: May 8, 1959
Producer: Charles Marquis Warren
Script: Fred Freiberger
Photography: John M. Nickolaus, Jr.
Editor: George Gittens
Guest Stars: Gary Merrill (Jed Mason), Robert Driscoll (Wilt Mason), Corey Allen (Mel Mason), Morris Ankrum (Dr. Tom Jackson), Don Haggerty (Mort Hendricks), Whit Bissell (Sam Harris), Bob Steele (Art Jameson), Eleanor Ayer (Mandy Harris), Ed Nelson (Kels Morgan), Ed Faulkner (Brett Mason), Olan Soulé (Frank Sanford), Guy Stockwell (Gregg Mason), Amzie Strickland (Bess Hargrove), Len Hendry (Store Owner)
Summary: After one of Favor's drovers, Pete Nolan, hurts himself falling from a horse, Favor and Rowdy set off for a nearby town called Provo to find a doctor. When they arrive, they find that Provo's streets are empty, but the local saloon is filled with people who are getting drunk. A merchant explains that the previous day the same group of people in the saloon broke into the Provo jail and lynched a prisoner named Mason. Now, they are trying to blot out their guilty consciences with alcohol. Before Favor and Rowdy can convince the town doctor to come with them to help Pete, Mason's family arrives in Provo, ready to kill anyone who might have participated in their kinsman's murder.

"Incident of the Dry Drive"

First Broadcast: May 22, 1959
Producer: Charles Marquis Warren
Script: John Dunkel
Photography: John M. Nickolaus, Jr.

Editor: Roland Gross
Guest Stars: Victor Jory (Jess Hode), Jean Inness (Carrie Hode), Ron Hagerthy (Jim Hode), Chris Alcaide (Gates)
Summary: A drought has left the Sedona Trail too arid to support cattle. Favor finds some land that has a stream on it, but the owner of the property, Jess Hode, is unwilling to allow access to his water unless Favor gives him half of his herd. At first, Favor wants to hold out and search for another source to feed his "water hungry" animals. There's no water to be found farther up the trail, though, and Favor finds himself wondering if he'll have to accept Hode's terms.

SEASON TWO, 1959–1960

"Incident of the Shambling Man"

First Broadcast: October 9, 1959
Producer: Charles Marquis Warren
Script: Charles Larson & Fred Freiberger, story by Charles Larson
Photography: John M. Nickolaus, Jr.
Editor: James Baiotto
Guest Stars: Anne Francis (Rose Wittman), Victor McLaglen (Harry Wittman), Gene Nelson (Dave Thompson), Robert Lowery (Lou Thompson), Harry Carey, Jr. (Tanner), Robert Karnes (Mel Simmons), Earle Hodgins (Judge James Kuff), Stephen Joyce (Vic), Ed Faulkner (Mason), Steve Thomas (Gene), Russell Trent (Gregg), Pamela Duncan (Woman), Bruce Wendell (Clerk)
Summary: Former prize fighter Harry Wittman lives with his daughter-in-law, Rose, on a desert ranch. After his long career in the ring, Harry now has significant brain damage. Sometimes, when he hears a loud sound, he thinks he's again in the ring and he swings at whoever's standing near him, including Rose. After Favor and Rowdy witness one of these attacks, they try to help Rose place Harry in an insane asylum. The drovers do not realize that Rose has been deliberately triggering Harry's attacks. With the old man institutionalized, she can sell the Wittman ranch and use the money to find a more interesting, cosmopolitan place to live.
Comment: "Incident of the Shambling Man" marks the final time McLaglen worked with his father, Victor (Harry); the actor would die on November 7, 1959, a month after this episode had its original broadcast. McLaglen had been a professional boxer before he became an actor; he is listed in the credits as "the Shambling Man."[28] This episode also features appearances by Andrew V. McLaglen's friends Harry Carey, Jr. (Tanner) and Ed Faulkner (Mason).

Hotel de Paree

Hotel de Paree ran for one season on CBS from the fall of 1959 to the summer of 1960.[29] Earl Holliman played the show's lead character, Sundance, a former outlaw who purchases a stake in the *Hotel de Paree* in Georgetown, Colorado. The inn's co-owners are a French woman named Monique Deveraux (Judi Meredith) and her daughter Annette (Jeanette Nolan). A skilled gunfighter, Sundance often leaves his duties at the Hotel de Paree to aid people in need. He wears a hat with a distinctive band of polished silver dollars that glint in the sun and occasionally blind his opponents. Strother Martin played Aaron Donager, a storekeeper who befriends Sundance. Sam Rolfe, one of the co-creators of *Have Gun, Will Travel*, served as the show's producer.

"Sundance and the Blood Money"

First Broadcast: January 1, 1960
Producer: Sam Rolfe
Script: Paul Savage
Photography: Frank Phillips
Editor: Fred Maguire
Music: Lucien Moraweck
Guest Stars: Russ Conway (Moss Coble), Ken Becker (Cal Eaton), Darryl Richard (Andy), Buck Young (First Miner), Victor Tayback (Second Miner), Mason Curry (First Townsman), Sheldon Allman (Second Townsmen), Joe Greene (Portly Man), Dick Myers (Ben)
Summary: A fugitive murderer is captured in Georgetown while the local marshal is out of town. Sundance is persuaded to hold the prisoner in the basement of the Hotel de Paree until the marshal returns. The killer escapes, however, and during his flight, a young boy is killed. Sundance sets out with Aaron to find the guilty man and bring him back to town.

"Sundance and the Greenhorn Trader"

First Broadcast: February 26, 1960
Producer: Sam Rolfe
Script: Jack Laird, based on a short story by William Gulick
Photography: Frank Phillips
Editor: Paul Weatherwax
Guest Stars: Richard Ney (Oliver Weatherford), Gordon Jones (Pemmican Joe), Roy Barcroft (Beartracks Conlon), Richard Devon (Chief Whitefeather), Dick Myers (Ben)
Summary: Sundance and Aaron have given $40 to Beartracks Conlon, an old trapper. In return, they are to share in the money Beartracks earns from the sale of any pelts he brings back from the mountains. At the end of the hunting season, though, their partner fails to show up in Georgetown. Sundance and Aaron then head into the mountains and find the trapper laid up with a hurt leg. The pair proceeds to take Beartracks's pelts, intending to trade them to a travelling merchant, but a series of mishaps hinder their efforts.

"Sundance and the Long Trek"

First Broadcast: April 22, 1960
Producer: Sam Rolfe
Script: Jack Jacobs
Photography: Frank Phillips
Editor: Fred Maguire
Guest Stars: Denver Pyle (Fred Taylor), Paul Burke (Tad Frisbee), Harry Carey, Jr. (Will Masters)
Summary: A posse comprised of a lawman, a businessman and a theatrical show promoter accuses Sundance of murdering a female singer in Denver.

FOUR

The Sixties

At the start of the sixties, McLaglen remained under contract at CBS, where he continued to contribute episodes to *Gunsmoke, Have Gun, Will Travel, Rawhide* and *Perry Mason*. In spite of his television commitments, he managed to direct four feature films during the first half of the decade: *Freckles* (1960), *The Little Shepherd of Kingdom Come* (1961), *McLintock!* (1963) and *Shenandoah* (1965). The commercial and critical success that greeted *Shenandoah* enabled McLaglen to move on from television and turn his attention exclusively to feature film direction after 1965. His credits during this busy period include *The Rare Breed* (1966), *Monkeys, Go Home!* (1967), *The Way West* (1967), *The Ballad of Josie* (1968), *The Devil's Brigade* (1968), *Bandolero!* (1968), *Hellfighters* (1968) and *The Undefeated* (1969).

Feature Films

Freckles—1960 (84 mins)

Producer: Harry Spalding, Associated Producers
Script: Harry Spalding, based on Gene Stratton-Porter's novel *Freckles*
Photography: Floyd Crosby (Color)
Editor: Harry Gerstad
Music: Henry Vars
Cast: Martin West (Freckles), Carol Christensen (Chris), Roy Barcroft (McLean), Steven Peck (Barbeau), Ken Curtis (Wessner), Jack Lambert (Duncan), Lorna Thayer (Miss Cooper), John Eldridge (Mr. Cooper)
Summary: McLaglen's fourth feature-length motion picture centers on a young man named Freckles. Severely burned as an infant, Freckles has only one hand. Despite this, he sets out to find work with a logging company in the wooded Limberlost section of northeast Indiana. Taken by the youth's intelligence and his earnest manner, the company's owner, Mr. McLean, hires Freckles on as a guard, having him patrol the forest with a rifle. One of the young man's tasks is to track down and drive out Barbeau, a charismatic French Canadian who leads a gang of timber thieves.

Living alone in a mountaintop cabin, Freckles spends his free time reading books. He also develops a friendship with Miss Cooper, a naturalist, and her attractive niece, Chris. Late in the summer, Barbeau and his cronies come into McLean's woods to cut down trees. After Freckles spots them, a gunfight commences and he and Barbeau shoot one another. The Canadian flees into the forest and Freckles follows, ready to kill him, but Barbeau bleeds to death from his wound before Freckles gets a chance. As a reward for his loyalty, Freckles receives a promotion, becoming a clerk for McLean's company.

Comment: McLaglen and his crew shot *Freckles* in the San Bernardino National Forest in southern California in the summer of 1960.[1] The movie features three actors who had worked with the director previously in the television shows *Have Gun, Will Travel* and *Gunsmoke*: Ken Curtis, Jack Lambert and Roy Barcroft. An adaptation of a 1903 novel by Gene Stratton-Porter, *Freckles* was updated by writer-producer Harry Spalding for contemporary audiences; many of the picture's protagonists use chainsaws, for instance, and move through the forest in jeeps and trucks. The one-armed Freckles doesn't drive, however. Instead, he covers the landscape on a horse, much like a cowboy hero in a Western.

By and large, *Freckles* provides viewers with a portrait of the logging industry that is positive. In the Limberlost territory, naturalists and lumberjacks enjoy friendships, and McLean and his men appreciate the forest's beauty and its wildlife — when Freckles isn't reading about the timber industry, he studies bird guides. But while the loggers may love the land, their ultimate goal is to exploit it, to cut down the trees and sell them, a process that has defaced the Limberlost's pristine condition. Ironically, it is Barbeau, the film's heavy, who cares most about the harmful impact McLean's activities have had. In one of the movie's more poignant scenes, he tells Freckles:

> My family was working this woods when the McLeans were fishing up north. We took what we needed and left the hills green. Who gave McLean the right to cut the land? If you don't know, I'll tell you: a little god he calls 'modern business.' There's another name for it, 'greed.' He calls us thieves, and maybe we are. But we take the lumber to live; we don't live to see how many trees we can cut. Let McLean show you his last year's cuttings. The forest gone. The land blackened for miles.... Nothing growing. Nothing planted. You're on the wrong side, Freckles. McLean is the biggest thief of us all.

Originally promoted by Twentieth Century–Fox as a movie for young audiences, *Freckles* is nevertheless a frequently violent picture. The film opens with a brutal fight between Ken Curtis's character, Wessner, and one of Barbeau's men. Another rough sequence transpires after Wessner goes to work for Barbeau and savagely attacks Freckles outside his cabin. The film's hero is not above viciousness himself. He responds to Wessner, for example, by pummeling him with his wooden arm, and conducts himself with similar resolve when he sets out to overpower — and kill — the renegade woodsman Barbeau in the picture's climactic chase sequence.

Reviews: "Though film generates very little suspense, there is a kind of appealing naiveté about it.... Under McLaglen's direction this simplicity is reflected in the performances which are wholesome and attractive but which don't give indication of what the actors may be capable." *Variety*, October 28, 1960.

Release: October, Twentieth Century–Fox

The Little Shepherd of Kingdom Come — 1961 (108 mins)

Producer: Maury Dexter, Associated Producers
Script: Barré Lyndon, based on John Fox, Jr.'s novel *The Little Shepherd of Kingdom Come*
Photography: Floyd Crosby (Color)
Editors: Jodie Copelan, Carl Pierson
Music: Henry Vars; songs "When Love is Young" and "The Little Shepherd of Kingdom Come" by Henry Vars and By Dunham

A scene from *The Little Shepherd of Kingdom Come* (Twentieth Century–Fox, 1961). Leading man Jimmie Rodgers appears in the foreground hoisting a revolver. Ed Faulkner, an actor McLaglen cast frequently in his film and television productions, is the Confederate officer on the stairwell.

Cast: Jimmie Rodgers (Chad), Chill Wills (Maj. Buford), Luana Patten (Melissa), Robert Dix (Caleb Turner), Ed Faulkner (Richard), George Kennedy (Dillon), Kenny Miller (Reuben), Shirley O'Hara (Mrs. Turner)

Summary: Chad is an orphan who lives with his dog, Luke, in the northern mountains of Kentucky. A farmer named Caleb Turner and his sister, Melissa, invite the boy to stay with them in their home in Kingdom Come, a valley settlement. Chad earns his keep tending sheep and helping Caleb work the land. When the older man heads down from the mountains to Lexington with a load of timber, Chad follows. But he stays behind after Maj. Buford, a gentleman planter who lives in the Bluegrass region outside the city, takes an interest in him. Yearning for a son, the major invites Chad to live in his home and pays for him to enroll in college, where the boy studies for a year.

The South's decision to secede from the Union and the subsequent outbreak of war brings this happy situation to an end. Though the state of Kentucky doesn't secede, many of Chad's friends in "the Bluegrass" side with the Confederacy, while Chad, who opposes slavery, decides to sign up with the North. The young man quickly distinguishes himself as a soldier, serving under his friend Caleb. But his convictions are tested when he meets Maj. Buford on the battlefield. After a stray bullet strikes Buford, the old man dies in Chad's arms. During the same skirmish, Caleb is also killed. Chad then decides to bury the men together, giving them a single headstone that tells future visitors that each man died valiantly. In the war's aftermath, Chad begins to court Melissa Turner and resolves to spend his life with her in Kingdom Come, a decision that frees him from the feeling of homelessness he has experienced his entire life.

Comment: Much of *The Little Shepherd of Kingdom Come* was shot on location in the San Bernardino National Forest, where McLaglen had filmed his previous feature *Freckles*.[2] Floyd Crosby served as director of photography on both pictures, as well. One of McLaglen's more obscure titles, the film was developed as a vehicle for Jimmie Rodgers, a popular singer at the time who had scored hits with the songs "Honeycomb" and "Kisses Sweeter than Wine." A native of Washington State, Rodgers struggled with the Kentucky accent he was asked to adopt for his role, and his performance weakens an otherwise strong film.[3] Fortunately, McLaglen managed to cast several strong supporting players, including Chill Wills, Robert Dix and Ed Faulkner, an actual native of Kentucky.[4] It should be noted, though, that Rodgers takes up a guitar early in the narrative and begins to sing, producing one of the few musical performances in McLaglen's oeuvre and one of the finer moments in this film. The song, titled "When Love is Young," was written by Henry Vars and By Dunham. Vars had already scored *Man in the Vault*, *Gun the Man Down* and *Freckles* for McLaglen, and in 1971 would collaborate again with the director on *Fools' Parade*.

The Little Shepherd of Kingdom Come is the first of McLaglen's movies that directly addresses war, a subject he returned to repeatedly in his film and television work over the next three decades. As he would in *Shenandoah* and *The Blue & The Gray*, which are similarly set during the Civil War period, McLaglen refuses in this picture to depict the conflict between the North and the South as a simple one between good and evil parties. While the movie frequently reminds the audience that the planters in Kentucky's Bluegrass country relied upon slavery for their success as businessmen, at the same time it doesn't hesitate to bring attention to commendable traits in these men's personalities. Chill Wills's interpretation of the Maj. Buford character, in particular, is quite sympathetic. The old man embraces Chad, providing him with a horse, fine clothes and education, for instance, and he does this in spite of his disapproving neighbors who show little more than disdain for the mountain boy.

It is the major's generosity that complicates Chad's response to the war. Though he opposes slavery and fights for the Union, Chad's unquestioning faith in the North's positions and policies starts to slip when he has to fight old friends like Maj. Buford. The boy reveals his conflicted point of view in one of the movie's final moments. Holding the dying Buford in his arms, he asks God to help him determine "my belonging place, the Bluegrass or the mountains," no longer certain about where his beliefs and loyalty lie. War can diminish and confuse people's political convictions, the film suggests, just as it can harden them.

Reviews: "Twentieth Century–Fox director Andrew MacLaglen [sic] conjures up an appealing old-fashioned atmosphere out of his Lexington society scenes. But, in a gently-coloured film, is most sharply skilful with his small Civil War battles through the woods." *Sydney Morning Herald*, December 17, 1961; "Pleasant without being too maudlin." *Motion Picture Guide*, 1699; "Slow moving version of the old chestnut which was first filmed in 1920 with Jack Pickford for Goldwyn and remade in 1928 by First National with Richard Barthelmess." *Western Movies*, 234.

Release: January, Twentieth Century–Fox

McLintock! — 1963 (127 mins)

Producer: Michael Wayne, Batjac Productions

Script: James Edward Grant
Photography: William H. Clothier (Color)
Editor: Otho Lovering
Music: Frank De Vol
Cast: John Wayne (McLintock), Maureen O'Hara (Katherine), Patrick Wayne (Devlin), Chill Wills (Drago), Yvonne De Carlo (Louise Warren), Stefanie Powers (Becky McLintock), Jack Kruschen (Birnbaum), Jerry Van Dyke (Matt Douglas, Jr.), Edgar Buchanan (Bunny), Chuck Roberson (Sheriff Lord), Perry Lopez (Davey Elk), Bruce Cabot (Ben Sage), Ed Faulkner (Young Ben Sage), Strother Martin (Agard), Michael Pate (Puma), Aissa Wayne

John Wayne and Maureen O'Hara play an unhappily married couple in *McLintock!* (Warner, 1963).

(Alice Warren), Bob Steele (Railroad Engineer), Hal Needham (Carter), Pedro Gonzales, Jr. (Carlos), Robert Lowery (Governor), H.W. Gim (Ching), Big John Hamilton (Fauntleroy Sage).

Summary: G.W. McLintock owns a spread of land that stretches across 200 square miles. One of the richest men in the Texas Territory, he's made his fortune as a cattle rancher. Although he's a husband and a father, he lives by himself in an enormous estate house surrounded by servants and friends. For the last two years, he's been separated from his Irish wife, Katherine, who suspects him of having slept around with other women. And his daughter, Becky, has been a college student, living in the East.

Following her graduation, Becky surprises Katherine when she tells her that she would like to live with her father. Angered by this, Mrs. McLintock heads out from Philadelphia to Texas and meets with G.W. She tells him that their daughter will be wasting her education and her opportunity for experiencing a satisfying life if she returns to this provincial corner of the country. Her efforts fail, though, and the rancher welcomes the ideas of having his daughter live with him. Katherine, in response, insists upon moving back into the family home. She refuses to share the bed with her husband, however, telling him, in fact, that she wants a divorce.

A few days before the Fourth of July, Becky arrives by train in McLintock, the town that has sprung up near her father's ranch. Her parents host a party to mark the occasion, and during the festivities, Becky becomes smitten with one of her father's ranch hands, Devlin Warren. A courtship soon follows, though the young woman, like her mother, has a volatile nature that quickly wears on Dev.

As these events take place at home, G.W. becomes aware that his friend Puma, a Comanche chief, is being forced with his tribe to relocate to a faraway reservation. G.W. elects to help Puma and his people escape from government custody before the relocation can commence. To do this, he and an old man named Bunny remove the lock from a railroad car that is carrying a cache of rifles. On Independence Day, as the town of McLintock hosts a rodeo, Puma and the other Comanches seize the guns from the train. They proceed to shoot up the town and ride off onto the range.

The uproar caused by the Indians' escape agitates Katherine and she responds by berating her husband. Tired of being mistreated, G.W. tells Katherine to behave. His forceful manner frightens her and she runs away from him, rushing down McLintock's main street. As G.W. follows, people along the sides of the street cheer, fed up with Katherine's bullying, as well. When he finally catches up with her, G.W. straddles his wife over his thighs and begins to spank her. He then starts from town for home. Humiliated and humbled, Katherine runs after him, eventually hopping into the back of her husband's wagon.

Comment: A Western comedy, *McLintock!* is the first of the five films McLaglen directed in which John Wayne played the lead. The movie was shot on location outside Tucson, Arizona, for Batjac, Wayne's production company.[5] Many of the actor's family members and friends contributed to the picture's creation. Wayne's son, Michael, served as the film's producer, while another son, Patrick, played the role of Devlin Warren. Longtime pals Bruce Cabot, Bob Steele and Big John Hamilton were given supporting roles, too, and Maureen O'Hara — Wayne's co-star in John Ford's *Rio Grande* (1950), *The Wings of Eagles* (1957) and *The Quiet Man* — was asked by the actor to play the role of his onscreen wife, Katherine.[6] The picture's screenwriter, James Edward Grant, was an old friend, as well, having worked for almost two decades with Wayne, scripting several of his best known pictures, including *Sands of Iwo Jima, Hondo, The Alamo* (1960) and *Donovan's Reef* (1963), the last film Wayne completed before he appeared in *McLintock!*, and the last picture the actor made with John Ford.

Upon *McLintock!*'s release in November 1963, reviewers noted similarities between the picture and *The Taming of the Shrew*, Shakespeare's play about a man named Petruchio who successfully subdues his vitriolic bride Katherina.[7] Critics also spotted parallels between *McLintock!* and Ford's *The Quiet Man*, which McLaglen himself had worked on a decade earlier as a second assistant director.[8] The resemblances between these pictures are extensive. Though *McLintock!* is set in Texas and *The Quiet Man* takes place in Ireland, both movies examine the strained love affairs between a boisterous American and his stormy Irish wife. Wayne and O'Hara played the male and female leads in each film, too. Both pictures also feature a prolonged sequence in which the husband character, exasperated by his wife's insolent manner, pursues the woman across the landscape and uses force to persuade her to become more compliant to his wishes.

The rough treatment Katherine receives in the final moments of *McLintock!* dates — and mars — this otherwise enjoyable film. As Nash and Ross point out in their *Guide to Motion Pictures*, "Wayne does a good job in this broad comedy, although it is doubted that the picture could have gotten away with the spanking scene if it were made today."[9] Sexism of this sort, it should be noted, had never appeared in McLaglen's earlier films, nor would it surface in later productions. As a matter of fact, in *The Rare Breed*— the picture O'Hara and McLaglen made together three years after *McLintock!*— the actress portrays a strong businesswoman who ignores the counsel and ridicule of her male companions, and eventually experiences great success as a cattle breeder. Similarly in *The Ballad of Josie*, Doris Day's eponymous heroine stands up to a crowd of hostile ranchers who try to block her from supporting herself. The case can certainly be made that *McLintock!* has a misogynistic streak, in other words, but labeling McLaglen a misogynistic director is something else.

Reviews: "[This] Batjac production has its infectious moments and should strike a responsive chord with audiences." *Variety*, November 13, 1963; "Well done, somewhat tongue-in-cheek, John Wayne vehicle which is sure to delight his fans." *Guide to Westerns*, 258; "An enormously popular film which thrives on action, humor, civic pride, just the right slice of slapstick, and a proper amount of drawing-room comedy, this remains one of John Wayne's most widely watched Westerns and a genre favorite." *Encyclopedia of Westerns*, 280; "There are some very funny sequences; the characters are reminiscent of those played by Wayne and O'Hara in Ford's *The Quiet Man*. It's loud, foolish, broad and enjoyable." *Western Films*, 232.

Release: November, United Artists
Availability: VHS, LD, DVD

Shenandoah—1965 (105 mins)

Producer: Robert Arthur, Universal Pictures
Script: James Lee Barrett
Photography: William H. Clothier (Color)
Editor: Otho Lovering
Music: Frank Skinner
Cast: James Stewart (Charlie Anderson), Doug McClure (Sam), Glenn Corbett (Jacob), Patrick Wayne (James), Rosemary Forsyth (Jennie), Philip Alford (Boy), Katharine Ross (Ann), Charles Robinson (Nathan), James McMullan (John), Tim McIntire (Henry), Paul Fix (Dr. Witherspoon), Denver Pyle (Pastor Bjoerling), George Kennedy (Fairchild), Dabs Greer (Abernathy), Lane Bradford (Tinkham), Bob Steele (Union Guard), Edward Faulkner (Union Sergeant), Eugene Jackson, Jr. (Gabriel), Rayford Barnes (Horace), Tom Simcox

Shenandoah (Universal, 1965) was the first of four pictures McLaglen made with James Stewart.

(Lt. Johnson), Kevin Hagen (Mule), Strother Martin (Engineer), James Best (Carter), Warren Oates (Packer), Harry Carey, Jr. (Jenkins)

Summary: Set in the final months of the Civil War, *Shenandoah* focuses on Charlie Anderson, a farmer who lives with his seven children (six sons and a daughter) in Virginia's Blue Ridge Mountains. A critic of slavery, Anderson has refused to join the Confederate army, keeping his sons out of it, as well. He finds himself caught up in the war nonetheless, after one of his sons, Boy, is misidentified by Union soldiers as a Rebel and sent off to a prison camp. Anderson and his children then set out to find the youth, though one of Anderson's sons, James, and his wife, Ann, stay behind at the farm to look after their newborn.

Hoping Boy is on board, the Andersons use force to stop a Union prison train that is loaded with captured soldiers. They don't find Boy, but one of the men on board is Sam, a Confederate officer who is married to Anderson's only daughter, Jennie. While the Andersons continue their search, Boy escapes his captors in the North. He soon finds himself on the battlefield, where he is injured. Fortunately, an old friend, a freed slave named Gabriel, helps Boy by pulling him out a firefight.

Eventually Anderson decides to stop the search. Before he and the others return home, however, a trio of Confederate deserters arrives at the family farm, asking James Anderson for water. When they realize the place is all but empty, the deserters kill James and his wife, Ann, though they spare the couple's baby. Another tragedy occurs a few days later: as Charlie Anderson and the others find the road that will take them home, a teenaged Rebel with a quick finger fires upon them, killing another Anderson son, Jacob.

The journey resumes and the Andersons soon arrive home, where they learn about the murder of James and Ann. The dead are then buried in the family plot. On a Sunday morning, Anderson hears church bells and summons the others on the farm to go with him to church.

As the service begins, a door opens and Boy hobbles in on a crutch. Happy and relieved, Anderson goes to his son and embraces him as the congregation begins to sing the hymn "Praise God, From Whom All Blessings Flow."

Comment: *Shenandoah* is McLaglen's second film about the American Civil War, his follow-up to *The Little Shepherd of Kingdom Come*. *Shenandoah* departs from the earlier film's sentimental portraits of soldiers on both sides of the conflict, emphasizing instead the tragic and absurd aspects of the conflict and the manner in which war hurts everyone, even men like Charlie Anderson who have no interest in participating in it. *Shenandoah* garnered positive reviews upon its release in the summer of 1965, and performed well at the box office, becoming the year's sixth highest earning motion picture.[10] In the decades since, the movie's realistic and frequently painful depictions of war have continued to draw attention from critics. Writing in 1992, for example, Gerard Molyneaux described *Shenandoah* as one of the "most powerful anti-war statement[s] of the sixties."[11]

Shenandoah continues to appeal to general audiences today, and it ranks with *McLintock!* as one of McLaglen's best known features. To a certain extent, the picture owes its popularity to leading man James Stewart, whose interpretation of Charlie Anderson is at once complex and sympathetic. As the film opens, Anderson appears to be little more than a stiff autocrat, who lectures and badgers his children at the dinner table, around the farm and even in church. As *Shenandoah* progresses, though, McLaglen gives Stewart numerous opportunities to show us that the character is not merely a bully, but a deeply concerned father. The search for Boy is one of the most explicit expressions of this paternal love. Anderson's refusal to keep his sons from fighting for the Confederacy is another. As the old farmer explains at one point to a Southern officer who has asked him to allow his sons to enlist:

ANDERSON: I've got 500 acres of good, rich dirt here. As long as the rains come and the sun shines, it'll grow anything I've a mind to plant. We've pulled every stump, cleared every field; and we've done it ourselves without the sweat of a slave.
JOHNSON: So?
ANDERSON: 'So?' So, can you give me one good reason why I should send my family, that took me a lifetime to raise, down that road like a bunch of damn fools to do somebody else's fighting?
JOHNSON: Virginia needs all of her sons, Mr. Anderson.
ANDERSON: That might be so, Johnson, but these are my sons!

Sadly, Anderson's efforts to spare his family from danger, on the whole, fail. Boy is captured and maimed in battle; James and Ann are murdered; and Jacob is killed by the young soldier. The farmer's decisions actually seem to contribute to these tragedies: the Confederate deserters would probably not dare to attack James and Ann at the farm, nor would the Rebel soldier feel the need to shoot Jacob in the woods, if Anderson and the others were not out looking for Boy in the first place. The deaths of these people seem even more wasteful, perhaps, because the search for the missing son is unsuccessful. Though Boy may return to the Shenandoah Valley at film's end, his escape from the Union prison camp and his subsequent flight home come about thanks to his own efforts, not his family's.

Reviews: "[D]espite a neuter title, [*Shenandoah*] packs drama, excitement and an emotional quality — particularly reflected in the climax — which should find better-than-average reception in the general market.... Under Andrew V. McLaglen's gutty direction the Robert Arthur production moves at quick tempo." *Variety*, April 14, 1965; "'Shenandoah' is a pretty good Civil War drama — an altogether respectable one.... It is also a careful picture, handsomely produced in excellent color by Universal. And as a dramatic allegory, underscoring the futility of war, it has a good cast, dominated by James Stewart, as the tough-minded head of an isolationist clan of Virginia farmers, pulled into the thick of the last Confederate

stand." *New York Times*, July 29, 1965; "Stewart is magnificent in a role that required enormous range and dimension to make it work well." *Encyclopedia of Westerns*, 387; "The greatness of 'Shenandoah' is gained through its calculated restraint, and thus it attains the heights in pathos, and the sublime aesthetically. It has a disciplined artistry; nothing obtrudes and no illusionist devices are employed." *John Ford and Andrew V. McLaglen*, 20; "James Stewart does one of his best roles in this fine Civil War drama that makes a few points about the futility of war as it entertains." *Motion Picture Guide*, 2878; "Well made, interesting and poignant melodrama with James Stewart giving a powerful performance as the patriarch." *Guide to Westerns*, 382; "[I]t's very well directed — one of McLaglen's best jobs — and quite satisfying as entertainment." *Western Films*, 291.
Release: June, Universal
Availability: VHS, LD, DVD

The Rare Breed—1966 (97 mins)

Producer: William Alland, Universal Pictures
Script: Ric Hardman
Photography: William H. Clothier (Color)
Editor: Russell F. Schoengarth
Music: Johnny Williams
Cast: James Stewart (Burnett), Maureen O'Hara (Martha), Brian Keith (Bowen), Juliet Mills (Hilary), Don Galloway (Jamie), Jack Elam (Simons), Ben Johnson (Jeff Harter), Alan Cailou (Taylor), David Brian (Elsworth), Perry Lopez (Juan), Harry Carey, Jr. (Mabry), Bob Gravage (Cattle Buyer), Larry Domasin (Alberto), Barbara Werle (Gert), Joe Ferrante (Esteban), Larry Blake (Auctioneer)
Summary: Sam "Bulldog" Burnett, a middle-aged cowhand, has come to St. Louis to attend the National Stockmen's 1884 Exposition. There he meets an English cattle breeder named Martha Evans and her daughter, Hilary. The women have come to the United States with Vindicator, a white-faced Hereford bull. Because Herefords lack horns, they are ideal for railroad transport, and the women hope this feature will draw interest from American investors. Vindicator is subsequently purchased at auction for $2,000 for a Texas cattleman named Alexander Bowen. Martha then hires Burnett to convey the bull to Texas, where she will attempt to crossbreed the Hereford with the Longhorn cows Bowen raises on his ranch.

Before leaving, Burnett makes a deal on the side with another rancher named John Taylor, who offers him $1,000 if he will steal Vindicator for him. On the trail to Texas, Burnett finds himself impressed not only by Vindicator's sturdiness, but Martha's strong personality, and he decides not to honor his deal with Taylor. When some of Taylor's hired men come to get the animal, the old cowhand uses chicanery and force to turn them away. He and his companions eventually complete the trek to Texas, where they meet the rancher Alexander Bowen.

Bowen is amused by the hornless bull, rather than impressed, and thinks it unlikely the animal will survive one winter in this part of the country, let alone breed. After setting Vindicator loose on the range, Bowen turns his attention to Martha, for whom he has taken a fancy. Winter soon arrives, bringing a blizzard, and Burnett heads out to find and save the hornless bull, but he is unsuccessful. As the hard season progresses, Bowen continues to court Martha, while his son, Jamie, pursues her daughter, Hilary. Once spring arrives, Burnett spots the missing bull's carcass in a patch of thawing snow. Bowen tries to console the American. If any of his longhorn cows have mated with Vindicator, Burnett can have the calves.

Spring turns into summer, and as Bowen continues his efforts to woo Martha, Burnett roams the landscape, searching for white-faced calves. He also buys a ranch, where he hopes to raise cattle with Martha. As summer comes to an end, he wonders if his efforts are in vain. At the same time, Martha begins to soften to Bowen's advances. But just as she agrees to marry him, Burnett shows up at Bowen's ranch, bringing in a calf that looks like a miniature version of Vindicator. The expression on Martha's face lets Bowen know that she is in love with Burnett, and he lets her go. The movie ends a moment later with a shot of Burnett's ranch, to a corral that is filled with Vindicator's white-faced heirs.

Comment: Much of *The Rare Breed*, McLaglen's second collaboration with Jimmy Stewart, was shot in Indio, California, where the director had filmed several episodes of *Have Gun, Will Travel* and *Gunsmoke*.[12] The picture's writer, Ric Hardman, was a veteran of television himself, having contributed scripts to programs like *Cheyenne*, *Lawman*, *Laredo* and *Rawhide*. Very much like the shows that were written for *Rawhide*, *The Rare Breed* chronicles the efforts taken by people to move cattle across the landscape. (McLaglen had directed six episodes for *Rawhide* from 1959 to 1962). But while a team of drovers in the television show worked their way each week from Texas to Missouri moving hundreds of animals, *The Rare Breed* inverts this pattern, having a single drover oversee the transport of one bull from Missouri to Texas.

The Rare Breed shares with one of McLaglen's later features, *The Last Hard Men*, a concern with what Nash and Ross have described as "the final days of the Wild West."[13] Set in 1884, *The Rare Breed* focuses in particular on the manner in which the arrival of technological innovation and industrialization — in this case, the spread of the railroad through rural America — precipitated the disappearance of men like Burnett, who had made their livings riding horses and moving longhorn cattle across the range. A character named Jeff Harter — a fellow cowpoke and a friend of Burnett — announces early in the movie: "One morning [we'll] wake up to a train whistle, and there won't be any more cattle drives. Yes, sir, in a few years it'll be gone; leastwise, the way we knew it." The coming of the railroads, in addition, has helped to make new cattle breeds — such as Herefords — attractive to American ranchers. As the auctioneer who sells Vindicator explains: "You'll notice the hornless condition being an innovation that should meet with the approval of each and everyone who must move or ship cattle." Ranchers who used railroad cars to transport their herds, that is, needed cattle that lacked horns in order to minimize the potential for injuries.

James Stewart looks for a lost bull in *The Rare Breed* (Universal, 1966).

Not everyone in the film is receptive to the idea of owning and raising hornless bulls, though. Burnett himself initially laughs at the mild-looking Vindicator, calling him a "knob-head" and "a useless hunk of gristle." The rancher Bowen regards the creature with similar disdain. For him, Herefords are a poor business investment because they aren't hearty enough to survive on the open Texas range. "I've lived half my life here. And I'll tell you," Bowen says, referring to Vindicator, "if [my] longhorns do not kill him, then the wolves and the winters will."

Burnett comes to recognize the possibility that Herefords might be successfully bred in Texas, however. "I think Vindicator is as good or better than any longhorn alive!" he declares at one point. And his subsequent decision to buy a ranch and raise Vindicator's heirs on it proves to be a smart one. As the film's final sequence shows us, the old drover's readiness to adopt new ideas about cattle rearing has not only made him prosperous, but happy, too.

Reviews: "'The Rare Breed' is a generally successful fictionalized blend of violence, romance, comedy, inspiration and oater Americana. The well-mounted, colorful William Alland production has good scripting, direction and performances.... Not a shoot-em-up, concentrating rather on personal conflicts, the Universal release has good-to-excellent b.o. prospects ... particularly in family and action markets where Stewart's 'Shenandoah' struck gold last year." *Variety*, February 2, 1966; "The movie has a good scenic look to it — McLaglen grew up under John Ford's tutelage and knows how to frame a composition ... it's very well performed by Stewart and Keith (the latter as a comically dour Scot) as two crusty frontiersmen vying for the affections of O'Hara. But the script is predictable." *Western Films*, 264.

Release: March, Universal Pictures
Availability: VHS, DVD

Monkeys, Go Home! —1967 (101 mins)

Presented by: Walt Disney
Co-Producer: Ron Miller, Walt Disney Productions
Script: Maurice Tombragel, based on G.K. Wilson's novel *The Monkeys*
Photography: William Snyder (Color)
Editor: Marsh Hendry
Music: Robert F. Brunner; "Joie de Vivre" by Robert B. Sherman and Richard M. Sherman, performed by Maurice Chevalier
Cast: Dean Jones (Henry "Hank" Dussard), Maurice Chevalier (Father Sylvain), Yvette Mimieux (Maria Riserau), Bernard Woringer (Marcel Cartucci), Clement Harari (Emile Paraulis), Marcel Hillarie (Mayor), Yvonne Constant (Yolande Angelli)
Summary: An American named Hank Dussard arrives in the south of France, having inherited an olive farm from his recently deceased mother. To save on labor costs, Dussard purchases four chimpanzees and trains them to pick his olive crop. He immediately finds himself at odds with his new community, in particular Marcel, a young socialist butcher who regards the newcomer and his animals as a threat to local business interests. Joined by Paraulis, a corrupt real estate agent, the butcher leads a campaign against Dussard, scrawling hostile slogans on walls around the town where much of the film's action takes place.

Dussard has his allies, however: a priest, a mayor and a young woman named Maria, who falls in love with the American. To win over the others in town, especially his fellow olive growers, Dussard offers to loan out the use of his monkey laborers for free. When it comes times to harvest the crops, though, the chimps run off. At first, the locals ridicule Dussard for his misfortune, but then the priest scolds them: "Who among you thinks of himself as a good neighbor? If you do, then consider for a moment your neighbor, the American. He staked his fortune and

Yvette Mimieux and Bernard Woringer in a scene from *Monkeys, Go Home!* (Disney, 1967).

his reputation on this venture, and lost.... Have you already forgotten he offered to share his monkeys with you, free of charge? Is this the way you return a kindness?" Chastened, the townsfolk begin to help the American. As everyone gets to work, Dussard and Maria decide to marry.

Comment: Although it's set in France, *Monkeys, Go Home!* was filmed at the Disney Studio in Burbank and the company's Golden Oak Ranch, making use of sets that were originally created for the *Zorro* television series.[14] The picture was just one of many produced for the studio in the sixties that featured chimpanzee characters; others included Robert Stevenson's *The Misadventures of Merlin Jones* (1964) and *The Monkey's Uncle* (1965) and Byron Paul's *Lt. Robin Crusoe, U.S.N.* (1966).[15]

Scripted by television writer Maurice Tombragel (*Annie Oakley*, *Bat Masterson*), *Monkeys, Go Home!* appears at first glance to be little more than a celebration of American-style capitalism. The Yankee businessman Dussard is at once individualistic and fearless, an innovator who shows the town how cheap labor can increase profits. His rivals, Marcel and Paraulis, in contrast, are presented as reactionary oafs who mouth Marxist clichés and sow anger amongst the other olive farmers. "Right here, do you believe me, in our own community an example of capitalist oppression," Marcel the butcher declares. "The American ... has imported slaves to undermine the economy of our village. Henry Dussard has brought in monkeys and trained them to pick olives." Marcel and Paraulis, moreover, lie, cheat and even steal with the least compunction. Early in the film, for instance, the butcher and the estate agent swipe a pair of bananas from a grocer. Presumably, McLaglen wants us to associate these two anti-capitalists with the story's other monkeys.

Dussard is far from flawless, however. Preoccupied with his ambitions, he ignores and rebuffs Maria's early efforts to woo him. "Money and work, is that all you think about?" she cries. He is similarly cold to his chimpanzees. For him, these creatures are "work chimps," no different from horses and other livestock. While Maria caresses and dresses the animals, Dussard barks orders at them and locks the creatures up in a small room. We find emotional aloofness of this sort in many McLaglen protagonists. G.W. McLintock in *McLintock!,* Chance Buckman in *Hellfighters* and Rafer Janders in *The Wild Geese,* for example, all devote more attention to their professional callings than their families, and as a result, they experience estrangement from the people who love them.

Dussard finally turns his attention to Maria and agrees to marry her, though, after the chimps run away from his farm, bringing his innovative approach to business to an abrupt end. Love blooms, it seems, when men like Dussard turn their thoughts away from money and work. The movie's ending may not explicitly denounce American capitalism, perhaps, but it doesn't endorse the practice either.

Reviews: "[F]ilm has the usual professional Disney blend of children, animals, humor and charm.... Andrew V. McLaglen, in a shift from oaters, shows another directorial facet in keeping the action going." *Variety,* Jan. 25, 1967; "Of 'Monkeys Go Home' perhaps the kindest thing to record is that they reached their destination without mishap! The antics of trained chimpanzees combined with the histrionic abilities of Maurice Chevalier is not a particularly inspiring formula — and certainly not one to sustain 101 minutes." *John Ford and Andrew V. McLaglen,* 23.

Release: February, Buena Vista Distribution Co.
Availability: VHS, DVD

The Way West—1967 (122 mins)

Producer: Harold Hecht, Harold Hecht Corp.
Script: Ben Maddow, Mitch Lindemann, based on A.B. Guthrie, Jr.'s novel *The Way West*
Photography: William H. Clothier (Color)
Editor: Otho Lovering
Music: Bronislau Kaper; title song by Kaper and Mack David, sung by The Serendipity Singers
Cast: Kirk Douglas (Tadlock), Robert Mitchum (Summers), Richard Widmark (Evans), Lola Albright (Rebecca Evans), Michael Witney (Johnnie Mack), Harry Carey, Jr. (McBee), Connie Sawyer (Mrs. McBee), Sally Field (Mercy), Michael McGreevey (Brownie), Roy Barcroft (Masters), Patric Knowles (Grant), John Mitchum (Little John), Jack Elam (Weatherby), Stefan Arngrim (Billy Tadlock), Peggy Stewart (Mrs. Turley), Stubby Kaye (Sam Fairman), Eddie Little Sky (Brave), Michael Keep (Brave), Gary Morris (Paw-Kee-Mah)
Summary: William J. Tadlock, a former United States senator, dreams of settling the Oregon Territory's Willamette Valley. To achieve this, he organizes a wagon train, recruiting more than a hundred families to make the trek. The Oregon Liberty Train, as he names it, sets out from Independence, Missouri, in the summer of 1846. Almost immediately, problems spring up for the party: the scout Tadlock hires to lead the train, Dick Summers, starts to lose his vision; one of the travelers in the group drowns during a river crossing; another traveler, John Mack, mistakes a young Sioux boy for a wolf and shoots him dead, arousing the wrath of the child's tribe.

As the journey progresses, Tadlock becomes increasingly tyrannical and ruthless. He insists upon having John Mack hanged. He forces the train to make a dangerous passage through the desert to save a week's time. He even strikes people who question his decisions. Eventually, the travelers rise up against Tadlock and replace him with Lije Evans, a farmer.

Thirty miles from the Willamette Valley, the pilgrims are forced to stop at the edge of a plunging canyon. An argument commences as Evans and the others decide on which move to make next. Should the Oregon Liberty Train descend the canyon and cross the river below, or abandon its original plans and head south to California?

The group chooses the former option. Evans then uses ropes and pulleys to lower the people, their animals and their wagons into the canyon. The last person to make the descent is Tadlock. On his way down, his rope is cut by the widowed wife of John Mack, and the senator falls to his death. Unwilling to pursue the deranged woman, the travelers bury Tadlock and resume the trip, soon arriving at their destination.

Sally Field in *The Way West* (United Artists, 1967), one of her first motion picture appearances.

Comment: *The Way West* is based upon A.B. Guthrie's novel of the same name, which received the Pulitzer Prize for Fiction in 1950.[16] Starring three of Hollywood's biggest "tough guy" stars — Kirk Douglas, Robert Mitchum and Richard Widmark — the picture was filmed in the summer of 1966 in central Oregon.[17] Despite strong performances from its leads and William H. Clothier's memorable footage of the Oregon landscape, the movie garnered poor reviews following its release in May 1967

Primarily, critics found fault with the film's narrative, complaining that it was long and melodramatic, and overly focused on the love lives of its characters. Large sections of the picture narrow on the efforts of Lije Evans's son, Brownie, to woo an insipid — and promiscuous — teenager named Mercy McBee, the "caravan's Lolita," as the *Los Angeles Times's* Kevin Thomas described her.[18] Mercy, however, is in love with John Mack, a frustrated husband who is unable to persuade his neurotic wife to sleep with him. The movie's older characters are beset with romantic urges, too. Tadlock tries to seduce Evans's wife, Rebecca, at one point. Similarly the scout, Dick Summers, talks frequently throughout the movie about taking a Blackfoot woman for a wife, and in the film's closing scene, he leaves the Liberty Train to follow up on this ambition.

Reviews: "Project probably looked good on paper, but washed out in scripting, direction and pacing. Incidents do not build to any climax; excepting the first and last reels, any others could be shown out of order with no apparent discontinuity. A lot of time, money and logistics — including use of national parks for some terrific location work — makes the final result all the more disappointing." *Variety*, May 17, 1967; "Not only are the incidents of conflict among the foreground travelers in the train fashioned to the concepts and the patterns of television Western serials, but they are directed by Mr. McLaglen and played by his brightly costumed cast in a style that almost brings into the picture the lights and cameras and all the stuff of artifice." *New York Times*, May 25, 1967; "The direction of Andrew V. McLaglen, who can do very well when he has a good script to work with, as was the case with 'Shenandoah,' is amiable as always.... If *The Way West* does not wholly succeed as drama, it is at least a well-made and wholly professional Hollywood Western. Western fans ... might enjoy it for that alone. Widmark and Mitchum are excellent in roles unusual for them and Douglas, as always, is a seasoned old hand." *Chicago Sun-Times*, Jun, 20, 1967.

Release: May, United Artists
Availability: VHS, DVD

The Ballad of Josie — 1968 (102 mins)

Producer: Norman Macdonnell, Universal Pictures
Script: Harold Swanton
Photography: Milton Krasner (Color)
Editor: Otho Lovering, Fred A. Chulack
Music: DeVol; "The Ballad of Josie" by Don Costa and Floyd Huddleston, sung by Ronnie Dante
Cast: Doris Day (Josie), Peter Graves (Jason Meredith), George Kennedy (Arch Ogden), Andy Devine (Judge Tatum), Robert Lowery (Whit Minick), William Talman (Charlie), David Hartman (Pruitt), Paul Fix (Alpheus Minick), Guy Raymond (Doc), Audrey Christie (Annabelle), Linda Meiklejohn (Jenny), Shirley O'Hara (Elizabeth), Timothy Scott (Klugg), Don Stroud (Bratsch), Elisabeth Fraser (Widow Renfrew), Harry Carey, Jr. (Mooney), Ed Faulkner (Livery Man), Teddy Quinn (Luther)
Summary: Josie Minick lives with her son, Luther, and her husband, Whit, in Arapaho, a frontier town in the Wyoming Territory. An abusive drunk, Whit comes home one night

from the local saloon and starts to menace Josie; to protect herself, she swats at him with a pool stick, accidentally knocking Whit down a flight stairs and killing him. A trial is subsequently held and Josie is acquitted. Whit's death leaves Josie without income, though, and her rich father-in-law, Alpheus, forces the widow to give young Luther over to him until she is financially stable.

Following her son's departure, Josie tries to find work at a newspaper, a bank and a restaurant, but she experiences little success. She then decides to raise cattle on a 450-acre spread she has inherited from her husband. But after a local rancher named Jason "Jace" Meredith warns her that she has neither the experience nor the toughness needed for this work, Josie reconsiders. A few days later, Jace and Josie take a carriage ride together. When they stop for a picnic, a flock of sheep wanders in from the range and surrounds them. "You know, it takes money, capital, brains and sweat to raise cattle," Jace says, "but any idiot with a two-bit dog and a Winchester can raise sheep."

Inspired by these remarks, Josie borrows money from the bank and purchases her own flock, a decision that enrages the cattlemen who own the land around her spread, including her friend Jace. The ranchers subsequently attempt to steal the sheep, but Josie fends them off with a pistol and a rifle, forcing the men to retreat to the hills that surround her house. A standoff follows that soon draws support from people across the country. Arapaho's female citizens march through the town with protest signs, for instance, and Jace heads out to Josie's ranch to help her keep the ranchers away. In addition, lawmakers in Washington, D.C., announce that they will deny Wyoming statehood if the conflict doesn't end. But the conflict does end, when one of the ranchers, a man named Ogden, offers to buy out Josie and help her start her own cattle ranching enterprise. The film then cuts to a parade in downtown Arapaho, to a shot of Josie, Jace and Luther riding together in a wagon. A campaign sign hangs from the side of their vehicle, announcing Jace's plans to run for U.S. Senate.

Comment: *The Ballad of Josie* was produced by Norman Macdonnell, one of the co-creators of the *Gunsmoke* radio program. Macdonnell had also played an important part in adapting *Gunsmoke* for CBS Television, as well, and served as the TV series' producer from 1956 to 1964 — the same years McLaglen directed for the show. Following his departure from *Gunsmoke*, Macdonnell became a producer at Universal Pictures, and one of the projects he was asked to oversee was a Western comedy, *The Epic of Josie*, with Doris Day set to play the lead. When McLaglen was approached about shooting the picture — he was under contact at Universal at the time — he accepted, happy about the opportunity to work with Macdonnell again.[19]

Filming commenced in February 1967, with Milton Krasner (*How the West was Won*) serving as director of photography.[20] The bulk of the picture's outdoor footage was shot in the San Fernando Valley outside Los Angeles, while interiors and street scenes were filmed in Universal City.[21] Prior to the movie's release in February 1968, Universal tweaked the original title, changing it to *The Ballad of Josie*, perhaps to better capitalize on Doris Day's popularity as a singer.

Much like McLaglen's *McLintock!*, *The Ballad of Josie* is filled with humorous moments, especially sight gags. When Josie walks through downtown Arapaho in a pair of men's jeans, for example, the town's conservative citizens are so shocked that they drop their groceries and stumble into horse troughs. The picture is not all laughs, however, especially when it addresses the problems women can experience when limits are placed upon their rights and freedoms by men. Many of the male characters who surround Josie strive to demoralize and manipulate her regularly. Her drunken husband tries to force sex on her. Her father-in-law takes away her son. Her friend Jace initially joins in with the other cattle ranchers to dispossess her of her sheep and her livelihood. Each of these efforts fails, though, in large part because Josie refuses to accept her status as a second-class person and stands up to her bullies. She swats back at her husband with the pool cue, sending him rolling down the stairs and killing him. She challenges the ranchers with drawn guns, and convinces them that she is as free to work her land as they are to work theirs. She secures an income for herself, as well, and retrieves Luther from her father-in-law.

Upon its release, *The Ballad of Josie* drew mixed reviews, with many critics dismissing it as a slight picture. Leo Sullivan in his review for *The Washington Post* complained, "There's nothing about [the film] that couldn't have been taken care of in the 54 minutes allotted to a Western series on TV."[22] Doris Day herself thought little of the picture and described it in her autobiography as "nothing more than a second-rate television western that required me to get up at four-thirty every morning."[23] But *The Ballad of Josie* has also received praise over the years, particularly for having a tough-minded female protagonist, a rarity in the Western genre. Phil Hardy has argued, for example, that "the film's central idea — Day as a feminist in turn-of-the-century Wyoming — and Day's performance transform the movie into a fascinating Western."[24]

Reviews: "'The Ballad of Josie' is a pleasant, innocuous Doris Day oater comedy about sheep-cattle range wars, and women's rights…. Action director Andrew V. McLaglen shows his talents in the few lively scenes; elsewhere, direction and script are plodding, acting routine." *Variety*, December 27, 1967; "An unusual Doris Day movie, in which she looks prettily worn out as the frontier widow who, having accidentally killed her violent, alcoholic husband, enrages local cattle barons by deciding to herd sheep — something, she is told, 'any idiot with a dog and a Winchester' can do. However uneasily between comedy and realism, with some boring male characters, this intriguing, uneven movie has some fine moments." *Rough Guide to Westerns*, 212–213

Release: February, Universal Pictures
Availability: DVD

The Devil's Brigade—1968 (132 mins)

Producer: David L. Wolper, Wolper Pictures, Ltd.
Script: William Roberts, based on a book by Robert H. Aldeman and Col. George Walton (U.S.A.R. Ret.)
Photography: William H. Clothier (Color)
Editor: William Cartwright
Music: Alex North
Cast: William Holden (Lt. Col. Robert T. Frederick), Cliff Robertson (Maj. Alan Crown), Vince Edwards (Maj. Cliff Bricker), Andrew Prine (Pvt. Theodore Ransom), Jeremy Slate (Sgt. Maj. Pat O'Neill), Claude Akins (Pvt. Rocky Rockman), Jack Watson (Cpl. Peacock), Richard Jaeckel (Pvt. Omar Greco), Bill Fletcher (Pvt. Bronc Guthrie), Richard Dawson (Pvt. Hugh McDonald), Tom Troupe (Pvt. Al Manella), Luke Askew (Pvt. Hubert Hixon), Jean-Paul Vignon (Pvt. Henri Laurent), Tom Stern (Capt. Cardwell), Harry Carey, Jr. (Capt. Rose), Michael Rennie (Lt. Gen. Mark Clark), Carroll O'Connor (Maj. Gen. Hunter), Dana Andrews (Gen. Walter Naylor), Gretchen Wyler (The Lady of Joy), Paul Busch (German Captain), Patric Knowles (Adm. Lord Mountbatten)
Summary: In the summer of 1942, Robert T. Frederick, a lieutenant colonel in the United States Army, is charged with creating a special fighting unit comprised of Canadian and American soldiers. Called the 1st Special Service Force, the group will be used by the Allies to try to

drive the Nazis out of Norway. Given only four months to prepare the men, Frederick faces an imposing obstacle. While the Canadians are all exemplary soldiers, the Americans are criminals and miscreants, and the two groups at first are unable to get along.

The lieutenant colonel manages to pull the regiment together, however, aided in part by his assistants, Maj. Bricker, an American, and Maj. Crown, an Irish officer serving with the Canadians. Training in Montana, the soldiers become adept at hand-to-hand combat, skiing and mountain climbing. Then Frederick learns that the mission to Norway has been cancelled. Hating to see the men's efforts go to waste, he persuades his superiors in Washington to send them to Italy instead, to conduct a raid on a small mountain town. The attack is successful and the soldiers bring back several prisoners. During an interrogation, a captured German officer refers to the soldiers as "devils," and thereafter the members of the 1st Special Service Force refer to themselves as the "devil's brigade." The men's prowess subsequently lands them another assignment and they are sent to Italy to knock out a German battalion that occupies a mountain along the route to Rome.

William Holden, star of *The Devil's Brigade* (United Artists, 1968).

Comment: *The Devil's Brigade* was spearheaded by David L. Wolper, a successful television producer who had overseen the creation of several notable documentaries about World War II, including *D-Day June 6, 1944* (1962), *France: Conquest to Liberation* (1965) and *Prelude to War* (1965). In his memoir *Producer*, Wolper explains that he became interested in the 1st Special Service Force after "an agent sent me the manuscript of a book ... entitled *The Devil's Brigade*," by Robert Aldeman and George Walton. "It was a terrific story and I made a deal with United Artists to produce it."[25] For the script, Wolper hired William Roberts, who'd worked on the screenplay for John Sturges's *The Magnificent Seven* (1960), which, like *The Devil's Brigade*, tells the story of a unit of fighting men who face a nearly impossible challenge.[26] Much of the picture was shot in the Wasatch Mountains area that surrounds Salt Lake City, Utah, as well as Camp W.G. Williams, a training camp administered by the Utah National Guard in Riverton, Utah.[27] The sequence in which the soldiers raid the Italian mountain town midway through the movie was filmed in Sant'Elia Fiume Rapido in central Italy.[28]

Though conditions on the mountains in Utah were windy and cold, shooting generally went smoothly. Leading man William Holden, however, was an alcoholic, which proved to be an occasional problem for McLaglen. The director recalled that "when the actor was drinking, his whole personality changed. He became garrulous, talkative, loud, outgoing. His performance, which at most times would be a hundred percent, became inept. He tottered on his feet, steeling himself to say the dialogue."[29] After the filmmakers moved to Italy to complete the film's remaining sequences, Holden's drinking grew worse. The actor's biographer Michelangelo

Capua explains that while in Utah, "Bill drank only wine ... when the crew moved to Italy, things suddenly changed and he started drinking vodka." At one point, Holden was so drunk, he became irate during a scene and turned a machine gun he was carrying on a crowd of bystanders and fired. Fortunately the gun was loaded with blanks, not live ammunition.[30]

The Devil's Brigade is the first film McLaglen made about World War II, a subject he returned to again with *The Sea Wolves, Breakthrough, Return from the River Kwai* and the television production *The Dirty Dozen: Next Mission*, a sequel to Robert Aldrich's *The Dirty Dozen*. In fact, *The Devil's Brigade* was faulted by some critics upon its release for bearing too close a resemblance to Aldrich's film, especially with its focus on misfit soldiers who, like those in *The Dirty Dozen*, undergo rigorous training before they head out for battle. In his memoir, Wolper claims that the parallels between the two pictures were coincidental, and that rather than being helped at the box office by its likeness to the earlier film, *The Devil's Brigade* suffered: "Unfortunately, [our picture] came out just a few months after the release of *The Dirty Dozen*, which was the same kind of story. It was a big hit and it killed us. We got lost in the wind."[31]

The similarities between the two films are extensive, however. Much like Maj. Reisman, the character Lee Marvin played in the original *The Dirty Dozen*, William Holden's Lt. Col. Frederick is by turns cynical and tough, but paternal, too, and his concern and affection for his men steadily increases as the film progresses. The American soldiers in both films are similarly unwilling at first to participate in the U.S. Army's efforts to defeat the Nazis, only agreeing to join the fight when they understand that doing so may reduce their jail sentences. In both films, as well, these hard-bitten characters grow increasingly committed to their efforts, many of them becoming ready and even willing to die as they carry on against the Nazi threat. Discipline, shared experience and a shared enemy, both films finally suggest, can have a potentially redeeming effect on men, turning criminals into heroes.

Yet one aspect of *The Devil's Brigade* departs significantly from *The Dirty Dozen*. In the earlier film, a single commander is charged with preparing twelve men and leading them into battle. In McLaglen's picture, in contrast, a single commander has the responsibility of preparing hundreds of men. If Frederick were dealing only with reprobates, perhaps, the task would probably be impossible. But a large part of the 1st Special Service Force is comprised of outstanding Canadian soldiers, "the handpicked best of the best-trained army in the world," as Frederick refers to them. The two groups despise one another initially. Yet friendships gradually develop when the Americans realize they stand to gain more by getting along with — and emulating — their rivals, than bickering with them.

Such is the case, for instance, with a character named Rocky Rockman. A loudmouth and a bully, early in the film Rocky sneers at the Canadians, dismissing them as soft and weak. But after a Canadian hand-to-hand combat instructor humiliates him, Rocky comes to understand that the systematic fighting methods of these soldiers from the north are superior to his own barroom brawling techniques. When he subsequently adopts these new techniques himself, and uses them successfully in battle, his contempt for the Canadians vanishes and he becomes friendly — even grateful — to them.

We find similar examples of rivalries transforming into friendships and allegiances throughout McLaglen's films. In *Bandolero!*, for example, the robbers Mace and Dee Bishop fight side-by-side with Sheriff July Johnson against a band of bandits. In *The Undefeated*, the Union colonel John Henry Thomas and the Confederate colonel James Langdon pair up to save themselves and their people from Mexican soldiers. And in *The Wild Geese*, the mercenary Pieter Coetzee repudiates his racist beliefs as he tries to save the life of the African leader Limbani.

Reviews: "Major drawbacks in the film are overexposure and later dramatic overkill.... The too-numerous brawls, well staged (Hal Needham was stunt supervisor), stand out as hyper-jazzy production numbers in an otherwise plodding screenplay." *Variety*, May 1, 1968; "Like *The Dirty Dozen* and *The Great Escape* ... *The Devil's Brigade* represents Hollywood's answer to a national longing for the earlier, more innocent times of World War II." *New York Times*, May 23, 1968.
Release: May, United Artists
Availability: VHS, LD, DVD

Bandolero!—1968 (106 mins)

Producer: Robert L. Jacks, Twentieth Century–Fox
Script: James Lee Barrett, from a story by Stanley Hough
Photography: William H. Clothier (Color)
Editor: Folmar Blangsted
Music: Jerry Goldsmith
Cast: James Stewart (Mace), Dean Martin (Dee), Raquel Welch (Maria), George Kennedy (July Johnson), Andrew Prine (Roscoe Brookbinder), Will Geer (Pop Chaney), Tom Heaton (Joe Chaney), Clint Ritchie (Babe), Denver Pyle (Carter), Sean McClory (Robbie), Harry Carey, Jr. (Cort), John Mitchum (Bath House Customer), Roy Barcroft (Bartender), Dub Taylor (Attendant), Perry Lopez (Frisco), Rudy Diaz (Angel), Donald Barry (Jack Hawkins)
Summary: As the film opens, Dee Bishop and his gang attempt to rob a bank in Val Verde, Texas. During the heist, a rich landowner named Stoner and his beautiful wife, Maria, wander into the bank. One of the bandits fires on Stoner and kills him. Hearing the shot, Val Verde's sheriff, July Johnson, rushes to the bank with his deputy Roscoe. The lawmen capture the robbers, bring them to jail and make plans for their execution.

In the desert outside Val Verde, Dee's brother Mace learns about the impending execution from a hangman who's been summoned to the town by Sheriff Johnson. Mace proceeds to murder the hangman, assume his identity and head to Val Verde himself, where he liberates Dee and the others. Mace then robs the town bank after Sheriff Johnson and a posse head out in pursuit of the fugitives.

On the trail to Mexico, Dee and his gang hijack a wagon, killing the driver and stealing food and supplies. The outlaws also kidnap the wagon's passenger, Maria Stoner. In love with Mrs. Stoner, Sheriff Johnson doubles down on his efforts to apprehend Dee once he learns about her abduction, pressing into Mexico with his

Raquel Welch, the female lead in *Bandolero!* (Twentieth Century–Fox, 1968).

posse. Mace heads into Mexico, too, and soon catches up with Dee. The two brothers, we learn, have been estranged for several years. In the Civil War, Dee rode with Quantrill's Raiders, a band of guerrillas that fought for the South, while Mace carried a gun for the Union.

Eventually Mace, Dee and the other fugitives seek shelter in a ghost town called Sabinas. Once there, Mace asks his brother to come with him to Montana, where the two can buy a spread and live as ranchers. Dee responds to the idea favorably, wondering if he might be able to establish a home there with Mrs. Stoner, with whom he's fallen in love. But then Johnson and his deputies arrive in Sabinas and succeed in capturing the two fugitives. Before the sheriff can move the outlaws from Sabinas, however, several Mexican *bandoleros* rush into the town. Johnson responds by freeing his prisoners and giving them arms. The strategy works and the *bandoleros* are beaten back and killed, but not before the Bishops are both fatally shot.

Comment: Filmed in the fall of 1967, *Bandolero!* is the only feature in which Dean Martin (Dee) and James Stewart (Mace) appeared together, though Stewart had made an appearance on Martin's popular TV show earlier that year.[32] At once violent and comic, *Bandolero!* is one of McLaglen's strongest Westerns, thanks in part to James Lee Barrett's tight script and William H. Clothier's gorgeous landscape photography. Much of the picture was shot in the red rock country surrounding the Glen Canyon National Recreation Area and the Lake Powell reservoir, which stretches between Utah and Arizona.[33] Sequences were also filmed in Brackettville, Texas, where John Wayne had shot *The Alamo* and John Ford made *Two Rode Together* (1961), the latter of which also featured Stewart.[34]

Like McLaglen's *The Undefeated* and *The Shadow Riders*, *Bandolero!* is set in the months following the conclusion of the Civil War. Neither of the Bishops have fared well from their experiences on the battlefield. Though Mace fought for the victorious Union, he is just as poor as his outlaw brother, and just as ready, it seems, to kill anybody who stands in his way as he pursues prosperity. Mace regards himself as his brother's moral superior, in fact, upbraiding Dee at one point for having joined William Clarke Quantrill and participated in the murderous siege of Lawrence, Kansas—an event that so shamed the Bishop brothers' mother, Mace explains, that it killed her. This disclosure fails to persuade Dee, however, that his character is in any way lower than Mace's. He complains: "One boy goes with Quantrill, the other goes with Sherman. One helps burn down a town, the other helps burn down a state. The one that burned down the town is the one that done in his mama."

The brothers nevertheless manage to reconcile despite their political differences. Primarily this is because they find themselves facing the same enemies, both the lawman Johnson and the *bandoleros* in Mexico. The brothers' affection for one another actually grows over the course of the film, especially after Mace asks Dee to buy land with him in Montana.

For Dee, by the way, the possibility of owning a ranch not only means living and working with his brother, but also a chance to start a family, an idea he begins to savor after Mrs. Stoner explains that she would like to come with him to Montana. Dee may be a killer who has repudiated the tenets of civilized society for years, but he seems to have the same yearnings for stability and love that characterize people who live within the law. July Johnson shares Dee's desires for companionship and love, too. Arguably, it is his affection for Mrs. Stoner, rather than his need to serve justice, which compels the sheriff to follow the Bishops into Mexico. At the same time, the sheriff's motives for making the dangerous journey may not be solely romantic. Unlike Dee, Johnson has learned that the widow has inherited land holdings from her slain husband, and if he can link himself with her, he stands to gain a fortune. The moral divisions between the film's heroes and heavies, we see, are neither great nor clear.

Reviews: "The settings ... are spectacular and fresh and captured marvelously by cinematographer William H. Clothier. There are nice performances by Stewart (who is incapable of

being uninteresting), by Dean Martin (sincere, lowkey, noncampy) and Kennedy. Miss Welch with a Spanish accent is earnest without being convincing." *Los Angeles Times*, July 5, 1968; "The film is rich in humour with an effective musical score by Jerry Goldsmith, and Andrew V. McLaglen achieved well-balanced portrayals from his highly competent cast." *John Ford and Andrew V. McLaglen*, 25.
Release: June, Twentieth Century–Fox
Availability: VHS, DVD

Hellfighters—1968 (121 mins)

Producer: Robert Arthur, Universal Pictures
Script: Clair Huffaker
Photography: William H. Clothier (Color)
Editor: Folmar Blangsted
Music: Leonard Rosenman
Cast: John Wayne (Chance Buckman), Katharine Ross (Tish), Vera Miles (Madelyn), Jim Hutton (Greg Parker), Jay C. Flippen (Jack Lomax), Bruce Cabot (Joe Horn), Edward Faulkner (George Harris), Irene Foster (Barbara Stuart), Edmund Hashim (Col. Valdez), Alberto Morin (Gen. Lopez), Alan Cailou (Harry York), Pedro Gonzales (Hernando)
Summary: Chance Buckman heads a company that puts out oil field fires around the world. This dangerous work has made Chance a rich man. He owns his own jet, lives in a luxury apartment and has girlfriends all over the globe. But his career has cost him his family: neither his daughter, Tish, nor his ex-wife, Madelyn, speak to him, though he loves them both.

During a job in Texas, Chance is badly injured and taken to the hospital. The doctors fear that he might die and place him under sedation. One of Chance's workers, a young firefighter named Greg Parker, decides to contact Tish and bring her to her father's side. At first, Tish and Greg dislike one another. But their feelings change quickly, and when Greg is later called to a fire in Louisiana, Tish follows him. The pair subsequently elopes once the fire is out. After the newlyweds return to Texas, they reveal to Chance about what they've done. Their news surprises him, but Chance likes the idea of having his favorite employee for a son-in-law.

A few days later, once Chance is out of the hospital, Madeyln Buckman flies in from San Francisco to meet Greg. At dinner, she warns Chance that the young couple's marriage is doomed — that Tish will never be able to accept her husband's dangerous work. But Tish has more of her father's blood in her than her mother's, and when Greg is called to a fire in Calgary, she joins him. On another job in Malaya, Greg hurts his leg and nearly loses his life. The accident forces Chance to think about his own mortality and the opportunities he's missed because of his work. He then decides to sell his company to Greg and re-marry Madelyn. Hired on as an executive at an oil company, Chance finds that his new life is a bit dull, but still enjoyable.

Greg continues to hop from country to county with Tish and a crew of firefighters. A job in Venezuela proves to be extremely difficult for him to complete, however. On state-controlled land, several well fires are burning simultaneously. Making the situation more complicated, anti-government rebels have scattered themselves around the oil fields, eager to thwart Greg's firefighting efforts. Greg calls on Chance for assistance and the older man agrees to fly down to Venezuela. When Chance tells Madelyn about his decision, she insists upon joining him. As the men get to work, the guerrillas attack, but the Venezuelan army manages to subdue them, allowing Chance, Greg and the others to stamp out the fires.

John Wayne and Katharine Ross play a father and daughter who like to put out oil fires in *Hellfighters* (Universal, 1968).

Comment: Though *Hellfighters* was not made for Batjac, John Wayne's production company, the actor's influence can be detected throughout this underrated film. Wayne had a say in who his co-stars in this film would be, requesting that Jim Hutton, Bruce Cabot and Ed Faulkner play his firefighting sidemen. These actors had all worked with Wayne on the picture he finished immediately prior to *Hellfighters*, *The Green Berets* (1968), which the Duke had not only starred in, but directed.[35] In *John Wayne: American*, Randy Roberts and James Stuart. Olson explain that Wayne also worked closely on the narrative with scenarist Clair Huffaker, who had previously scripted two pictures for the actor, Michael Curtiz's *The Comancheros* (1961) and Burt Kennedy's *The War Wagon* (1967). Wayne, in particular, asked for the sequence in which Chance and the others are forced to work on the wells in Venezuela as guerrillas attack them.[36]

While some critics panned the film for being slow and devoting too much of its narrative to the private lives of its heroes, *Hellfighters* has its share of interesting moments, especially the numerous firefighting sequences. In order to depict these activities accurately, Wayne, McLaglen, Huffaker and the film's producer, Robert Arthur, consulted regularly with a real "wild well control" specialist, Paul N. "Red" Adair, who also served as the model for Wayne's character, Chance Buckman. The picture's special effects coordinators Fred Knoth, Whitney McMahan and Herman Townsley were similarly concerned with achieving visual realism, and used thousands of gallons of diesel oil and raw propane to create flames that rose 125 feet into the air.[37] One of the film's finer moments appears in the opening sequence, when an oil well explodes at night, filling the screen with an orange and yellow blaze as oil field workers scatter for cover, some of them in flames themselves.

Reviews: "Producer Robert Arthur has latched onto an appropriate topic for his John Wayne starrer that adroitly intermingles exciting action and suspense with interesting characters.... Wayne enacts one of those hardy stalwarts who fights blazoning oil wells wherever they occur throughout the world, and Arthur has developed his idea realistically, backed by Andrew V. McLaglen's know-how direction." *Variety*, November 27, 1968;

Release: December, Universal Pictures
Rating: G
Availability: VHS, LD, DVD

The Undefeated — 1969 (119 mins)

Producer: Robert L. Jacks, Twentieth Century–Fox
Script: James Lee Barrett, based on a story by Stanley Hough
Photography: William H. Clothier (Color)
Editor: Robert Simpson
Music: Hugo Montenegro
Cast: John Wayne (John Henry Thomas), Rock Hudson (James Langdon), Roman Gabriel (Blue Boy), Lee Meriwether (Margaret), Tony Aguilar (Rojas), Ben Johnson (Short Grub), Marian McCargo (Ann Langdon), Melissa Newman (Charlotte Langdon), Harry Carey, Jr. (Webster), Paul Fix (Gen. Masters), Edward Faulkner (Anderson), John Agar (Christian), Michael Vincent (Bubba), Bruce Cabot (Newby), Royal Dano (Sanders), Bob Gravage (Hicks)
Summary: In the days following the end of the Civil War, John Henry Thomas, a Union colonel, resigns his commission and sets out with the men who served under him to round up wild horses, which he plans to sell to the U.S. Army. Thomas and the others manage to capture 3,000 animals, but the government agents who are sent to buy the horses try to

cheat the colonel and the arrangement collapses. Thomas then makes a deal with Maximilian, the emperor of Mexico, who needs the horses to help his army suppress an uprising being led by his nemesis Benito Juarez.

As Thomas and his men head into Mexico to deliver the animals, they meet James Langdon, a former Confederate colonel. Langdon explains that Maximilian has invited him and the hundred or so soldiers he commanded in the war to serve in Mexico as mercenaries. As the old warriors become acquainted, bandits descend on Langdon's camp. Thomas and his men come to Langdon's aid and the attack is thwarted. To express his gratitude, Langdon invites the Yankees to join them for a Fourth of July celebration. Before anyone even has a chance to eat, however, a massive brawl breaks out, with Thomas's and Langdon's men thrashing each other in the dirt. Despite the fight, the colonels establish a friendship and show goodwill to one another when they part.

As Thomas heads south with his horses, Langdon and his party proceed to Durango, where they meet Gen. Rojas, a representative for Maximilian. Rojas invites Langdon and his companions to enter his fort. Once everyone is inside, though, the general reveals that he is in fact a Juarista, committed to Maximilian's overthrow. Now trapped, Langdon is told that he must persuade Col. Thomas to deliver his 3,000 horses to the Juaristas, or Langdon's people will all be executed. Langdon then leaves the fort and looks for the other colonel. When he finds him, he is relieved to learn that Thomas is ready to provide help. Thomas and his men proceed to turn their herd of horses toward Durango, but they are met by a line of soldiers loyal to Maximilian. A vigorous fight follows and Maximilian's men are crushed. Thomas subsequently delivers the horses to Rojas and the prisoners are released.

Comment: Much like Chance Buckman, the protagonist John Wayne played in McLaglen's *Hellfighters*, Col. John Henry Thomas is a rugged businessman, whose pursuits lead him into dangerous situations: while Buckman puts out oil fires as guerrillas shoot at him, Thomas transports wild horses through a war zone. Like Buckman, as well, Thomas surrounds himself with men whose loyalty to him is absolute. Wayne, of course, had made a point of playing strong leaders like this on the screen since the forties, long before he ever had McLaglen direct a film for him. In Edward Dmytryk's *Back to Bataan* (1945), for example, the actor had played a character named Col. Madden who inspires a band of Philippine commandos to undermine the occupation of their country by Japanese forces. In Howard Hawks's *Hatari* (1962), Wayne was Sean Mercer, a commercial hunter who traps animals in Africa with a team of assistants. And in his own *The Green Berets*, Wayne played Mike Kirby, an ageing colonel who fights the Vietcong alongside young soldiers who regard him as a sort of father.

In these earlier films, Wayne's characters all strive to serve what they believe is the public good. Chance Buckman's firefighting saves lives and oil wells, protecting both the environment and the business interests of his clients. Sean Mercer fills the zoos of the world with exotic animals, enabling visitors to learn about wildlife and become interested in protecting it. And for Col. Kirby, the war against the North Vietnamese advances the objectives of American foreign policy.

Thomas's decision to deliver his horses to Maximilian, in contrast, seems to be driven by little more than a desire to earn money for himself and his men, an action that hinges on sedition. Before setting out on the trip, that is, a government official warns the colonel that trading with Mexico's emperor violates U.S. law. The treasonous aspects of his arrangement with Maximilian aren't lost upon Thomas either. Shortly after the colonel and his band of former soldiers cross into Mexico, he jokes, "We got Maximilian on one hand and Juarez on

John Wayne and Lee Meriwether in *The Undefeated* (Twentieth Century–Fox, 1969).

the other, and bandits in between. On top of that, we're Americans in Mexico taking a cavy of horses to a very unpopular government. Why should we expect trouble?" Yet Thomas's ambitions are never realized. Instead of providing the animals to Maximilian, he and his men trade them to the Juaristas for the freedom of Langdon's people. "People's lives matter more [to them] than money or comfort," writes Gary Hoppenstand in his essay "Hollywood Cowboys and Confederates in Mexico."[38] With its message that even would-be war profiteers and quasi-traitors like Thomas and his men can act selflessly, *The Undefeated* stands out, perhaps, as one of McLaglen's more optimistic films.

Reviews: "Basically wrong is the whole uneven mood of the film. Neither Wayne nor Hudson seems to know whether they are in a light comedy or a serious drama." *Variety*, October 1, 1969; "Although not of the same caliber as other Andrew V. McLaglen ventures ... this big (some have called it 'lumbering') production does benefit from a reliable group of character actors (many of them Wayne film regulars)." *Encyclopedia of Westerns*, 454; "[T]he movie is not one of Wayne's best, although it does have exciting sequences and excellent supporting cast, topped by one-time 'B' Western comedy sidekick, Dub Taylor." *Great Western Pictures II*, 387.

Release: October, Twentieth Century–Fox
Rating: G
Availability: VHS, LD, DVD

Series Television

Gunsmoke

McLaglen was one of *Gunsmoke*'s most prolific directors in the first half of the sixties, shooting 49 episodes for the series before leaving the program in 1965. During this time, *Gunsmoke* underwent several changes. At the start of the series' seventh season (1961–1962), the producers expanded the show's running time from 30 minutes to 60 minutes, hoping to improve ratings. In the next season (1962–1963), Burt Reynolds was added to the cast to play the blacksmith Quint Asper. Then in the tenth season (1964–1965), Ken Curtis joined the regular cast as the affable mule skinner Festus Haggens. That same season, *Gunsmoke* also lost one of its central characters, Chester, after actor Dennis Weaver quit the program to pursue new projects and roles.[39]

Season Six, 1960–1961

"The Blacksmith"

First Broadcast: September 17, 1960
Producer: Norman Macdonnell
Script: John Meston
Photography: Fleet Southcott
Editor: Al Joseph
Music: Jerry Goldsmith
Guest Stars: George Kennedy (Emil), Anna-Lisa (Gretchen), Bob Anderson (Tolman), Wesley Lau (Willy), Herb Patterson (Spooner)
Summary: A cattle rancher named Tolman covets a piece of land owned by Emil, a blacksmith who lives in Dodge. On Emil's wedding night, Tolman attacks the blacksmith's new bride Gretchen, hoping this will scare her and Emil out of town. Instead of running, the blacksmith stands up to the rancher, beating him up in a fistfight.
Comment: Kennedy (Emil) made his first of many appearances on *Gunsmoke* in this episode. A friend of McLaglen, the actor had parts in the features *The Little Shepherd of Kingdom Come*, *Shenandoah*, *The Ballad of Josie*, *Bandolero!*, *Fools' Parade* and *Cahill, United States Marshall*. Composer Jerry Goldsmith wrote the music for this episode; he would collaborate again with McLaglen on *Bandolero!* and *The Last Hard Men*.

"Small Water"

First Broadcast: September 24, 1960
Producer: Norman Macdonnell
Script: John Meston
Photography: Fleet Southcott
Editor: Otto Meyer
Guest Stars: Trevor Bardette (Finn), Warren Oates (Seth), Rex Holman (Leroy)
Summary: Dillon and Chester are charged with bringing a murderer named Finn Pickett to Dodge for trial. En route, Finn tries to escape and the marshal shoots him dead. To ward off conflict with the slain man's brothers, Dillon and Chester pay a visit to Finn's father, Leroy. During their conversation with Leroy, Dillon becomes convinced that the old man, like his dead son, is a murderer. Dillon and Chester then take Leroy into custody. As the three men start for Dodge, the remaining Pickett brothers surround them, intent on helping their father escape.

"Say Uncle"

First Broadcast: October 1, 1960
Producer: Norman Macdonnell
Script: John Meston
Photography: Fleet Southcott
Editor: Otto Meyer
Guest Stars: Gene Nelson (Hutch), Dorothy Green (Nancy), Richard Rust (Lee), Harry Lauter (Martin), Roy Barcroft (Farr), Dabbs Greer (Jonas), James Rawley (Man)
Summary: Lee Nagel and his father Martin have come to Dodge to open a general store. Shortly after their arrival, Martin's ne'er-do-well brother, Hutch, shows up. When a keg of nails falls on Martin and kills him, young Lee suspects his uncle of foul play. His misgivings increase when Hutch proposes to Lee's widowed mother, Nancy. At the couple's wedding reception, Lee confronts his uncle about the crime and Hutch responds by throwing a knife at him. Dillon and Chester witness the attack, arrest the groom and lead him off to jail.

"The Badge"

First Broadcast: November 12, 1960
Producer: Norman Macdonnell
Script: John Meston, story by Marian Clark
Photography: Fleet Southcott
Editor: Al Joseph
Music: Leith Stevens
Guest Stars: John Dehner (Rack), Conlan Carter (Augie), Harry Swoger (Ike), Allan Lane (Mac), Mike Mikler (Charlie)
Summary: A bank robber named Rack and his sidekick Augie ambush Dillon on the trail that leads out of Dodge. After deciding to keep the lawman as a prisoner, the criminals start for Texas. Along the way, Dillon manages to make a friend of Augie, persuading him to cut the ropes that bind his wrists and feet. Once free, the marshal kills Rack. Then he heads back to Dodge with Augie.

"Shooting Stopover"

First Broadcast: October 8, 1960
Producer: Norman Macdonnell
Script: John Meston, story by Marian Clark
Photography: Fleet Southcott
Editor: Al Joseph
Guest Stars: Anthony Caruso (Gurney), Patricia Barry (Laura), Robert Brubaker (Jim Buck), Paul Guillofoyle (Reverend)
Summary: Dillon and Chester must transfer Gurney, a suspected killer, from Dodge City to Wichita on a stagecoach that is carrying a large shipment of gold. After a group of bandits attacks them, Dillon and the other travelers take cover in a rest station.

"Ben Tolliver's Stud"

First Broadcast: November 26, 1960
Producer: Norman Macdonnell
Script: John Meston, story by Norman Macdonnell

Photography: Fleet Southcott
Editor: Otto Meyer
Guest Stars: John Lupton (Ben), Jean Ingram (Nancy), Roy Barcroft (Jake), Hank Patterson (Carl)
Summary: Ben Tolliver works for a cantankerous rancher named Jake Creed. The two men do not get along, in part because Tolliver is in love with Creed's daughter and wants to marry her. After Tolliver quits his job, Creed refuses to pay him the money he's owed. Ben, in turn, takes a horse from Creed's ranch, infuriating his former employer.

"Bad Sheriff"

First Broadcast: January 7, 1961
Producer: Norman Macdonnell
Script: John Meston
Photography: Fleet Southcott
Editor: Al Joseph
Guest Stars: Russell Arms (Hark), Kenneth Lynch (Gance), Harry Carey, Jr. (Turloe), Don Keefer (Chet), Lane Chandler (Sam)
Summary: Sheriff Gance and his deputy, Turloe, pursue and capture a stagecoach robber. Instead of bringing in the bandit and jailing him, they decide to hold onto him and the money he's taken. The crooked lawmen's ambitions are frustrated when they run into Dillon on the trail outside Dodge.
Comment: This was not the first time Carey, Jr. (Turloe) turned in a role as an inept lawman for McLaglen. In the director's 1956 feature *Gun the Man Down*, the actor played a dimwitted deputy and in a 1959 episode of *Have Gun, Will Travel* ("The Posse"), he portrayed a cowardly sheriff.

"Kitty Shot"

First Broadcast: February 11, 1961
Producer: Norman Macdonnell
Script: John Meston
Photography: Fleet Southcott
Editor: Otto Meyer
Music: Bernard Herrmann
Guest Stars: George Kennedy (Jake Bayloe), Rayford Barnes (Helm), Joseph Mell (Bill Pence)
Summary: Two train robbers, Helm and Jake, get into a fight with one another at the Long Branch. Jake draws, fires his gun and inadvertently shoots Miss Kitty. He shoots Helm, too, killing him. Jake then sets out for the prairie, hoping to elude justice. Dillon follows the fugitive closely, prepared to kill him if necessary.

"Stolen Horses"

First Broadcast: April 8, 1961
Producer: Norman Macdonnell
Script: John Meston, story by Norman Macdonnell
Photography: Fleet Southcott
Editor: Otto Meyer
Music: Jerome Moross
Guest Stars: Buck Young (Jim Redig), Shirley O'Hara (Mrs. Kurtch), Jack Lambert (Tebow),

Guy Raymond (Abe), Henry Brandon (Quick Knife), Charles Seel (Jed Cuff), Alex Sharp (Acker), Eddie Little Sky (Brave)

Summary: With help from an Indian chief named Quick Knife, Dillon and Chester head to a ranch where a fugitive murderer has taken an old farmer hostage.

"Long Hours, Short Pay"

First Broadcast: April 19, 1961
Producer: Norman Macdonnell
Script: John Meston
Photography: Fleet Southcott
Editor: Al Joseph
Music: Fred Steiner
Guest Stars: John Larch (Serpa), Lalo Rios (Little Fox), Allan Lane (Capt. Graves), Dawn Little Sky (Squaw), Steve Warren (Sergeant), Frank Sentry (Crooked Knife), Fred McDougall (Tracker)
Summary: In the prairieland outside Dodge, Dillon captures Serpa, a crooked businessman who sells rifles illegally to a band of Pawnee Indians. As the marshal leads his prisoner back to town, some Pawnees show up and attack. They free Serpa and tie Dillon to the ground. The marshal manages to escape and re-captures Serpa, whom he then turns over to the custody of the U.S. Cavalry.

SEASON SEVEN, 1961–1962

"Harpe's Blood"

First Broadcast: October 21, 1961
Producer: Norman Macdonnell
Script: John Meston
Photography: Fleet Southcott
Editor: Otto Meyer
Guest Stars: Peter Whitney (Cooley), Evans Evans (Jenny), Dan Stafford (Kyle), Conlan Carter (Jeff), Warren Kemmerling (Carr), Moira Turner (Sarah)
Summary: Kyle Cooley has a crush on Jenny Troupe, a beautiful, blonde-haired saloon girl who works at the Long Branch. Kyle wants to marry her, but he faces a serious obstacle: Jenny already has a husband, a rancher named Neil Carr. To correct the situation, Kyle murders Carr and frames his brother Jeff for the crime.
Comment: "Harpe's Blood" brings to mind such *films noirs* as Billy Wilder's *Double Indemnity* (1944) and Orson Welles's *The Lady from Shanghai* (1947), which also feature blonde *femme fatale* leads who use the promise of sex and money to lure men into trouble. The actress who plays Jenny in this episode is Evans Evans. She would later marry director John Frankenheimer; like McLaglen, Frankenheimer was a contract director at CBS in the late fifties and early sixties.[40]

"Long, Long Trail"

First Broadcast: November 4, 1961
Producer: Norman Macdonnell
Script: Kathleen Hite
Photography: Fleet Southcott
Editor: Otto Meyer

Guest Stars: Barbara Lord (Sarah Drew), Mabel Albertson (Gody Baines), Alan Baxter (Lou Hacker), Peggy Stewart (Fan Hacker), Robert Dix (Jamie)

Summary: Sarah Drew has come from Boston to Kansas to visit her fiancé Jamie, a cavalry officer who is stationed in a remote fort 150 miles north of Dodge. Sarah wants Dillon to take her to the fort. Along the way, the two encounter numerous obstacles, including an Indian attack and a prairie fire. They also fall in love.

"Indian Ford"

First Broadcast: December 2, 1961
Producer: Norman Macdonnell
Script: John Dunkel
Photography: Fleet Southcott
Editor: Otto Meyer
Guest Stars: Pippa Scott (Mary Tabor), R.G. Armstrong (Capt. Benter), Roy Roberts (Tabor), Anthony Caruso (Lone Eagle), Robert Dix (Spotted Wolf), John Newton (Sgt. Cromwell), Lane Chandler (Trumbull), Dawn Little Sky (Indian Woman)

Summary: Trumbull, an old mountain man, is crossing the prairie when he spots a band of Indians slaughtering a buffalo. One of the people in the group appears to be a white woman. Trumbull makes his way to Dodge to tell Dillon about what he's seen. The marshal immediately wonders if the woman might be Mary Tabor, a local woman who was abducted by a Cheyenne war party during a stagecoach holdup a year earlier.

"The Do-Badder"

First Broadcast: January 6, 1962
Producer: Norman Macdonnell
Script: John Meston
Photography: Fleet Southcott
Editor: Al Joseph
Music: Leith Stevens
Guest Stars: Abraham Sofaer (Harvey Easter), Strother Martin (Gene Bunch), Adam Williams (Slim Trent), Warren Oates (Chris Kelly), James Nusser (Louie Pheeters), H.M. Wynant (Sam Smith), Harry Bartell (Charlie Fess), Mercedes Shirley (Mary Pickett), James Anderson (Bert Case), Roy Engel (Ed Greeley), Shug Fisher (Harry Obie), Richard Reeves (Red), Craig Duncan (Pete), Glenn Strange (Sam)

Summary: Harvey Easter has been prospecting for gold in the Rocky Mountains for the last ten years. Now a rich man, he feels compelled to persuade the residents of Dodge to lead commendable lives and work hard. His efforts are met with hostility from the townsfolk, rather than gratitude.

"Cody's Code"

First Broadcast: January 20, 1962
Producer: Norman Macdonnell
Script: John Meston
Photography: Fleet Southcott
Editor: Otto Meyer
Guest Stars: Gloria Talbot (Rose), Anthony Caruso (Cody Durham), Wayne Rogers (Brach), Robert Knapp (Dukes), Ken Becker (Koger), Ollie O'Toole (Postmaster), Robert Gravage (Citizen), Richard Bartell (Hank)), Don Russell (Harry)

Summary: Rose Loring is a saloon girl in the Long Branch. One night she is attacked by a drunken cowboy and Brach Tracy, a customer in the bar, steps up to defend her. Rose, in turn, falls in love with Brach, though she is engaged to Cody Durham, a kindly-mannered carpenter. Cody's pleasant personality vanishes when he learns about Rose's love for Brach and the couple's plan to leave Dodge.

"Old Dan"

First Broadcast: January 27, 1962
Producer: Norman Macdonnell
Script: Kathleen Hite
Photography: Fleet Southcott
Editor: Otto Meyer
Music: Wilbur Hatch
Guest Stars: Edgar Buchanan (Dan Witter), William Campbell (Luke), Philip Coolidge (Lem), Hugh Sanders (Thede), Dorothy Neumann (Mrs. Bales), Joe Haworth (Gates)
Summary: Dan Witter is a hard-bitten alcoholic, but his charismatic manner impresses Doc Adams. With Doc's help, the old man gets a job in town, working as a store clerk. His appetite for drink is too great, though, and he soon goes on a bender, after stealing a supply of vanilla extract from his employer. A second chance for work and sobriety surfaces when a rancher named Lem hires Dan to help out on his farm. Sadly, it doesn't take long before Dan falls off the wagon again. This time, though, he also kills a man — Lem's son.
Comment: Edgar Buchanan (Dan) appeared as Bunny Dull in *McLintock!* William Campbell (Luke) starred as Tommy Dancer in McLaglen's first feature, *Man in the Vault*; he worked with the director in the seventies on the *Hec Ramsey* series, as well. Campbell had also played a pilot in Wellman's *The High and the Mighty* (1954), one of the pictures McLaglen was assigned to as a first assistant during his time at Wayne-Fellows Productions in the early fifties.

"The Gallows"

First Broadcast: March 3, 1962
Producer: Norman Macdonnell
Script: John Meston
Photography: Fleet Southcott
Editor: Otto Meyer
Music: Rene Garriguenc
Guest Stars: Jeremy Slate (Pruit), Joseph Ruskin (Judge), Robert J. Stevenson (Ax), Richard Shannon (Gamer), James Nusser (Louie Pheeters), Orville Sherman (Sheriff), William Challee (Feist), Nancy Walters (Gal), Ollie O'Toole (Milt), Robert Gravage (Hangman)
Summary: Pruit Dover, a poor cowboy, delivers a load of freight to Ax Parsons in Dodge. Rather than pay Pruit for his work, Parsons draws a knife on the cowboy. Dover responds by killing him. Despite the lack of witnesses and compelling evidence, a judge convicts Dover of murder and sentences him to death. Dillon suspects that Dover lacks the temperament to stab a man in cold blood, but he nevertheless agrees to convey the condemned man to Hays City, where his execution is scheduled. En route, the conscience-stricken marshal decides to set Dover free, but the prisoner refuses to go, arguing that he would rather be dead than live the life of a fugitive. Disgusted with himself and Dover's situation, Dillon turns his charge over to the sheriff in Hays City and leaves town immediately, unwilling to watch the poor man hang.

Comment: Jeremy Slate (Pruit) worked again with McLaglen on *The Devil's Brigade* and the television movie *Stowaway to the Moon*.

"Wagon Girls"

First Broadcast: April 7, 1962
Producer: Norman Macdonnell
Script: John Meston
Photography: Fleet Southcott
Editor: Al Joseph
Music: Fred Steiner
Guest Stars: Constance Ford (Florida), Ellen McRae (Polly), Arch Johnson (Feester), John Marshall (Emma), Kevin Hagen (Bowman), William Schallert (Capt. Grant), Ben Wright (Sgt. Pickens), Dabbs Greer (Mr. Jonas), Rayford Barnes (Lee), Joseph Perry (Harve), William Wellman, Jr. (Pvt. King), Buck Young (Cpl. Stone), Gilman Rankin (Chief Red Knife)
Summary: Dillon heads out from Dodge to find a pair of thieves who've stolen a merchant's cashbox. He soon stumbles across a young woman named Polly, who's been sleeping behind a bush on the trail. Polly has run away from a wagon train that is transporting several women to Colorado; the leader of the train, a man named Feester, has been harassing her. Polly explains to Dillon that Feester promised the women who have come with him that they will find rich miners waiting to marry them in Denver. Dillon suspects that this is a scam, that in reality the women will be forced into working as dancehall girls and, perhaps, prostitutes. The marshal then returns Polly to the wagon train, but he stays on in order to help her and the other women avoid their unhappy fate.
Comment: This episode's plot recalls William A. Wellman's *Westward the Women* (1950), another story in which a wagon train is used to convey female passengers across the western frontier. In Wellman's film, the wagon master (played by Robert Taylor) is an honest man who transports his passengers to California to marry farmers. Wellman's son, Bill Wellman, Jr., briefly appears in this episode as a cavalryman. Ellen McRae (Polly) is better known as Ellen Burstyn, the star of William Friedkin's *The Exorcist* (1973) and Martin Scorsese's *Alice Doesn't Live Here Anymore* (1974). "Ellen McRae" itself is a stage name. Burstyn's birth name is Edna Rae Gillooly.[41]

"The Summons"

First Broadcast: April 21, 1962
Producer: Norman Macdonnell
Script: Kathleen Hite, story by Marian Clark
Photography: Fleet Southcott
Editor: Otto Meyer
Guest Stars: John Crawford (Loy Bishop), Robert J. Stevenson (Cape), Myron Healey (Moseley), Bethel Leslie (Rose-Ellen), Cal Bolder (Dawkins), Percy Helton (Duffer), Shug Fisher (Telegrapher)
Summary: Loy Bishop guns down his outlaw friend, Jake Mosley, and heads to Dodge to collect a $1,000 reward. Having never heard of Mosley, Dillon locks up Bishop for murder. When the marshal finds out the dead man really was wanted, he frees Bishop. The assassin is subsequently spurned by the folks of Dodge as he waits to collect his reward money.

162 Andrew V. McLaglen

"The Dreamers"

First Broadcast: April 28, 1962
Producer: Norman Macdonnell
Script: John Meston
Photography: Fleet Southcott
Editor: Otto Meyer
Guest Stars: Liam Redmond (Cairn), J. Pat O'Malley (Fogle), Valerie Allen (Annie), Cece Whitney (Julia), Gage Clarke (Mr. Botkin), Shug Fisher (Obie), Perry Cook (Barkeep), Glenn Strange (Sam)
Summary: A pair of prosperous gold miners comes into Dodge to check on the status of their assets in the town bank and have a drink at the Long Branch. One of the men, Henry Cairn, falls in love with Kitty the moment he sees her. He declares that he will marry her, but she turns away his advances. Cairn then purchases a neighboring saloon to lure Kitty's customers away: if he can break her financially, he hopes, she will acquiesce and agree to be his wife. The plan succeeds only in bankrupting Kitty and she is temporarily forced to shutter the Long Branch.
Comment: An otherwise unremarkable episode, "The Dreamers" features an unusually expressive flashback sequence that deserves consideration. Toward the end of the program, Dillon and Kitty are standing in the Long Branch's nearly empty, shadow-draped barroom. After Dillon says goodnight and leaves, Kitty moves across the floor, glancing at the furniture and walls. Her voice materializes on the soundtrack: "Yeah," she says, "they sure were roaring times in here all right." The camera then draws close on Kitty's face and the flashback begins. Following a dissolve, we see Kitty standing atop a staircase, looking down at the saloon. Flooded with light and filled with customers, the Long Branch is now a merry place. As a piano plays, Kitty descends the stairs. The camera, mounted to a jib, follows and pans to the floor. A saloon girl dances on a tabletop, spinning in a circle. Sitting nearby is Doc Adams, who drinks beer as he watches a pair of men fight. The camera then drifts over to the bar, where Chester is standing, smiling as a bartender smashes a bottle over a drunk's head. Another man moves across the barroom, firing a gun into the ceiling. Dillon snatches the weapon, throws it to the ground and starts toward the bar to get a drink. At this point, the camera pulls back and we see a different saloon girl dancing on a table. Everyone is happy, especially Kitty, who grins as she watches the merriment in the room. The likelihood that anything like this would ever happen in the Long Branch is nil, but the heightened, dreamy nature of the memory gives us a greater understanding of what the saloon means to Kitty and how its closing has hurt her.

"The Prisoner"

First Broadcast: May 19, 1962
Producer: Norman Macdonnell
Script: Robert E. Thompson
Photography: Fleet Southcott
Editor: Otto Meyer
Guest Stars: Andrew Prine (Billy Joe), Nancy Gates (Sarah), Conrad Nagel (Major), Ed Nelson (Seth), Dabbs Greer (Mr. Jonas), Rayford Barnes (Jellicoe), William Phipps (Ham), Charles Fredericks (Hunk), William Corrie (Waiter), Dorothy Neumann (Mrs. Pierson), Cathy Merchant (Sally), Ollie O'Toole (Postmaster), Chris Whitman (Mrs. Thurmon), John Close (Turner)

Summary: An escaped convict named Billy Joe Arlen stops in Dodge for a drink. After starting a fight in the Long Branch, he is told by Dillon to leave town. A few days later, the marshal learns that Billy Joe is an escaped convict. Dillon then sets out to find the fugitive and soon apprehends him on a ranch owned by a man named Maj. Owens. Before Dillon can start back to Dodge with the prisoner, Owens appears and accuses Billy Joe of murdering his son. He asks Dillon to turn Billy Joe over to him, but the marshal refuses, arguing that vigilantism is never justified. Undeterred, the major and another son, Seth, make plans to wrest Billy Joe from Dillon's custody.

Comment: Andrew Prine (Billy Joe) had parts in *The Devil's Brigade*, *Bandolero!* and *Chisum*.

SEASON EIGHT, 1962–1963

"Quint Asper Comes Home"

First Broadcast: September 29, 1962
Producer: Norman Macdonnell
Script: John Meston
Photography: Fleet Southcott
Editor: Otto Meyer
Guest Stars: Burt Reynolds (Quint), Angela Clarke (Topsanah), Michael Keep (Chief), William Zuckert (Asper), Myron Healey (Mike), Harry Carey, Jr. (Grant), Lane Bradford (Bob), Earle Hodgins (Dobie), Dabbs Greer (Mr. Jonas), Robert Hinkle (Cowboy), Foster Brooks (Ed), Michael Barrier (Brave), Henry Beckman (Duff), John Vari (Leader), James Doohan (Davit), Ed Peck (Semple), Robert Gravage (Charlie), Glenn Strange (Sam)
Summary: Quint Asper's father is white and his mother is Comanche. After some racist drifters murder his father, Quint makes an oath to destroy as many white men as he can. To do this, he joins up with his mother's tribe and participates in massacres for three years. During a raid on some buffalo hunters, however, he is shot. Dillon subsequently finds the injured Quint and takes him into Dodge, where Doc Adams nurses the bitter young man back to health. When Quint returns to the Comanches, he finds that he no longer has the ability to murder whites. Dejected by the tribe, Quint heads back to Dodge where Dillon welcomes him and tries to set him up in business.
Comment: In this episode, Burt Reynolds (Quint) made his *Gunsmoke* debut; he stayed with the show until 1965, the same year McLaglen left the program.[42] Robert Gravage (Charlie) had parts in McLaglen's *The Rare Breed*, *The Undefeated* and *"something big."*

"Jenny"

First Broadcast: October 13, 1962
Producer: Norman Macdonnell
Script: John Meston
Photography: Fleet Southcott
Editor: Al Joseph
Guest Stars: Ruta Lee (Jenny), Ron Hayes (Zel), John Duke (Flack), James Nusser (Louie Pheeters), Barry Cahill (Chuck), Ken Hudgins (Pete), Monte Montana, Jr. (Joe)
Summary: A bank robber named Zel Meyers and his girlfriend, Jenny, come to Dodge. After Zel loses $1,500 in a poker game, he assaults the man who won his money in an alley, killing him. Though there are no witnesses, Dillon suspects Zel is guilty of the crime and locks him up. Separated from Zel, Jenny turns her attention to the marshal and tries to seduce him.

"The Trappers"

First Broadcast: November 3, 1962
Producer: Norman Macdonnell
Script: John Dunkel
Photography: Fleet Southcott
Editor: Al Joseph
Guest Stars: Strother Martin (Billy), Richard Shannon (Tug), Doris Singleton (Irma), Robert Lowery (Idaho), Lane Chandler (Luke), Chal Johnson (Tom), Robert Brubaker (Jim Buck), Glenn Strange (Sam)
Summary: Billy and Tug make their living poaching game on tribal land. After Tug is attacked and stabbed by an Indian, his partner abandons him, certain the injured man will die. Billy then heads to Dodge where he sells the pelts he and Tug have collected for $6,000. The high sum he earns draws the attention of a local dressmaker named Irma and her swindler boyfriend, Idaho Smith. As the two crooks scheme to separate Billy from his money, Dillon learns that Tug is still alive and he brings the wounded trapper into Dodge. Once Tug recovers his strength, he heads out to find — and punish — his former partner.
Comment: Robert Lowery (Idaho) played the Texas governor in *McLintock!* and Doris Day's husband in *The Ballad of Josie*.

"Phoebe"

First Broadcast: November 10, 1962
Producer: Norman Macdonnell
Script: John Meston
Photography: Fleet Southcott
Editor: Otto Meyer
Guest Stars: Virginia Gregg (Phoebe), Joan Freeman (Annie), Don Megowan (Oliver), Phyllis Coates (Rose), Gregg Palmer (Hulett), Harry Raybould (Casper), Dick Peabody (Simsie), John McLiam (Sam Kinney), Phil Chambers (Ned), Marilyn Harvey (Mary), Glenn Strange (Sam)
Summary: Phoebe Strunk and her four psychopathic sons prey on farmers and travelers, killing them for their money. When the Strunk family abducts a young girl, Dillon and Quint set out from Dodge to rescue her, tracking the kidnappers through the rain.
Comment: McLaglen returned to the "kidnapped female" theme in *Bandolero!*, having Dean Martin and a gang of violent criminals abduct Raquel Welch. Unlike the cruel Strunks, Martin's character not only experiences remorse for seizing the woman, but also falls in love with her. Kidnappings surface in McLaglen's *"something big," The Last Hard Men, The Shadow Riders* and *Sahara*, too.

"Abe Blocker"

First Broadcast: November 24, 1962
Producer: Norman Macdonnell
Script: John Meston
Photography: Fleet Southcott
Editor: Otto Meyer
Guest Stars: Chill Wills (Abe Blocker), Wright King (Bud), Dabbs Greer (Mr. Jonas), Harry Carey, Jr. (Jake), Miranda Jones (Mary Groves), Robert Adler (Emmett), Marshall Reed (Sam Vestal), Lane Bradford (Gant), Wallace Rooney (Dan Binney), Chuck Roberson (Joe), Glenn Strange (Sam)

Summary: Abe Blocker lives off the rugged land outside Dodge, hunting game, sleeping under the trees, making his own "mountainshine." The arrival of farmers and their transformation of the wilderness into pastures and crops have upset him to the point of madness, prompting him to terrorize the newcomers. Though sympathetic to Abe's concern for the land, Dillon decides to bring the old man in from the forest and put him behind bars.

Comment: Chill Wills (Abe) had roles in McLaglen's *The Little Shepherd of Kingdom Come* and *McLintock!*

"Us Haggens"

First Broadcast: December 8, 1962
Producer: Norman Macdonnell
Script: Les Crutchfield
Photography: Fleet Southcott
Editor: Al Joseph
Guest Stars: Ken Curtis (Festus), Denver Pyle (Haggens), Elizabeth MacRae (April), Billy Hughes (Timmy), Howard Wright (Dietzer)
Summary: As Dillon hunts for a killer named "Black" Jack Haggens, he is joined by a drifter named Festus Haggens. Festus explains that he is the fugitive's nephew and that he blames his uncle for the death of his brother and now wants revenge.
Comment: This episode marks Ken Curtis's first performance on *Gunsmoke* as Festus. Festus would become a regular character on the series in the subsequent season and stay on the show until *Gunsmoke*'s cancellation in 1975. McLaglen recommended Curtis for the role of Festus.[43]

"False Front"

First Broadcast: December 22, 1962
Producer: Norman Macdonnell
Script: John Meston, story by Hal Moffett
Photography: Fleet Southcott
Editor: Al Joseph
Guest Stars: Andrew Prine (Clay), William Windom (Hill), Art Lund (Heber), Charles Fredericks (Senator), Shary Marshall (Rita), Wallace Rooney (Dale Binney), Robert Fortier (Ray Costa), Brett King (Hank), K.L. Smith (Pete), William Bryant (Joe), Roy Thinnes (Harry), Michael Mikler (Bill)
Summary: Paul Nill is a cynical newspaperman who bets Nick Heber, a professional gambler, that he can persuade the residents of Dodge that a young laborer named Clay Tatum is a dangerous gunfighter. If Clay can maintain the masquerade and stay alive for two weeks, Heber will pay Nill $1,000. But if Clay can't do this, Nill must pay the same to Heber.

"The Renegades"

First Broadcast: January 12, 1963
Producer: Norman Macdonnell
Script: John Meston
Photography: Fleet Southcott
Editor: Al Joseph
Guest Stars: Audrey Dalton (Lavinia), Ben Wright (Colonel), Jack Lambert (Brice), Donald Barry (McIver), John Pickard (Poole), Ed Faulkner (Sergeant), Linda Hutchins (Ruth), Bob Steele (Sam Gordon), Alan Dexter (Trask), Joseph Bassett (Leader)

Summary: Quint is hired to ride shotgun on a stage that is headed for Oklahoma. One of the passengers is Lavinia Pate, the daughter of a cavalry officer. A bigot, Lavinia treats Quint with disdain because his mother was a Comanche. When a gang of robbers attacks the coach, Quint rescues Lavinia and afterward the woman begins to reconsider her attitude toward Native Americans.

Comment: Donald "Red" Barry (McIver) was a contract player at Republic Pictures in the forties who appeared in Western programmers like *The Apache Kid* (1941) and *Outlaws of Santa Fe* (1944), and the serial *Adventures of Red Ryder* (1940). McLaglen later cast him as Jack Hawkins in *Bandolero!* Bob Steele (Sam Gordon) also appeared in several "B" Westerns for Republic in the thirties and forties, including *The Colorado Kid* (1937) and *Billy the Kid in Texas* (1940). Steele had small parts in McLaglen's *McLintock!* and *Shenandoah*.[44]

"Two of a Kind"

First Broadcast: March 16, 1963
Producer: Norman Macdonnell
Script: Merwin Gerard
Photography: Robert Pittack
Editor: Al Joseph
Guest Stars: Richard Jaeckel (O'Ryan), Michael Higgins (Finnegan), Kent Smith (Bealton), Earle Hodgins (Judge), Ben Wright (Harris), Garry Walberg (Anson), John Mitchum (Wills), Glenn Strange (Sam), Bee Tompkins (Girl)
Summary: O'Ryan and Finnegan are longtime friends who have turned against one another over a woman. Irish immigrants, the two share ownership of a salt mine outside Dodge. When their feud turns violent, a judge orders them to look out for another: if one of the men should die under suspicious circumstances, the other will be charged with murder. The judge's decision prompts a group of corrupt speculators to turn their sights on Finnegan. If they can kill him, O'Ryan will hang, and ownership of the salt mine will be turned over to them.
Comment: Richard Jaeckel (O'Ryan) had parts in McLaglen's *The Devil's Brigade*, *Chisum* and *The Dirty Dozen: Next Mission*.

"With a Smile"

First Broadcast: March 30, 1963
Producer: Norman Macdonnell
Script: John Meston, story by Bud Furillo & George Main
Photography: Frank Phillips
Editor: Al Joseph
Guest Stars: James Best (Dal), R.G. Armstrong (Maj. Cree), Sharon Farrell (Lottie), Linden Chiles (Pat), Dick Foran (Sheriff), Dan Stafford (Kelly), Robert J. Stevenson (Foy), Gilman Rankin (Waiter), James Nusser (Louie Pheeters), Jay Della (Cowboy)
Summary: Dal Cree is the spoiled son of a rich landowner named Maj. Cree. After one of the women who work in the Long Branch reproves him, Dal shoots her dead and is soon arrested. Unable to accept that his son may be a killer, Maj. Cree attempts to win a reprieve for him. Failing, he asks Dal to accept his imminent death with courage, to walk to the scaffold "with a smile." As it becomes apparent that his son hasn't got a strong enough personality for this, the major persuades the sheriff who is overseeing the hanging to trick Dal into believing that he will be allowed to escape and flee to Mexico.

"Quint-Cident"

First Broadcast: April 27, 1963
Producer: Norman Macdonnell
Script: Kathleen Hite
Photography: Frank Phillips
Editor: Al Joseph
Guest Stars: Mary La Roche (Willa), Ben Johnson (Ben Crown), Don Keefer (Nally), Catherine McLeod (Lizzie), Ollie O'Toole (Telegrapher)
Summary: As Dillon and Quint bring Ben Crown, a suspected murderer, back to Dodge, they find a woman named Willa burying several family members in a plot behind her house. The men take care of the widow as best they can, preparing food and tending to the graves. But when they ask Willa to join them as they start again for town, she declines. Later, Quint stops by to visit and provide Willa with some food. She misinterprets his concern as an expression of romantic desire. Around the same time, Ben Crown is released from jail in Dodge, after Dillon determines that Crown is not guilty of murder. Crown then heads to Willa's house and assaults her. Instead of attributing the attack to Crown, Willa blames Quint.
Comment: Ben Johnson (Crown) first worked with McLaglen on *Wild Stallion* (1952), a low-budget Western directed by Lewis D. Collins on which McLaglen served as an assistant director. Johnson would subsequently appear in McLaglen's *The Rare Breed*, *Chisum* and *"something big."*

"The Odyssey of Jubal Tanner"

First Broadcast: May 18, 1963
Producer: Norman Macdonnell
Script: Paul Savage
Photography: Frank Phillips
Editor: Al Joseph
Guest Stars: Beverly Garland (Leah), Peter Brick (Jubal), Denver Pyle (Aaron), Kevin Hagen (Hobie), Gregg Palmer (Fletcher), George Selk (Moss Gimmick), Hal Needham (Cowboy)
Summary: Dirt farmer Aaron Larker has fallen in love with saloon girl Leah Brunson. On the same night Aaron proposes to Leah, a drunken buffalo hunter named Collie Fletcher punches the farmer in the head, fracturing his skull and killing him. While tracking Collie, Dillon finds an injured man lying beneath a tree on the trail, named Jubal Tanner. A former Confederate soldier, Tanner explains that Collie shot him and stole his horse. Embittered by the war, Tanner shows no gratitude to the marshal as he's brought in to Dodge. His surly manner arouses the anger of the people he meets in town, including Leah, the saloon girl who was engaged to Aaron Larker. But when Leah is attacked by her dead fiancé's lovestruck brother, Hobie, Tanner gallantly defends her, stopping Hobie with a bullet. Tanner may not be as self-centered or as hardhearted as he's seemed, Leah realizes, and she wonders if the two might someday find happiness together.

"The Quest for Asa Janin"

First Broadcast: June 1, 1963
Producer: Norman Macdonnell
Script: Paul Savage
Photography: Frank Phillips

Editor: Al Joseph
Music: Van Cleave
Guest Stars: Anthony Caruso (Macklin), Richard Devon (Janin), Jack Lambert (Scotsman), George Keymas (Pardee), Joseph Siroloa (Leroy), James Nusser (Louie Pheeters), Gene Darfler (Dave), Harry Carey, Jr. (Colridge), Lane Chandler (Warden), Ed Faulkner (Deputy), Pedro Gonzalez Gonzalez (Bartender)
Summary: Dave Ingalls has been convicted of murdering his girlfriend, but Dillon is certain the man is innocent. His hunches are confirmed when he learns from a drifter that a man named Asa Janin has admitted that he is the killer. Dillon soon sets out to Texas to find Janin. But will he find him before Ingalls hangs?
Comment: Pedro Gonzalez Gonzalez briefly appears in this episode as a bartender. He and McLaglen first worked together on the features *Ring of Fear* and *The High and the Mighty*, when McLaglen was an assistant director under contract at Wayne-Fellows Productions. Gonzalez Gonzalez also appeared in the first two features McLaglen directed, *Man in the Vault* and *Gun the Man Down*, as well as the later pictures *Hellfighters* and *Chisum*.

SEASON NINE, 1963–1964

"Lover Boy"

First Broadcast: October 5, 1963
Producer: Norman Macdonnell
Script: John Meston
Photography: Frank Phillips
Editor: Otto Meyer
Music: Fred Steiner
Guest Stars: Sheree North (Avis), Ken Curtis (Kyle), Alan Baxter (Ab), Carol Bryon (Terry), Richard Coogan (Luke), Allan Hunt (Boy)
Summary: Kyle Kelley has a hearty appetite for women. Upon his arrival in Dodge, he fixes his attention on Avis Fisher, a pretty, married woman who doesn't love her husband, a dirt farmer named Ab. Kyle and Avis begin to see one another in the afternoons and Ab becomes suspicious. When Kyle suggests that he and Avis can start out for Colorado together and enjoy a new life if someone killed Ab, Avis responds with enthusiasm. Tragedy soon follows.

"Easy Come"

First Broadcast: October 26, 1963
Producer: Norman Macdonnell
Script: John Meston
Photography: Frank Phillips
Editor: James Baiotto
Guest Stars: Andrew Prine (Sippy), Carl Reindel (Calhoun), George Wallace (Tobin), Dave Willock (Clerk), Charles Briggs (Riley), Orville Sherman (Wib Smith), Chubby Johnson (Barr), David Manley (Parks), Sam Edwards (Morff), K.L. Smith (King), Dallas Mitchell (Cowboy), Shug Fisher (Harry), Peggy Rea (Lady)
Summary: Elmo Sippy is an itinerant grafter whose potential for cruelty is belied by his mild appearance. After losing big in a card game at the Long Branch, he heads out from Dodge on a crime spree, robbing and killing several men. As Dillon and Chester search for Sippy outside town, the murderer returns to Dodge, looking to win his money back at the poker table.

"Prairie Wolfer"

First Broadcast: January 18, 1964
Producer: Norman Macdonnell
Script: John Dunkel
Photography: Frank Phillips
Editor: Otto Meyer
Guest Stars: Noah Beery, Jr. (Nate Guthrie), Don Dubbins (Wendt), Holly McIntire (Sarah), Fred Coby (Charlie), Glenn Strange (Sam), James Drake (Dude)
Summary: Festus Haggens is hired by some cattlemen to eliminate wolves that have been attacking their cows on rangeland outside Dodge. A rancher named Guthrie takes a dislike to Festus, arguing that the "prairie wolfer" covets his daughter. He also charges Festus with killing cows and selling the beef on the black market. In reality, Guthrie is the one who is guilty of this crime.
Comment: In this episode, Ken Curtis made his second appearance as Festus on *Gunsmoke*. Festus would remain on the series as a regular character until *Gunsmoke*'s cancellation in 1975. In the thirties, Noah Beery, Jr. (Guthrie) was McLaglen's classmate at Cates School in Carpinteria, California.[45]

"Once a Haggen"

First Broadcast: February 1, 1964
Producer: Norman Macdonnell
Script: Les Crutchfield
Photography: Frank Phillips
Editor: Al Joseph
Guest Stars: Slim Pickens (Bucko), Elizabeth McRae (April), John Hudson (Curly), Kenneth Tobey (Fickett), Roy Barcroft (Pop), Howard Wendell (Judge)
Summary: A drummer named Fickett comes to Dodge and wins big in a poker game at the Long Branch. Festus and his cowhand pal, Bucko, joke about robbing Fickett as they set out for a night of drinking. The next morning, Fickett is found dead in his room, and the evidence Dillon finds at the crime scene indicates that Bucko is the murderer. A trial follows and the jury finds Bucko guilty, condemning him to the gallows. Festus and his girlfriend, April, then make an effort to save their friend, but they use different means. While April searches for evidence that will prove the cowboy is innocent, Festus uses a gun to spring Bucko from the town jail.
Comment: Ken Curtis sings on several occasions in this episode. Curtis actually got his start in the entertainment industry as a singer. In the forties, he performed with the Tommy Dorsey Band and also the Sons of the Pioneers, a cowboy music act.[46]

"No Hands"

First Broadcast: February 8, 1964
Producer: Norman Macdonnell
Script: John Meston
Photography: Frank Phillips
Editor: Otto Meyer
Guest Stars: Denver Pyle (Pa), Strother Martin (Timble), Kevin Hagen (Emmett), Rayford Barnes (Jess), Conlan Carter (Ben), Wright King (Lon), Orville Sherman (Wib Smith), James Nusser (Louie Pheeters), Shug Fisher (Barkeep), Mark Murray (Boy), Glenn Strange (Sam)

Summary: Timble is an impoverished wood carver who lives in a shack near Dodge with his dog. As he crafts a sign for Miss Kitty, a bit of wood strikes Timble in the eye, and Doc Adams takes him up to his office to tend the injury. While the doctor treats his patient, a deranged drifter named Pa Ginnis enters the office and tells Doc to fix his son's injured leg immediately. Doc declines, explaining that he needs to finish up with Timble's eye first. Enraged, Pa Ginnis and his sons promise to vent their anger on the little wood carver. When they get their chance, they stomp his hand, destroying his livelihood.

"May Blossoms"

First Broadcast: February 15, 1964
Producer: Norman Macdonnell
Script: Kathleen Hite
Photography: Frank Phillips
Editor: Otto Meyer
Guest Stars: Lauri Peters (Mayblossom), Charles Gray (Lon), Richard X. Slattery (Greer), Sarah Selby (Ma Smalley), Roger Torrey (Feeder)
Summary: Mayblossom Haggens has come up to Dodge from Texas to marry her second cousin, Festus, to whom she's been engaged since she was born. Unaware of this arrangement himself, Festus nevertheless elects to help Mayblossom and find her a place to live. Sadly, an itinerant carpenter named Lon Harder hates Festus, having lost to him at the poker table; and for revenge, Harder rapes Mayblossom. When Festus learns about this, he murders the carpenter, a crime that Marshal Dillon ultimately chooses to overlook.

"The Bassops"

First Broadcast: February 22, 1964
Producer: Norman Macdonnell
Script: Tom Hanley
Photography: Frank Phillips
Editor: Otto Meyer
Guest Stars: Robert J. Wilke (Kelby), Warren Oates (Deke), Mickey Sholdar (Tommy), James Griffith (Harford), Eunice Pollis (Mellie), James Nusser (Louie Pheeters), Ollie O'Toole (Telegrapher), Robert Bice (Wilson), Glenn Strange (Sam), Patricia Joyce (Donna Lee)
Summary: Dillon apprehends Kelby, a fugitive killer. As they make their way to Dodge, the criminal attacks the marshal on the side of a hill. Both men fall from their horses, injuring their heads and losing consciousness. Dillon also loses his badge in the scuffle. A short time later, a drifter named Deke Bassop finds the two men lying in the dirt. Bassop starts for Dodge, towing them from his wagon on a travois. Kelby returns to consciousness first and tells his rescuer that he is a United States marshal and that Dillon is his prisoner. When Dillon wakes up, he makes the same claim. Unable to determine which man is telling the truth, Bassop keeps the two tied together and continues toward Dodge.

"The Kite"

First Broadcast: February 29, 1964
Producer: Norman Macdonnell
Script: John Meston
Photography: Frank Phillips
Editor: Al Joseph

Music: Richard Shores
Guest Stars: Lyle Bettger (Polk), Michael Higgins (Cassidy), Allyson Ames (Clara), Betsy Hale (Letty), Sarah Selby (Ma Smalley), Burt Douglas (Bryan), Glenn Strange (Sam)
Summary: When a sinister rider shows up at her prairie home, Clara Cassidy tells her daughter Letty to hide. The stranger, a bank robber named Polk, subsequently shoots Clara dead and sets out to Dodge, unaware that Letty has witnessed the crime. Once the child's father returns home and discovers the murder, he takes Letty to Dodge, hoping she will recognize the killer. The strategy is not only ineffective, but dangerous, as it alerts Polk to the child's existence and the threat she poses to him.

"Now That April's Here"

First Broadcast: March 21, 1964
Producer: Norman Macdonnell
Script: Les Crutchfield
Photography: Frank Phillips
Editor: Otto Meyer
Guest Stars: Elizabeth MacRae (April), Royal Dano (Bender), Hal Baylor (Grody), Vic Perrin (Argus), Glenn Strange (Sam)
Summary: Called out of town, Dillon asks Quint to watch his office for him. That night, Festus's girlfriend, April, witnesses some men hiding a corpse in a barrel. She tells Quint and Festus about this, but they refuse to believe her. When Dillon returns, he listens to April's remarks carefully and takes action.
Commentary: Royal Dano (Bender) appeared in McLaglen's *The Undefeated*, playing the Confederate officer who tells John Wayne's character Col. Thomas that the Civil War has ended. Dano also appears briefly in *Cahill, United States Marshal* as a hermit.

"The Promoter"

First Broadcast: April 25, 1964
Producer: Norman Macdonnell
Script: John Meston
Photography: Frank Phillips
Editor: Otto Meyer
Music: Tommy Morgan
Guest Stars: Vic Perrin (Huckaby), Allen Case (Lieutenant), Robert Fortier (Sergeant), Don Collier (Price), Larry Blake (Shell), Peggy Stewart (Daisy), Gregg Palmer (Jake), Wilhelm von Homburg (Otto), John Newman (Johnny Towers), James Nusser (Louie Pheeters), Shug Fisher (Obie), Hank Patterson (Hank)
Summary: Henry Huckaby, a poor farmer, imagines he has a better chance of getting rich if he moves to Dodge. After losing much of his money in a poker game, he decides to promote a prizefight between a drifter and a recently discharged cavalry scout. Boxing is illegal in Kansas, however, and when Dillon calls an end to the match, Huckaby forgoes his dream of making easy money and returns to his farm.

"The Warden"

First Broadcast: May 16, 1964
Producer: Norman Macdonnell
Script: Les Crutchfield

Photography: Frank Phillips
Editor: Otto Meyer
Guest Stars: George Kennedy (Stark), Anthony Caruso (Bull Foot), Julie Parrish (Cool Dawn), Chris Connelly (Trainey), Ollie O'Toole (Telegrapher)
Summary: Bull Foot is a swindler who pretends to sell his daughter, Cool Dawn, to a drifter named Stark. Stark demands revenge after Cool Dawn runs off from him and returns to her father's home.

"The Other Half"

First Broadcast: May 30, 1964
Producer: Norman Macdonnell
Script: John Dunkel
Photography: Frank Phillips
Editor: Otto Meyer
Guest Stars: Lee Kinsolving (Jess Bartell/Jay Bartell), Donna Anderson (Nancy), Paul Fix (Sam Bartell), Patric Knowles (MacIntosh), Larry Blake (Mr. Hoover), Dave Cass (Minister), Robert Gravage (Barney)
Summary: When Jay Bartell is murdered, his twin brother, Jess, presses Dillon to find the killer. As the marshal conducts his investigation, Jay begins to act erratically, fighting with people, yelling at his father, even proposing to his dead brother's fiancée. Eventually Dillon wonders if the young man's strange behavior may actually be an expression of a guilty conscience.

SEASON TEN, 1964–1965

"Crooked Mile"

First Broadcast: October 3, 1964
Producer: Norman Macdonnell
Script: Les Crutchfield
Photography: Frank Phillips
Editor: Otto Meyer
Music: Rudy Schrager
Guest Stars: George Kennedy (Degler), Royal Dano (Praylie), Katharine Ross (Susan)
Summary: Susan Degler's father hates Indians. When Susan falls in love with Quint, Degler reacts with anger because the blacksmith's mother is Comanche. Learning that Susan plans to marry Quint, Degler recruits one of his kin to go to Dodge and persuade Quint to miss the wedding, killing him if he refuses.
Comment: McLaglen cast Ross (Susan) to play the role of Ann in *Shenandoah*, her first big screen role. Ross would gain fame later in the sixties for her appearance as Dustin Hoffman's love interest in Mike Nichols's *The Graduate* (1967).[47] She again worked with McLaglen on *Hellfighters* and two television productions in the eighties, *The Shadow Riders* and *Travis McGee*.

"Chicken"

First Broadcast: December 5, 1964
Producer: Norman Macdonnell
Script: John Meston
Photography: Frank Phillips

Editor: Otto Meyer
Music: Fred Steiner
Guest Stars: Glenn Corbett (Dan Collins), Gigi Perreau (Lucy), John Lupton (Carl), L.Q. Jones (Brady), Lane Chandler (Morgan), Dave Willock (Becker), Lane Bradford (Davis), Chubby Johnson (Rogers), Roy Barcroft (Roy), Michael Keep (Willis), John Pickard (Phelps), Bob Steele (Coe)
Summary: A group of travelers mistakenly credits a cowpoke named Dan Collins with singlehandedly stopping a stagecoach robbery. Collins enjoys the attention he receives from the story, especially when he visits Dodge, where he's treated as a hero. One morning in town, Collins meets and falls in love with a young woman named Lucy Benton, who lives on a farm with her crippled brother, Carl. When Lucy refuses his advances, Collins concludes that she's afraid of him and his reputation as a killer. Wanting to correct this perception, he visits the woman on her farm and tells her the truth, confessing that he's not only a liar, but a coward, too. Shortly after Collins leaves the Bentons' farm, Lucy and her brother are visited by Wes Morgan, a neighboring rancher who wants to scare the pair off of their land. To get this done, Morgan has brought along several armed thugs. When Collins turns and sees what's happening, he's faced with a hard choice: run away to safety or risk his life to help the Bentons.
Comment: Glenn Corbett (Collins) had parts in McLaglen's *Shenandoah*, *Chisum* and *The Log of the Black Pearl*. Lane Chandler (Morgan) appeared in McLaglen's *The Little Shepherd of Kingdom Come* and *One More Train to Rob*.

"Bank Baby"

First Broadcast: March 20, 1965
Producer: Norman Macdonnell
Script: John Meston
Photography: Frank Phillips
Editor: Otto Meyer
Guest Stars: Jacques Aubuchon (Bert), Gail Kobe (Grace), Virginia Christine (Bess), Hampton Fancher (Milton), Roy Roberts (Mr. Botkin), Harry Carey, Jr. (Fisher), William Boyett (Harry), Cliff Ketchum (Teller)
Summary: Tired of being poor, Bert Clum decides to rob a bank in Dodge with his wife, Bess. Before he heads into town, he kidnaps a baby from the Fishers, a family traveling across Kansas in a wagon train. Clum figures that if Bess holds the baby in her arms during the robbery, the bank's guard will be less likely to shoot at them when they make their escape. A bigot, Mr. Fisher assumes that only an Indian would abduct a white baby: he even accuses Quint Asper of playing a role in the crime. Fisher's theories and actions prove to be a distraction for Dillon as he tries to find the real kidnappers.

Have Gun, Will Travel

Have Gun, Will Travel in the sixties continued to earn the same high ratings it enjoyed in the previous decade. Few changes were introduced during this period, with the show's producers continuing to have episodes shot on location in rugged landscape settings like Bend, Oregon and Lone Pine, California. But the program was cancelled in 1963, after Richard Boone decided he was no longer interested in playing the role of Paladin. Before the start of the series' fourth season (1960–1961), Kam Tong, the actor who played Paladin's helpful friend Hey Boy, left *Have Gun* to appear on another CBS program, *Mr. Garlund*. Actress Lisa Lu replaced him, playing a character Paladin called "Hey Girl." Following the cancellation of *Mr. Garlund* in the spring of 1961, Kam Tong returned to *Have Gun* to reprise his role and the Hey Girl character disappeared.[48]

Season Four, 1960–1961

"Love's Young Dream"

First Broadcast: September 17, 1960
Producer: Frank R. Pierson
Script: Jay Simms
Photography: Frank Phillips
Editor: Everett Sutherland
Guest Stars: Ken Curtis (Monk), Lorna Thayer (Augusta), Mike Mazurki (Power), Hal Needham (Bartender)
Summary: An ill-mannered itinerant named Monk trades his life in the wilderness for San Francisco to collect on an inheritance, a share in a saloon in upscale Nob Hill.
Comment: In this episode, Monk makes his second appearance on *Have Gun, Will Travel*. Curtis first played the character in the series' third season (1959–1960), in an episode titled "The Naked Gun," which McLaglen also directed. A scruffy troublemaker, Monk would serve as the model for the Festus character Curtis played on *Gunsmoke* from 1964 to 1975.[49]

"A Head of Hair"

First Broadcast: September 24, 1960
Producer: Frank R. Pierson
Script: Harry Julian Fink
Photography: Frank Phillips
Editor: Everett Sutherland
Music: Jerry Goldsmith
Guest Stars: Ben Johnson (John Anderson), Trevor Bardette (Chagra), George Kennedy (Lt. Bryson), Donna Books (Mary Grange), Chuck Hayward (Cheyup), Olan Soulé (Manager)
Summary: A band of Nez Percé Indians has abducted a white woman for her golden hair. Paladin hires on an Indian scout from an army post named John Anderson to help him find her. Although he is white, Anderson considers himself a member of the Sioux nation because of the many years he spent living with the tribe. His life ruined by drink, Anderson longs to prove to himself and others that he is still a strong warrior.

"The Tender Gun"

First Broadcast: October 22, 1960
Producer: Frank R. Pierson
Script: Jay Simms
Photography: Frank Phillips
Editor: Everett Sutherland
Guest Stars: Jeanette Nolan (Maude), Lou Antonio (Greve), Tom Reese (Yates), Herbert Patterson (Heck), Don Keefer (Corcoran)
Summary: Sheriff Maude Smugley owns a spread that is rich with oil. Because the sheriff has refused to sell her land to him, a speculator named Yates has recruited several gunmen to change the old lady's mind. The sheriff asks Paladin to help her with her problem, even

pleading with him to kill the others, though he refuses at first. When the hired guns descend on the town jail and begin to fire at him and the sheriff, however, Paladin changes his mind.

"Fogg Bound"

First Broadcast: December 3, 1960
Producer: Frank R. Pierson
Script: Shimon Wincelberg, based on *Around the World in Eighty Days* by Jules Verne
Photography: Frank Phillips
Editor: Everett Sutherland
Music: Fred Steiner
Guest Stars: Patric Knowles (Phileas Fogg), Peter Whitney (Maj. Proctor), Jon Silo (Jean Passepartout), Arlene McQuade (Aouda)
Summary: Phileas Fogg, the hero of Jules Verne's 1873 novel *Around the World in Eighty Days*, makes an appearance in this episode. Having missed his train from San Francisco to Reno, Fogg hires Paladin to serve as a guide, leading him and his entourage through the Sierras. Reaching Reno is not the only challenge facing Fogg. He is also being followed by a violent drifter who covets the money that the world traveler carries in one of his bags.

"The Legacy"

First Broadcast: December 10, 1960
Producer: Frank R. Pierson
Script: Robert E. Thompson
Photography: Frank Phillips
Editor: Samuel Gold
Guest Stars: Roy Barcroft (Carter), Harry Lauter (Crawford), Harry Carey, Jr. (Burton), Chuck Roberson (Pike), George Kennedy (Tarnitizer).
Summary: Paladin joins a group of vigilantes as they search for a fugitive named Tarnitizer. After Paladin shoots Tarnitizer, the dying man has a will quickly drawn up, which bequeaths his entire fortune to Paladin, if, and only if, the gunfighter stays alive on the trail back to town. Eager to claim Tarnitizer's fortune for themselves, the vigilantes take measures to capture — and kill — Paladin.

"The Fatal Flaw"

First Broadcast: February 25, 1961
Producer: Frank R. Pierson
Script: Jack Laird
Photography: Frank Phillips
Editor: Samuel Gold
Guest Stars: Royal Dano (Curley Ashburne), Jena Engstrom (Cassandra), Miguel de Anda (Salazar), Allyn Joslyn (McKendrick)
Summary: Paladin and a marshal named McKendrick have captured Curley Ashburne, a professional criminal. Bringing Curley down from the mountain where's he been hiding is proving to be difficult. Not only has the marshal been shot, but a heavy snowstorm has come in. The three men seek shelter in an abandoned shack. Curley's hands may be restrained, but he is free to speak, and he uses his words to torment the marshal and tempt him into betraying his duties as a lawman.

"Bearbait"

First Broadcast: May 13, 1961
Producer: Frank R. Pierson
Script: Robert E. Thompson
Photography: Frank Phillips
Editor: Samuel Gold
Music: Jerome Moross
Guest Stars: Judi Meredith (Sally), Martin West (Bunk), Stephen Roberts (Sheriff), Richard Rust (Sim), Ralph Reed (Bert), Frank Ferguson (Kincaid), Jack Tesler (Father)
Summary: While completing a job for a client in a rural western town, Paladin meets a young barmaid named Sally who pleads with him to take her to San Francisco. The woman changes her mind when three young cowhands ridicule Paladin and threaten his life. Paladin subsequently neutralizes the bullies, and Sally asks him again to take her to San Francisco. The gunfighter, disappointed by her fickleness, scolds the young woman instead.
Comment: McLaglen manages to invest this episode with suspense and poignancy, despite the mundane premise of its plot. Sally may be flighty, but the barmaid is nevertheless a sympathetic character, as she longs to leave home because her saloon owner father mistreats her and pays her poor wages. To a certain degree, Sally anticipates the central character in McLaglen's *The Ballad of Josie*, a housewife whose abusive husband has limited her ability to make choices for herself and enjoy life fully. Martin West, the lead in McLaglen's *Freckles*, plays one of the heavies in this episode.

"The Road"

First Broadcast: May 27, 1961
Producer: Frank R. Pierson
Script: Frank R. Pierson
Photography: Frank Phillips
Editor: Otto Meyer
Music: Rene Garriguenc
Guest Stars: Trevor Bardette (Hensoe), Gene Lyons (Merton), Perry Cook (Sibley), Joel Crothers (John), Ben Wright (Beaman), George Kennedy (Preston)
Summary: Paladin is traveling through the mountains for an unspecified reason. Needing a place to sleep, he pays for a night in a group tent along a mountain trail. His sleep is interrupted by a man who tries to pick his pocket. When Paladin complains, the owner of the tent fails to take action and the gunfighter leaves the camp. Infuriated by the accusations that have been leveled at him, the pickpocket sets out after Paladin, bushwhacks him and takes his gun. He then forces Paladin into the woods and commences to pursue him like a hunter following prey.

"Long Way Home"

First Broadcast: February 4, 1961
Producer: Frank R. Pierson
Script: Shimon Wincelberg
Photography: Frank Phillips
Guest Stars: Ivan Dixon (Spruce), John Milford (Hutton), Rayford Barnes (Deputy), William Talman (Sheriff)
Summary: Isham Spruce, a freed slave, left his wife and daughter in Georgia to earn a living

wage in the West. But when a racist co-worker taunted him, he responded by killing the man. Now Paladin and an angry sheriff's posse are in pursuit of Spruce. While the others are eager for his head, Paladin regards the fugitive as a tragic figure and tries to help him.

Comment: Actor William Talman plays a sheriff in this episode; Talman had worked with McLaglen on several episodes of *Perry Mason* in the fifties. He subsequently appeared in McLaglen's *The Ballad of Josie*.

"The Siege"

First Broadcast: April 1, 1961
Producer: Frank R. Pierson
Script: Jack Curtis
Photography: Frank Phillips
Editor: Everett Sutherland
Music: Rene Garriguenc
Guest Stars: David J. Stewart (Kessler), Perry Lopez (Bobby Joe), Robert Karnes (Tyler), Mike Kellin (Alvah), Russ Bender (Doctor), Brad Weston (Theo)
Summary: The Brent brothers have a predilection for poisoning the water supply in a desert town outside Phoenix. To keep their wells free of poison, the locals have to pay the brothers protection money. Tired of this situation, some townsfolk capture the youngest of the Brents, Bobby Joe. Anticipating retribution from the other Brents, the town hires Paladin to watch over the prisoner.
Comment: Perry Lopez (Bobby Joe) appeared in *McLintock!*, *The Rare Breed* and *Bandolero!*

"My Brother's Keeper"

First Broadcast: May 6, 1961
Producer: Frank R. Pierson
Script: Jay Simms
Photography: Frank Phillips
Editor: Samuel Gold
Music: Lucien Moraweck
Guest Stars: Wright King (Cull), Betsy Jones-Moreland (Topaz), Ed Nelson (Rack), Karly Swenson (Sheriff), Ben Wright (Boggs), Otto Waldis (Kress), Allen Wood (Forbes)
Summary: After a puma attacks him, Paladin lies on the ground, nearly dead. Two drifters stumble upon the stricken gunfighter, but instead of helping him, they steal his horse and the $2,500 he's carrying in his saddle. Paladin manages to keep himself alive and starts out to find the two men, ready to reclaim his lost possessions and deliver revenge.

"The Uneasy Grave"

First Broadcast: June 3, 1961
Producer: Frank R. Pierson
Script: Jack Curtis
Photography: Frank Phillips
Editor: Samuel Gold
Music: Lucien Morwaeck
Guest Stars: Pippa Scott (Kathy), Werner Klemperer (Leander), Lillian Bronson (Mrs. Johnson), Don Beddoe (Marshal), Wolfe Barzell (Figaro), Steve Warren (Hex), William Bryant (Loafer), Robert Gibbons (Manager), Shirley O'Hara (Lady)

Summary: Riding along a country road, Paladin finds a young woman named Kathy digging a grave. The man she is burying was her fiancé; she explains that Leander Johnson, one of the most powerful men in nearby Johnsonville, murdered him. Saddened by the woman's story and attracted to her beauty, Paladin starts with Kathy for Johnsonville, where they are met with indifference and hostility by the local citizens. Paladin soon finds himself facing the sadistic Leander Johnson, as well.

"Soledad Crossing"

First Broadcast: June 10, 1961
Producer: Frank R. Pierson
Script: Don Ingalls
Photography: Frank Phillips
Editor: Everett Sutherland
Music: Rene Garriguenc
Guest Stars: Ed Faulkner (Bud McPhater), Natalie Norwick (Jody), Ken Curtis (Strickland), Walker Edmiston (Mr. Grant), Chuck Roberson (Man), Irma Sundrey (Woman)
Summary: A high bounty has been set for the capture of the McPhater brothers, a pair of murderous religious fanatics who have been terrorizing Oregon. Paladin heads out to capture the two. When he finds them, though, one of the brothers is dead, perhaps from diphtheria. Paladin then apprehends the surviving McPhater, whose name is Bud, and the two make their way to the nearest town, which lies on the other side of the Soledad River. An official stops them before they can cross the river, explaining that anyone who may have been exposed to diphtheria is forbidden from coming near the town. As a result, the gunfighter is forced to linger along the riverbank with his psychopathic prisoner, exposing himself, perhaps, to a disease that can kill him.
Comment: At once obsessed with the Bible and capable of great malice, Ed Faulkner's character, Bud McPhater, perhaps brings to mind the sinister pastor Robert Mitchum portrayed in Charles Laughton's *The Night of the Hunter* (1955). Tall and striking, Faulkner worked often with McLaglen, appearing in films like *The Little Shepherd of Kingdom Come, McLintock!, Shenandoah, The Ballad of Josie, Hellfighters, The Undefeated, Chisum* and *"something big."* Faulkner also worked with McLaglen on episodes of *Gunsmoke, Everglades, Rawhide* and *The Lieutenant*, as well as the television movies *The Log of the Black Pearl* and *Stowaway to the Moon*.

SEASON FIVE, 1961–1962

"The Vigil"

First Broadcast: September 16, 1961
Producer: Frank R. Pierson
Script: Shimon Wincelberg
Photography: Frank Phillips
Editor: Everett Sutherland
Guest Stars: Mary Fickett (Adella Forsythe), George Kennedy (Deke), Dan Stafford (Reamer)
Summary: A nurse asks Paladin to lead her to a desert mine where several men have been injured. Before they reach the site, the travelers come upon two vagrants standing over a freshly dug grave. The man in the grave, one of them explains, was killed earlier in the day by an Indian. Paladin suspects otherwise.

"The Revenger"

First Broadcast: September 30, 1961
Producer: Frank R. Pierson
Script: Robert E. Thompson
Photography: Frank Phillips
Editor: Samuel Gold
Guest Stars: Anthony Caruso (Solomon), Rayford Barnes (Jelly), Harry Carey, Jr. (Conlon), Janet Lake (Lydia), Russell Arms (Ralph Turner), Shug Fisher (Atman)
Summary: After Paladin receives a request for his services from a secretive client, he boards a stagecoach and sets out for Yuma. Riding with him is an unpleasant group of passengers: an incompetent sheriff, his cutthroat prisoner, an ill-tempered woman and her alcoholic husband. As the stage moves through the desert, it is set upon by bandits. When the sheriff kills one of these men, the situation grows more dangerous. Solomon, the leader of the bandits, explains that his dead comrade had been certain that one of the passengers on board the stage had murdered his wife. But the sheriff's bullet silenced him before he could point out who the killer is. For the sake of justice, one of the passengers must now give up his or her life. Who will it be?

"The Race"

First Broadcast: October 28, 1961
Producer: Frank R. Pierson
Script: Peggy and Lou Shaw
Photography: Frank Phillips
Editor: Samuel Gold
Music: William Lava
Guest Stars: Ben Johnson (Crabbe), Michael Pate (Tamasun), John Hopkins (Cowboy), Stewart East (Checker), Vana Leslie (Blonde)
Summary: Sam Crabbe owns a large cattle spread, but he wants to expand his holdings. To do this, he has approached a tribe of Indians that owns the land that lies adjacent to his. Rather than offering to buy out his neighbors, Crabbe makes an unusual proposition to Tamasun, the tribe's chief: he and the chief will race a pair of horses and the winner will lay claim to both properties. As each man can pick a rider, Crabbe goes to Paladin, aware of his reputation as a horseman.

"Ben Jalisco"

First Broadcast: November 18, 1961
Producer: Frank R. Pierson
Script: Harry Julian Fink
Photography: Frank Phillips
Editor: Samuel Gold
Guest Stars: Charles Bronson (Ben Jalisco), Coleen Gray (Lucy), John Litel (Armstedder), Lane Chandler (John Tay), Rick Silver (Will Tay), Chuck Roberson (Carly)
Summary: Ben Jalisco, a murderous bounty hunter, is sent to jail thanks to his wife Lucy's testimony. After he escapes, Jalisco returns home, looking for her. Fortunately, the gallant Paladin sets himself up as Lucy's protector.

"The Brothers"

First Broadcast: November 25, 1961
Producer: Frank R. Pierson
Script: Robert E. Thompson
Photography: Frank Phillips
Editor: Samuel Gold
Guest Stars: Buddy Ebsen (Bram Holden), Paul Hartman (Possum Corbin), Peggy Stewart (Edna Raleigh), Ed Faulkner (Bodyguard #1), Hal Needham (Bodyguard #2), Stuart East (Rider)
Summary: A widow asks Paladin to track down Bram Holden, the murderer of her husband. The gunfighter agrees to the job and locates Holden in a desert town. On the trail back to San Francisco, the two are met by Possum, an elderly prospector. Insistent that Bram Holden is his brother, and that he is guilty of stealing his gold and killing his sweetheart, Possum shoots Holden dead. Paladin and Possum then proceed to Elko, Nevada, where Paladin plans to turn the old timer over to the authorities. Outside the city, a stranger approaches their wagon and Possum insists that this man is also his brother, guilty of stealing his gold and killing his sweetheart. Realizing that Possum is deranged, Paladin prevents his companion from attacking the man, and they continue on to Elko.

"A Knight to Remember"

First Broadcast: December 9, 1961
Producer: Frank R. Pierson
Script: Robert Dozier
Photography: Frank Phillips
Editor: Everett Sutherland
Guest Stars: Hans Conreid (Don Esteban), Robert Carricart (Dirty Dog), Dolores Donlon (Dukinea), Wright King (Alessandro)
Summary: Eccentric Don Esteban, a member of the Mexican gentry, believes that he is Don Quixote, the fictional hero of Miguel de Cervantes's great novel. Concerned for his welfare, the Don's family hires Paladin to find the elderly gentleman and bring him back to Mexico.

"The Mark of Cain"

First Broadcast: January 13, 1962
Producer: Frank R. Pierson
Script: Shimon Wincelberg
Photography: Frank Phillips
Editor: Everett Sutherland
Music: Rene Garriguenc
Guest Stars: Phillip Coolidge (Dr. Avatar), Roy Barcroft (Jake Trueblood), Iphigenie Castiglioni (Pina), Olive Carey (Woman), Rick Silver (Harrison), Dale Ishimoto (Tomuchin)
Summary: An advocate for phrenology, Dr. Avatar believes that the shape of a person's head can be used to understand the nature of his or her personality. Eager to examine the skulls of killers, the doctor has come from Italy to America to examine Jake Trueblood, a legendary gunslinger. Avatar hires Paladin to help him locate Trueblood in the desert. Convinced that the old man's measurements validate the claims of phrenology, Avatar asks Paladin to kill Trueblood and cut off his head. Instead, Paladin turns his gun on his wacky client.

Comment: This episode features an appearance by Olive Carey, the widow of actor Harry Carey and mother of McLaglen's friend and frequent collaborator, Harry Carey, Jr. Like her husband and her son, Olive Carey was a member of John Ford's "stock company" of actors, with roles in *The Searchers*, *The Wings of Eagles* and *Two Rode Together*.[50]

"The Hunt"

First Broadcast: February 3, 1962
Producer: Frank R. Pierson
Script: Herman Groves
Photography: Frank Phillips
Editor: Samuel Gold
Music: Fred Steiner
Guest Stars: Leonid Kinskey (Radachev), Joan Elan (Vanessa Stuart), John Mitchum (Niki), Hank Patterson (Jesse)
Summary: A Russian prince named Radachev has come to America to find adventure and excitement. As he explains to Paladin, "The only thing that amuses me in this world is danger." He offers the gunfighter $5,000 to play a game with him in the forest. "I hunt you. You hunt me," he says. Paladin refuses to cooperate at first, but he is forced to change his mind when the prince insists on playing the game anyway
Comment: Filmed on location in Bend, Oregon, this episode features an uncredited appearance by McLaglen's friend Ed Faulkner as a cavalry officer.

"The Man Who Struck Moonshine"

First Broadcast: March 24, 1962
Producer: Frank R. Pierson
Script: Barry Trivers
Photography: Frank Phillips
Editor: Everett Sutherland
Guest Stars: William Conrad (Moses Kadish), Phyllis Avery (Mrs. Kadish)
Summary: In an effort to please his wife, Moses Kadish has sworn off drink for one year. To help himself stay dry, he has built a cabin in a remote mountain canyon. Unfortunately, the well in his front yard draws whiskey out of the ground instead of water. When Kadish shares some of the whiskey with Paladin, and tells his guest about its mysterious source, the gunfighter sets out to find an explanation. Kadish's cabin, Paladin learns, sits upon a cache of whiskey barrels. The drunkard responds to this news by destroying the reserve. When the liquor's owner discovers what has happened, he pays a visit to Kadish, seeking revenge.
Comment: Conrad (Kadish) played the role of Matt Dillon on the *Gunsmoke* radio show.[51]

"Silent Death, Secret Death"

First Broadcast: March 31, 1962
Producer: Frank R. Pierson
Script: Jack Laird
Photography: Frank Phillips
Editor: Samuel Gold
Guest Stars: Robert Emhardt (Hodges), Michael Pate (Chief), Shug Fisher (Wilhoit), John Holland (Courtney Burgess), Regina Gleason (Beatrice), Russ Bender (Arthur)

Summary: Beatrice Burgess has not seen her brother, Hodges, for seven years and she hires Paladin to find him. After a two month search, the gunfighter learns that Hodges has created his own private militia, which he houses in a vast fort. When Paladin finds the fort, he discovers that typhoid has killed everyone in it except for two men. Determining if one of these men is Hodges proves to be difficult, as one of them is delirious and the other may be a liar.

"Hobson's Choice"

First Broadcast: April 7, 1962
Producer: Frank R. Pierson
Script: Robert E. Thompson
Photography: Frank Phillips
Editor: Everett Sutherland
Music: Van Cleave
Guest Stars: Milton Selzer (Nobel), Parley Baer (Thurber), Olan Soulé (Cartwright), Ollie O'Toole (Drunk), Titus Moede (Hartman), Harrison Lewis (Barber)
Summary: Alfred Nobel, the creator of dynamite, is a guest at the Hotel Carlton. The scientist hires Paladin to track down several bottles of nitroglycerine that have been inadvertently labeled and sold as medicinal tonic. After the bottles are recovered, a shortsighted businessman surprises and robs Paladin at gunpoint, making off with the nitroglycerin, which he plans to sell. Before he gets far, though, the bottles explode.

"Coming of the Tiger"

First Broadcast: April 14, 1962
Producer: Frank R. Pierson
Script: Anthony Wilson
Photography: Frank Phillips
Editor: Samuel Gold
Music: Lucien Moraweck
Guest Stars: Marc Marno (Minoru), Teru Shimada (Takara), James Hong (Priest), Bob Okazaki (Osata), Fuji (Samurai), Gerald Milton (Sam), William Wellman, Jr. (Billy), Beulah Quo (Mrs. Osata), Setsuko Yamaji (Tikara)
Summary: Unhappy with the second-class status of Asian people in America, a Buddhist priest and his samurai companion are sent from Japan to sow dissent in San Francisco. When Paladin's friend Takura learns about this plan, he seeks the gunfighter's assistance, asking him to stop the two agitators from entering the country at the Mexican border.

"Invasion"

First Broadcast: April 28, 1962
Producer: Frank R. Pierson
Script: Peggy and Lou Shaw
Photography: Frank Phillips
Editor: Everett Sutherland
Guest Stars: Robert Gist (Gavin O'Shea), Lew Brown (Michael Mahoney), Douglas Lambert (Danny Mahoney), Robert Gibbons (Government Official), Roy Roberts (Sheriff), Vicki Benet (French Woman)
Summary: Gavin O'Shea, an Irish nationalist, has come to America to raise funds and recruit

supporters for his efforts to drive the British out of Ireland. When the U.S. State Department learns that O'Shea is planning an attack on Canada (a British colony), Paladin is hired to confront and persuade the radical to change his mind.

Comment: This episode is one of the few in the series that focuses on overtly political subject matter. Interestingly, Paladin responds to O'Shea and his anti-colonial views sympathetically, though he prevents the old rebel from realizing his objectives. Liberty may be a worthy pursuit, the episode suggests, but it must not come at the cost of law and stability.

"Pandora's Box"

First Broadcast: May 19, 1962
Producer: Frank R. Pierson
Script: Archie L. Tegland
Photography: Frank Phillips
Editor: Everett Sutherland
Guest Stars: Martin West (Billy Joe), Mary Munday (Decora), Lorna Thayer (Hanna), Robert Stevenson (Woody), Ken Curtis (Lucky Laski), Lewis Martin (Client), Jamie Brothers (Jon)
Summary: Billy Joe is a fugitive killer and his father wants Paladin to bring him to justice. The gunfighter locates the young man on a bluff above a wagon camp with his gun aimed at the people below. When Paladin takes the young man down to the camp, the colorful characters there recognize him. Angry with Paladin for holding Billy Joe, they bully and cajole the gunfighter until he removes the handcuffs around his prisoner's wrists. Rather than being grateful to these people, Billy Joe strikes at a woman in the group with a machete and kills her. Paladin quickly re-captures the young man and the two resume their trek.

SEASON SIX, 1962–1963

"The Fifth Bullet"

First Broadcast: September 29, 1962
Producer: Robert Sparks
Script: Harry Julian Fink
Photography: Frank Phillips
Editor: Tony De Marco
Guest Stars: Ben Johnson (Bartlett), Dorothy Dells (Emmy), Shug Fisher (Hotel Keeper), Peter Boone (Johnny)
Summary: Bartlett is released from prison after eight years for manslaughter. Waiting for him at the prison door is Paladin, who has promised the ex-convict's wife that he will bring Bartlett home alive. This is no easy feat, as the father of the people Bartlett killed has hired gunmen to track down Bartlett and murder him.

"A Place for Abel Hix"

First Broadcast: October 6, 1962
Producer: Robert Sparks
Script: Don Ingalls, story by John Kneubuhl
Photography: Frank Phillips
Editor: Samuel Gold
Guest Stars: Robert Blake (Lauro), Paul Tripp (Reverend Harper), Jean Engstrom (Mrs. Hix),

Kevin Hagen (Judd Bowman), Stewart East (Man), Bill Hart (Olney), Jerry Gatlin (Weaver), Hal Needham (Zimmer), Tom Sweet (Moon), Linda Cordova (Linda)

Summary: Abel Hix, one of the fastest guns in the West, has been killed under suspicious circumstances. Paladin is asked to sort out Hix's investments, making sure the dead man's heirs receive the money he's left to them. Suspecting that a local businessman may have murdered the gunslinger, Paladin and a Mexican boy named Lauro investigate the circumstances leading up to Hix's death.

Comment: Robert Blake (Lauro) was a child actor, best known for being one of the kids in the Our Gang series of films.[52] He and McLaglen had worked together previously in the forties, on *Dakota* and *Out California Way*, when McLaglen was a production clerk at Republic.

"The Bird of Time"

First Broadcast: October 20, 1962
Producer: Robert Sparks
Script: Don Ingalls
Photography: Frank Phillips
Editor: Samuel Gold
Music: Van Cleave
Guest Stars: George Matthews (Ahab Tyson), John Hoyt (Stryker), Francis DeSales (Doc Kelly), Dal Jenkins (Youth), Hal Needham (Man)

Summary: Paladin is riding along a trail when he finds a man hanging by his wrists from a tree. Paladin learns that the man's name is Stryker and his enemy, Ahab Tyson, has done this to him. Once Paladin frees Stryker, the two separate. Later, Paladin captures Tyson. Before the gunfighter can turn him over to the authorities, though, Stryker appears and shoots Tyson. Paladin responds with his own gun, killing Stryker. Fatally injured, Tyson asks the gunfighter to take him to his old home in the mountains, a town called Blue Sky, where he can die in peace. When the men arrive, they see that the once lively Blue Sky has become a ghost town, in part because Tyson murdered several people there a decade earlier, including his wife.

Comment: This episode takes its title from a verse that appears in *The Rubaiyat of Omar Khayyam*, which Paladin quotes in the program's final moments: "The Bird of Time has but a little way/To fly — and Lo! the Bird is on the Wing."

"The Predators"

First Broadcast: November 3, 1962
Producer: Robert Sparks
Script: Harry Julian Fink
Photography: Frank Phillips
Editor: Samuel Gold
Music: Richard Shores
Guest Stars: Richard Jaeckel (John Tyree), Ellen Willard (Girl), James Griffith (Marauder), Lester Maxwell (Boy)

Summary: Paladin tracks down suspected criminal John Tyree in a sandstorm. He and Tyree quickly find themselves without water, and together they scour the desert landscape, searching unsuccessfully for streams and wells. When the pair wanders up to a ranch house with a well out front, the occupants inside — a woman and her young brother — welcome them with gunfire, fearful Paladin and his captive may belong to a band of roving killers who are also combing the desert for water.

"Shootout at Hog Tooth"

First Broadcast: November 10, 1962
Producer: Robert Sparks
Script: Herbert Meadow
Photography: Frank Phillips
Editor: Samuel Gold
Guest Stars: Patrick McVey (Clanahan), Steven Piccaro (Chapineau), Les Damon (Tillbury), Chris King (Morrissey), Hal Baylor (Perrin), Doodles Weaver (Hildreth), Ralph Bernard (Partridge)
Summary: A trio of gunfighters has taken over Hog Tooth, and the town's leaders ask Paladin for help. Arriving on the Fourth of July, Paladin uses his brain and a box of fireworks, rather than gunplay, to free Hog Tooth from its unwanted guests.

"Penelope"

First Broadcast: December 8, 1962
Producer: Robert Sparks
Script: Shimon Wincelberg
Photography: Frank Phillips
Editor: Everett Sutherland
Guest Stars: Joanna Barnes (Penelope), Lawrence Dobkin (Lacey), Jester Hairston (Euclid), Jack Doner (Man), Ivan Bonar (Bartender)
Summary: A genteel alcoholic named Oliver Lacey confronts Paladin in the lobby of the Hotel Carlton, and tells him that he's been in Mexico for the last year searching for gold. Now, Lacey wants to get back to his ranch and his wife, Penelope. Before he can head home, though, the drunkard passes out. Lacey's servant then appears, telling Paladin that Penelope has been keeping company with other men since her husband's departure. Anticipating trouble, the gunfighter rushes off to the Lacey ranch to warn Penelope about her spouse's imminent return.
Comment: Shimon Wincelberg's witty script pays homage to Homer's epic poem *The Odyssey*, which also features a character named Penelope who is left alone for a long period of time by her husband. The name "Oliver Lacey," moreover, bears a phonetic resemblance to "Ulysses," the name of Penelope's husband in Homer's poem.

"The Treasure"

First Broadcast: December 29, 1962
Producer: Robert Sparks
Script: Herb Meadow and Robert E. Thompson
Photography: Frank Phillips
Editor: Samuel Gold
Music: Nathan Scott
Guest Stars: Jeanne Cooper (Edna Harden), Jim Davis (Long) DeForest Kelley (Deakin), Lee Van Cleef (Corbin), Bob Woodward (Gruber), Buck Taylor (Eddie), Stewart East (Waiter)
Summary: Jess Harden has been sentenced to prison for eight years, having stolen $80,000 from a bank in a town called War Lance. The money was never recovered and Harden's

wife, Edna, believes that he hid it in War Lance. When she learns about her husband's release from prison, Edna decides to go to the town, eager to rendezvous with him — and the loot. She hires on Paladin to join her there, for both protection and advice.

"Brotherhood"

First Broadcast: January 5, 1963
Producer: Robert Sparks
Script: Herb Meadow and Albert Ruben
Photography: Frank Phillips
Editor: Everett Sutherland
Music: Lucien Moraweck
Guest Stars: Charles Bronson (Jim Redrock), Michael Keep (Abe Redrock), Myron Healey (Stennis), Max Mellinger (Mossman), Shug Fisher (Kroll), Dawn Little Sky (Wife), Warren Joslin (Driver)
Summary: Two Indian brothers find themselves at odds with each another. One of them, Jim, is a sheriff; the other one, Abe, is a criminal. Jim offers Paladin $200 to apprehend his brother and bring him in to justice, a job Paladin completes with ease. But then, after a band of racist vigilantes kidnap Abe and prepare to lynch him, the sheriff and the gunfighter work together to set the prisoner free.

"The Burning Tree"

First Broadcast: February 9, 1963
Producer: Robert Sparks
Script: Robert and Wanda Duncan
Photography: Frank Phillips
Editor: Samuel Gold
Music: Rene Garriguenc
Guest Stars: Elinor Donahue (Letty May), Paul Fix (Stinchcomb), Whit Bissell (Fairchild), George Brenlin (Eph), Duane Grey (Abner), Joe Madrid (Boy)
Summary: Paladin tracks down and apprehends Fairchild, a habitual murderer who preys on women. On the road to Wichita, Paladin and Fairchild stop in a small town for food and lodging. When the pair is turned away from a boarding house, Paladin asks Stinchcomb, the local sheriff, to hold Fairchild in his jail. The sheriff agrees, but then makes a strange offer: he would like to buy Fairchild from Paladin for $100. To keep his town safe, Stinchcomb explains, he regularly provides a band of Osage Indians with prisoners. The Indians subsequently kill these men beneath a burning tree and use their scalps in burial rituals. Appalled, Paladin rejects the offer, angering the sheriff and the town's other citizens.

"Caravan"

First Broadcast: February 23, 1963
Producer: Robert Sparks
Script: Jay Simms
Photography: Frank Phillips
Editor: Samuel Gold
Music: Rene Garriguenc
Guest Stars: Miriam Colon (Punya), Dolores Faith (The Rani), Cliff Osmond (Koro), Carmen D'Antonio (Satri), Ross Sturlin (Caro), Hal Needham (Indian)

Summary: Driven out of India by revolutionists, a queen hires Paladin to lead her and her entourage from San Francisco to a settlement in the desert. The gunfighter accepts the job because he is fond of the queen's beautiful assistant, Satri. The journey is threatened when someone pours the group's entire supply of water into the sand. Paladin at first suspects the queen's male bodyguard is guilty of this crime. The true culprit, though, is Satri, a discovery that breaks Paladin's heart.

"The Eve of St. Elmo"

First Broadcast: March 23, 1963
Producer: Don Ingalls
Script: Jay Simms
Photography: Frank Phillips
Editor: Everett Sutherland
Music: Rene Garriguenc
Guest Stars: Warren Stevens (Col. Draco), Brett Somers (Myra), Chris Alcaide (Brock), Jerry Summers (Collie), P.L. Smith (Sven), George Kennedy (Brother Grace)
Summary: Col. Draco is a rich landowner and a bully. Confined to a wheelchair, he insists on exerting control over the water supply in the town where he lives. Brock March and his son, Collie, refuse to abide by Draco's demands and they have begun to build their own wells. Brock, in fact, is responsible for the colonel's paralysis, having shot him eight months earlier in a fight over water rights. Making the situation more unpleasant, Draco's sister, Myra, is in love with Brock. To restore his authority, Draco offers Paladin a large fee if he will kill the Marchs. The gunfighter finds himself tempted at first, but he turns down the job and chooses instead to try to help the feuding families reconcile. This decision enrages Draco, prompting the crippled colonel to miraculously rise from his chair and reach for his gun, which he turns on Paladin.
Comment: Paladin's encounter with the Dracos and the Marchs takes place on the first of June — the day before St. Elmo's feast day — hence the episode's title. St. Elmo, better known, perhaps, as St. Erasmus, was a fourth century Italian bishop who performed and experienced several miracles during his lifetime, including visits from angels. Paladin is told early in the episode that the residents of Draco's town believe that if they pray to St. Elmo and provide him with an acceptable gift, he will perform a miracle for them.[53]

"Face of a Shadow"

First Broadcast: April 20, 1963
Producer: Robert Sparks
Script: Robert C. Dennis
Photography: Frank Phillips
Editor: Samuel Gold
Music: Rene Garriguenc
Guest Stars: Enid Jaynes (Darklis), Lee Van Cleef (Golias), Roy Barcroft (Jim Sherwood), Rayford Barnes (Canning), Harry Carey, Jr. (Earl Tibner), Nestor Paiva (Dan Tibner), Richard Reed (Dimitri), William Woodson (Craft)
Summary: Paladin protects a band of gypsies from vigilantes who suspect them of having robbed and murdered a rancher.
Comment: This was the series' last original broadcast; CBS would follow this episode with several re-runs before pulling *Have Gun, Will Travel* permanently from its lineup in September 1963.[54]

Perry Mason

McLaglen contributed only one episode to the *Perry Mason* show in the sixties, "The Case of the Clumsy Clown," in contrast to the six he directed between 1958 and 1959. The program was broadcast during the series' fourth season (1960–1961).

"The Case of the Clumsy Clown"

First Broadcast: November 5, 1960
Producer: Seeleg Lester
Script: Sam Neuman
Photography: Frank Redman
Editor: Richard Cahoon
Guest Stars: Douglas Henderson (Felix), Chana Eden (Lisa), Walter Sande (Judd Curtis), Jerry Franklin (Robert Clarke), Ken Curtis (Durant), Russ Thompson (Ring Master), Lillian Bronson (Judge), Kenneth Tobey (Deputy D.A. Alvin)
Summary: Judd Curtis and Robert Clarke own a circus together. Neither man is fond of the other and each would like to buy out the other's share, but the cost is too great for either of them to cover on their own. They begin to collect money from their employees and friends — whoever can raise the money to buy out the other first will take ownership of the circus. Before this can come about, Curtis is shot dead during a performance by a clown named Felix. Or so everyone thinks. Felix swears that he was on a train bound to San Francisco when the shooting happened, and therefore someone else, wearing his clothes and makeup, must be the murderer. To prove his innocence, Felix goes to Mason for help.
Comment: Series regular William Talman, who frequently played Mason's courtroom nemesis Hamilton Burger, does not appear in this episode. According to the *Los Angeles Times*, Talman had been arrested in March 1960 for attending a party in Hollywood where drugs were being used, and CBS Television, in response, dropped the actor from the *Perry Mason* cast. Talman was eventually acquitted and he and the Hamilton Burger character returned to the show in January 1961, after this episode was filmed.[55]

Gunslinger

Developed and produced by Charles Marquis Warren, *Gunslinger* was a mid-season replacement series first broadcast by CBS in February 1961; it was not renewed for a second season. Tony Young played the show's lead character, Cord, a private contractor who tracks down fugitive criminals for the Army in the New Mexico Territory in the years immediately following the Civil War.[56] Other characters included Capt. Wingate (Preston Foster), Pico McGuire (Charles Gray), Amby Hollister (Midge Ware), Billy Urchin (Dee Pollock) and Murdock (John Pickard).[64] McLaglen directed the series' premiere episode, "The Buried People."

"The Buried People"

First Broadcast: February 9, 1961
Producer: Charles Marquis Warren
Script: John Dunkel and Louis Vittes, story by John Dunkel
Photography: John M. Nickolaus, Jr.
Editor: James Baiotto, Ray Williford
Guest Stars: Royal Dano (El Señor), Fay Spain (Martha), George Kennedy (Sheriff), Roy

Barcroft (Taggert), Myron Healey (Carger), Russ Bender (Hanton), Ed Faulkner (Corporal), Lane Chandler (Town Marshal)

Summary: With Pico and Bill, Cord searches for a sadistic doctor who performed strange experiments on Union soldiers in a Confederate prison camp during the Civil War.

Everglades

A syndicated series produced by United Artists, *Everglades* was on the air from 1961 to 1962, with only 36 episodes produced.[57] Starring Ron Hayes, the show chronicled the exploits of Lincoln Vail, a police constable who fights crime in the swamps of fictional Everglades County, Florida, riding about on an airboat. The series was the brainchild of Budd Schulberg, the Academy Award–winning screenwriter whose credits included *On the Waterfront* (1954) and *A Face in the Crowd* (1957).[58]

"Primer for Pioneers"

First Broadcast: Fall 1961
Producer: Stuart Schulberg
Script: Budd Schulberg
Photography: Fleet Southcott
Editor: Stanford Tischler
Guest Stars: R.G. Armstrong (Luther Jacks), Jena Engstrom (Memory), Nancy Rennick (Angie), Ed Faulkner (Dispatcher)
Summary: Luther Jacks lives with his three children deep in the swamp. Luther regards modern society as a threat and wants to shield his kids from it, keeping them out of school. When a truant officer is shot at the Jacks's home, Vail pays the family a visit, bringing toys, clothing and books for Luther's children. The gesture infuriates Luther and he draws his gun on Vail.
Comment: This episode's director of photography, Fleet Southcott, worked frequently with McLaglen on *Gunsmoke* and *Have Gun, Will Travel*. Ed Faulkner, who appeared in several television programs and features McLaglen directed, briefly appears in this program as a police dispatcher. R.G. Armstrong (Luther) would work again with McLaglen in the eighties on the television movie *The Shadow Riders*.

Rawhide

McLaglen directed five episodes of *Rawhide* in the fifties, but just one in the sixties, "Deserter's Patrol," which was first broadcast during the program's fourth season (1961–1962). Cast regular Clint Eastwood (Rowdy Yates) does not appear in this episode, though Eric Fleming (Gil Favor) does.

"Deserter's Patrol"

First Broadcast: February 9, 1962
Producer: Endre Bohem
Script: Louis Vittes
Photography: Jack Swain
Editor: James Baiotto
Music: Don Ray
Guest Stars: Don Megowan (Corporal Cochran), Jock Gaynor (Ogalla), Russ Conway (Hiller), Russell Arms (Marshall), Robert Dix (Kano), Bob Duggan (Sgt. Regan), Dan Stafford

(Henderson), Conlan Carter (Baines), Edward Faulkner (Rutledge), Eugene Martin (Acoma), William White (Davis), Hal Needham (Corporal Williams), Barney Hale (Sentry), Harry Carey, Jr. (Walsh)

Summary: Favor helps organize a prisoner swap between the U.S. Army and a band of Pawnee Indians. Ironically, the American soldiers are each guilty of desertion, but their commanding officer wants them saved because he needs men.

Comment: Robert Dix (Kano) played Caleb Turner in *The Little Shepherd of Kingdom Come*.

The Lieutenant

Launched in the fall of 1963, *The Lieutenant* ran for one season on NBC.[59] The show was created by Gene Roddenberry, who would develop *Star Trek* later in the decade. Roddenberry got his start in television as a writer, scripting several episodes of *Have Gun, Will Travel*, many of which were directed by McLaglen.[60] *The Lieutenant* featured Gary Lockwood as Lt. William Rice, a United States Marine Corps officer stationed at Camp Pendleton in southern California. Several episodes of the program were in fact filmed at Camp Pendleton, the same location where McLaglen had assisted director Allan Dwan on *Sands of Iwo Jima* in 1949.[61]

"The Proud and the Angry"

First Broadcast: September 28, 1963
Producer: Gene Roddenberry
Script: Jerome B. Thomas
Photography: Paul Ivano
Editor: Robert James Kern
Guest Stars: Robert Vaughn (Rambridge), Rip Torn (Kasten), Chris Connelly (Russell), Richard Rust (Grace), Bob Davis (Crosse), Gilbert Green (McAdams), Barnaby Hale (Cook), Miranda Jones (Nancy)
Summary: A sergeant named Kasten trains new marines. When Kasten is suspected of mistreating his men, Rice poses as a newly enlisted grunt and watches the sergeant to determine if official action should be taken.
Comment: Robert Vaughn (Rambridge) subsequently played the role of Sen. Reynolds in McLaglen's 1981 miniseries *The Blue & The Gray*. Rip Torn (Kasten) played Gen. Ulysses S. Grant in the same production.

"To Take Up Serpents"

First Broadcast: October 19, 1963
Producer: Gene Roddenberry
Script: Jay Simms
Photography: Paul Ivano
Editor: Robert James Kern
Guest Stars: John Alderman (Fiske), Tom Simcox (Parker), Anna-Lisa (Maria), Pat Priest (Diane), William O'Connell (Wade), Michael Ryan (Johnson)
Summary: Rice faces a personal and professional crisis after he discovers that he experiences vertigo when he flies, a potential career killer for a USMC officer.
Comment: This episode's title alludes to Mark 16:18 in the King James Version of the Bible: "They shall take up serpents; and if they drink any deadly thing, it shall not hurt them; they shall lay hands on the sick, and they shall recover." Faith, the passage suggests, can

produce miracles for believers. Tom Simcox (Parker) played the role of Lt. Johnson in McLaglen's *Shenandoah*.

"Tour of Duty"

First Broadcast: March 7, 1964
Producer: Gene Roddenberry
Script: Art Wallace
Photography: Paul Ivano
Editor: Robert James Kern
Guest Stars: Louis Nye (Green), Kelly Thordsen (Reynolds), Ricardo Montalban (Reading), Edward Faulkner (Logan), Marian Collier (Marton), Carey Foster (Jan), Bobby Pickett (Alvin C. Hopgood)
Summary: Rice faces censure from his superiors when he decides not to prosecute a young marine for misconduct.
Comment: One of the actors in this episode's cast is Bobby Pickett, the singer-songwriter who scored a hit with the novelty song "Monster Mash" in 1962.[62]

"The War Called Peace"

First Broadcast: April 11, 1964
Producer: Gene Roddenberry
Script: Anthony Wilson
Photography: Paul Ivano
Editor: Robert James Kern
Guest Stars: Denver Pyle (Morrissey), Lloyd Bochner (Denning), Donna Anderson (Laura Ann), John Marley (Bardel), Tom Drake (Curtis), Ed Long (Hoving)
Summary: Rice masquerades as a bureaucrat to determine if a top secret missile program has been compromised.

The Virginian

Produced for NBC, *The Virginian* was unusual among TV Westerns as its programs ran for 90 minutes. Starring James Drury as the show's unnamed central character, *The Virginian* was on the air from 1962 to 1971.[63] Each episode chronicled the exploits of cowhands and cattle drovers who work and live on the Shiloh Ranch in Medicine Bow, Wyoming. Among the other actors who appeared on the show regularly were Lee J. Cobb as the ranch's owner, Judge Henry Garth, and Doug McClure, who played a cowhand named Trampas. McLaglen only shot one episode for *The Virginian*, "Smile of a Dragon," which was broadcast during the series' second season (1963–1964).

"Smile of a Dragon"

First Broadcast: February 26, 1964
Producer: Don Ingalls
Script: Cy Chermak and Don Ingalls, story by Borden Chase
Photography: Lionel Lindon
Editor: Edward A. Biery
Guest Stars: Richard Carlson (Marden), Buck Taylor (Plumb), Frank Overton (Umber), Phyllis Coates (Mrs. Marden), Patricia Morrow (Ellie), Stephen Price (Jonathan), Kam Tong (Ming Yang), Miyoshi Umeki (Kim Ho)

Summary: A stagecoach is robbed and Trampas is misidentified as one of the bandits. A vindictive sheriff named Marden pursues the young man through the landscape, forcing him to seek help from a family of Chinese immigrants. When Trampas manages to track down the actual criminals, he learns that Marden himself is a member of the gang.

Comment: In this episode, McLaglen draws attention to problems caused by racial prejudice: the immigrants who help Trampas are regularly mistreated because they are Asian. McLaglen returned to this theme in his 1971 feature *One More Train to Rob*. "Smile of a Dragon" features an appearance by Kam Tong, who'd starred as Hey Boy on *Have Gun, Will Travel*. Doug McClure (Trampas) would have a prominent role in McLaglen's *Shenandoah*, playing Rosemary Forsyth's husband, Sam. Series regulars James Drury and Lee J. Cobb do not appear in this episode.

Wagon Train

Wagon Train premiered on NBC in September 1957. In 1962, the program moved to ABC, where it stayed until its cancellation in 1965. Set in the years following the Civil War, *Wagon Train* followed the efforts of a team of men who transport travelers from St. Joseph, Missouri to California. Ward Bond served as the series' first wagon master, Maj. Seth Adams, but after Bond's death in 1961, a new wagon master, Chris Hale (John McIntire), was introduced.[64] Other characters included Flint McCullough (Robert Horton), Bill Hawks (Terry Wilson) and Cooper Smith (Robert Fuller). McLaglen filmed only one episode for *Wagon Train*, "The Silver Lady," which was broadcast during the series' eighth and final season (1964–1965).

"The Silver Lady"

First Broadcast: April 25, 1965
Script: Dick Nelson
Photography: Walter Strenge
Editor: Gene Palmer
Guest Stars: Michael Burns (Morgan Earp), Don Collier (Wyatt Earp), Don Galloway (Virgil Earp), Vera Miles (Anne Reed), Arthur O'Connell (Charlie Loughlin), Henry Silva (Doc Holliday)
Summary: In this episode, Cooper Smith shares a story with Bill Hawks about the famed Earp brothers and an incident in which a stagecoach carrying silver rolled over and killed a female passenger.
Comment: Vera Miles (Anne Reed) would again work with McLaglen on the feature *Hellfighters* and the telefilm *Travis McGee*.

FIVE

The Seventies

The seventies started well enough for McLaglen with the release of four cowboy pictures—*Chisum* (1970), *One More Train to Rob* (1971), *"something big"* (1971) and *Cahill, United States Marshal* (1973)—and a crime melodrama, *Fools' Parade* (1971). But afterward, new offers to direct big pictures failed to materialize, prompting McLaglen to return to television after an eight year break. Among the TV shows he worked on in the mid seventies were *Banacek*, *Hec Ramsey* and *The Fantastic Journey*. During this period, McLaglen also had the opportunity to direct a pair of modestly budgeted films, *Mitchell* and *The Last Hard Men*, but neither of them generated significant returns at the box office. Then, in 1977, McLaglen was asked by British producer Euan Lloyd to helm *The Wild Geese*, an expensive action-adventure about mercenaries that proved to be an enormous commercial hit. Thanks to this success, McLaglen again found himself in high demand as a motion picture director as the decade came to an end.

Feature Films

Chisum—1970 (111 mins)

Producer: Andrew J. Fenady, Batjac Productions
Script: Andrew J. Fenady, based on his story "Chisum and the Lincoln County Cattle War"
Photography: William H. Clothier (Color)
Editor: Robert Simpson
Music: Dominic Frontiere; "Ballad of John Chisum" by Andrew J. Fenady and Dominic Frontiere, sung by Merle Haggard
Cast: John Wayne (John Chisum), Forrest Tucker (Lawrence Murphy), Christopher George (Dan Nodeen), Ben Johnson (James Pepper), Glenn Corbett (Pat Garrett), Bruce Cabot (Sheriff Brady), Andrew Prine (Alex McSween), Patric Knowles (Henry Tunstall), Richard Jaeckel (Jess Evans), Lynda Day (Sue McSween), Geoffrey Deuel (Billy "The Kid" Bonney), Pamela McMyler (Sallie Chisum), John Agar (Amos Patton), Lloyd Battista (Neemo), Robert Donner (Bradley Morton), Ray Teal (J.B. Wilson), Edward Faulkner (Dolan), Ron Soble (Charley), John Mitchum (Baker), Glenn Langan (Col. Dudley), Alan Baxter (Gov. Sam Axtell), Alberto Morin (Juan), William Bryant (Jeff), Pedro Armendariz, Jr. (Ben), John Pickard (Sgt. Braddock), Abraham Sofaer (Chief White Buffalo), Gregg Palmer (Riker), Hank Worden (Elwood), Pedro Gonzalez Gonzales (Mexican Rancher), Jim Burk (Trace), Eddy Donno (Cass)

Summary: John Chisum owns a sprawling ranch in Lincoln County in the New Mexico Territory. Unmarried, the rancher has devoted his energies entirely to his business in the years since the Civil War, making himself rich. Never interested in having a family of his own, he nonetheless enjoys close friendships with his employees and his neighbors, especially a fellow cattleman named Tunstall.

Chisum's status as Lincoln County's most powerful resident is threatened, however, by the arrival of Lawrence Murphy, a wealthy speculator who uses his money to destroy local businesses, buy up land, install lawmen who answer to him and purchase the loyalty of the New Mexico Territory's governor. Free to sidestep the law, Murphy and his men begin to use violence to undermine Chisum, stealing his horses, rustling his cattle, even killing his friend Tunstall.

The murder of Tunstall leads to Murphy's undoing. Tunstall has been acting as a mentor to William "Billy the Kid" Bonney, trying to help the young man overcome his outlaw tendencies. Upon the old man's death, Billy sets out for revenge, certain of Murphy's culpability. He starts off by killing a sheriff named Brady and a pair of deputies whom he believes has murdered his friend under Murphy's orders. A massive manhunt commences, but Billy stays on in Lincoln County, in part because he wants to see Murphy's blood, but also because he's fallen in love with Chisum's niece, Sallie, who has recently come to live with her uncle.

One night, Billy breaks into a store owned by Chisum to steal some blasting dynamite, which he plans to use against Murphy. He's quickly spotted by one of Murphy's men, Nodeen, who has replaced Brady as Lincoln County's sheriff. A standoff follows, with Billy and some of his friends trading shots with Nodeen and his deputies. When Chisum learns about the clash, he and his ranch hands run a herd of cattle through downtown Lincoln, which forces Nodeen and his men to scatter, allowing Billy to escape.

Following this, Chisum tracks down Murphy. The two brawl and Murphy is killed after falling from a second floor balcony. Chisum then returns his ranch. There, Chisum's niece Sallie reveals that she is now romantically interested in Pat Garrett, one of the men who has helped her uncle defeat Murphy. As Sallie makes plans to start a family, Chisum starts out alone on one of his horses to the top of a hill, where he surveys the vast spread of land he continues to own and control.

Comment: On his commentary for the DVD edition of *Chisum*, McLaglen explains that the film was shot entirely in Durango, Mexico. *Chisum* marks the final time McLaglen collaborated with cinematographer William H. Clothier. He and McLaglen had first worked together as employees at Wayne-Fellows Productions on pictures like Wellman's *Island in the Sky*, *The High and the Mighty*, and *Track of the Cat*. Clothier lensed McLaglen's first two pictures, *Man in the Vault* and *Gun the Man Down*, as well as the bulk of the pictures McLaglen made in the sixties, including *McLintock!*, *Shenandoah*, *The Rare Breed* and *Bandolero!* Following *Chisum*, Clothier worked on just three more pictures (all with John Wayne): Howard Hawks's *Rio Lobo* (1970), George Sherman's *Big Jake* (1971) and Burt Kennedy's *The Train Robbers* (1973), before retiring permanently from motion picture work.[1]

A Batjac production, *Chisum* was scripted by Andrew J. Fenady. Fenady had previously written for the *Hondo* television series (ABC, 1967–1968); starring Ralph Taeger, the show was produced by Batjac and it featured characters who had first appeared in the motion picture *Hondo*, in which Wayne had starred.[2] Fenady based *Chisum*'s narrative on actual events that occurred in the New Mexico Territory in the 1870s, when cattle barons John Chisum and Lawrence Murphy waged a bloody battle over disputed land, using men like Sheriff William Brady, Dan Nodeen, William Bonney and Pat Garrett to achieve their goals.[3] The film's indebtedness to and its readiness to, exaggerate, upon real history links it to *The Alamo*, a 1960 picture directed by Wayne in which he played frontiersman Davy Crockett.

Chisum also resembles *McLintock!*, the first movie Wayne and McLaglen made together as actor and director. Most obviously, both films take their titles from their central characters' last names. But the two movies also focus on individualistic protagonists who have managed to succeed financially in the American frontier, transforming the wilderness into farms and ranches. Yet while G.W. McLintock is secure in his position as a landowner, so much so that he has a town named after him, Chisum must protect his land and his neighbors from Murphy and his confederates. The rancher is at first reluctant, however, to take action against his rival, preferring discussion and mediation to conflict and violence. This unwillingness to challenge Murphy, even after Tunstall is killed, proves to be extremely frustrating for Chisum's close friend Pepper, who complains to him: "[A]ll this speechifying, storekeeping, prayer-meeting don't amount to spit in the river. There's only one thing that's going to make this territory know who's bull of the woods." The "one thing" Pepper refers to, of course, is the use of force, and once Chisum recognizes that Murphy will not respond to diplomacy, he decides to follow Pepper's counsel and take action. When this point is reached, by the way, the rancher cries, "Let's break out some Winchesters!" and soon blood and smoke seep through the streets of Lincoln.

Among *Chisum*'s admirers was Richard Nixon.[4] The president referred to the film in a 1970 address he gave in Denver:

> Over the last weekend I saw [*Chisum*].... [A]s I looked at that movie, I said, "Well, it was a very good western, John Wayne is a very fine actor and it was: a fine supporting cast. But it was just basically another western, far better than average movies, better than average westerns."
>
> I wondered why it is that the western survives year after year after year. A good western will outdraw some of the other subjects. Perhaps one of the reasons, in addition to the excitement, the gun play, and the rest, which perhaps is part of it but they can get that in other kinds of movies but one of the reasons is, perhaps, and this may be a square observation — is that the good guys come out ahead in the westerns; the bad guys lose.
>
> In the end, as this movie particularly pointed out, even in the old West, the time before New Mexico was a State, there was a time when there was no law. But the law eventually came, and the law was important from the standpoint of not only prosecuting the guilty, but also seeing that those who were guilty had a proper trial.[5]

It has to be noted, however, that in the New Mexico Territory depicted in this movie, laws do exist, and men like Brady and Nodeen are paid to enforce them. But these two are not interested in acting honestly, and it is their dereliction ultimately which prompts Chisum to restore order to Lincoln County on his terms — with fists and rifles. As William F. Buckley remarked in a 1970 column, "what is notable about 'Chisum' is that the good guys win and the bad guys lose BECAUSE the good guys take the law into their own hands."[6] John Chisum and his "good guy" friends, in short, are vigilantes, and violent ones at that.

Reviews: "[T]hough historically backdropped, film is a rehash of the time-honored western formula of the heavy out to move in and take over all the hero has suffered and fought for. What is most important is that it's entertainment, not dependent upon a sleazy story line or contrived efforts at sensationalism." *Variety*, June 24, 1970; "A traditional action-packed western starring Wayne in the title role, playing the same rugged character he had played in dozens of his other films." *Motion Picture Guide*, 420; "As Chisum, Wayne dominates the screen with his usual vigor, warmth, and a largely avuncular manner. Yet when he finally deals with the vicious Lawrence Murphy ... it is with the grit, honor, and uncompromising toughness worthy of John Wayne at his best." *Encyclopedia of the Western*, 87; "Big, brawling John Wayne oater; quite entertaining and one of his last really exciting vehicles." *Western Movies*, 74.

Release: June, Warner Bros.
Availability: VHS, LD, DVD
Rating: G

One More Train to Rob—1971 (108 mins)

Producer: Robert Arthur, Universal Pictures
Script: Don Tait and Dick Nelson, story by William Roberts
Photography: Alric Edens (Color)
Editor: Robert Simpson
Music: David Shire; song "Havin' Myself a Fine Time" by Richard Maltby, Jr. and David Shire, sung by Tim Morgan
Cast: George Peppard (Harker Fleet), Diana Muldaur (Katy), John Vernon (Nolan), France Nuyen (Ah Toy), Steve Sandor (Jim Gant), Soon-Talk Oh (Yung), Richard Loo (Mr. Chang), Robert Donner (Adams), John Doucette (Monte), C.K. Yang (Wong), Marie Windsor (Louella), Timothy Scott (Slim), Joan Shawlee (Red), Hal Needham (Bert Gant), Harry

George Peppard as the affable bandit Hark Fleet in *One More Train to Rob* (Universal, 1971). With Pamela McMyler, left.

Carey, Jr. (Red), Jim Burk (Skinner), Ben Cooper (1st Deputy), Ray Dimas (Herbert), Guy Lee (Sen), Charles Seel (Reverend), George Chandler (Conductor), Pamela McMyler (Cora Mae), Merlin Olsen (Eli Jones), Phil Olsen (Phil Jones)

Summary: Hark Fleet is a professional train robber. Prior to a job one night, he checks into a hotel that doubles as a brothel in order to establish an alibi for himself. He then sneaks out and meets up with his girlfriend, Katy, putting her on an outbound train beside a travelling drummer named Tim Nolan. Hark commences to hold up the train with several assistants. When the robbers empty the bank box they find on board, they stash the money in Katy's suitcase. Nolan, it turns out, is in cahoots with Hark and Katy, and he sees that the stolen money is safely removed from the train at a subsequent stop.

Following the robbery, Hark returns to the brothel. When the police come by later to ask him if he's had any role in the crime, Hark tells them he's been at the hotel all night. The sheriff accepts Hark's alibi. But before he leaves, two enormous men, the Jones brothers, storm Hark's room. They tell Hark that he has left their sister, Cora Mae, with child and if he hopes to live, he'd better marry her. Unwilling to say goodbye to his life as a bachelor, Hark tries to escape, but as he does so he injures the sheriff. As a result of this, Hark is pursued, captured and taken to the local jail. While in custody, he marries Cora Mae and, shortly after this, receives a three year prison sentence. Cora Mae later visits Hark at the penitentiary, where she tells him that his sentence is grounds for having their marriage annulled. She adds that she was never pregnant in the first place and reveals that Hark's friend and partner, Tim Nolan, encouraged her to feign the pregnancy in order to prompt Hark to leave his life as a criminal behind and forfeit his share of the recent robbery.

As Hark serves his term, Nolan adopts the life of a gentleman, buying a home and a ranch, as well as marrying Hark's girlfriend, Katy. When Hark's good behavior prompts the officials at the prison to parole him early, the convict sets out to find Nolan and exact revenge. As he makes his way to Calador, California, where Nolan is now living, he watches as a gang of crooks tries to rob a lode of gold from a family of Chinese miners. Anticipating the attack, the miners have loaded up their wagon with rocks instead of ore. The robbers respond by killing some of the miners and kidnapping Mr. Chang, the miners' leader. Hark offers to help the miners, but they have little reason to trust him and they turn him away.

Hark then makes his way to the Nolans' home. Nolan and Katy are both surprised that their former friend has been released from prison. They agree to put him up for a time, but when Hark asks for his share of the money from the long ago train robbery, Nolan says that he cannot give it to him. The money has been invested and is not accessible at the moment. Hark soon learns the truth, however, that Nolan is actually deeply in debt, and to stay solvent, he has been pleading with the miner Mr. Chang to lend him money. But the old man has been unwilling to help, and for this reason, it is Nolan who has had Mr. Chang kidnapped.

Hark then decides that in order to ensure his revenge against Nolan, he must help the Chinese miners successfully deliver their gold to San Francisco, making sure that Nolan never gets the chance to seize it for himself. Hark then sets out at first to win the miners' trust and respect. To do this, he frees a Chinese woman who has sold herself into bondage to a local brothel and delivers her to the miners. He also rescues Mr. Chang from his captors. These actions persuade the miners that Hark is sincere about his desire to help and they allow him to show them how to protect themselves from robbers like Nolan.

Despite Hark's efforts, Nolan manages to swipe a large portion of gold from the miners anyway. Undiscouraged, Hark and the miners commandeer a train that is headed for San Francisco. They load the remaining portion of their gold on board and then, when the train rolls into Calador, they watch as Nolan loads the gold he's stolen on board the same car where the miners' gold has been stowed. After this, Hark approaches Nolan and his men and forces them at gunpoint from the car. The miners are then free to make their way to San Francisco with all of their gold. A gunfight follows in which Nolan is fatally shot. As he dies, Nolan asks Hark to marry Katy and borrow money from Mr. Chang to keep the ranch in Calador financially afloat.

Comment: *One More Train to Rob* features a hero whose personality arouses both our distaste and admiration. A professional criminal, Hark Fleet earns his living with a gun, bullying defenseless passengers on trains. Nevertheless, when he learns about the family of Chinese miners who've been exploited and menaced by violent criminals — men who think and act much in the same way as he — he directs his energies toward helping the miners, enabling them to bypass their enemies and deliver their gold to buyers in San Francisco. Hark reveals the better aspects of his personality, as well, when he frees the Chinese prostitute from the madam who has purchased her, though he himself, ironically, is a frequent patron of brothels.

Protagonists with contradictory personalities like Hark come to the aid of vulnerable people frequently in McLaglen's movies. In *The Undefeated*, for instance, bad tempered John Henry Thomas forgoes his ambitions to sell horses to the Emperor Maximilian in order to liberate Col. Langdon's family and friends from Juarista insurgents. Likewise in *Breakthrough*, Sgt. Steiner, a member of the vicious German Wehrmacht, stands up to his commanding officer and defends several French villagers who have been put in harm's away. Hark also brings to mind Rem Anderson, the bank robber hero of McLaglen's *Gun the Man Down*. Hark and Rem are both career criminals, for instance, who are betrayed by a partner following a heist. Both characters are sent to prison, and once they are released, they find that the men who betrayed them have become romantically involved with their lady friends. In each film, as well, the protagonists forgive the women who have forsaken them.

Though *One More Train to Rob* is scored with violence and tragedy — the plight of the trapped prostitute, in particular — it ranks as one of McLaglen's more overtly comic pictures. Much of the picture's humor arises from Hark's mannerisms, especially the pleasure he takes in being a train robber. We find an instance of Hark relishing his wicked ways, for example, when Tim Nolan discloses that he's poorly invested and lost the money from the train robbery they coordinated years earlier.

> NOLAN: The bank in San Francisco won't extend me a note. I owe them a hundred thousand dollars and with my holdings worth five times that, they're waiting like vultures to swoop down and foreclose.
> HARK: Tim, how many times have I tried to tell you that banks are not to do business with, they're to rob.

One More Train to Rob was produced during a period when "funny" cowboy pictures of this sort were enjoying a vogue. Hollywood had been producing comic Westerns for decades — among them Buster Keaton's *Go West* (1925), Leo McCarey's *Ruggles of Red Gap* (1935) and George Marshal's *Destry Rides Again* (1939). But after the release of Ellis Silverstein's commercially and critically successful *Cat Ballou* in 1965, Western-themed farces and spoofs were turned out in fairly high number, among them Fielder Cook's *A Big Hand for the Little Lady* (1966), Burt Kennedy's *Support Your Local Sheriff* (1969), Gene Kelly's *Cheyenne Social Club* (1970) and Mel Brooks's *Blazing Saddles* (1974). *One More Train to Rob* is not McLaglen's first Western comedy, however. That distinction belongs to 1963's *McLintock!"*

Reviews: "*One More Train to Rob* is a sometimes tongue-in-cheek, bawdy, fast-shootin' western with comedic overtones.... Enough novelty is inserted both in story line and character development to keep audiences engaged." *Variety*, April 7, 1971; "Because it is too lax, too slow, too mechanical, too timid in its inventions, *One More Train to Rob* never becomes funny. And because it never becomes funny it has no way really to contain or control the violence that is its other side and that falls after a while from the level of rugged amiability to mere blood lust." *New York Times*, June 3, 1971; "The direction is fast paced, managing to blend the vengeance theme with that of the Chinese gold nicely, and Peppard gives a solid performance as the antihero." *Motion Picture Guide*, 2269.

Release: May, Universal Pictures
Rating: GP

Fools' Parade—1971 (98 mins)

Alternate Title: *Dynamite Man from Glory Jail*
Producer: Andrew V. McLaglen, James Lee Barrett (uncredited), Stanmore Productions, Penbar Productions
Script: James Lee Barrett, from the novel *Fools' Parade* by Davis Grubb
Photography: Harry Stradling, Jr. (Color)
Editor: David Bretherton, Robert Simpson
Music: Henry Vars
Cast: James Stewart (Mattie Appleyard), George Kennedy (Doc Council), Anne Baxter (Cleo), Strother Martin (Lee Cottrill), Kurt Russell (Johnny Jesus), William Windom (Sizemore),

Lobby poster for *Fools' Parade* (Columbia, 1971). The picture drew strong reviews, but stumbled at the box office.

Mike Kellin (Steve Mystic), Kathy Cannon (Chanty), Morgan Paull (Junior), Robert Donner (Willis Hubbard), David Huddleston (Homer Grindstaff), Dort Clark (Enoch Purdy), James Lee Barrett (Sonny Boy), Richard Carl (Police Chief), Arthur Cain (Prosecuting Attorney), Paul Merriman (Fireman), Walter Dove (Engineer), Pete Miller (Trusty), George Metro (Train Dispatcher), Suzann Stoehr (Bank Teller), John Edwards (Bank Clerk)

Summary: Mattie Appleyard, a convicted murderer, has spent the last 40 years of his life in a state penitentiary in Glory, West Virginia. Over the course of his sentence, Mattie has always had jobs. Thanks to his frugality, he's put away $25,000, which he keeps in a bank in downtown Glory. With the money, he wants to open a store with two friends he's made in prison, Lee Cottrill, an old bank robber, and Johnny Jesus, a teenager unjustly convicted of rape.

Mattie, Lee and Johnny are all released on the same day. At Glory's railroad station, an official from the prison named Doc Council gives Mattie a check for his money. He then tells Mattie to leave the town on a train with Lee and Johnny and never come back. After the train departs, Mattie comes to realize that his check can only be cashed in Glory.

As it turns out, Council and a crooked banker named Homer Grindstaff have been siphoning Mattie's savings for themselves. Council is so set on keeping Mattie's money that he's hired some thugs to murder the old man. Aided by a conductor named Hubbard, who's been paid off by Council, the killers board the train that carries the ex-convicts out of Glory. In an effort to outwit these people, Mattie pretends that a divine entity of some sort has also entered the train, which only he can see. The ruse works and Mattie, Lee and Johnny flee the train. They manage to make off with some dynamite, as well, which Mattie earlier took from a mining equipment supplier who was also riding on the train. The three friends then sneak back into Glory. The next morning, Mattie confronts the banker, Grindstaff, and orders him to cash his check. At first Grindstaff refuses, but he complies when Mattie reveals that he has several sticks of TNT strapped to his belly.

As Lee and Johnny wait for Mattie along the railroad tracks outside of town, they are approached by a drifter who tells them about a barge on the nearby river where they can sleep with women and drink liquor. Lee cannot resist the offer and he leaves Johnny. Once inside the floating cathouse, Lee meets Cleo, a blousy madam with a single prostitute in her employ, a young girl named Chanty. As Lee enjoys himself, Mattie reunites with Johnny and they head together to Cleo's.

Simultaneously, a posse led by Council scours the riverbank, eventually tracking the fugitives to the boat with the help of a bloodhound named Joy, who adores Johnny and eagerly follows his scent. While Cleo distracts Council, Mattie, Lee and Johnny make off on a skiff. From Council, Cleo learns about the money Mattie has taken from the bank. She then permits Council to force himself on Chanty.

Worried about Chanty's safety, Johnny persuades Mattie to return to the barge. When the men realize that Council has departed, they climb aboard. Cleo now explains to them that if they want her to remain silent, Mattie must turn the money he took from the bank over to her. Instead, Mattie gives Cleo a box of dynamite he's brought with him, telling her it's filled with cash. As the men leave with Chanty moments later, Cleo fires a pistol at the lock on the box to open it. The subsequent explosion destroys her and the barge.

Mattie and his friends then return to town, climb into a box car at a railroad depot and fall asleep, confident the train will carry them away. When they wake up, though, they realize the train hasn't left the station. Even worse, they spot Doc Council's car sitting close by. When Joy, the bloodhound who loves Johnny, picks up the boy's scent, she leads Council to the train, prompting Mattie and the others to run. Fortunately, they are soon spotted by the train conductor, Hubbard, who earlier helped the gunmen board the train and threaten Mattie.

Hubbard now feels guilty for his actions and decides to help the fugitives, delivering them to an empty, old house in the countryside.

Council eventually finds the group, though, helped again by Joy the bloodhound. When the animal runs inside to find Johnny, Council opens fire and Mattie is struck by a bullet. Johnny, in response, hurls a stick of dynamite at Council. Joy mistakes the dynamite for a real stick, retrieves it, and brings it back into the house. Acting quickly, Mattie hurls the dynamite out the window. The explosive lands right in front of Council, killing him.

Mattie, Lee and Johnny are subsequently captured and placed in jail, and Mattie's money is returned to Homer Grindstaff at the bank in downtown Glory. During a hearing the next day, the judge on duty becomes convinced that Mattie has been the victim of a great crime perpetrated by Council and Grindstaff. Mattie is then released and escorted to the Glory bank, where he collects his $25,000. Grindstaff, in turn, is arrested and led to jail. Mattie, Lee, Johnny and Chanty then board the next train out of Glory. As the train starts from the station, Joy the bloodhound appears and bounds down the tracks, as eager as ever to be with her friend Johnny. The friends are happy to have the dog with them and they help her onto the train.

Comment: *Fools' Parade* marks McLaglen's fourth collaboration with scenarist James Lee Barrett, who'd supplied the scripts for *Shenandoah*, *Bandolero!* and *The Undefeated* and later *"something big."* Barrett also co-produced *Fools' Parade* with McLaglen, and appears briefly on the screen, playing the vagabond who lures Johnny and Lee to Cleo's barge on the river.

Just as he did for *Shenandoah* and *Bandolero!*, which similarly featured James Stewart in the lead, Barrett builds the plot of *Fools' Parade* around a chase. In *Shenandoah*, Charlie Anderson searches for his lost son Boy in the Virginia mountains. In *Bandolero!*, Sheriff July Johnson (played by George Kennedy) follows the fugitive Bishop brothers into Mexico. And in *Fools' Parade*, Doc Council (also played by George Kennedy) scours West Virginia's coal country for Mattie, Lee and Johnny.

Fools' Parade was filmed in the fall of 1970 on location in Moundsville, West Virginia, the home of the West Virginia State Penitentiary.[8] The movie is an adaptation of a 1969 novel written by Davis Grubb. Grubb also authored the 1953 novel *The Night of the Hunter*, the source for a 1955 *film noir* thriller of the same name, which Charles Laughton directed. In the cinematic version of *The Night of the Hunter*, Robert Mitchum played a character named Harry Powell, a violent criminal who murders a young mother and obsessively pursues her children through the West Virginia landscape, much as Council pursues Mattie, Lee and Johnny in *Fools' Parade*. Harry Powell and Doc Council are both religious fanatics, as well, inclined to pray and quote scripture as they plan out murders.

One of McLaglen's favorite films, *Fools' Parade* nevertheless sank at the box office, unable to attract contemporary audiences.[9] As Richard Schickel noted in his review for *Life*, "*Fools' Parade* is a movie that flies in the face of fashion. Its setting is small-town and rural; it has a strong, straightforward narrative line; its characters — although carrying heavy (and perhaps too obvious) symbolic weights — are essentially simple and unsophisticated souls, mostly of the older generation; it is directed by Andrew V. McLaglen in an old-timey style that his father, Victor ... would have felt very comfortable with. In short, it has little going for it in today's market, beyond the fact that it is suspenseful, surprising, entertaining."[10]

With its sentimental ending, its cast of graying stars and Harry Stradling, Jr.'s unembellished camerawork, *Fools' Parade* does indeed seem "old-timey" when we compare it to contemporary releases like Mike Nichols's *Catch-22* (1970), Robert Altman's *M*A*S*H* (1970) and William Friedkin's *The French Connection* (1971). Each of these pictures self-consciously subverted conventional storytelling structures and dispensed with the polished visual style that characterized the work of earlier mainstream Hollywood directors like Ford, Farrow and Wellman, under whom McLaglen had learned his craft. At the same time, *Fools' Parade* seems to be very much of its time. Freed from the restrictions imposed upon content and language by the Production Code, which the Motion Picture Association of America had dropped in 1968, McLaglen introduces material into the film that once would have drawn censure, including depictions of prostitution and rape.[11] Moreover, the protagonists in this picture, far from being heroic in any traditional sense, are alienated individuals—a murderer, a bank robber and a convicted (albeit unjustly) sex offender—who not only kill the psychopathic Doc Council, but receive amnesty from prosecution afterward.

In the next picture they made together, *"something big,"* McLaglen and Barrett would again build a narrative around likeable outcasts who commit serious crimes with impunity. But unlike the unlucky trio in *Fools' Parade*, whose actions are precipitated by the criminal conduct of other people, the protagonists in *something big*—a band of kidnappers, robbers and murderers—break laws and flout social mores simply because doing so seems to make them happy.

Reviews: "'Fools' Parade' has certain merit as a suspense melodrama, but lacks strong development and in transition from novel to screen loses the mounting power that should have characterized unfoldment." *Variety*, June 23, 1971; "Andrew V. McLaglen's 'Fools' Parade' is one of those films, very rare in recent years, that restores faith in ordinary movie-going as a reasonable and even privileged way of passing time." *New York Times*, August 19, 1971; "[A] very nicely done piece of storytelling whose narrative flow is flecked with moments that are vivid, bizarre and surprising and with characters who are the same." *Los Angeles Times*, August 22, 1971; "[M]uch of it has a gritty, Bonnie and Clyde-like feel for the grassroots impact of depression-era desperation on law and order." *American*, October 2, 1971, 235; "Stewart is superb as the tough old ex-con replete with a removable glass eye and so, too, is Baxter, in a scant part as a floozy." *Motion Picture Guide*, 891.

Release: July, Columbia Pictures
Rating: GP

"something big"—1971 (107 mins)

Producer: Andrew V. McLaglen, James Lee Barrett (uncredited), Cinema Center Films, Stanmore and Penbar Productions
Script: James Lee Barrett
Photography: Harry Stradling, Jr. (Color)
Editor: Robert Simpson
Music: Marvin Hamlisch; title song by Burt Bacharach and Hal David, sung by Mark Lindsay
Cast: Dean Martin (Joe Baker), Brian Keith (Col. Morgan), Honor Blackman (Mary Anna Morgan), Carol White (Dover MacBride), Ben Johnson (Jesse Bookbinder), Albert Salmi (Johnny Cobb), Don Knight (Tommy MacBride), Joyce Van Patten (Polly Standall), Judi Meredith (Carrie Standall), Denver Pyle (Junior Frisbee), Merlin Olsen (Sgt. Fitzsimmons), Robert Donner (Angel Moon), Harry Carey, Jr. (Joe), Ed Faulkner (Capt. Tyler), Paul Fix (Chief Yellow Sun), Armand Alzamora (Luis), David Huddleston (Malachi Morton), Bob Steele (Teamster No. 3), José Angel Espinoza (Emilio Estevez), Robert Gravage (Sam), Chuck Hicks (Corporal James), John Kelly (Barkeeper)
Summary: A native of Pittsburgh, Joe Baker now lives in the Southwest, where he makes his living robbing stagecoaches with a ragtag crew and a pet dog named Tuffy. He's promised to himself that he will return to Pennsylvania and his fiancée, a woman named Dover MacBride, once he's accomplished "something big." But four years have passed and he has

Dean Martin (right) spends a moment with Judi Meredith (left) and Joyce Van Patten (center) in "*something big*" (National General, 1971).

yet to achieve his goal. When Baker receives a letter from Dover telling him that she is coming to collect him and take him back home, Baker begins to feel desperate. If he can't pull off "something big" soon, he may never have the chance to fulfill his dream.

In a saloon, Baker shares his anxiety with Johnny Cobb, a fugitive outlaw. Years have passed since Cobb has slept with a woman. If Baker can deliver a female companion to him, Cobb explains, he will give him a Gatling gun. Baker has recently learned that a Mexican bandit named Estevez has been storing loot in a nearby town. With a Gatling gun, Baker can overwhelm Estevez and his gang and make himself and his friends rich. This is the "big" opportunity he's been seeking. Although the idea of finding, kidnapping and handing a woman over to Cobb troubles Baker, he agrees to the deal.

Baker and his men are soon stopping every passing stagecoach they see, looking for passengers who might be suitable for Cobb. Their luck is poor at first, but they eventually seize a coach that is carrying a beautiful woman, an Easterner named Mary Anna. After they make off with the prisoner, Baker discovers that Mary Anna is the wife of Col. Morgan, chief officer of Fort Dry Wells, a nearby desert outpost for cavalry horse soldiers. Morgan is scheduled to retire soon, and Mary Anna has come out to this corner of the southwest to rejoin her husband. Once the colonel learns about his wife's abduction, he summons a scout, a man named Bookbinder, and the two head out to find Mary Anna and capture Baker.

Impressed by Mary Anna's intelligence and beauty, Baker changes his mind about turning her over to Cobb. His interest in getting the Gatling gun persists, though. Ironically, Mary Anna has grown fond of Baker and she encourages him to follow through on his meeting with Cobb, taking the gun by force if necessary. Baker's desire for the gun increases even more after his fiancée, Dover, abruptly arrives by stagecoach at Fort Dry Wells. When Baker hears about her arrival, he goes to her, and learns that he must leave for Pittsburgh within a couple of days, or she will marry someone else.

Baker sets out again to rendezvous with the fugitive outlaw, Cobb. But just around the same time, Col. Morgan and Bookbinder meet Cobb on a trail and discover the Gatling gun he's pulling in a wagon. Morgan commences to arrest Cobb. This gun, he says, was recently stolen from a federal arsenal in Texas. When Cobb lets on that he is planning to trade the weapon to Baker, Morgan says that he will let Cobb go if Cobb will lead him to Baker. Cobb agrees and takes the colonel to the outlaw, surprising Baker. Mary Anna is then turned over to her husband. The colonel insists upon taking Baker and the Gatling gun back to Fort Dry Wells, as well. Mary Anna comes to Baker's aid, however, and she convinces Morgan to give him his chance to do "something big."

Baker and his gang proceed to take the weapon and attack the village where the bandit Estevez is hiding. After killing Estevez and driving his men out of the town, Baker and his men find Estevez's stash of gold and jewels in a church. Happy with himself for finally achieving "something big," Baker starts out for Pittsburgh with Dover. Joining them in the stagecoach are Mary Anna and Col. Morgan.

Comment: Like *Fools' Parade*, "*something big*" was co-produced by McLaglen and James Lee Barrett, who also wrote the script. As mentioned in the preceding citation, the two movies resemble one another closely. Both are by turns sentimental and dark, featuring scenes of great violence. In *Fools' Parade*, the malevolent prison administrator Doc Council chases ex-convict Mattie Appleyard and his friends through the West Virginia mountains; in "*something big*," the eccentric cavalry officer Morgan tracks the roguish kidnapper Joe Baker through the Texas desert. In *Fools' Parade*, Mattie walks free after holding up a bank and killing his nemesis Doc Council; in "*something big*," Joe is given permission by Morgan to use his Gatling gun to pillage and plunder a Mexican village.

Barrett also scripted three earlier pictures for McLaglen, *Shenandoah*, *Bandolero!* and *The Undefeated*. Notably, kidnapping and abductions play important roles in these films, just as they do in "*something big*." In *Shenandoah*, for example, Union forces apprehend and incarcerate Charlie Anderson's son Boy after they mistake him for a Confederate soldier. Dee Bishop (another role for Dean Martin) takes Mrs. Stoner hostage in *Bandolero!* and brings her with him to Mexico. And in *The Undefeated*, the Juaristas apprehend Col. Langdon's supporters and threaten to kill them with a firing squad. The abductions depicted in these earlier films all lead to injury and death. Boy returns from the prison camp with a terrible limp; Dee Bishop is shot to death; and the Juaristas are destroyed by Col. Thomas and his men.

Joe Baker's kidnapping of Mary Anna Morgan, in contrast, is cast in a milder light. Baker not only escapes punishment for this crime, but, rather bizarrely, he finds an advocate in Mary Anna, who tells her husband to give Baker his Gatling gun and permit him to raid the town where Estevez keeps his loot. When Morgan hesitates at first with his response to her, Mary Anna gestures to the gun and cries, "Let him have it!" Cowed by her strength apparently, the old army officer soon consents. Mary Anna's ability to exert herself effectively here might arouse our admiration, perhaps, were it not for the fact that she is helping a man who has done something despicable to her.

Reviews: "Weak Dean Martin oater." *Variety*, November 10, 1971; "[The film] occasionally

recalls the sentimentality of John Ford, with mock seriousness, as well as the inane cheeriness of those TV Westerns whose heroes never die, but just go into reruns." *New York Times*, January 22, 1972; "Unfortunately, 'Something Big' gives off rather stale and aimlessly mercenary vibrations. Barring a climactic gun battle that's both uncalled for and excessively violent in this generally unserious comedy-adventure context, there's nothing particularly disagreeable about the film. At the same time there's nothing to distinguish it." *Washington Post*, November 22, 1971; "An enjoyable Western from the prolific team of Barrett and McLaglen, who, with this film, begins to parody John Ford." *The Western*, 335.
Release: November, National General Pictures
Rating: PG

Cahill, United States Marshal—1973 (103 mins)

Producer: Michael A. Wayne, Batjac Productions
Script: Harry Julian Fink and Rita M. Fink, story by Barney Slater
Photography: Joseph Biroc (Color)
Editor: Robert L. Simpson
Music: Elmer Bernstein; song "A Man Gets to Thinkin'" by Elmer Bernstein and Don Black, sung by Charlie Rich
Cast: John Wayne (J.D. Cahill), George Kennedy (Fraser), Gary Grimes (Danny), Neville Brand (Lightfoot), Clay O'Brien (Billy Joe), Marie Windsor (Mrs. Green), Morgan Paull (Struther), Dan Vadis (MacDonald), Scott Walker (Ben Tildy), Denver Pyle (Denver), Jackie Coogan (Charlie), Rayford Barnes (Pee Wee Simser), Dan Kemp (Joe Meehan), Harry Carey, Jr. (Hank), Walter Barnes (Sheriff Grady), Paul Fix (Old Man), Pepper Martin (Hard Case), Vance Davis (Negro), Ken Wolger (Boy), James Nusser (Doc), Murray MacLeod (Gordine)
Summary: Widower J.D. Cahill has two young sons, Danny and Billy Joe. A United States marshal, Cahill frequently leaves his home in Baird, Texas, to hunt for fugitives. His frequent trips have aroused the resentment of his oldest son, Danny, who has fallen in with a group of criminals headed by a man named Fraser.

While Cahill is in the mountains rounding up a gang of bank robbers, Danny, Fraser and some of Fraser's friends are arrested following a drunken brawl in a local saloon. As the bunch waits in their cells, little Billy Joe Cahill sets fire to a stable in downtown Baird, prompting the town's sheriff, his deputies and nearly everyone else in town to rush to the blaze. Billy Joe then heads to the jail to free his brother. Danny subsequently explains to Billy Joe that Fraser and the prisoners want to rob the local bank, which is now unprotected thanks to the fire. Though Billy Joe questions his brother's judgment, he gives up the keys to the cell.

Led by Fraser, the little group proceeds from the jail to the town's bank. As the men and the boys get to work, a passerby recognizes what is happening and notifies the sheriff, who runs off from the fire to stop the robbery. The sheriff and another man are then killed. Following this, Fraser hands the money from the bank over to Billy Joe and tells him to hide it. He and the others then head back to the jail and lock themselves into their cells.

The next morning, Cahill comes in from the mountains with his prisoners and learns about the fire and the killings from the previous night. Gordine, the acting sheriff, explains that a search for the robbers has yielded no results. After hearing this, Cahill finds out from Gordine that Danny has been locked up for fighting. Gordine then decides to allow the boy and the others to go. Eager to find the robbers, Cahill deputizes Danny, wanting him by his side for help. The marshal later approaches a friend, a Comanche Indian named Lightfoot, and

John Wayne under attack in *Cahill, United States Marshal* (Warner, 1973).

hires him on a as a scout. The three depart for the mountains, where they soon find a band of men around a campfire. Cahill suspects these people are the bank robbers, though Danny tries to convince him differently. Unsure of what to make of his son's reticence, Cahill starts back for Baird with the men, who are subsequently tried and sentenced to death by hanging.

While Cahill, Danny and Lightfoot are in the mountains, Fraser pays a visit to Billy Joe, asking him where he's hidden the money from the bank job. The boy refuses to give the outlaw an answer and runs away from him through the town during a rain storm. Billy Joe is soon taken with pneumonia. Undiscouraged, Fraser sneaks into the boy's bedroom and demands information from him. Now, though, Billy Joe says that he doesn't remember where he hid the money, but he will show Fraser once he's back on his feet.

When Billy Joe is well, he reveals to Danny that the money is buried in a forest cemetery. Now certain his sons were involved in the bank robbery, Cahill follows the two into the woods when they go to get the money, bringing Lightfoot with him. The men spring on Danny and Billy once the money is out of the ground, startling them, but the boys rush off and head out for Fraser's hideout in a distant canyon. The bandit is not there, though, and the kids wait, ready to return his share to him. Soon Cahill and Lightfoot track the boys to the same canyon, but before they can enter it, one of Fraser's men attacks them, wounding Cahill and killing Lightfoot.

That night, Fraser and his associates return to their camp, where they are met by the Cahill brothers. Unhappy with the idea of only getting a portion of the bank robbery money from Danny and Billy, Fraser threatens the two, demanding that they tell him where the rest of the cash is hidden. The sudden arrival of Cahill puts an end to Fraser's efforts, however. A firefight commences and Fraser flees. Cahill then tells his sons to take him to the spot where the rest of the money has been stashed. The boys consent and lead their father to the hiding place. As they dig into the ground, Fraser reappears. Another firefight follows and this time Fraser is killed. As Danny, Billy Joe and Cahill set back for Baird with the stolen money, the boys ask their father if they will be sent away to a reformatory or remain with him at home. If the latter, they hope that Cahill will spend more time with them than he has previously.

Comment: *Cahill, United States Marshal* is the fifth and final film on which McLaglen and John Wayne worked together as director and star. The picture was shot in late 1972 and early 1973 in Durango, Mexico, with Joseph Biroc serving as the film's director of photography.[12] William H. Clothier, who'd lensed the first four McLaglen-Wayne features, had retired the previous year.[13] The picture's cast includes several actors with whom Wayne had been making pictures since the forties: Paul Fix (*Dakota*), Marie Windsor (*The Fighting Kentuckian*), Hank Worden (*Fort Apache*, 1948) and Harry Carey, Jr. (*3 Godfathers*). The cast also features several players McLaglen frequently used during his days at CBS — Denver Pyle, Rayford Barnes, James Nusser and George Kennedy.

Much like *McLintock!* and *Hellfighters*, which Wayne and McLaglen also made together, *Cahill, United States Marshal* focuses on the problems that arise when a family patriarch devotes too much time and attention to his work. But while in *McLintock!* and *Hellfighters* the characters G.W. McLintock and Chance Buckman damage their relationships with their wives, Cahill strains his relationship with his two young sons. In this picture, in fact, Cahill attributes some responsibility to his wife for his obsessive work habits. As he explains to Danny, his harshest critic: "I don't want what I'm saying to sound like I'm making excuses. There's no excuse for negligence. No excuse for a man ignoring his duty, either. Your mother — God bless her. When she was dying, the last thing she said on earth was, 'Go get 'em, J.D.' And I've been going and getting them [fugitive criminals] ever since 'til it's no longer just my job, it's part of my life."

Cahill, United States Marshal is not the first film directed by McLaglen that draws a link between troubled youths and absent father figures. In *Chisum*, William Bonney takes to killing people after the murder of his mentor, John Tunstall. We can interpret Bonney's murderous behavior as a twisted expression of love for Tunstall, perhaps, motivated as it is by a desire to avenge his death. Danny and Billy Joe, on the other hand, agree to help Fraser and the other robbers out of frustration with their father, and, it seems, a desire to punish him. As Danny tells his younger brother in advance of the job: "To hell with J.D. Cahill. Let's go rob ourselves a bank, Billy Joe."

Reviews: "John Wayne held back from usual activities by problems of fatherhood, but okay for Wayne fans." *Variety*, June 12, 1973; "[A] tacky Western of drowsy pace." *New York Times*, July 12, 1973; "While not of the same caliber as some later Wayne westerns (*Chisum, The Cowboys, The Shootist*), this is still an enjoyable film. By combining the twin complexities of fatherhood and law enforcement, a new theme is added to Wayne's screen arsenal." *Encyclopedia of Westerns*, 70; "McLaglen's directing is, as always, efficient and amiable and appears effortless in its seamless smoothness." *Western Films*, 130.

Release: July, Warner Bros.
Rating: PG
Availability: VHS, DVD

Mitchell — 1975 (97 mins)

Producer: R. Ben Efraim, Essex Enterprises Ltd.
Script: Ian Kennedy Martin

Photography: Harry Stradling, Jr. (Color)
Editor: Fred A. Chulack
Music: Larry Brown and Jerry Styner; song "Mitchell" by Steve Hoffman, Larry Brown and Jerry Styner, sung by Hoyt Axton
Cast: Joe Don Baker (Mitchell), Martin Balsam (Cummins), John Saxon (Deaney), Linda Evans (Greta), Merlin Olsen (Benton), Morgan Paull (Salvatore Mistretta), Harold J. Stone (Tony Gallano), Robert Phillips (Chief Pallin), Buck Young (Aldridge), Rayford Barnes (Tyzack), Todd Bass (Child), Jerry Hardin (Desk Sergeant), Sidney Clute (Rudy), Vicky Peters (Helena), Duffy Hambleton (Edmondo Bocca), John Ashby (Burglar), Bill Sullivan (Townsend), Jim B. Smith (O'Hagen), Charles Glover (Danziger), Charles Tamburro (Helicopter Pilot), Gary Combs (Helicopter Officer), Stan Stone (Sergeant), Tom Larence (Patrolman)
Summary: When Walter Deaney, an affluent lawyer, returns to his home, he finds a burglar rooting through drawers and stealing silverware. Instead of alerting the police, Deaney shoots the thief in cold blood, killing him. In response, the Los Angeles police department sends one of its detectives, Mitchell, over to Deaney's house. As he interviews Deaney, Mitchell begins to wonder if the lawyer may have murdered the burglar.

When he shares his thoughts with his supervisor, Chief Pallin, Mitchell learns that Deaney is already being investigated by the federal government for other crimes, and for this reason, the detective should turn his attention to a different case. The chief later sends Mitchell to Bel Air to monitor a suspected mobster named Cummins, who may be involved in trafficking heroin. Simply staking out Cummins house is too boring for Mitchell, however, and he confronts the old man, asking him directly about his business and his links to dope suppliers in Mexico.

An alcoholic, Mitchell stays in his apartment and gets drunk when he isn't watching Cummings. One night, he receives a visit from a beautiful call girl who calls herself Greta. At first, Mitchell suspects that Cummins has secured Greta's services, using her to bribe him. In reality, Deaney has been paying for the prostitute in an effort to discourage Mitchell from further investigating the events that led up to the burglar's death in his home. When Mitchell realizes this, he tells the lawyer that he cannot be bought off. Deaney decides then that Mitchell must be killed, and to do this, he solicits Cummins's help. Cummins agrees and leads Mitchell out to a dune buggy racing park, where Mitchell strands his car in a stream. A short time later, Deaney appears in a dune buggy. He tries to hit Mitchell with it, but the vehicle flips and explodes, killing Deaney.

Following this, Mitchell confronts Cummins at the gangster's home, threatening to take him into custody, along with his servant Benton. The old racketeer tries to bargain with the cop. If Mitchell will let him go, he will tell him where he can pick up and a confiscate a delivery of heroin. He explains that Mitchell can then use the heroin to make contact with and apprehend one of Cummins's gangster associates, Mistretta. But the offer is a ruse. The heroin Mitchell picks up is actually chalk and Cummins tips off Mistretta, telling him that Mitchell is looking for him. Mistretta in turn captures Mitchell, but the detective manages to escape with help from a police helicopter. Suspecting that Cummins and Benton will make a break for Mexico on a yacht, Mitchell has the helicopter fly over the ocean. Once he spots the men, Mitchell has himself lowered onto their boat, where he kills Benton, then Cummins.

Comment: From 1956 to 1965, McLaglen contributed nearly 100 episodes to CBS's *Gunsmoke*, a show in which central character Matt Dillon, a personable United States marshal, devotes his energies to helping people. A model of clemency and mercy, Marshal Dillon stands out as one of the most idealized lawman characters in television history. In McLaglen's feature films, however, police characters often conduct themselves in an unappealing manner. In *Bandolero!*, for example, the incompetent sheriff July Johnson allows Mace Bishop to liberate a gang of killers and rob a bank. In *Chisum*, Sheriffs Brady and Nodeen and their deputies serve as a sort of private militia for Lawrence Murphy. And in *The Last Hard Men*, the chief constable on a Navajo reservation takes a bribe from a fugitive killer.

Although the crime fighting hero in *Mitchell* is committed to eliminating heroin and the people who sell it from the streets of Los Angeles — a commendable objective — he generally fails to arouse our admiration, as well. A bully and a drunk, Mitchell empties ashtrays on the street, sleeps with a call girl, ignores the rules of due process, to say nothing of the ill-fitting suit he wears. And while Mitchell's refusal to behave appropriately understandably frustrates his enemies, he also irks the people with whom he works, including his supervisor, who declares at one point: "People don't like you, Mitchell. I wonder why. I don't care for you much myself."

Upon its release in September 1975, *Mitchell* generally received unfavorable reviews, with critics objecting in particular to Joe Don Baker's turn as the hero.[14] *Mitchell*'s reputation was not helped either when in 1993 a truncated version of the film was savaged by the satirical cable television show *Mystery Science Theater 3000*.[15] Despite these dismissals, *Mitchell* is an entertaining picture, with several memorable moments, especially the chase scene during which Deaney tries to kill Mitchell with a dune buggy and the later sequence when the detective uses a helicopter to pursue Cummins and Benton over the open sea.

Reviews: "Except for its gloss productions values and snappily executed special effects, 'Mitchell' is a woebegone adventure, a waste of some first rate screen talent and a smudge on the otherwise workmanlike record compiled by Andrew McLaglen." *Variety*, September 10, 1975; "It is not easy to sustain interest in an action film in which the action sequences generate little excitement and the dramatic sequences — due to second-rate writing and half-hearted acting — have no power." *Los Angeles Times*, September 26, 1975; "Director Andrew McLaglen has a created a coarse film. The hoary theme of good guy overcoming all obstacles is wedded to an end-justifies-means mentality that permits 90 minutes of blameless killings." *Ottawa Citizen*, October 28, 1975.

Release: September, Allied Artists
Rating: R
Availability: VHS, DVD

The Last Hard Men — 1976 (97 mins)

Producer: Walter Seltzer and Russell Thacher, Twentieth Century–Fox
Script: Guerdon Trueblood, based on novel *Gun Down* by Brian Garfield
Photography: Duke Callaghan (Color)
Editor: Fred Chulack
Music: Jerry Goldsmith
Cast: Charlton Heston (Sam Burgade), James Coburn (Zach Provo), Barbara Hershey (Susan Burgade), Jorge Rivero (Cesar Menendez), Michael Parks (Sheriff Noel Nye), Larry Wilcox (Mike Shelby), Thalmus Rasulala (George Weed), Morgan Paull (Portugee Shiraz), John Quade (Will Gant), Robert Donner (Lee Roy Tucker), Christopher Mitchum (Hal Brickman), David Herrera (Storekeeper)
Summary: Convicted killer Zach Provo is serving a prison sentence in Yuma, Arizona, where he and his fellow inmates spend their days under the desert sun laying railroad track. Feigning an injury one day, Zach falls to the ground. As a guard approaches, Provo strikes at

James Coburn (center) and a group of prisoners try to escape from their captors in *The Last Hard Men* (Twentieth Century–Fox, 1976).

him with a railroad spike, killing the man. An uprising follows, with the prisoners slaying their captors and escaping.

News of the escape soon reaches the city of Tucson, where retired lawman Sam Burgade lives with his daughter, Susan. It was Burgade who captured Provo years earlier and sent him to Yuma, following a shootout in which Provo's wife was killed. Certain that the killer is bound to pass through the Tucson area, Burgade meets with the current sheriff, whose name is Noel Nye. He persuades Nye to set a trap for Provo, telling him to put a false announcement in the newspaper about a gold shipment that is to be delivered to Tucson by train. When Provo reads about the shipment, Burgade reasons, he will likely strike the train. But instead of gold, the bandit will find Burgade, Nye and a posse ready to stop him.

Provo is not fooled by the announcement, and while the lawmen are busy working on their plan, he goes to Burgade's home, where he finds the old man's daughter, Susan. Provo then kidnaps Susan, eager to inflict as much pain on Burgade as he can as payback for the death of his wife, which he believes the former sheriff caused. Fearing retaliation from Burgade, Provo's cronies talk about abandoning him, but he convinces them to stay on, explaining that he has stashed a great sum of money from a past robbery on a nearby Navajo reservation. If they will accompany him to the reservation, Provo promises to pay each of them $4,000 for their loyalty. Impressed by Provo's offer, the others agree to stay on and help.

Once Burgade realizes Susan has been taken by Provo, he organizes a posse comprised of Sheriff Nye, Nye's deputies and Susan's fiancé, Hal. The group soon heads into the desert, following the kidnappers' tracks. After Provo and his men reach the Navajo reservation, Provo secures help from the local police, bribing them with some of the money he's stashed on their land. Soon after, Burgade's posse arrives at the reservation. Because this land lies outside of Sheriff Nye's jurisdiction, however, Nye tells his deputies to return with him to Tucson, leaving Burgade and Hal to go after Susan on their own.

The two eventually track the young woman's kidnappers to a large hill. Hiding in a copse of trees at the bottom of the hill, Burgade and Hal strategize, uncertain over which actions they should take. Aware of the men below, Provo tries to draw them out by having two of his own men rape Susan on the side of the hill. The poor woman's father starts to rush out to help her, but he is knocked out cold by Hal, who reasons that Burgade will get killed if he leaves the safety of the trees, and if he gets killed, Susan's chances for survival will disappear completely.

After Burgade regains consciousness, he and Hal wait for night to fall. They decide then to set the arid hill on fire by lighting brush, a development that forces many of the kidnappers to panic and expose themselves to Burgade's and Hall's guns. As daylight returns, Burgade and Hal move up the hill, trading shots with the few men who are still alive, killing them. Simultaneously, Provo skulks across the rocky terrain with Susan, but he abandons her when he spots Burgade. The bandit and the lawman proceed to exchange fire, each man hitting the other. Provo is soon killed and Burgade, gravely injured, falls into a deep canyon. Moments later, Hal and Susan find the dying man and try to help him.

Comment: *The Last Hard Men* was filmed in Arizona — in Tucson, Old Tucson and Nogales — in late fall 1975. The film is an adaptation of *Gun Down*, a 1971 novel by Brian Garfield. Garfield was asked to tweak the film's shooting script, which had been written by Guerdon Trueblood. In 2010, Garfield recalled:

> Trueblood essentially had scenarized the novel — he'd just put it in screenplay form, but hadn't changed anything. That would have come in the next draft, but he was under contract to go to Europe to do a writing job there. So he couldn't do rewrites, or go on location with the film that was then working-titled BURGADE. So I ended up doing that, to the extent that it needed doing — mainly it was just discarding long speeches (you can have those in a novel but not in a movie) and condensing scenes and setting some things aside. We did most of this on the set while shooting, and to tell the truth I wasn't called on to do much. Most of the changes were obvious ones. I do remember one scene in which Heston was supposed to deliver a half-page of dialogue about how he hated growing old. Heston threw out virtually all the dialogue and replaced it with (a) digging a pair of glasses out of his pocket to read a telegram, and (b) having trouble getting on his horse. It was a much more effective way to convey the same information. I wasn't there for the whole shoot; they'd already shot the Old Tucson sequences and the prison break. I arrived when the production moved to the border country west of Nogales, and we filmed the chase sequence that makes up roughly the last two-thirds of the movie. Again, what little I did was mainly help cut dialogue out of the script.

The Last Hard Men, the title under which the film was eventually released, was not the first McLaglen picture on which the writer worked. In 1962, Garfield had "signed on for a day's work as an extra in *McLintock!*," which was also shot in Arizona.[16]

Of all the films and television shows about the Old West that McLaglen made over his long career, *The Last Hard Men* is the most violent. The picture opens with Provo shoving a railroad spike into a guard's throat and ends with Burgade falling and smashing his body against some boulders. In between, several characters hurt and kill each other, every detail graphically captured by the camera. One of Provo's band of thugs, for instance, has his ear shot off, while another of his cronies is shot fatally at point blank range. The most distressing violence in the story, though, materializes when Provo sets his men on Susan, assaulting her before the eyes of her helpless father and her fiancé.

The savagery presented here is so intense, so unlike anything else that we find in McLaglen's other work, that *The Last Hard Men* perhaps brings to mind the string of "ultraviolent" movies Sam Peckinpah directed in the late-sixties and early-seventies, films like *The Wild Bunch*, *Straw Dogs* (1971) and *Bring Me the Head of Alfredo Garcia* (1974), in which depictions of physical cruelty and injury occur often.[17] James Coburn and Charlton Heston had in fact appeared together in Peckinpah's *Major Dundee* (1965), and Coburn had played one of the leads in Peckinpah's *Pat Garrett and Billy the Kid* (1973).

Reviews: "'The Last Hard Men,' one of the few westerns turned out by a major studio in the last couple of years, doesn't exactly herald a return to the great tradition of western filmmaking, but it is a fairly good actioner with handsome production values and some thoughtful overtones." *Variety*, April 21, 1976; "Credit Andrew McLaglen, the late Victor McLaglen's son, with infusing this movie with a nice element of suspense, but he also has to take the blame for the mindless blood-letting which occurs as Burgade picks off the lives, one by one, of Provo's sleazy companions, leaving only Provo, naturally, to the last." *Miami News*, May 23 1977; "The cast gives believable and realistic performances, with script and direction contributing a sleek smoothness." *Motion Picture Guide*, 1609; "Solid performances by Coburn and Heston and good directing by Andrew V. McLaglen elevate this handsomely produced western punctuated with revenge and violence." *Encyclopedia of the Western*, 241.

Release: June, Twentieth Century–Fox
Availability: DVD
Rating: R

The Wild Geese—1978 (132 mins)

Producer: Euan Lloyd, Various Entertainment Trading Co., Richmond, Victory Films
Script: Reginald Rose, based on the novel *The Wild Geese* by Daniel Carney
Photography: Jack Hildyard (Color)
Editor: John Glen
Music: Roy Budd; song "Flight of The Wild Geese" written and performed by Joan Armatrading; "Rafer's Theme" by A. Borodin; "Dance of Death" written and performed by Jerry and Marc Donahue
Cast: Richard Burton (Col. Faulkner), Roger Moore (Lt. Shawn Fynn), Richard Harris (Capt. Rafer Janders), Hardy Kruger (Lt. Pieter Coetzee), Stewart Granger (Sir Edward Matherson), Winston Ntshona (President Limbani), Thomas Baptiste (Mboya), John Kani (Sgt. Jesse), Jack Watson (Sandy Young), Frank Finlay (The Priest), Kenneth Griffith (Witty), Barry Foster (Balfour), Ronald Fraser (Jock), Ian Yule (Tosh), Patrick Allen (Rushton), Rosalind Lloyd (Heather), David Ladd (Sonny), Paul Spurrier (Emile), Jeff Corey (Mr. Martin), Brook Williams (Samuels), Percy Herbert (Keith), Glyn Baker (Esposito), Syndey Chama (Clark), Ken Gampu (Alexander), Jane Hylton (Mrs. Young), Taks Senekal (East German Officer), Martin Grace (East German Officer), Terry Wells (Cuban Officer), Joe Cole (Derek), Fats Bookholane (Tribal Elder), John Alderson (Randy)
Summary: British merchant banker Edward Matherson is trying to develop a copper mining operation in Zembala, a country in central Africa. He cannot commence with his plans because the nation's leader, President Julius Limbani, has been kidnapped by the Zembalan

army, which is headed by the ruthless Col. Mboya. Unable to negotiate with Mboya, Matherson decides to have Limbani rescued, with the hope that he will be eventually be restored to power. To make this come about, the businessman invites Allen Faulkner, an aging, alcoholic mercenary, to his home in London, and asks him to assemble a team of professional soldiers who can free Limbani from the military camp where he is being held.

Faulkner accepts the offer and gets to work. Among the people he recruits are two old friends, Rafer Janders and Shawn Fynn. Janders, at first, is reluctant about taking the work. Instead of fighting other people's battles, he would prefer to sell art works and spend time with his young son, Emile. Fynn, on the other hand, takes the job right away. He has recently been running errands for a crime family in London, an occupation that disgusts him.

Faulkner, Janders and Lloyd proceed to interview and hire dozens of men, after which they head to Africa, where they train and prepare for the mission. The time quickly comes for the mercenaries to attack. Catching Mboya's men off guard, they overtake the camp and find Limbani, who is close to death and unable to walk. One of the mercenaries, a white South African named Coetzee, volunteers to carry Limbani out of the camp on his shoulders. Ironically, Coetzee is a racist and an advocate for apartheid, who takes pleasure in insulting the enfeebled president with his views about white supremacy.

Fearing capture from Mboya's soldiers, Faulkner moves his team through the bush quickly, directing the men to an airfield, where Matherson has said he will send a plane to collect them. But while the mercenaries have been at work rescuing Limbani, the businessman has been communicating with Col. Mboya, who's become willing to grant him access to Zembala's copper deposits. For this reason, Matherson no longer needs Limbani to be freed. Moreover, he recognizes that if Faulkner and the others never return to London, he won't need to pay them. He then decides to cancel the flight that will pick the men up and get them out of Zembala.

When Faulkner and the others realize what has happened, they return to the bush, trying to elude Mboya's soldiers. Again Coetzee carries Limbani, and the two argue back and forth, but the shared danger they experience causes the hatred between them to soften. Coetzee even starts to question the value and viability of apartheid and racial segregation. The size of the Zembalan troops soon proves to be too much for Faulkner and the others, and many of the men are killed, including Coetzee. The mercenaries continue to run, eventually finding a village. Shortly after their arrival, Limbani dies. A Roman Catholic priest, eager to get the mercenaries out of the village, tells Faulkner, Fynn and Janders where they can find an old cargo plane, which they can use to escape.

Getting to the plane is nearly impossible because the fields surrounding it are filled with Mboya's soldiers. Faulkner sends Fynn, an experienced pilot, ahead to secure the plane. Faulkner, Janders and the remaining mercenaries then try to work their way to the plane, using their guns to hold back the Zembalans. Nearly all of the men make it, except for Janders, who is unable to jump into the plane as it rolls down the airstrip. With Mboya's men rushing toward him, Janders recognizes that he is doomed. He pleads with Faulkner to look out for his son Emile, and asks his friend to kill him with his gun, which Faulkner does. The plane takes off after this and Fynn sets a course south, hoping to find a friendly place to land.

Several months later, Faulkner sneaks into Matherson's London home. He explains that he wants to be paid for his services and takes a large sum from a safe. Then he shoots the old man dead. Sometime later, Faulkner goes to the boarding school where Emile Janders is a student. The two begin to walk together and talk about the boy's dead father.

Comment: *The Wild Geese* was produced by Euan Lloyd, a Briton who'd been working in the movies since the thirties. In the early sixties, Lloyd had served as a vice president at Highroad Productions, a film production company owned by the writer-producer Carl Foreman. One of Highroad's biggest hits during Lloyd's time with the company was *The Guns of Navarone* (1961), a World War II actioner starring Gregory Peck, David Niven, Anthony Quinn and Anthony Quayle.[18]

In his DVD commentary for *The Wild Geese*, Lloyd explains that in 1971 or 1972, after he'd establish himself as an independent producer, he was eager to make a "big" adventure picture like *The Guns of Navarone*, with a wartime backdrop and "a large cast of international players." Several years followed before Lloyd found a story that interested him — an unpublished novel about a band of mercenaries by Rhodesian novelist Daniel Carney. A friend had passed on the manuscript to Lloyd in London. "Well, I read it as quickly as I could. I was leaving for America that night and I took it with me.... I read it twice on the plane to Los Angeles." Convinced the story had the potential for being a hit, Lloyd secured the film rights from Carney. The producer then spent two years developing the picture, securing financing, overseeing the creation of a script and casting the film. Among the actors he signed for the picture, which was given the title *The Wild Geese*, were Richard Burton, Roger Moore, Richard Harris, Hardy Kruger and Stewart Granger. He asked McLaglen to direct the picture in part because John Ford, a friend of Lloyd, had praised McLaglen's talents as a filmmaker to him many years earlier.

The Wild Geese was shot in Africa and Britain in the fall of 1977, and in the summer of 1978, it had its premiere in South Africa.[19] In advance of the picture's release, *The Wild Geese* was marketed as a blood-and-guts action movie. One of the lobby posters prepared for the film featured the four principals — Burton, Moore, Kruger and Harris — hoisting machine guns, with a tag line beneath them declaring: "The dogs of war.... The best **** mercenaries in the business." To a certain extent, the *Wild Geese* is a film that appeals to audiences who enjoy on-screen depictions of violence and lively action sequences, for instance the commandos' storming of the camp where Limbani is held prisoner and the climactic scene in which Mboya's men besiege the airstrip. Several critics were in fact bothered by these depictions of Faulkner and his men at work, arguing the movie sensationalized — and romanticized — the soldier of fortune business. Ray Conlogue of the *Globe and Mail*, a Canadian paper, complained, for instance, that the movie is "a great but dishonest shoot-up that merely feeds fantasies," while the *Washington Post*'s Bart Mills dismissed it as "a film that glorifies mercenaries."[20]

Accusations that *The Wild Geese* glorifies professional soldiers and the work they do may be overstated, however. Though the picture does indeed make the lives of these men look exciting on several occasions, it also draws attention to the great danger that attends their profession. After Matherson hires Faulkner early in the picture, we have to remember, the colonel creates a unit of about fifty men. Many of these men are subsequently killed in Zembala, some of them experiencing horrific, painful deaths. Arthur Witty, the group's medic, is hacked to death by Mboya's men with machetes, for instance, and Coetzee dies slowly from a bullet wound in his chest. The carnage is so great that when Fynn eventually manages to fly the men out of Zembala, only a dozen of the original group have survived. Making the deaths of these men more wasteful is the overall futility of their mission. Just after their plane takes off, that is, President Limbani dies. Not only have Faulkner and his men been betrayed by their employer Matherson, but whatever hope there may have been for restoring a democratically elected leader to power in Zembala no longer exists. Their efforts — and their deaths — have yielded nothing.

Reviews: "Euan Lloyd's uppercase actioner, centered on a caper by mercenaries in Africa, attempts to be a cornucopia of tried boxoffice hooks but ultimately fails to meld its comedy adventure, pathos, violence, heroics — or even its political message — into a credible whole." *Variety*, May 24, 1978; "McLaglen is a straightahead filmmaker, and he doesn't beat around

the African bush. Though more than two hours long, 'The Wild Geese' is adroitly paced, thanks to a sturdily structured script by Reginald Rose." *Newsweek,* November 27, 1978; "[T]he picture has an expensive look befitting the marketable big-name starts, but the screenplay is overloaded by its attempt to blend action, comedy, violence, and pathos." *Toledo Blade,* November 14, 1978.
Release: November, Allied Artists
Rating: R
Availability: VHS, DVD

Television Movies

Stowaway to the Moon—1975 (95 mins)

Broadcast: CBS, January 10, 1975
Producer: John Cutts, Mor-Film Fare, Inc.
Script: John Booth and William R. Shelton, based on William R. Shelton's novel *Stowaway to the Moon: The Camelot Odyssey*
Photography: J.J. Jones (Color)
Editor: John Schreyer
Music: Pat Williams
Cast: Lloyd Bridges (Charlie Engelhardt), Jeremy Slate (Rick Lawrence), James McMullan (Ben Pelham), Morgan Paull (Dave Anderson), Michael Link (E.J.), John Carradine (Avril), James Callahan (Smathers), Walter Brooke (Whitehead), Keene Curtis (Tom Estes), Edward Faulkner (Eli Mackernutt), Jon Cedar (Hans Hartman), Barbara Faulkner (Mary Mackernutt), Stephen Rogers (Joey), Charles "Pete" Conrad, Jr. (Himself)
Summary: Eager to experience space flight, young E.J. Mackernut sneaks himself onto a manned NASA rocket that takes off from Cape Canaveral in Florida. As the rocket makes its way to the moon, one of the astronauts on board finds E.J. hiding in a trash bin. The discovery prompts the astronauts and their NASA supervisors to cancel the planned landing. But E.J. asks the chiefs at Mission Control to reconsider, arguing that his presence will not interfere with the astronauts' efforts to collect important rocks on the moon's surface. Later, after one of the astronauts becomes ill, E.J. actually plays a part in salvaging the mission, and when he returns to Earth, he enjoys a hero's welcome.
Comment: The improbability of its plot doesn't prevent *Stowaway to the Moon* from being an excellent film that is at once amusing and suspenseful. Much of the picture was shot on location at the Kennedy Space Center, making use of real NASA facilities, including a launch pad. Editor John Schreyer also cut in vintage footage from actual Apollo space flights. Several NASA personalities contributed to the picture, too. Joe W. Schmitt, a Space Flight Equipment Specialist for NASA, served as the film's technical advisor, and Pete Conrad, the third astronaut to walk on the moon, has a small on-screen role as a TV newsman.[21] One of just two productions McLaglen directed with a science fiction theme (the other being the pilot episode of *The Fantastic Journey* television series), *Stowaway to the Moon* features several actors the director had worked with previously in both feature films and television: Ed Faulkner (*Shenandoah, The Undefeated*), Jeremy Slate (*The Devil's Brigade*) and John Carradine (*Gunsmoke, Have Gun, Will Travel*). The source for the telefilm's script is *Stowaway to the Moon: The Camelot Odyssey,* a 1973 novel by William Roy Shelton.
Reviews: "'Stowaway to the Moon' ... is exceptional not merely because it's one movie-for-TV that's actually suitable for children but because it's so exhilarating an adventure. And

not only is it a refreshing change of pace from the formula suspense thrillers but also a lively celebration of the power of the imagination and the value of the intellect." *Los Angeles Times*, January 10, 1975.

Murder at the World Series—1977 (97 mins)

Broadcast: ABC, March 20, 1977
Producer: Cy Chermak, ABC Circle Films
Script: Cy Chermak
Photography: Richard C. Glouner (Color)
Editor: John F. Link, Richard A. Harris
Music: John Cacavas
Cast: Lynda Day George (Margot Mannering), Murray Hamilton (Harvey Murkison), Karen Valentine (Lois Marshall), Gerald S. O'Loughlin (Moe Gold), Michael Parks (Larry Marshall), Janet Leigh (Karen Weese), Hugh O'Brian (The Governor), Nancy Kelly (Alice Dakso), Johnny Seven (Severino), Tamara Dobson (Lisa), Joseph Wiseman (Sam Druckman), Bruce Boxleitner (Cisco), Larry Mahan (Gary Vawn), Cooper Huckabee (Frank Gresham), Maggie Wellman (Kathy), Cynthia Avila (Jane Torres), Monica Gayle (Barbara Gresham), Lisa Hartman (Stewardess).
Summary: After the Houston Astros baseball club declines to sign a player named Cisco, the young man, made insane by anger, sets out to spoil the team's chances of beating the Oakland Athletics in the World Series. To do this, Cisco tries to sabotage the Series's last two games at the Houston Astrodome, abducting and murdering innocent people. Among Cisco's victims is a waitress named Kathy, whom he mistakes for a ball player's wife.
Reviews: "'Murder at the World Series' ... is a terrorist suspenser that's well enough made to be diverting but is also disturbing because it could give the unbalanced some dangerous ideas." *Los Angeles Times*, March 18, 1977; "Andrew V. McLaglen draws upon his years of big-screen experience to make 'Murder at the World Series' come alive despite inevitable contrivances. Indeed, this fast-paced film does posses scope and does manage to let us get to know an awful lot of people in a very brief period of time." *Washington Post*, March 18, 1977.

Series Television

The NBC Mystery Movie

In 1971, NBC launched *The NBC Mystery Movie* on Sunday nights. An "umbrella" TV series, *The NBC Mystery Movie* provided viewers with an opportunity to watch what Tim Brooks and Earle Marshall have described as "a number of rotating series that appeared in the same time slot on different weeks." Episodes had 90-minute and 120-minute running times. Each of the programs produced for the show followed the efforts of law enforcement professionals and private detectives who investigate and solve crimes. *Columbo*, *McCloud* and *McMillan and Wife* comprised the show's lineup during the inaugural season. High ratings prompted NBC to introduce a second edition of the *Mystery Movie* to its broadcast schedule on Wednesday nights during the show's second season, and new productions like *Madigan*, *Cool Million*, *Banacek* and *Hec Ramsey* were added to the rotation. *The NBC Mystery Movie* would stay on the air for another three seasons and the network continued to develop and introduce new offerings. Later series included *Tenafly*, *Farrady & Company*, *The Snoop Sisters*, *Amy Prentiss*, *McCoy*, *Quincy, M.E.*, and *Lanigan's Rabbi*. McLaglen contributed four productions to *The*

NBC Mystery Movie during the show's third and fourth seasons (1973–1975), directing episodes of *Banacek*, *Hec Ramsey* and *Amy Prentiss*.[22]

Banacek

Created by Anthony Wilson, *Banacek* was part of *The NBC Mystery Movie*'s rotation from fall 1972 to fall 1974.[23] George Peppard played the series' titular hero, a self-employed private investigator who hires himself out to insurance companies. Working in Boston, Banacek would search for stolen precious goods that had been indemnified by his clients; finding these items (e.g. rare coins, art, vehicles) spared the insurers from having to pay out enormous claims to policy holders. Other characters in the series included Banacek's love interest, Carlie Kirkland (Christine Belford), his driver, Jay Drury (Ralph Manza), and his friend Felix Mulholland (Murray Matheson), a high-end bookseller. Prior to *Banacek*, Peppard and McLaglen worked together in 1971 on the feature film *One More Train to Rob*.

"The Three Million Dollar Piracy"

First Broadcast: NBC, November 21, 1973
Producer: Howie Horwitz
Script: Stanley Ralph Ross and Robert Van Scoyk, story by Jack Turley
Photography: Sam Leavitt
Editor: Robert Watts
Music: Dick DeBenedictis
Guest Stars: Linden Chiles (Henry DeWitt), Don Knight (Isaac Porter), Dick Gautier (Mario Fratelli), Arlene Martell (Diana Maitland), Hal Buckley (Sanborn), Titos Vandis (Capt. Larkos), Martin Kosleck (Bruno), Susan Damante (Leona Sanborn), Rudy Challenger (Lt. Trask), Lada Edmund, Jr. (Lila Porter), Jean Manson (Wilda Porter), Byron Morrow (Max), Hal Baylor (Foreman)
Summary: A shah has commissioned a Boston artisan to craft a magnificent, bejeweled coach for his imminent wedding. Valued at $3 million, the coach is to be shipped across the ocean to North Africa. Shortly after it is loaded onto the ship, the coach vanishes, practically before the eyes of Henry DeWitt, an executive with the Boston Insurance Company. Banacek learns about the disappearance through a source and gets to work quickly. When he isn't chasing leads, he flirts with Carlie, who has recently become engaged to DeWitt.
Comment: Although the plot for "The Three Million Dollar Piracy" is built around Banacek's investigation, McLaglen and writers Ross and Van Scoyk direct a great deal of attention to Banacek's private life, focusing in particular on his pursuits of women who are connected to other men, including not only Carlie, but an actress named Diana Maitland (Arlene Martell), the woman for whom the shah has had the wedding coach built. Banacek is more interested in sex, it seems, than conventional morality, a trait he shares with Hark Fleet, the outlaw character he played in McLaglen's *One More Train to Rob*.
Availability: DVD

"Rocket to Oblivion"

First Broadcast: February 12, 1974
Producer: Howie Horwitz
Script: Robert Van Scoyk
Photography: Sam Leavitt
Editor: Albert J. Zuniga

Music: Hal Mooney
Guest Stars: Linda Evans (Cherry Saint-Saens), Andrew Prine (Wardlow), Don Gordon (Buck Powell), Tom Drake (Roger Fashion), Phillip Carey (Art Gallagher), Roy Poole (Det. Garrett), George Murdock (Cavanaugh), Dick Van Patten (Donald Morgan), Polly Middleton (Beautiful Girl), Robert Rothwell (Officer Lonigan), Jayne Kennedy (Girl Demonstrator), Jimmy Joyce (Eddie)
Summary: An eccentric engineer named Tom Wardlow sets up a display at the Science and Industry Expo in Boston, hoping to find a buyer for a new rocket engine he has designed. Just as Wardlow prepares to present his invention to a group of potential investors, the lights in the building go out; when they return, his rocket engine is gone. Because the $5 million machine is insured by the Boston Insurance Company, Banacek is notified and commences an investigation, eventually tracing the theft to an ex-professional football player and a crooked scientist.
Comment: McLaglen would again direct Linda Evans (Cherry) in *Mitchell*, which went into production in the fall of 1974, just about six months after this episode had its broadcast.[24] "Rocket to Oblivion" also features two actors McLaglen had worked with previously: Andrew Prine (Wardlow), who'd starred in numerous television shows (*Gunsmoke, Have Gun, Will Travel*) and features (*Bandolero!, The Devil's Brigade*) McLaglen helmed in the sixties, and Dick Van Patten (Morgan), who'd appeared in an early episode of *Rawhide* ("The Power and the Plow").
Availability: DVD

Hec Ramsey

Hec Ramsey was developed for producer Jack Webb's Mark VII productions.[25] The program was set in New Prospect, Oklahoma, in the early twentieth century, with Richard Boone playing the show's lead, an aged deputy whose training in forensic science helps him solve crimes. Among the other players in the cast were Rick Lenz, who played Oliver Stamp, the sheriff of New Prospect, and Harry Morgan, who played Amos Coogan, the town barber. *Hec Ramsey* ran for two seasons (1972–1974) before NBC removed the series from the *Mystery Movie* lineup.[26]

Scar Tissue (95 mins)

First Broadcast: March 10, 1974
Producer: Harold Jack Bloom
Script: Mann Rubin
Photography: Robert Hauser
Editor: Edward Bierry
Music: Fred Steiner
Guest Stars: Chill Wills (Sam McDade), Kurt Russell (Matthias Kane), William Campbell (Vince Alexander), Dick Haymes (Hobbs), Charles Aidman (Bannister), Hilarie Thompson (Betsy), Jason Evers (Peter Jones), Albert Salmi (John Rhodes)
Summary: Matthias Kane hates his father and has told people he wants to kill him for having abandoned him and his mother years earlier. When Kane's dead body is found in New Prospect, suspicion falls on the angry young man.
Comment: "Scar Tissue" features several actors McLaglen had previously directed in motion pictures: Kurt Russell (*Fools' Parade*), Albert Salmi ("*something big*"), Chill Wills (*McLintock!*) and William Campbell (*Man in the Vault*).

Amy Prentiss

Jessica Walter, star of the short-lived *Amy Prentiss*, one of the rotating programs in NBC's *Mystery Movie* series (Universal Television).

Amy Prentiss ran for one season (1974–1975) on *The NBC Mystery Movie*. The show's central character (Jessica Walter), after which the series took its name, served as the San Francisco Police Department's chief of detectives. *Amy Prentiss*'s regular cast was made up of the officials and investigators who work with the chief— Det. Contreras (Johnny Seven), Det. Tony Russell (Steve Sandor), Det. Rod Pena (Arthur Metrano). Prentiss's daughter Jill (Helen Hunt) also had a recurring role.[27] The *Amy Prentiss* character was first introduced on *Ironside* (1967–1975), an NBC series about a wheelchair-bound investigator who also works for the San Francisco Police Department.[28]

"The Desperate World of Jane Doe"

First Broadcast: December 22, 1974
Producer: Cy Chermak
Script: Elinor Karpf, Steven Karpf
Photography: Alric Edens
Guest Stars: Gwenn Mitchell (Joan Carter), Corrine Camacho (Judyth Payson), Harvey Jason (Fleishman), Cameron Mitchell (Satin Charlie), Don Murray (Connors), Andrew Prine (Mel Kay), Joyce Van Patten (Mrs. Hyser)
Summary: Connors is a drunk who embarrasses himself at a party with his obnoxious behavior. The next morning, he finds a dead woman in his home. The investigating officers conclude quickly that Connors is the killer, an opinion Amy Prentiss doesn't share.

The Wonderful World of Disney

In 1954, Walt Disney Productions launched *Disneyland*, an anthology television program for young audiences. Over its long run, the series found a home on all three of the era's national television networks, appearing first on ABC, then NBC and finally CBS. Comprised of cartoons, single episode dramas, serials and documentaries, the show remained on the air until 1983 under various names, including *The Magical World of Disney*, *Walt Disney's Wonderful World of Color*, *Walt Disney Presents* and *Walt Disney*. From 1969 to 1979, the program was called *The Wonderful World of Disney*, with episodes appearing as a part of NBC's Sunday night lineup.[29] McLaglen helmed two first-run productions for *The Wonderful World of Disney*, "The Bluegrass Special" and "Trail of Danger."

"The Bluegrass Special"

First Broadcast: May 22, 1977
Producer: James Algar, Walt Disney Productions

Script: Sheldon Stark, based on a story by James Algar
Photography: Duke Callaghan
Editor: Gordon D. Breanner
Music: Buddy Baker
Cast: William Windom (Phil Wainright), Celeste Holm (Deirde), Devon Ericson (Penny), Davy Jones (Davey), James Gleason (Billy Joe), Shug Fisher (Harvey), Ed Faulkner (Dan), John R. McKee (Jerry)
Summary: Penny Wainright wants to be a jockey. She comes closer to realizing this dream after her father purchases a horse called Woodhill. Feisty and mean, Woodhill refuses to be handled by men, but he likes Penny and allows her to ride him. With Penny in the saddle, in fact, Woodhill runs like a champion. With her father's permission, Penny decides to enter Woodhill into a race called the Bluegrass Special. Unfortunately, a track official, concerned about Woodhill's temperamental manner, won't let the horse participate in the race. Some jockeys ridicule Penny over this. She, in turn, challenges them to a race on a training track, which she and Woodhill win.
Comment: McLaglen's *Sahara* is similarly concerned with a young female who enters into a race against men. In *Sahara*, however, the race involves automobiles, not horses. William Windom (Wainright) played the role of Sizemore in McLaglen's *Fools' Parade*.
Availability: VHS, DVD

"Trail of Danger"

First Broadcast: March 12, March 19, 1978
Producer: James Algar
Script: Calvin Clements, Jr., from a story by H.L. Davis
Photography: Duke Callaghan
Editor: Gordon D. Breanner
Music: Buddy Baker
Cast: Larry Wilcox (Beech Carter), Jim Davis (Pop Apling), Robert Donner (Sheep Boss), David Ireland (Hand), Tom Hiler (Ice Man), Charles Hoagland (Old Timer)
Summary: Two cowboys are hired to move a herd of wild horses across a 180-mile stretch during the winter. Along the way they encounter numerous challenges, including wild animals, bad weather and hostile sheepherders.
Comment: Larry Wilcox (Beech), best known for his role as Jon Baker on the *CHiPS* television show, first worked with McLaglen in 1975 on the feature *The Last Hard Men*. He also appeared in the director's 1985 telefilm *The Dirty Dozen: Next Mission*. Jim Davis (Pop) appeared in "The Treasure," a 1962 episode of *Have Gun, Will Travel* that McLaglen directed. Robert Donner (Sheep Boss) had also worked with McLaglen in previous television productions, as well as the films *Fools' Parade*, *"something big"* and *The Last Hard Men*.

Pilot Episodes and Series Premieres

The Log of the Black Pearl—1975 (86 mins)

Broadcast: NBC, January 4, 1975
Producer: William Stark, Black Pearl Productions, Mark VII Limited, Universal Television
Script: Harold Jack Bloom, story by Harold Jack Bloom, Eric Bercovici, Jerry Ludwig
Photography: Gabriel Torres (Color)
Editor: Robert Leeds

Music: Laurence Rosenthal

Cast: Ralph Bellamy (Capt. Fitzsimmons), Kiel Martin (Chris Sand), Jack Kruschen (Jocko Roper), Glen Corbett (Michael Devlin), Anne Archer (Lila Bristol), Henry Wilcoxon (Alexander Sand), John Alderson (Eric Kort), Edward Faulkner (Fenner), Pedro Armendariz, Jr. (Archie Hector), José Angel Espinosa (Benjamin Velasquez)

Summary: Alexander Sand operates a maritime salvage company that searches for treasure below the sea. When he dies, Sand leaves his grandson, Chris, an enormous schooner called the Black Pearl, which is moored in Mexico. A Los Angeles stockbroker, Chris plans to sell the ship in order to pay off his grandfather's extensive debts. To get an estimate of the Black Pearl's worth, he hires a consultant, an old sailor named Fitzsimmons. As the two men review the Black Pearl's logs, they realize that Alexander Sand had been on the verge of locating a stash of Swiss gold in the Tropic of Cancer. Chris and Fitzsimmons decide then to put together a crew and set out on the Black Pearl to find the loot. Their efforts are thwarted by an American businessman named Devlin, who is also aware of the sunken gold and wants the treasure for himself.

Comment: *The Log of the Black Pearl* was made for Jack Webb's production company, Mark VII Limited. NBC chose not to pick up the program as a series. Shot on location in Mexico, the telefilm features gorgeous footage of the open sea, the shoreline and an actual street carnival set on the scenic streets of Mazatlan.[30] *The Log of the Black Pearl* provided McLaglen with the opportunity to direct several actors he knew and had worked with on earlier productions. Jack Kruschen (Jocko) played Jake Birnbaum, the chess-playing storekeeper in McLaglen's *McLintock!* And Glenn Corbett (Devlin) appeared as Pat Garrett in McLaglen's *Chisum. The Log of the Black Pearl* also marks one of the last times the director collaborated with supporting actor Ed Faulkner (Fenner), who'd been working with McLaglen in film and television projects since the fifties.

Banjo Hackett—1976 (96 mins)

Alternate Title: *Banjo Hackett: Roamin' Free*
Broadcast: NBC, May 3, 1976
Producer: Bruce Lansbury, Bruce Lansbury Productions, Columbia Pictures Television
Script: Ken Trevey
Photography: Al Francis
Editor: Dann Cahn, David Wages
Music: Morton Stevens
Cast: Don Meredith (Banjo Hackett), Ike Eisenmann (Jubal), Chuck Connors (Sam Ivory), Jennifer Warren (Mollie Brannen), Dan O'Herlihy (Tip Conaker), Jeff Corey (Judge Janeway), Gloria DeHaven (Lady Jane Gray), L.Q. Jones (Sheriff Tadlock), Jan Murray (Jethro Swain), Anne Francis (Flora Dobbs), Slim Pickens (Lijah Tuttle), David Young (Elmore Mintore), Richard Young (Luke Mintore), John O'Leary (Mister Creed), Jeff Morris (Jack O'Spades), John Anderson (Moose Matlock), Kenneth O'Brien (Wiley Pegram), Britt Leach (Carpenter), Shirley O'Hara (Postmistress), Elizabeth Perry (Grace Nye), Doodles Weaver (Old Turkey), Stan Haze (Blacksmith)

Summary: Benjamin Johnson "Banjo" Hackett is a loner who drifts from town to town, making his living trading horses. After he finds out that his sister has died, he tracks her son, Jubal, to an orphanage. Seeing that Jubal has been mistreated by the orphanage's director, Banjo takes the boy out of the home. He learns from Jubal that an Arabian horse Banjo gave him, a mare named Dido, has been sold at auction to pay for the debts Jubal's mother left behind when she died. Dido, it turns out, is pregnant with a foal and a rich horse breeder is ready to pay $10,000 for her. Banjo and Jubal then set out to find the missing animal, but their efforts are hindered by Sam Ivory, an outlaw who wants the horse himself.

Comment: An announcement that appears in the production's closing credits says that the outdoor sequences in *Banjo Hackett* were shot in Los Padres National Forest, in Santa Barbara County, California. The forest is located close to the city of Carpinteria, the home of Cates School, where McLaglen was a student in the late thirties. Don Meredith (Banjo) had been a successful player in the National Football League from 1960 to 1968, spending his entire career as a quarterback with the Dallas Cowboys.[31] Richard Young (Luke Mintore) would later play the role of Prince Malko in *Eye of the Widow*, McLaglen's last film. *Banjo Hackett* was not picked up as a series by NBC.

Availability: DVD

Royce — 1976

Broadcast: CBS, May 21, 1976
Producer: William T. Philips, MTM Enterprises
Script: Jim Byrnes
Photography: Edward Plante
Editor: Jim Byrnes
Music: Jerrold Immel
Cast: Robert Forster (Royce), Mary Beth Hurt (Susan Mabry), Moosie Drier (Stephen Mabry), Teri Lynn Wood (Heather Mabry), Michael Parks (Blair Mabry), Eddie Little Sky (White Bull), Dave Cass (Dent)
Summary: Royce is a white man who has spent much of his life living with and learning outdoor survival skills from a Comanche tribe. When a woman and her two sons are abandoned in rural Kansas, Royce comes to their aid, leading them through the wilderness to California.
Comment: *Royce* was made for Mary Tyler Moore's MTM Productions. This Western-themed, hour-long pilot had its broadcast on CBS, marking the first time the network had carried one of McLaglen's show since his departure from *Gunsmoke* in 1965. *Royce* was not picked up as a regular series.[32]

Code R

Code R ran on CBS from January 1977 to June 1977. McLaglen directed the series' hour-long pilot episode. *Code R* was an adventure show, set on the Channel Islands of California, the best known of which is Catalina. The show depicted law enforcement and emergency professionals aiding and rescuing people in distress. Regular cast members included Tom Simcox, James Houghton and Martin Kove.[33]

"High Adventure"

Broadcast: January 26, 1977
Producer: Edwin Self, Warner Bros. Television
Script: Edwin Self
Photography: Sam Leavitt
Music: Lee Holdridge

Guest Cast: Susanne Reed (Suzy), Ben Davidson (Milbank), Robbie Rundle (Bobby), W.T. Zacha (Harry), Ted Gehring (Jerome Popkin), Stephen Oliver (Jacobson), Frank Salsedo (Willie), Dennis Bowen (Jerry), Pat Anderson (Danielle)

Summary: This episode introduces the show's principal characters at work, helping tourists and locals. The problems they respond to include roving wildlife, a stranded swimmer and a runaway hot air balloon.

The Fantastic Journey

A science fiction series, *The Fantastic Journey* premiered on NBC in February 1977. The program followed a group of marine biologists who take their boat into the Bermuda Triangle. After their ship wrecks on a strange island, the scientists learn that they have passed through a mystical portal into a place where time is scrambled; among the other residents on the island are people from the long ago past and the distant future. McLaglen directed the series' pilot, "The Vortex." *The Fantastic Journey* was cancelled in April 1977.[34]

"The Vortex"

Broadcast: February 3, 1977
Producer: Leonard Katzman, Bruce Lansbury Productions, Ltd., Columbia Pictures Television
Script: Michael Michaelian, Katharyn Michaelian and Merwin Gerard, story by Merwin Gerard
Photography: Sam Leavitt
Editor: William O. Cairncross and Richard Rabjohn
Music: Robert Prince
Cast: Scott Thomas (Dr. Paul Jordan), Susan Howard (Mara), Jared Martin (Varian), Carl Franklin (Dr. Fred Walters), Karen Somerville (Jill), Ike Eisenmann (Scott Jordan), Leif Erickson (Ben Wallace), Don Knight (Paget), Ian McShane (Cambden), Gary Collins (Dar-L), Mary Ann Mobley (Rhea), Jason Evers (Atar), Lynn Borden (Enid), Jack Stauffer (Andy), Byron Chung (George), Tom McCorry (Scar), Mike Road (Voice of the Source)
Summary: Led by marine biologist Dr. Paul Jordan, a team of researchers sets out on a ship called the Yonder to conduct research in the Atlantic. After the scientists enter the region of the ocean called the Bermuda Triangle, their ship breaks apart and sinks. The survivors wash up on the shore of an island, where they are met by a man named Varian, a doctor who uses music to cure injuries. Varian explains that men and animals from different periods in the earth's history exist simultaneously on the island. Varian, for example, is from the twenty-third century. Elsewhere on the island are some sailors from the sixteenth century, who kidnap the Yonder's captain and a couple of scientists. With Varian's help, Dr. Jordan and his son, Scott, rescue the captives. Almost immediately, they find themselves facing a new adversary, a monster called The Source that consumes human beings for energy.
Comment: Bruce Lansbury is credited with creating *The Fantastic Journey* in the program's opening credits. Lansbury had served as producer on the unsold pilot for *Banjo Hackett*, which McLaglen also directed. Child actor Ike Eisenmann (Scott) appeared in both productions, as well.

SIX

The Eighties

In the eighties, McLaglen travelled the world extensively, directing motion pictures in India, the Middle East, Asia and Europe. He helmed several television productions, as well, including a pair of miniseries, *The Blue & The Gray* and *On Wings of Eagles*, which garnered the director some of the best reviews of his career. Despite these successes, McLaglen left filmmaking in 1989, trading his life behind the camera for a quieter existence in Friday Harbor, Washington, where he continues to live today.

Feature Films

ffolkes—1980 (99 mins)

Producer: Elliott Kastner, Cinema Seven Productions Ltd.
Script: Jack Davies, from his novel *Esther, Ruth & Jennifer*
Photography: Tony Imi (Color)
Editor: Alan Strachan
Music: Michael J. Lewis
Cast: Roger Moore (ffolkes), James Mason (Admiral Brindsen), Anthony Perkins (Kramer), Michael Parks (Shulman), David Hedison (King), Jack Watson (Olafsen), George Baker (Fletcher), Jeremy Clyde (Tipping), David Wood (Herring), Faith Brook (Prime Minister), Lea Brodie (Sanna), Anthony Pullen Shaw (Ackerman), Philip O'Brien (Webb), John Westbook (Dawnay), Jennifer Hilary (Sarah), John Lee (Phillips), Brook Williams (Helicopter Pilot), Sean Arnold (Schmidt), Mathias Kilroy (Olsen), Lindsay Campbell (Shaw), Jonathan Nuth (Kirk), Robert Swan (Miller), William Abney (Gail)
Summary: A gang of hijackers led by a madman named Lew Kramer overtakes a supplies ship in the North Sea that services an enormous oil production platform. If the British government fails to deliver a £25 million pound ransom to him, Kramer will blow up the platform, an act that will result in the deaths of hundreds of people and the likely destruction of the northern European coastline.

The Prime Minister of Britain consults with her advisors about the best actions to take and learns that the Royal Navy lacks the resources and training needed to eliminate the threat Kramer poses. One of her counselors then suggests that the government should consider the services of Rufus Excalibur ffolkes, the head of a private company called ffolkes fusiliers, which specializes in counter-terrorism operations.

When ffolkes is approached about the situation, he agrees to help and is soon flown out from his private castle to London, where he meets with the prime minister and a Royal Navy admiral named Brindsen. ffolkes begins to counsel his new clients about the best ways to defeat Kramer, arguing for subterfuge and cunning. In particular, ffolkes asks to be allowed to pose as a British officer and accompany Brindsen as the admiral negotiates with Kramer on board the hijacked supplies ship. When he and the admiral have Kramer's attention, some of ffolkes's fusiliers will storm and overtake the captive ship.

Once ffolkes and Brindsen meet with Kramer, however, Kramer says that he does not like ffolkes's face and has him sent by helicopter from the supplies ship to the oil production platform. Undaunted, ffolkes dons a wet suit and swims back to the supplies ship. Unknown to him, several of his men set out for the ship at the same time. Almost simultaneously, ffolkes and the commandos board the ship. Covered head to toe in wet suits and masks, the men do not recognize each other at first, and the employer and his employees begin to attack one another. Nevertheless, the raid is ultimately successful, with ffolkes and his fusiliers killing many of Kramer's men with their bare hands, knives and harpoons. When ffolkes eventually makes his way to the ship's control room, he fires a harpoon into Kramer's chest. Almost dead, Kramer reaches for the button that will blow up the oil platform. Fortunately, ffolkes manages to dismantle the detonator before he can succeed and Kramer dies.

Comment: Filmed along the coast of Ireland, *ffolkes* marks McLaglen's second collaboration with Roger Moore.[1] The actor and director had first worked together two years earlier in South Africa on *The Wild Geese*. Moore was one of the world's most recognizable actors in the late-seventies, thanks to his recurring role as the secret agent 007 in the James Bond film series. In pictures like *The Man with the Golden Gun* (1974) and *The Spy Who Loved Me* (1977), Moore had interpreted Bond with great charisma, playing a tuxedoed gallant with an appetite for beautiful women. In *ffolkes*, however, the actor subverts the debonair image of Bond he'd created. Rather than pursuing women, ffolkes reviles them, preferring instead the company of cats. His face buried beneath a billowy beard, he makes a point of eschewing gentlemanly conduct whenever he can, taking pleasure in shocking people with his rudeness. When he is visited at his castle home by the priggish Admirable Brindsen, for instance, ffolkes insists upon having a drink, thought it is not yet even noon. Even worse, he takes his liquor straight from the bottle, declaring, "We drink scotch here the way it should be drunk — neat."

In his favorable review of the picture, the *Washington Post*'s Gary Arnold wrote, "One can understand why Roger Moore might have leaped at the opportunity to play ffolkes. The character's eccentricities are so plentiful, beginning with the spelling of his name, that Moore probably felt liberated from the rigidities of the James Bond role while embodying a similar kind of heroic gent."[2] At the same time, however, subtle references to Moore's career as Bond can be spotted throughout *ffolkes*. Attentive viewers will note, for instance, that one of Moore's co-stars is David Hedison (King), an actor who'd shared the screen with Moore as Bond's CIA friend Felix Leitner in *Live and Let Die* (1973). On at least one occasion, as well, composer Michael J. Lewis inserts bits of composer John Barry's distinctive main theme from *Goldfinger* (1964) — the first Bond film — into his otherwise original score.[3]

Spiked with action and clever humor, *ffolkes* is one of McLaglen's best features, thanks not only to Moore's memorable performance, but also Anthony Perkins's as the spiteful villain Kramer. Michael Parks shines, as well, playing Kramer's nearsighted number two, Harold Shulman. His face distorted by a pair of enormous eye glasses, Harold follows after Kramer devotedly through much of the picture, offering him reassuring words constantly, even stroking his boss's forearm at one point.

Reminiscent, perhaps, of the men who hijack a subway car in Joseph Sargent's *The Taking of Pelham One Two Three* (1974), Kramer and his cronies are criminals who behave like terrorists. And though Kramer declares that his intentions are apolitical and that he only wants the money he can extort from the British government, the damage inflicted on the British economy and government will be profound if Kramer follows through with his plans to blow up the oil production platform. There is much more at stake, in other words, than the equipment and human lives Kramer is threatening to destroy. A bit surprisingly, perhaps, the British government turns to a private contractor, rather than its own military and law enforcement assets, to neutralize Kramer. In this respect, ffolkes departs again from the James Bond film series; Bond, after all, is a government employee.

ffolkes may succeed in defeating Kramer — an act for which he is personally thanked by Britain's prime minister in the film's final scene — but his outlandish methods and personality, along with his frequently poor judgment, hardly arouse our confidence. Early in the sequence during which he and his men begin to liberate the hijacked ship, for example, ffolkes is mistaken by one of his people for one of Kramer's. In the resulting scuffle, ffolkes throws his own employee, rather needlessly, over the ship's side into the ocean. ffolkes's contempt for women is so pervasive, as well, that he cannot accept at first that a female crew member who saves his life later in the same sequence is in fact a woman. "You look like a boy. You act like a boy," he insists. Only later, when he shoves his rescuer under a hot shower in an effort to save her from hypothermia does he realize his error. "By casting James Bond's Roger Moore as a misogynist, by showing the special agent as a social misfit," notes Laura Kay Palmer, "*ffolkes* ... reminds us that the man to whom England owes all is not necessarily the type one would have for tea."[4]

Reviews: "The action sequences are tense and well-handled, especially the underwater work." *Variety*, April 23, 1980; "As though doing penance for his voluptuous escapades as the Saint and, more recently, in four James Bond films, Roger Moore has permitted himself to be cast as a cat-loving, needlepoint-working misogynist who leads a team of freelancing commandos.... The screenplay, adapted by Jack Davies from his own novel, can't decide whether it's all a joke." *New York Times*, April 18, 1980; "'folkes' is an admirably crisp, incisive counter-terrorist thriller." The *Washington Post*, April 21, 1980; "Roger Moore, the blandly handsome James Bond, hardly seems a likely actor for this colorful role, but he gives it his liveliest try." *Pittsburgh Post-Gazette*, April 21, 1980.

Release: April, Universal Pictures
Availability: VHS, DVD
Rating: PG

Breakthrough—1981 (115 mins)

Alternate Title: *Sergeant Steiner*
Producer: Achim Seelus, Alex Winitsky, Wolf C. Hartwig, Palladium-Rapid
Script: Peter Berneis and Tony Williamson
Photography: Tony Imi (Color)
Editor: Raymond Poulton
Music: Peter Thomas
Cast: Richard Burton (Sgt. Steiner), Robert Mitchum (Col. Rogers), Rod Steiger (Gen. Webster), Curt Jurgens (Gen. Hoffman), Helmut Griem (Maj. Stransky), Michael Parks (Sgt. Anderson), Klaus Loewitsch (Krueger), Veronique Vendell (Yvette), Joachim Hansen (Kirstner)
Summary: Rolf Steiner is a German sergeant who leads a band of commando fighters during

World War II. As the film opens, Steiner's superior officer, Maj. Stransky, sends the sergeant and his men into a railroad tunnel to sabotage a Soviet train. Inside the tunnel, however, the soldiers are met by an oncoming tank and three of them are killed. Once he and the other survivors return to their camp, Steiner strikes Stransky, blaming him for the soldiers' deaths.

Steiner is subsequently sent to German headquarters, where an officer named Gen. Hoffman threatens him with various punishments for his insubordinate conduct. Nevertheless, the general recognizes that Steiner is a brave soldier with a distinguished record, and to the sergeant's surprise, Hoffman gives him a leave of absence—a two-week holiday in Paris. During this break, Steiner not only spots Stransky at a café, but sleeps with the major's lady friend.

Just as Steiner prepares to leave Paris, Allied forces invade Normandy, heralding the end of Germany's dominance in Western Europe. Rather than return to Russia, Steiner is sent to St. Boulogne, a provincial town in the north of France, which is still under the German military's control. A division of American tanks, however, now surrounds the town, preparing to attack. Not long after his arrival, Steiner is summoned to meet again with Gen. Hoffmann, who tells the sergeant that Adolf Hitler will be visiting St. Boulogne in the next few days. A group of officers, he explains, are plotting to assassinate the Fuehrer.

Contemptuous of Hitler and his policies, Steiner agrees to help. He proceeds to make contact in the woods outside St. Boulogne with Col. Rogers, the officer in charge of the American tank division that surrounds the town. Steiner reveals the plot to the officer, asking him to delay the attack on St. Boulogne until after Hitler is killed.

Before the plans for the assassination can proceed, though, many of the conspirators are exposed and Gen. Hoffman kills himself. The German High Command then dispatches Maj. Stransky to St. Boulogne to replace Hoffman. Stransky decides immediately that something must be done about Col. Rogers's tank division. Rather than sending soldiers out to attack the tanks, though, Stransky orders them to set explosives throughout St. Boulogne, which they will detonate once the American tanks enter the town. He then orders the town's citizens at gunpoint to stand on the street and welcome the Americans as they arrive, hoping this will trick Col. Rogers into thinking the Germans have abandoned St. Boulogne.

Wanting to protect the lives of these people, Steiner turns against Stransky, killing him. Col. Rogers's tanks soon roll through the town and a vigorous battle follows, ending with victory for the Americans. Steiner and Col. Rogers subsequently meet on one of St. Boulogne's ravaged streets where they briefly chat about the horrible costs of war. Steiner then walks off, heading out of the town alone.

Comment: *Breakthrough* is the sequel to *Cross of Iron*, a World War II-era story directed by Sam Peckinpah about an enlisted soldier in the German Wehrmacht named Rolf Steiner. Released in 1977, *Cross of Iron* follows Steiner, his colleagues and the vindictive Maj. Stransky as they fight and eventually retreat from advancing Russian troops along the Eastern Front. Peckinpah's biographer David Weddle notes that the movie "became the biggest-grossing picture in Germany and Austria since *The Sound of Music*." *Cross of Iron* stumbled in the States, however. "The public wasn't interested in a World War II movie that cast the Germans in a sympathetic light and ended on ... a bleak and nihilistic note."[5]

Cross of Iron's producer Wolf C. Hartwig was nevertheless happy with the picture's performance and decided to make a sequel. Instead of using Peckinpah again, though, he signed McLaglen to direct. Richard Burton, one of the leads in McLaglen's previous picture *The Wild Geese*, was cast as Steiner, replacing James Coburn, who'd played the role in the earlier film. American actors Robert Mitchum (Rogers) and Rod Steiger (Webster) were recruited,

Promotional poster for *Breakthrough* (Maverick, 1981), a sequel to Sam Peckinpah's *Cross of Iron*.

as well. The picture was shot in Berlin and Vienna in 1978 and released the next year in Europe and performed well, as *Cross of Iron* had. But nearly three years would pass before Hartwig secured a distribution deal in the United States and the picture struggled to find an audience on this side of the Atlantic — just as Peckinpah's had.[6]

Of McLaglen's numerous treatments of war as a theme, *Breakthrough* is certainly the bleakest. While pictures like *Shenandoah*, *The Devil's Brigade* and *Return from the River Kwai* resemble *Breakthrough* with the emphasis they place on the physical and psychological suffering that war begets, these pictures all end on comparatively happy notes. In *Shenandoah*, Boy returns home safely to his father's farm, following his long stay in a prison camp. Despite incurring heavy losses, the soldiers in *The Devil's Brigade* overtake their German adversaries. And in *Return from the River Kwai*, the Allied prisoners of war, albeit starving and sick, are spared from being displaced to Japan.

But in *Breakthrough*, success is elusive. Hitler survives, while his would-be assassins are killed. St. Boulogne is liberated, but the effort levels the town to the ground. And though Steiner survives the danger and violence he encounters throughout the film, his insistence upon protecting the French villagers from Stransky and his readiness to help the Americans invade the town ultimately cost him the parts of life that seem to matter to him most, his career in the army and the comradery he enjoys with his fellow soldiers. To underscore the isolation Steiner has created for himself, McLaglen and cinematographer Tony Imi close the film with a shot of the sergeant walking through St. Boulogne alone, his expressionless face surveying the devastated streets and the twisted bodies of men who once fought beside him.

Reviews: "The screenplay serves less here as the base for spectacular fireworks (as it was in the Peckinpah pic) but moves more into human fields of tension. There is still enough tough action though to satisfy patrons who are looking for it.... McLaglen [leads] his stars and cast ... so subtly that the strived-for human emotions really become captivating." *Variety*, March 21, 1979; "McLaglen directs his action sequences with a flair for stunts and a knowledge of his audience, but he always manages to give us a closer look into his characters, and Burton is developed rather well." *Deseret News*, May 22, 1981.

Release: Maverick Pictures, 1981
Rating: PG
Availability: VHS

The Sea Wolves — 1981 (120 mins)

Alternate Title: *The Sea Wolves: The Last Charge of the Calcutta Light Horse*
Producer: Euan Lloyd, Lorimar
Script: Reginald Rose, based on James Leasor's novel *Boarding Party*
Photography: Tony Imi (Color)
Editor: John Glen
Music: Roy Budd; song "The Precious Moments" by Richard Addinsell and Leslie Bricusse, sung by Matt Monro
Cast: Gregory Peck (Lt. Col. Lewis Pugh), Roger Moore (Capt. Gavin Stewart), David Niven (Col. Bill Grice), Trevor Howard (Jack Cartwright), Barbara Kellermann (Mrs. Cromwell), Patrick Macnee (Maj. Yogi Crossley), Kenneth Griffith (Wilton), Patrick Allen (Colin Mackenzie), Wolf Kahler (Trompeta), Robert Hoffmann (U-Boat Captain), Dan Van Husen (First Officer), George Mikell (Ehrenfels Captain), Jurgen Andersen (First Officer), Bernard Archard (Underhill), Martin Benson (Mr. Montero), Faith Brook (Mrs. Grice), Allan Cutherbertson (Melborne), Edward Dentith (Lumsdaine), Clifford Earl (Sloane), Rusi

Ghandi (The Governor), Percy Herbert (Dennison), Patrick Holt (Barker), Donald Houston (Hilliard), Glyn Houston (Peters), Victor Langley (Williamson), Terence Longdon (Malverne), Michael Medwin (Radcliffe), Morgan Sheppard (Lovecroft), John Standing (Finley), Graham Stark (Manners), Keith Stevenson (Manuel), Jack Watson (Maclean), Moray Watson (Breene)

Summary: In early 1943, several British merchant ships are torpedoed by German u-boats in the Indian Ocean. Britain's Special Operations Executive (SOE), a clandestine intelligence outfit, sends one of its men, Col. Lewis Pugh, to the state of Goa on the Indian subcontinent to determine who is supplying the u-boats with information about the merchant ships' locations. Joined by Capt. Gavin Stewart, also of the SOE, Pugh soon learns that the *Ehrenfels*, a German commercial vessel floating in one of Goa's coastal harbors, is the likely source. Because Goa is a colony of Portugal, a country that has retained its neutrality during the war, international law forbids the British military from doing anything to stop the transmissions.

The danger posed by the *Ehrenfels* is so great that Pugh and Stewart decide to sidestep the law. With the blessing of their superiors at the British Ministry of Economic Warfare, the two go to Calcutta to recruit volunteers from the Calcutta Light Horse (CLH), a part-time territorial unit in the British Indian Army comprised of middle-aged and elderly men. With these men, Pugh wants to sail up from Calcutta to Goa into the harbor where the *Ehrenfels* is moored. Pugh and the volunteers will then board the ship, destroy the transmitter and set off explosives that will sink the ship into the sea.

Though Pugh is initially vague about the details of the mission, the members of the CLH are eager to assist him. Because of their age, they have been prohibited — much to their displeasure — from actively participating in the war. Soon Pugh has twenty or so volunteers, among them Bill Grice, an experienced navy man. Under Grice's supervision, a group of volunteers steals a tired freighter named the *Phoebe* from the port of Calcutta and starts for Goa, leaving Pugh behind to transport other members of the CLH up the coast by train.

As Pugh finalizes his plans in Calcutta, Capt. Stewart and an elderly Light Horse man named Jack Cartwright coordinate a series of events in Goa, which they hope will attract the attention of the sailors on the *Ehrenfels* and lure many of them to shore in advance of the *Phoebe*'s arrival. One of these efforts includes providing all sailors who visit a harbor brothel with complimentary services. A lothario, Stewart spends the little free time he has in Goa trying to seduce a British widow named Mrs. Cromwell. But Mrs. Cromwell, in truth, is a Nazi agent, and when Jack Cartwright finds her one evening rifling through Stewart's room, she stabs the old man to death. Hours later, Stewart discovers the truth about Mrs. Cromwell and shoves a knife into her belly, killing her.

Pugh eventually rejoins Grice and the others on the *Phoebe*, and the group sails into Goa's harbor and locates the *Ehrenfels*. Stewart's efforts to draw the ship's crew to shore have been effective, and Pugh and his aging commandos find only a few men on board. Nevertheless, the effort to take the ship is difficult, with several members of the CLH getting killed or taking injuries. Once Pugh finds and destroys the transmitter, he and the others return to the *Phoebe*. A series of mines that have been attached to the *Ehrenfels*'s hull commences to explode and fires erupt, forcing the ship's surviving crew to jump overboard. Pugh pities these sailors, but does nothing to help them. Instead, he looks after the CLH men on the *Phoebe* and commends them for their fine work.

Comment: *The Sea Wolves* is based on actual events that occurred in March 1943, which British writer James Leasor documented in his 1978 book *Boarding Party: The Last Action of the Calcutta Light Horse*. The film is McLaglen's second and final collaboration with independent producer Euan Lloyd, who'd overseen the production of *The Wild Geese*. Unsurprisingly, perhaps, *The Sea Wolves* and *The Wild Geese* share a number of similarities. In addition to the references to animals in their titles, both pictures were written by scenarist Reginald Rose and feature musical scores by Roy Budd; actors Roger Moore, Jack Watson and Kenneth Griffith also appeared in both pictures, too. The plots of *The Wild Geese* and *The Sea Wolves* parallel one another, as well; in each, a small band of determined men — their youth many years behind them — sets out on a dangerous mission that yields success, but not without extensive casualties.

The Sea Wolves also brings to mind J. Lee Thompson's *The Guns of Navarone* (1961), a film on which Lloyd had worked two decades earlier.[7] Set during World War II, the two pictures both depict the efforts of Allied saboteurs, rather than traditional soldiers, as they confront German enemies. Gregory Peck and David Niven had starring roles in each film, too. Two decades separate the films, however, and actors Peck and Niven, as well as the characters they play in *The Sea Wolves*, are quite a bit older than they are in the earlier picture. The presence of these aging protagonists often lends *The Sea Wolves* a slightly comic tone. Shortly after the Light Horse volunteers agree to give their help to Pugh, for example, McLaglen inserts several shots of the men wheezing and straining as they try to get themselves into shape. On board the *Phoebe*, as well, we watch the men complain about seasickness and even throw up over the ship's side.

Despite its humorous sequences, *The Sea Wolves* is still a war picture. And much as he does in *The Devil's Brigade* and *Breakthrough*, McLaglen reminds

In ***The Sea Wolves*** (United Artists, 1981) Gregory Peck, David Niven and Roger Moore recruit a group of middle-aged volunteers to sink a German ship during World War II.

us throughout this film that war often yields tragic and horrific outcomes. Pugh's friend Jack Cartwright loses his life to the Nazi agent Mrs. Cromwell, for example, and several of the Light Horse volunteers are severely injured, some even killed, after they board the *Ehrenfels*. And though the German sailors on the *Ehrenfels* function as the villains in this movie, their efforts to save their own lives once their ship has begun to explode are pitiable. The frightening sight of these men throwing themselves into the dark water without life jackets even prompts Col. Pugh, the engineer of this situation, to refer to the men as "poor devils."

Interestingly, Pugh uses the term "poor devils" earlier in the film, as well, over drinks with his friend, Bill Grice, at the Calcutta Light Horse's clubhouse. In this scene, Grice reveals to Pugh that he's become frustrated over his inability to contribute more to the war effort and that he longs to lead an exciting life like Pugh's. At first, Pugh cannot understand his friend's envy and Grice continues:

> GRICE: What happened to your wife and daughter in Coventry—
> PUGH: Come off it, Bill.
> GRICE: I'm sorry, Lewis. I didn't mean to open up old wounds. But you do have some opportunity for revenge.
> PUGH: Oh, good God. If I have to kill some poor devils, it's not revenge. It doesn't really diminish my anger or my grief. Not one bit.

Pugh's somber regard for war, we might note, is a trait he shares with a number of other characters who appear in McLaglen's cinema, ranging from the morally conflicted Union soldier Chad in *The Little Shepherd of Kingdom Come* to the compassionate Japanese major who anguishes over the welfare of the Allied prisoners in *Return from the River Kwai*. Each of these men has seen too much of combat and its horrors to ever regard war as an occasion for adventure, fun or revenge.

Incidentally, McLaglen's youngest daughter, Mary, makes a brief on-screen appearance in *The Sea Wolves*, playing a woman who works for the British Ministry of Economic Warfare. Mary McLaglen also had small parts in her father's *ffolkes*, as well as *Chisum*, a picture in which her brother, Josh, appeared, too.

Reviews: "[The film] teems with romantic heroism routinely told." *Variety*, July 9, 1980; "'The Sea Wolves' ... takes its style from its content, being full of slightly forced, cheery, sentimental bravado and patriotism of its over-the-hill characters, whose very over-the-hillness keeps one's interest flagging until the final assault on the floating Nazi spy center." *New York Times*, June 5, 1981; "The film's suspense is wonderfully sustained and its conclusion as boisterously successful as a Mardi Gras (which it much resembles)." *Nation*, June 27, 1981.
Release: June, United Artists
Availability: VHS, DVD
Rating: PG

Sahara—1984 (111 mins)

Producer: Menahem Golan, Yoram Globus, Cannon Group
Script: James R. Silke
Photography: David Gurfinkel (Israel), Armando Mannuzzi (London) (Color)
Editor: Michael J. Duthie
Music: Ennio Morricone
Cast: Brooke Shields (Dale Gordon), Lambert Wilson (Jaffar), Horst Bucholz (Von Glessing), John Rhys-Davies (Rasoul), Ronald Lacey (Beg), Cliff Potts (String), Perry Lang (Andy),

John Mills (Cambridge), Steve Forrest (R.J. Gordon), Yehuda Elboym (Dramm), Yossef Shiloah (Halef), Gabi Amrani (Omar)

Summary: R.J. Gordon, an engineer who designs cars, lives in Detroit with his teenage daughter Dale. Nearly broke, Gordon needs to secure financial backing for his latest car, a roadster called the Gordon-Packard. To land a deal with a potential investor, the engineer decides to enter the car into a race that traverses the unpaved roads of the Sahara desert. Before he can do this, though, Gordon is severely injured in an accident. As he lies dying in the hospital, he asks Dale to race the car herself.

Dale agrees, and following her father's death, she and a pair of engineers who worked for Gordon set sail for Africa with the Gordon-Packard. Because the organizers of the Sahara rally have forbidden women from participating, Dale disguises herself with a fake moustache and a trilby hat that hides her long hair. After the race commences, she dramatically lets down her hair for her rivals to see, and speeds into the West African desert.

A band of Bedouin nomads, led by a man named Rasoul, soon besiege and capture Dale's little group. Aroused by Dale's beauty, Rasoul orders the young woman to be delivered to his tent, where he plans to take her virginity. Fortunately, Rasoul's nephew, Jaffar, learns about Dale and decides to protect her. A sheik, Jaffar has dominion over the tribe, and his wishes stand. At the same time, custom demands that Jaffar must marry Dale, an idea that doesn't sit well with the young American.

Dale nevertheless comes to the aid of her captors later when a rival band of nomads attacks Jaffar's camp with a machine gun that has been mounted to an armored car. During the battle, she grabs some sticks of dynamite from the trunk of the Gordon-Packard and plants them in the ground. When the armored car draws near, Dale fires a rifle at one of the explosive bundles and blows up the vehicle. Dale's heroics do nothing to help her own situation, though. Insistent upon having Dale marry his nephew, Rasoul tortures Dale's engineer companions until the young woman agrees. A wedding quickly follows and that night Dale and Jaffar consummate their marriage.

The next morning, however, Dale wakes up before everyone else in the camp. She climbs into the Gordon-Packard and makes off, hoping to return to the race. She is soon stopped by Lord Beg, leader of the group that earlier attacked Jaffar's camp, who hates Dale because she destroyed his armored car. He proceeds to take her to an underground cell, which he stocks with wild cats. Jaffar soon learns about his new wife's predicament and starts out to find her, bringing along some warriors from his tribe. He finds Beg's camp and a terrific battle erupts. As the fighting continues, Jaffar locates Dale and rescues her from her cell. Following this, she jumps into the Gordon-Packard and sets off to finish the race.

Despite the troubles she's faced, Dale still manages to win the rally, narrowly beating a German rival named Von Glessing. Confident now that her father's car will receive the recognition and financial support she thinks it deserves, Dale turns away from the finish line and heads back into the desert to return to Jaffar.

Comment: British director John Guillermin (*The Blue Max*, *Towering Inferno*) was initially signed by Cannon to direct *Sahara*, but he left the production after principal photography began. Some of Guillermin's footage nevertheless made it into the film's final cut, in particular the early sequences that take place in Detroit, which were actually shot outside London.[8]

Following Guillermin's departure, producer Menahem Golan recruited McLaglen, who filmed the picture's remaining sequences in Israel, shooting extensively in the Judean Hills outside Jerusalem and the Negev desert.[9] Golan played a sizeable role throughout *Sahara*'s creation, having developed the original idea for the film's plot. A profile of the production that appeared in *People* explains that Golan "was inspired both by Rudolph Valentino's 1921

Brooke Shields as Dale Gordon in *Sahara* (Columbia, 1983), much of which was shot on location in Israel.

silent classic *The Sheik* and by the temporary disappearance of Margaret Thatcher's son in the Sahara during a car rally last winter [1982]. 'Brooke eees dee most bew-tee-fool creature on earth,' says Golan, known for his B-movies and bad temper. 'She eees dee genie of dee desert.... We are not afraid here of clichés. I want a bew-tee-fool romantic blockbuster where all Amereee-can keeds will identify.'"[10]

Though McLaglen came onto the production late and Golan exerted substantial control over the script, *Sahara* still displays several stylistic and thematic markers that distinguish the director's other work. Though the film is at once a story about an automobile race and a love affair, for example, it visually recalls the Westerns McLaglen made with cinematographer William H. Clothier in the sixties—*Bandolero!* and *Chisum* come to mind—thanks to the frequency with which shots of the landscape desert and men on horseback fill the screen. The picture's opening may be one of the most striking sequences in all of McLaglen's cinema, with footage of Beg and his marauders using rifles and wild cats to chase down and kill a family of nomads. The horror of the massacre is contrasted and augmented by the immense beauty of the location where it takes place, the desert sand forming soft, pink waves around the poor people's slain bodies. Ennio Morricone's elegiac score in the background, rich with orchestral strings, enhances the sense of tragedy that emerges from this memorable scene even further.

Sahara also recalls another pair of films McLaglen made in the sixties—*The Rare Breed* and *The Ballad of Josie*—as it features a strong female protagonist who makes a point of defying expectations and restrictions that have been set before her by society as a result of her gender. In *The Rare Breed*, Martha Price proceeds with selling the bull Vindicator after her husband dies, though the male buyers she approaches at first refuse to take her seriously because she is a woman. In *The Ballad of Josie*, Josie is maligned and attacked by her male neighbors after she leaves behind the "female" profession of waiting tables to go into business as a rancher. And in *Sahara*, Dale Gordon — her name itself has an epicene quality — refuses to let the Sahara rally's organizers' prohibition against female drivers stop her from competing in the race. Dale not only engages in an activity that custom has set aside for men, but manages to persuade others that she actually is a man, adopting masculine mannerisms and concealing her femininity with makeup and props. Once she no longer needs to trick her peers, however, Dale abandons her masquerade with a flourish, tossing her racing cap onto the roadway after the rally's start, allowing her long hair to tumble free in the wind. Dale can act like a man when she needs to, the film infers, but, at the same time, she is not unhappy with being a woman.

Reviews: "'Sahara ... is silly but it's also spellbinding — a fun, fantasy-adventure yarn, full of gloss, animals and those sweeping desert sands." *Los Angeles Times*, March 3, 1984. "The script is the worst ... with overused chases and fights, and feeble humor." *Deseret News*, March 8, 1984.

Release: March, Columbia
Availability: VHS
Rating: PG

Return from the River Kwai — 1989 (101 mins)

Producer: Kurt Unger, Leisure Time
Script: Sargon Tamimi and Paul Mayersberg, based on the book *Return from the River Kwai* by Joan and Clay Blair, Jr.
Photography: Arthur Wooster (Color)
Editor: Alan Strachan
Music: Lalo Schifrin; "Japanese Theme" composed and produced by Kitaro
Cast: Edward Fox (Maj. Benford), Denholm Elliott (Col. Grayson), Christopher Penn (Lt. Crawford), Tatsuya Nakadai (Maj. Harada), George Takei (Lt. Tanaka), Nick Tate (Lt. Comm. Hunt), Timothy Bottoms (Seaman Miller), Michael Dante (Comm. Davidson), Richard Graham (Sgt. Perry), Etsushi Takahashi (Capt. Ozawa), Alexandre Blaise (Exec. Officer Clancy), Masato Nagamori (Lt. Yamashita), Pierre Valderon (Frenchman in Saigon), Patricia Edmondson, Sheila McLaglen, Lolita Mirpuri (Ladies in Saigon)
Summary: Lt. Tanaka of the Japanese Imperial army has been charged with building a bridge across the Kwai River, which runs between occupied Thailand and Burma. His workforce is comprised of Allied prisoners of war. As the project nears completion, a squadron of American planes bombs the bridge, destroying it.

A pilot in the raid named Lt. Crawford takes fire from the Japanese. Forced to jump from his plane and parachute into the jungle below, Crawford is subsequently rescued by some farmers who bring him to a nearby village and turn him over to a Briton named Col. Grayson who has been training the locals in guerrilla fighting methods.

Enraged by the loss of the bridge, Tanaka decides to punish the prisoners he oversees, ordering three of them to be shot by a firing squad. Before the executions can commence, another Japanese officer, Maj. Harada, intervenes, sparing the men. He then explains to Tanaka that all healthy prisoners in the work camp are to be transported by train to Vietnam and, later, boat to Japan. Maj. Benford, a British doctor, is charged with determining who is fit to make the trip.

While the Japanese officers continue with their plans to move the prisoners, Col. Grayson asks the pilot Crawford to lend his support to the Thai resistance by helping him blow up a railroad trestle used by the Japanese. At first unwilling, Crawford eventually has a change of heart, and he joins Grayson and the guerrillas. When they find the trestle, they place explosives under the tracks which they detonate as a train approaches — the same one carrying Tanaka, Harada and the prisoners. A firefight follows in which Grayson is killed. Shortly after this, Tanaka's soldiers capture Crawford.

Once the trestle is repaired, the train resumes its journey and eventually reaches the coastal city of Saigon. As the prisoners are being fed, Crawford shares his meal with an elderly beggar. From the old man, Crawford learns where a local airfield is located and later escapes. He manages to board a Japanese plane and takes off, but mechanical problems arise, forcing him to crash. He stays alive on the open sea in a raft before a British submarine rescues him.

Following Crawford's escape, the other prisoners are boarded into the hull of a civilian cargo ship. The heat inside the boat is terrible, and the doctor Maj. Benford protests, worried that these conditions will kill the prisoners. Despite the objections of Maj. Harada, the ship's captain, a man named Ozawa, insists upon keeping the men below. Accompanied by a pair of commercial freighters, Capt. Ozawa's ship soon starts out for Japan. As night falls, the flotilla is detected by the same submarine crew that rescued Crawford. At first, the submarine's executive officer wants to torpedo Capt. Ozawa's ship, arguing that it is a military vessel. But Crawford pleads with him to refrain from this, trying to convince him that imprisoned Allied soldiers are probably on board. The officer agrees to hold off on the attack temporarily.

As Crawford pleads with the executive officer, the prisoners on board Ozawa's ship decide to rise up against their captors, fearing they will die if they remain any longer in the sweltering hull. Maj. Benford, up to this point, has been uninterested in forcefully challenging Tanaka and the other Japanese officers, but now he joins in, helping the others overwhelm the ship's deck. As this revolt takes place, the executive officer on the submarine orders his men to torpedo one of the other freighters in the flotilla. Just as Benford and the prisoners take control of their ship, they inadvertently steer it into the torpedo's path. An explosion follows, the ship begins to sink and everyone on board jumps into the water. Fortunately, many of the prisoners survive, thanks to rafts and other floating objects. Crawford and the crew in the submarine proceed to search for and rescue the men all through the night and next morning.

Comment: *Return from the River Kwai* is an adaptation of a 1979 book by historian Clay Blair, Jr., and his wife, Joan. Published under the title *Return from the River Kwai*, the book recounts a nautical disaster during World War II that led to the deaths of hundreds of Allied prisoners of war in the Gulf of Thailand. Like the POWs in this film, these men were forced by their Japanese captors to work on the Burma Railway, which Imperial Japan developed during the war to move its soldiers between Thailand and Burma. In 1944, approximately 2,000 of these prisoners were loaded onto ships that were to carry them to Japan, where they were to be used for other projects. As the vessels headed out, a group of American submarines — unaware of the human cargo on board — torpedoed the convoy. The survivors were subsequently rescued over the next several days.

Return from the River Kwai is not a sequel to David Lean's Academy Award-winning film *The Bridge on the River Kwai* (1957), despite the similarities in the films' titles. While McLaglen's movie is based, albeit loosely, on a historical source, Lean's film is an adaptation of a 1952 fictional novel by Pierre Boulle called *The Bridge Over the River Kwai*. The likenesses between the two narratives' titles, however, was enough to trouble the estate of Sam Spiegel — Spiegel had produced *The Bridge on the River Kwai*— and a lawsuit was filed against Kurt Unger, the producer of *Return from the River Kwai*, in an effort to get him to change the title. Unger ultimately refused to yield, but the legal troubles he encountered prevented him from securing a distributor for *Return from the River Kwai* in the United States.[11]

Return from the River Kwai is one of many films directed by McLaglen in which individuals try to free themselves from captivity. In *The Last Hard Men* and *Sahara*, for instance, Sue Burgade and Dale Gordon both struggle to escape from sadistic kidnappers, and in *Bandolero!* Dee Bishop and his gang flee the gallows and attempt to lose themselves in Mexico. We also find characters like the pilot Lt. Crawford throughout McLaglen's films, who are similarly concerned with the welfare and safety of imprisoned people. G.W. McLintock in *McLintock!* arms and frees a band of Indians as they are forcefully relocated by federal officials to a reservation. Charlie Anderson heads out to recover his son, Boy, from an army prison camp in *Shenandoah*. And the mercenaries in *The Wild Geese* remain committed to delivering President Limbani from Zembala, undeterred even when they realize their client has no intention of paying them for their services.

Sheila McLaglen, the director's fourth wife, appears briefly in *Return from the River Kwai*, playing a European woman who takes tea in a café in Saigon.

Reviews: "'Return' was shot entirely in Philippines. All tech credits are good, including Arthur Wooster's crisp lensing, aerial footage by Kevan Ross Lind and Lalo Schifrin's score." *Variety*, April 12–18, 1989; "McLaglen ... has not made the obliquest reference to Lean's POW classic. Standard WW2 adventure is all we get." *War Films*, 158;

Release: April (London), Rank Film Distributors
Availability: VHS, DVD

Eye of the Widow—1991 (96 mins)

Alternate Title: *L'Oeil de la Veuve*
Producer: Daniel Carillo, Adlar Productions
Script: Joshua Sauli, from the novels *Roman Vengeance* and *The Ayatollah's Widow* by Gérard de Villiers
Photography: Arthur Wooster
Editor: Luce Grunenwaldt
Music: Hubert Roistang, Yvan Jullien
Cast: Richard Young (Malko Linge), F. Murray Abraham (Kharoun), Mel Ferrer (Frankenheimer), Ben Cross (Nassiri), Terence Ford (Milton Brabeck), Annabel Schofield (Sharnilar), Paul Smith (Elko), Rick Hill (Chris Jones), Patrick Macnee (Marcus), Felicity Dean (Victoria), Ashley Richardson (Ingrid), Susanna Hofmann (Alexandra), Nabila Khashoggi (Vanya), Elvira Neustaedtl (Anna), Benjamin Feitelson (Kashani), Mike Marshall (Klaus), Norbert Blecha (Werner), Christina Klingler (Countess), Sacha Lighter (Cardinal)
Summary: Malko Linge, an Austrian prince, is hosting a dinner party at his castle when a band of terrorists strikes. A trained killer who occasionally works as a contractor for the CIA, Linge drives the attackers out, but not after much of his home is destroyed and several guests are killed or injured.

Malko is soon contacted by his handlers at the CIA. The head of the group that stormed his castle, he learns, is a man named Nassiri. Malko's previous involvement in anti-terrorist activities in Libya probably prompted the siege. The CIA wants to find Nassiri because he has connections to a shadowy figure named Kharoun, who is set on killing as many people as he can in order to undermine global stability. If Malko will agree to search for Nassiri, the CIA will pay him well. Needing money to repair his castle, Malko accepts the assignment.

One of the people who may be able to help Malko locate Nassiri is a young widow named Sharnilar, who's gone into hiding since her husband, an arms dealer, was murdered by Nassiri and his supporters. These same men tortured and mutilated Sharnilar, gouging out one of her eyes before she managed to escape from them. Malko eventually tracks the widow to Corsica, off the coast of France. Sharnilar agrees to help him find Nassiri, making available her dead husband's supply of explosives.

Malko proceeds to comb the Cote d'Azur for Nassiri. Through the course of the search, the prince discovers that Kharoun has come into the possession of biological weapons, which he plans to use soon. Complicating the situation, Sharnilar has agreed to marry Kharoun, unaware, perhaps, of his sinister intentions.

Comment: His Serene Highness Malko Linge is the protagonist in a series of espionage novels by French novelist Gérard de Villiers.[12] Prince Malko lives in an old castle and to cover the costs of maintaining the property, he works as a part time operative for the CIA. *Eye of the Widow* is an adaptation of two Malko Linge novels, *Roman Vengeance* (1981) and *The Ayatollah's Widow* (1985).

Eye of the Widow was filmed on location in the spring and summer of 1989 throughout Europe. After principal shooting wrapped, producer Daniel Carillo had additional footage shot and edited the picture without McLaglen's input, prompting the director to distance himself from the project.[13] Although *Eye of the Widow* is in many ways an Andrew V. McLaglen film in name only, viewers will note that Malko Linge is just one of many "hero for hire" characters to appear in the director's oeuvre, with others that include *Have Gun, Will Travel*'s Paladin, the mercenaries in *The Wild Geese* and the former army colonel Arthur Simons, who leads a team of amateur commandos into Tehran in the television miniseries *On Wings of Eagles*.

Release: Summer (France), Europex
Availability: VHS, DVD

Television Movies

Louis L'Amour's The Shadow Riders—1982 (96 mins)

Alternate Title: *The Shadow Riders*
Broadcast: CBS, September 28, 1982
Producers: Verne Nobles, Dennis Durney, Pegasus Group, Columbia Pictures Television
Script: Jim Byrnes, based on a story by Louis L'Amour
Photography: Jack Whitman
Editor: Bud Friedgen
Music: Jerrold Immel
Cast: Tom Selleck (Mac Traven), Sam Elliott (Dal Traven), Ben Johnson (Uncle Jack Traven), Katharine Ross (Kate Connery), Geoffrey Lewis (Maj. Ashbury), Jeffrey Osterhage (Jess Traven), Gene Evans (Col. Hammond), R.G. Armstrong (Sheriff Gillette), Marshall Teague (Lt. Butler), Robert B. Craig (Laird), Ben Fuhrman (Devol), Jane Greer (Ma Traven), Harry Carey, Jr. (Pa Traven), Dominique Dunne (Sissy), Natalie May (Heather), Jeannetta Arnette (Southern Belle), Owen Orr (Frank King), Kristina David (Renfro Damsel), Joe Capone (Sgt. Ballock), Scanlon Gail (Yankee Officer),
Summary: Mac and Dal Traven return together to their family ranch in Texas following the conclusion of the Civil War. Though Mac fought for the Union and Dal for the Confederacy, the two men's affection for one another enables them to ignore their ideological differences.

Once they arrive home, they learn that outlaws have kidnapped their younger brother, Jesse, and their two young sisters, as well as Dal's longtime girlfriend, Kate.

The leader of the kidnappers is a man named Ashbury. A Confederate officer during the war, Ashbury plans to trade the captives to Maximilian, Emperor of Mexico, in exchange for money and guns, which he and his men can then use to attack the United States. To facilitate this, Ashbury heads down to the Texas coastline with his prisoners. There, he meets a smuggler named Holliday, who proceeds to ship the Traven girls to Mexico. The men leave Kate behind on the Texas beach, however, in the custody of Ashbury's men.

Dal and Mac soon find Kate and free her. They also reunite with their brother Jesse, who's managed to escape the bandits on his own. When Kate tells Dal and Mac that their sisters have been taken to Mexico, the Travens realize that they will need the help of their Uncle Jack, a professional criminal whose knowledge of Mexico is superior to theirs. Uncle Jack is in prison, however, and the Travens are forced to use dynamite to spring him. Following this, the Travens proceed into Mexico, where they find their sisters and rescue them.

Comment: Produced for CBS, *The Shadow Riders* is based on an original story by the Western novelist Louis L'Amour. The picture was produced and written by Jim Byrnes, who had brought L'Amour's novel *The Sacketts* to television in 1979 — Tom Selleck (Mac), Sam Elliott (Dal) and Jeffrey Osterhage (Jesse) played the leads in both telefilms.[14] McLaglen's final Western, *The Shadow Riders* features several actors who had been working with the director for decades: Ben Johnson (Uncle Jack), Harry Carey, Jr. (Pa Traven) and Katharine Ross (Kate). The production also features a brief appearance by actress Jane Greer (Ma Traven), her first and only appearance in a McLaglen film.

The Shadow Riders somewhat resembles McLaglen's *The Undefeated*, which similarly features an unreconstructed Confederate officer who heads to Mexico to conduct business with Maximilian. But while Col. Langdon in the earlier film is a sympathetic character, driven as he is by an urge to support and help the men who served under him during the war, Ashbury in *The Shadow Riders* is a violent, political fanatic, whose hatred of the Union prompts him to engage in despicable behavior. *The Shadow Riders* was filmed on location in Northern California.[15] In the picture's closing credits, McLaglen's son Josh is listed as "Assistant to the Director."

Availability: VHS, DVD

The Dirty Dozen: Next Mission — 1985 (95 mins)

Broadcast: NBC, February 4, 1985
Producer: Harry R. Sherman, MGM/UA Television
Script: Michael Kane
Photography: John Stanier
Editor: Alan Strachan
Music: Richard Harvey
Cast: Lee Marvin (Maj. Reisman), Ernest Borgnine (Gen. Worden), Ken Wahl (Valentine), Larry Wilcox (Tommy Wells), Sonny Landham (Sam Sixkiller), Richard Jaeckel (Bowren), Rolf Saxon (Robert Wright), Wolf Kahler (Dietrich), Crispin Denys (Schmidt), Gavan O'Herlihy (Perkins), Ricco Ross (Dregors), Jay Benedict (Didier Le Clair), Michael Paliotti (Baxley), Paul Herzberg (Reynolds), Jeff Harding (Sanders), Sam Douglas (Anderson)
Summary: In 1944, Allied intelligence becomes aware of a plot by the Nazis to assassinate Hitler. Fearing his death will actually lengthen the war, the leaders of the Allied war effort decide to frustrate the assassination. To bring this about, Gen. Sam Worden of the U.S. Army tells one of his officers, Maj. Reisman, to organize a special commando outfit com-

prised of twelve soldiers who have been sentenced by the army to death or long terms in prison. Gen. Worden explains to Reisman that a Nazi general named Dietrich has been given the task of killing Hitler. If Reisman's men can find and stop Dietrich in time, their sentences might be commuted.

The major proceeds to select the soldiers for the assignment and train them in the English countryside. Upon Gen. Worden's orders, Reisman's men are sent to occupied France in a plane. Once they land, though, they are spotted and attacked by German soldiers. The men who survive press on, eventually tracking Gen. Dietrich to a train depot, where Reisman orders one of them, a sniper named Dregors, to fire at the officer. Dregors's task becomes more difficult when an unexpected plane arrives in a nearby field and one of its passengers turns out to be Hitler himself.

Comment: *The Dirty Dozen: Next Mission* is a sequel to Robert Aldrich's *The Dirty Dozen* (1967). A first-rate, suspenseful production, the telefilm was nevertheless maligned by many critics who faulted it for resembling Aldrich's picture too closely, or not enough. *The Dirty Dozen: Next Mission* brings McLaglen's own *Breakthrough* to mind, as well; in that picture, though, the protagonists strive to kill Hitler, rather than save him.

Much of *Next Mission* was shot on location in rainy England, with vintage planes, armored cars and trains.[16] The telefilm marks McLaglen's first collaboration with Lee Marvin after *Seven Men from Now*, which McLaglen had co-produced for John Wayne's Batjac Productions almost thirty years earlier. A ratings success for NBC, *The Dirty Dozen: Next Mission* was followed by two more made-for-TV sequels, both directed by Lee H. Katzin, *The Dirty Dozen: The Deadly Mission* (1987) and *The Dirty Dozen: The Fatal Mission* (1988).

Reviews: "A strong performance by Lee Marvin, reprising his role from the MGM film, dominates the actioner, but that's not enough to compensate for the overall lackluster quality." *Variety*, February 13, 1985; "[I]t's a great yarn ... with plenty of action and some very tense moments." *San Diego Union*, Feb 7, 1985.

Availability: VHS, DVD

Lee Marvin as Maj. Reisman in the telefilm *The Dirty Dozen: Next Mission* (MGM/UA Television, 1985).

Miniseries

The Blue & The Gray—1982 (381 mins)

Broadcast: CBS, November 14, 16, 17, 1982
Producers: Hugh Benson, Harry Thomason, A Larry White and Lou Reda Production, Columbia Pictures Television
Script: Ian McLellan Hunter, story by John Leekley and Bruce Catton; based in part on Catton's *Reflections on the Civil War*
Photography: Al Francis (Color)
Editors: Fred A. Chulack, Bud Friedgen
Music: Bruce Broughton
Cast: Stacy Keach (Jonas Steele), John Hammond (John Geyser), Julia Duffy (Mary Hale), Robin Gammell (Jacob Hale, Sr.), David Harper (James Hale), Julius Harris (Preacher), Gregg Henry (Lester Bedell), Cooper Huckabee (Matthew Geyser), James Carroll Jordan (Thaddeus Lowe), Brian Kerwin (Malachy Hale), William Lucking (Capt. Potts), Charles Napier (Maj. Harrison), Walter Olkewicz (Pvt. Grundy), Penny Peyser (Emma Gayser), Duncan Regehr (Capt. Randolph), David Rounds (Christopher Spencer), Christopher Stone (Maj. Fairbairn), Diane Baker (Evelyn Hale), Kathleen Beller (Kathy Reynolds), Lloyd Bridges (Ben Geyser), Rory Calhoun (Gen. George Meade), Colleen Dewhurst (Maggie Geyser), David Doyle (Col. Phineas Wade), Michael Horton (Mark Geyser), Warren Oates (Maj. Wells), Gerald S. O'Loughlin (Sgt. O'Toole), Geraldine Page (Mrs. Lovelace), Dan Shor (Luke Geyser), Rip Torn (Gen. Ulysses S. Grant), Robert Vaughn (Sen. Reynolds), John Vernon (Secretary of State Seward), Sterling Hayden (John Brown), Paul Winfield (Jonathan Henry), Gregory Peck (Abraham Lincoln), Bruce Abbott (Jake Jr.), Royce D. Applegate (Cell Reporter), Walter Brooke (Gen. Haupt), Janice Carroll (Mary Todd Lincoln), Fredric Cook (Capt. Grimes), William Brian Curran (Dr. Bennett), Gregg Palmer (Bull Run Colonel), George O. Petrie (Court Clerk), Jordan Rhodes (Pennsylvania Colonel), Warwick Sims (Count Von Ziller), Fred Stuthman (George), Peter Von Zerneck (Prussian General), Maggie Wellman (Nell), M.C. Gainey (Sykes), John Petlock (Judge Parker), Alex Harvey (Cavalry Colonel), Steve Nevil (Johnny Reb), Len Wayland (Field General), Noble Willingham (Cavalry General), Ebbe Roe Smith (Bates), Diane Sommerfield (Luanna), Tom Stern (Regular Union Major), John Voldstad (Mooney), John Dennis Johnston (Lt. Hardy), Veronica Redd (Hattie), Robert Suymonds (Gen. Robert E. Lee), William Wellman, Jr. (Lt. Murcer), Paul Harper (Lamar), Peter Jason (Sgt. Ogilvie), Lyle Armstrong (Lincoln's Advisor)
Summary: A southerner who objects to slavery, John Geyser refuses to serve for the Confederacy during the Civil War. Geyser still sees and experiences plenty during this violent period as an artist-journalist who produces graphic accounts of historic actions on and off the battlefield for magazine readers. Among the events he witnesses are the trial and execution of John Brown right before the war starts, the Battle of Bull Run and the freeing of slaves. He and his friend, Jonas Steele, a Union officer, witness the death of Abraham Lincoln, as well. In addition to actual events from history, the telefilm brings attention to the private lives of Geyser and Steele, depicting their happy moments and personal tragedies, including love affairs, health problems and the losses of loved ones.
Comment: *The Blue & The Gray* was the subject of a lengthy feature in the *Los Angeles Times*, which noted that "the teleplay is largely an account of the war's impact on a personal level, a logical approach to a bloody conflict that halved a nation, split families and turned 40 percent of its participants into casualties."[17] The miniseries also made the cover of *TV*

Guide. The production marks the first time Gregory Peck (Lincoln), the star of McLaglen's *The Sea Wolves*, appeared in a television film.[18] *The Blue & The Gray* was also one of the last productions on which Sterling Hayden (John Brown) appeared. Hayden had previously worked with McLaglen on *Kansas Pacific* and *Hellgate*, when McLaglen was still a first assistant director. William Wellman, Jr. and Maggie Wellman, the children of McLaglen's mentor William A. Wellman, also appear in the cast.

Reviews: "What veteran director Andrew V. McLaglen does best is show the devastating impact of war on the battlefield. His battle sequences are superbly staged, widening the small screen to show panoramic chaos and carnages as flesh is torn and bodies go flying." *Los Angeles Times*, November 12, 1982.

Availability: VHS, DVD

On Wings of Eagles—1986 (261 mins)

Broadcast: NBC, May 18, 19, 1986
Producer: Lynn Raynor, Edgar Scherick Productions, Taft Entertainment
Script: Sam Rolfe, based upon Ken Follett's *On Wings of Eagles*
Photography: Robert Steadman
Editor: Alan Strachan
Music: Laurence Rosenthal
Cast: Burt Lancaster (Simons), Richard Crenna (H. Ross Perot), Paul LeMat (Coburn), Louis Giambalvo (Paul Chiapparone), Jim Metzler (Bill Gaylord), Esai Morales (Rashid), James Sutorius (Joe Poche), Robert Wightman (Keane Taylor), William Bumiller (Rich Gallagher), Cyril O'Reilly (Pat Scully), Lawrence Pressman (Bill Gayden), Alan Fudge (Merv Stauffer), John Doolittle (Glen Jackson), Karen Carlson (Ruth Chiapparone), Diane Salinger (Emily Gaylord), Patrick Collins (John Howell), Bob Delegall (Ron Davis), Constance Towers (Margot Perot), Martin Doyle (Jim Schwebach), Karen Landry (Cathy Gallagher), Patricia McCormack (Liz Coburn), Mary Apick (Mrs. Nourbash), Parviz Sayyad (Dadgar), Kabir Bedi (Mohammad), Raul Miranda (T.J. Marquez), Pedro Armendariz, Jr. (Mr. Dobuti), Diana Bracho (Mrs. Dobuti), Sebastian Ligarde (Aide #1), Gregory Garland (Aide #2), Elia Domenzain (Mrs. Abolhassan), Martin LaSalle (Majid), Ramon Alvarez (U.S. Colonel), Alfred Sevilla (Habib), Miguel Angel Fuentes (Large Kurd), Marcos Russek (Rebel Officer), John Sterlini (Deputy), Julio Ahuet (Leader), Alberto Rodriguez (School Rebel), Carlon Cardan (Turkish Officer), Steve Franken (Mort Myerson), Dennis Bell (Dick Douglas), Richard A. Crenna (Ross Perot, Jr.), Steven Spencer (Lou Goetz), Dorothy Plummer (Lulu May Perot), Joy Rogers (Kathy), Erika Carlsson (Ann Tercel), Jennifer Sibly (Nurse), Manuel Ojeda (Commandant)
Summary: American billionaire H. Ross Perot's company Electronic Data Systems (EDS) has come to Iran to build an enormous computer network for the government. Late in 1978, as the Shah's grip on power starts to slip, Perot decides to move his employees out of Tehran, the Iranian capital. But two EDS executives—Paul Chiapparone and Bill Gaylord—are apprehended and imprisoned by an official named Dadgar, who suspects the men have been engaged in illegal activity of some sort, though he's unwilling or unable to provide evidence against them. At first, Perot solicits help from the U.S. Department of State, but he is told very little can be done. Perot then approaches a retired army colonel, Arthur "Bull" Simons, and asks him to spring the two executives from prison.

Simons agrees and with Perot's counsel puts together a commando unit comprised of EDS employees, picking men who've had combat experience. Simons soon leads the EDS people into Iran. With help from an Iranian man named Rashid, the colonel and his amateur commandos free Chiapparone and Gaylord. Pursued by Dadgar, Simons and the others struggle to get out of the country, taking a pair of trucks through a mountain pass to Turkey. When they reach the border, Perot is there to meet them. An armed standoff with Dadgar follows, but the official eventually relents and permits the men to cross into Turkey. The Americans, now safe and free, fly to the U.S., where they are met by their relieved families on an airstrip.

Comment: *On Wings of Eagles* is McLaglen's final television production. The film received an Emmy nomination for Outstanding Miniseries. Filled with action, humor and political intrigue, the program's script was written by Sam Rolfe, the creator of the 1960s spy show, *The Man from U.N.C.L.E.* Rolfe also created *Have Gun, Will Travel*, one of the shows McLaglen worked on most frequently when he was a contract director at CBS in the late fifties and early sixties.[19]

On Wings of Eagles is an adaptation of popular writer Ken Follett's account of actual events that occurred during the Iranian Revolution. H. Ross Perot himself approached Follett's publisher, William Morrow, about having the Welsh author write a book about his and Col. Simons's efforts to rescue the EDS employees. Follett was intrigued by the storyline and agreed to do it; when the book was published in 1983, it became a bestseller.[20] Though Follett has written several popular titles in the years since, his best known book, perhaps, is a spy thriller, *Eye of the Needle* (1978). Careful viewers will note that an airline employee in the telefilm can be seen reading *Eye of the Needle* when Perot boards a flight to Iran.

On Wings of Eagles was shot in Mexico City and Toluca, a mountainous area that lies to the southwest of the capital city.[21] Many of the film's supporting cast members and extras are Mexican, including Pedro Armendariz, Jr. (Mr. Dobuti), who'd earlier worked with McLaglen on the pilot for *Log of the Black Pearl* and *The Undefeated*, both of which were shot in Mexico, as well.[22]

Reviews: "Very smartly turned out, rivetingly suspenseful and devoid of most of the padding and stalling that plague long-form TV dramas, 'Eagles' is a gung-ho adventure, and one that is not, thankfully, a get-even story. It's not about getting even — and the dialogue is free of demagogic, anti–Iranian rants — it's about getting justice, those who got it and those for whom it was gotten. The getting is darn good." *Washington Post*, May 17, 1986; "If "On Wings of Eagles" makes any philosophical point, it is that boldness, bravery, and ingenuity — combined with money, power, and privilege — can overcome almost any bureaucracy and all odds. And in the process, provide material for a thrilling ... caper movie." *Christian Science Monitor*, May 16, 1986.

Availability: VHS

Pilot Episodes

Travis McGee—1983 (98 mins)

Broadcast: ABC, May 18, 1983
Producer: George Eckstein, Hajeno Productions, Warner Bros. Television
Script: Sterling Siliphant; from John D. MacDonald's novel *The Empty Copper Sea*
Photography: Jack Whitman
Editor: Richard Bracken
Music: Jerrold Immel
Cast: Sam Elliott (Travis McGee), Gene Evans (Meyer), Barry Corbin (Sheriff Ames), Richard Farnsworth (Van Harder), Geoffrey Lewis (John Tuckerman), Amy Madigan (Billy Jean Bailey), Vera Miles (Julie Lawless), Katharine Ross (Gretel Howard), Marshall Teague (Nicky Noyes), Maggie Wellman (Mishy Burns), Walter Olkewicz (Bright Fletcher)

Summary: When Van Harder, a charter captain with a reputation for drinking, passes out and crashes his boat, his passenger, a shady land developer named Hub Lawless, is thrown into the ocean and disappears. Lawless is presumed dead, but his insurance company — and Van's friend, Travis McGee, a self-described "human salvage" specialist — suspect the developer may have faked his own death and fled to Mexico with other people's money.

Comment: Travis McGee is the creation of crime writer John D. MacDonald. The character appeared in more than 20 novels, among them *The Girl in the Plain Brown Wrapper* (1968), *The Dreadful Lemon Sky* (1975) and *The Empty Copper Sea* (1978), upon which this telefilm's plot is based.[23] McGee is a self-employed contractor who hires himself out to people who need help finding lost objects, people and so forth. In this respect, McGee resembles two other fictional heroes that appeared in television shows McLaglen directed, the suave gunslinger Paladin in *Have Gun, Will Travel* and the private investigator Thomas Banacek of the *Banacek* series. Though the literary McGee lives in South Florida, the McGee in this production calls Ventura, California, home. Parts of *Travis McGee* were actually filmed in Ventura Harbor.[24] *Travis McGee* was conceived as a pilot for a series for ABC, but the show was never picked up. The production's female leads, Vera Miles and Katharine Ross, had appeared together previously in McLaglen's *Hellfighters*.

Reviews: "[D]eftly written made-for-tv movie that [can] be enjoyed for its own sake." *Variety*, May 25, 1983; "The trouble with the film is that while it does initially involve viewers, it loses them quickly. It isn't until the last 15 minutes that the payoffs come, and by then it's hard to still care." *Pittsburgh Post-Gazette*, May 18, 1983.

Appendix I: Appearances in Documentaries

John Wayne and "Chisum"—1970

Producer: Professional Films
Availability: DVD
Note: Follows the making of *Chisum* on location in Durango, Mexico, with extensive footage of McLaglen working with actors and crew, including cinematographer William H. Clothier. Included as an extra on Warner's 1998 DVD release of the film.

Stars' War: The Flight of the Wild Geese—1978

Producer: Iain Johnstone, Varius Entertainment Trading Co.
Availability: DVD
Note: Included on Thirtieth Anniversary DVD edition of *The Wild Geese*; chronicles the film's production on location in Africa.

The Hollywood Greats: John Wayne—1983

Producer: Margaret Sharp, BBC TV
Note: British made-for-television production about the actor, featuring on-screen commentary from McLaglen, Kirk Douglas, Harry Carey, Jr., and Ronald Reagan.

The Making of 'The Quiet Man'—1992

Producer: Leonard Maltin, Mark Lamberti, Lamberti Productions Corp.
Availability: VHS and DVD
Note: Produced to mark *The Quiet Man*'s fortieth anniversary. McLaglen gives an interview in which he discusses his memories of working beside John Ford and Maureen O'Hara.

The Duke & The General—1998

Producer: Cara Entertainment, Spy Guise Video

Availability: VHS
Note: Features interviews with actors John Wayne and James Stewart and directors Mark Rydell and McLaglen. Includes footage of Stewart and McLaglen on the set of *Fools' Parade*.

Dobe and a Company of Heroes— 2002

Producer: Tony Schweikle, National Film Network
Availability: DVD
Note: Summary of Harry Carey, Jr.'s career in films and television, with on-screen commentary from people who worked with the actor, including McLaglen, George Kennedy and Tom Selleck.

The Joy of Ireland— 2002

Producer: Michael Gillis, Artisan Home Entertainment
Availability: DVD
Note: Featurette produced to mark *The Quiet Man*'s fiftieth anniversary; appears on Republic's 2002 Collector's Edition release of the motion picture on DVD.

Budd Boetticher: A Man Can Do That— 2005

Producer: Dave Kehr, Bruce Ricker, Rhapsody Films
Availability: DVD
Note: Profile of Boetticher's career originally produced for Turner Classic Movies, an American cable television channel. The profile is featured in a DVD set called *The Films of Budd Boetticher*, which Sony released in 2008. In addition to McLaglen, Clint Eastwood, Quentin Tarantino and Taylor Hackford provide on-screen commentary about Boetticher and his films.

The Making of The High and the Mighty— 2005

Producer: Batjac Productions, Inc., Paramount Home Video
Availability: DVD
Note: Documentary featured in Paramount's 2005 DVD release of *The High and the Mighty*. In a segment called "The Batjac Story: Part 1 (1953–1961)," McLaglen speaks about the manner in which John Wayne helped him with his career.

The Making of Island in the Sky— 2005

Producer: Batjac Productions, Inc., Paramount Home Video
Availability: DVD
Note: Featurette included on Paramount's 2005 DVD release of *Island in the Sky*. McLaglen and actors Harry Carey, Jr. and Michael Wellman remember their experiences working on the picture.

The Making of McLintock!— 2005

Producer: Batjac Productions, Inc., Paramount Home Video
Availability: DVD
Note: Featured on Paramount's Special Collector's Edition of *McLintock!*, which was released on DVD in 2005. McLaglen, Stefanie Powers, Maureen O'Hara and John Wayne's family members share their memories of the production.

John Ford/John Wayne: The Filmmaker and The Legend — 2006

Producer: Kenneth Bowser, Thirteen/WNET
Availability: DVD
Note: Produced for PBS's *American Masters* television series, this program examines Wayne and Ford's creative partnership, with commentary provided by McLaglen, Peter Bogdanovich, Martin Scorsese and others.

100 Years of John Wayne — 2007

Producer: Elizabeth Daly, Jeff Hildebrandt, Starz! Encore Entertainment
Note: Brief survey of Wayne's career produced for Encore Westerns, an American cable television channel. Among on-screen personalities are McLaglen and several members of Wayne's family.

Appendix II: Stage Productions

Founded in 1989, the San Juan Community Theatre is located in downtown Friday Harbor, Washington.[1] McLaglen has been volunteering as a director for the theatre since 1992. Prior to this, he had no experience directing for the stage. The theatre's productions feature actors, set designers, stagehands and other crew who live in Washington State's San Juan Islands. The first production McLaglen helmed for the theatre, *Shenandoah*, is a musical adaptation of his 1965 film. His sixth production, *Twelve Angry Men*, was penned by Reginald Rose, the same writer who scripted McLaglen's *The Wild Geese* and *The Sea Wolves*. From 1994 to 2000, McLaglen also sat on the San Juan Community Theatre's Board of Trustees. Since 2000, Merritt Olsen has served as the Theatre's Executive Director. Olsen provided the following list of plays McLaglen has directed for the theatre and information about their production dates.

1992: *Shenandoah*
Author: James Lee Barrett
Summary: A Virginia farmer looks for his missing son during the Civil War.

1995: *Uncle Vanya*
Author: Anton Chekhov
Summary: The overseer of a farm in provincial Russia falls in love with his employer's wife.

1996: *Private Lives*
Author: Noël Coward
Summary: A man and woman who were once spouses both remarry. On their honeymoons, they cross paths and resume their love affair.

1997: *Mister Roberts*
Author: Adapted by Thomas Heggen and Joshua Logan from Thomas Heggen's novel
Summary: An officer on a supplies ship yearns to experience combat during World War II.

1998: *Chapter Two*
Author: Neil Simon
Summary: A divorcée and a widower reluctantly begin a love affair in New York City.

1999: *Twelve Angry Men*
Author: Reginald Rose
Summary: A juror persuades his colleagues to acquit a man who is being tried for murder.

2000: *Death of a Salesman*
Author: Arthur Miller
Summary: A distressed salesman commits suicide in a misguided attempt to help his family.

2001: *Lost in Yonkers*
Author: Neil Simon
Summary: Two teenagers are forced to live with their despotic grandmother.

2002: *Lend Me a Tenor*
Author: Ken Ludwig
Summary: Panic runs through an opera company when its featured singer accidentally overdoses on pills and wine.

2003: *To Kill a Mockingbird*
Author: Adapted by Christopher Sergel from Harper Lee's novel
Summary: A white lawyer in the Deep South defends an African American man who has been unjustly charged with rape.

2004: *Funny Money*
Author: Ray Cooney
Summary: Trouble befalls an accountant who mistakenly brings home a briefcase that doesn't belong to him.

2004: *The Nerd*
Author: Larry Shue
Summary: An architect is surprised to learn that a man who once saved his life on the battlefield is a hopeless nerd.

2005: *Plaza Suite*
Author: Neil Simon
Summary: An anthology production featuring a trio of stories about men and women who rendezvous in a luxury suite in New York's Plaza Hotel.

2006: *On Golden Pond*
Author: Ernest Thompson
Summary: Old resentments surface when a woman visits her elderly parents at their vacation home.

2007: *Over the River and Through the Woods*
Author: Joe DiPietro
Summary: A young man thinks about moving from the New York area to Seattle, an idea that upsets his grandparents.

2008: *Rumors*
Author: Neil Simon
Summary: The Deputy Mayor of New York's plans for hosting a party come undone after he shoots himself in the ear.

2009: *The Odd Couple*
Author: Neil Simon
Summary: Two men with clashing personalities share an apartment in New York City.

Chapter Notes

Preface

1. Harry Carey, Jr., *Company of Heroes* (Metuchen, NJ: Scarecrow, 1994), 192.

Chapter 1

1. McLaglen's middle name is Victor. "The director keeps the 'V' in the middle of his name as memorial to his father, the Oscar-winning screen actor, Victor McLaglen." From ffolkes, 1980, press kit.
2. Bob Thomas, Associated Press, "Macho Director is Part of Rare Breed," *Pittsburgh Post-Gazette*, April 25, 1980.
3. Andrew V. McLaglen, interviews with author, March 15, 2009, March 9, 2010, and telephone interview, August 23, 2010. McLaglen became an American citizen in 1941.
4. Victor McLaglen, *Express to Hollywood* (London: Jarrolds, 1934), 232–234, 241, 245–246, 251–254.
5. From "Andrew V. McLaglen — The Pro," an interview between Joyner and the director that appears in *The Westerners* (Jefferson, NC: McFarland, 2009), 63.
6. Barry Monush, *The Encyclopedia of Hollywood Film Actors* (New York: Applause Theatre and Cinema Books, 2003), 489.
7. See Victor McLaglen, *Express*, 270, and Harry T. Brundidge, *Twinkle, Twinkle, Movie Star!* (New York: E.P. Dutton, 1930; reprint, New York: Garland, 1977), 51.
8. See Sheila Graham, "Boxing is McLaglen's Sore Point," *Hartford Courant*, March 12, 1936, and Yana Ungermann-Marshall, *La Cañada* (San Francisco: Arcadia, 2006), 100.
9. Abe Greenberg, "Voice of Hollywood: Now Meet Andy McLaglen," *Citizen-News* [Hollywood], February 24, 1968. See also Myrtle Gebhart, "Hollywood Protects Itself against Kidnappers," *Los Angeles Times Magazine*, April 3, 1932.
10. Victor McLaglen, *Express*, 18–20.
11. "Andrew V. McLaglen: Last of the Hollywood Professionals," an interview between Dixon and the director that appears in *Senses of Cinema*, http://archive.sensesofcinema.com/contents/09/50/andrew-v-mclaglen-interview.html (August 10, 2009). See also Gebhart, "Hollywood Protects." Victor McLaglen won an Academy Award in the Best Actor category for his portrayal of Gypo Nolan in *The Informer*. Monush, *Film Actors*, 489.
12. Henryk Hoffman, *"A" Western Filmmakers* (Jefferson, NC: McFarland, 2000), 156–157. See also Joyner, "The Pro," *Westerners*, 62.
13. "McLaglen is Making New Spat Film," *Citizen-News* [Hollywood], March 20, 1963.
14. "Another McLaglen on His Way Up," *Toledo Blade*, May 7, 1967.
15. McLaglen, interview with author, March 10, 2010.
16. David Rothel, *Richard Boone: A Knight Without Armor in a Savage Land* (Madison, NC: Empire, 2000), 95.
17. "Making New Spat Film."
18. *The Wild Geese*, press kit, 1978.
19. McLaglen, interview with author, March 9, 2010.
20. McLaglen, telephone interview with author, August 23, 2010.
21. For a brief overview of the Selective Service System in the forties, see Susanna McBee, "The Hullabaloo is Old Hat to Hershey," *Life*, August 20, 1965: 28–29.
22. Dixon, "Hollywood Professionals."
23. McLaglen, interview with author, March 9, 2010.

24. Joyner, "The Pro," *Westerners*, 64.
25. See "Engagements," *Los Angeles Times*, March 22, 1943, and "Andrew V. M'Laglen's Wife Wins Divorce," *Los Angeles Times*, July 13, 1945.
26. *McLintock!*, 1963, press kit.
27. McLaglen, interview with author, March 9, 2010.
28. Dixon, "Hollywood Professionals."
29. See Associated Press, "Actor's Son Now Can Remarry His Wife," *Modesto Bee*, June 11, 1958, and "Actress Veda Ann Borg Sues for Divorce," *Los Angeles Times*, February 26, 1957.
30. Fred Landesman, *The John Wayne Filmography* (Jefferson, NC: McFarland, 2004), 84.
31. McLaglen, interview with author, March 15, 2009.
32. McLaglen, telephone interview with author, August 23, 2010. See also The American Film Institute, *The American Film Institute Catalog of Motion Pictures Produced in the United States, Feature Films, 1941–1950*, exec. ed. Patricia King Hanson (Berkeley: University of California Press, 1997), 79.
33. Dixon, "Hollywood Professionals."
34. McLaglen, interview with author, March 9, 2010. See also Dixon, "Hollywood Professionals."
35. Landesman, *Wayne Filmography*, 305.
36. Herb Fagen, *Duke, We're Glad We Knew You* (New York: Citadel, 2009), 88.
37. Michael Munn, *John Wayne: The Man Behind the Myth* (New York: New American Library, 2004), 136.
38. Joyner, "The Pro," *Westerners*, 64.
39. Maureen O'Hara, *'Tis Herself: A Memoir* (New York: Simon & Schuster, 2004), 159, 161, 162.
40. Dan Ford, *Pappy: The Life of John Ford* (Englewood Cliffs, NJ: Prentice Hall, 1979), 242–244.
41. From "The Making of 'The Quiet Man,'" Republic, 1992.
42. Stephen B. Armstrong, "Andrew V. McLaglen Looks Back," interview in *Classic Images*, April 2009, 82.
43. *James Arness: An Autobiography* (Jefferson, NC: McFarland, 2001), 81.
44. Ronald L. Davis, *Duke: The Life and Image of John Wayne* (Norman, OK: University of Oklahoma Press, 1998), 164.
45. Randy Roberts and James Stuart Olson, *John Wayne: American* (New York: Free Press, 1995), 378.
46. Armstrong, "Looks Back," 81.
47. Donald Shepherd, Robert Slatzer and Dave Grayson, *Duke: The Life and Times of John Wayne* (New York: Citadel, 2002), 191.
48. Frank T. Thompson, *William A. Wellman* (Metuchen, NJ: Scarecrow, 1983), 73.
49. See Roberts and Olson, *American*, 398–403.
50. Davis, *Life and Image*, 174.
51. Roberts and Olson, *American*, 409.
52. William A. Wellman, *A Short Time for Insanity* (New York: Hawthorn, 1974), 96.
53. McLaglen, telephone interview with author, August 23, 2010.
54. Amy Louise Wood, *Lynching and Spectacle: Witnessing Racial Violence in America* (Chapel Hill: University of North Carolina Press, 2009), 225.
55. *Variety*, November 10, 1954.
56. *Behind the Myth*, 162.
57. Donald Clark and Christopher P. Anderson, *John Wayne's The Alamo: The Making of the Epic Film* (Secaucus, NJ: Carol Pub., 1995), 16.
58. Lee Server, *Robert Mitchum: Baby, I Don't Care* (New York: St. Martin's, 2001), 281.
59. Armstrong, "Looks Back," 82.
60. Joyner, "The Pro," *Westerners*, 68.
61. Armstrong, "Looks Back," 81.
62. Joyner, "The Pro," *Westerners*, 68.
63. Dixon, "Hollywood Professionals."
64. McLaglen, interview with author, March 15, 2009.
65. Andrew V. McLaglen, personal notes, shooting script for *Gun the Man Down*, 1956. See also Joyner, "The Pro," *Westerners*, 68.
66. Joyner, "The Pro," *Westerners*, 69.
67. *Autobiography*, 101.
68. McLaglen's signing with CBS is one of several announcements featured in an entertainment report titled "Shelley Winters and Pat Hingle Signed for 'Inspired Alibi,'" which appeared in *New York Times*, January 26, 1957.
69. Rothel, *Richard Boone*, 94, 193.
70. Ibid., 94.
71. Armstrong, "Looks Back," 81.
72. McLaglen, interview with author, March 15, 2010.
73. "Victor M'Laglen, Screen Star, Dies," *New York Times*, November 8, 1959.
74. See *The Devil's Brigade*, 1968, press kit and *The Way West*, 1967, press kit.
75. From *The Making of The High and the Mighty*, a documentary that appears on Paramount's 2005 Special Collector's Edition release of *The High and the Mighty* on DVD.

76. O'Hara, *Herself*, 234. See also Davis, *Life and Image*, 246–250.
77. *Behind the Myth*, 245–246.
78. Roberts and Olson, *American*, 498.
79. Joyner, "The Pro," *Westerners*, 71.
80. Gary Fishgall, *Pieces of Time* (New York: Scribner, 1997), 302. Fishgall notes that the title of the film Stewart wanted McLaglen to direct was *Fields of Honor*, rather than *Seals of Honor*. A blurb published in *The Hollywood Reporter*—"Famed Sons of Like Men Signed to Pic," August 7, 1964—refers to the project as *Fields of Honor*, as well.
81. Joyner, "The Pro," *Westerners*, 71.
82. "War's Over—Movie Company Departs for California Location," *Eugene Register-Guard*, August 21, 1964.
83. See "Andrew McLaglen Inks 5-Pix U Deal," *Hollywood Reporter*, December 21, 1965, and Thomas, "Another McLaglen on His Way Up."
84. Fishgall, *Pieces of Time*, 305.
85. Lowell E. Redelings, "Andrew McLaglen: Theatreman's Alter Ego," *Motion Picture Herald*, February 15, 1967.
86. "Andrew McLaglen Inks 5-Pix U Deal."
87. *The Way West*, press kit.
88. See "3rd Generation McLaglen," *Hollywood Reporter*, July 20, 1966. For information on Sharon's wedding, see "Zinnemann, McLaglen Troth Told," *Los Angeles Times*, December 4, 1966, and "Zinnemann, McLaglen Vows Read," *Los Angeles Times*, January 30, 1967. In "Andrew V. McLaglen: Last of the Hollywood Professionals," McLaglen explains to Wheeler Winston Dixon that his daughter Sharon was "for 20 years ... a script analyst at Warner Brothers, and after that was a script analyst for ten years at MGM."
89. Tony Thomas, *The Films of Kirk Douglas* (Secaucus, NJ: Citadel Press, 1991), 221.
90. Server, *Baby*, 407–408.
91. McLaglen, interview with author, March 15, 2009.
92. See Michael Coyne, *The Crowded Prairie* (New York: St. Martin's, 1998), 138.
93. "Cinema: Dry Well," *Time*, February 21, 1969.
94. McLaglen, interview with author, March 15, 2009.
95. Roberts and Olson, *American*, 569–570.
96. Munn, *Behind the Myth*, 295.
97. Ibid., 572–573.
98. "John Wayne Rides Again in Chisum," July 30, 1970.
99. Roberts and Olson, *American*, 577.
100. Marc Eliot, *Jimmy Stewart: A Biography* (New York: Harmony, 2006), 377.
101. *Jimmy Stewart: A Life in Film* (New York: St. Martin's, 1993), 164.
102. Andrew V. McLaglen, personal notes, shooting script for *"something big,"* 1971. See also William Schoell, *Martini Man* (Dallas: Taylor, 1999), 265–266.
103. McLaglen, telephone interview with author, August 23, 2010.
104. Wayne Warga, "Real West Re-created South of the Border," *Los Angeles Times*, December 17, 1972.
105. Roberts and Olson, *American*, 583.
106. Writing in 1979, Christopher Wicking and Tise Vahimagi noted, "In recent years, McLaglen ... has suffered from the decline of the western — and TV has supplemented his movie career." *The American Vein, Directors and Directions in Television* (New York: E.P. Dutton, 1979), 102. For information on *The NBC Mystery Movie*, see Tim Brooks and Earle Marsh, *The Directory to Prime Time Network and Cable TV Shows* (New York: Ballantine, 2007), 952.
107. *Richard Boone*, 95.
108. "Andrew McLaglen to Direct Joe Don Baker Starrer," *Box Office*, December 2, 1974.
109. McLaglen, interview with author, March 15, 2009.
110. Charlton Heston, *The Actor's Life: Journals, 1956–1976* (New York: E.P. Dutton, 1978), 454–458.
111. Brian Garfield, e-mail message to author, February 13, 2010.
112. "Love-Death Western," *New York Times*, April 24, 1976.
113. "The Last Hard Men," *Variety*, April 21, 1976. See also Michael Munn, *Charlton Heston* (New York: Robson, 1986), 180.
114. Garfield e-mail.
115. McLaglen, interview with author, March 10, 2010.
116. Thomas, "Macho Director" (see chap. 1, n. 2). One of McLaglen's neighbors in Friday Harbor was Ernest Gann, who'd scripted two films on which McLaglen had worked during his time at Wayne-Fellows Productions, *Island in the Sky* and *The High and the Mighty*. See Simon Perry, "Characterizations Key Angles in Today's Action Films: McLaglen," *Variety*, June 20, 1979.
117. McLaglen, interview with author, March 15, 2009. See also Cliff Goodwin, *Behaving Badly* (London: Virgin, 2002), 176.
118. Paul Iredale, Reuters, "Burton, Buddies Back in the Bush," *Los Angeles Times*, November 17, 1977. McLaglen subsequently gave Mary small on-screen parts in *ffolkes* and *The Sea Wolves*.

119. "Andrew V. McLaglen," *Los Angeles Herald-Examiner*, November 24, 1978.
120. From Lloyd's commentary on *The Wild Geese*, Thirtieth Anniversary Edition, DVD, 2004.
121. "Producer Lloyd Knew He Had Right Characters," *Lewistown Evening Journal* [Maine], September 9, 1978.
122. From Lloyd's DVD commentary for *The Wild Geese*. See also Len D. Martin, *The Allied Artists Checklist* (Jefferson, NC: McFarland, 1993): x.
123. Associated Press, "Gunga Again," *Citizen* [Ottawa], February 1, 1978.
124. Donald Spoto, *Laurence Olivier: A Biography* (New York: Cooper Square Press, 2001), 393–394. See also Dale Pollock, "'Inchon!'— Shooting for the Moonies," *Los Angeles Times*, May 16, 1982. Terrence Young eventually took up the director's reigns for *Inchon!* The film premiered at the Cannes Film Festival in 1982.
125. Jerry Roberts, *Robert Mitchum: A Bio-Bibliography* (Westport, CT: Greenwood, 1992), 156.
126. David Weddle discusses the production history of *Cross of Iron* in *If they Move... Kill'em!* (New York: Grove, 2001), 504–513
127. *ffolkes*, press kit. See also Roger Moore, *My Word is My Bond: A Memoir* (New York: Collins, 2008), 230, and Thomas, "Macho Director."
128. McLaglen, interview with author, March 9, 2010. See also Robert Kistler, "John Wayne Dies at 72 of Cancer," *Los Angeles Times*, June 12, 1979.
129. Associated Press, "Gregory Peck Stars," *Windsor Star* [Ontario], October 15, 1979. See also Goodwin, *Behaving Badly*, 178.
130. Associated Press, "Civil War Film Being Edited for Next Fall," *Pittsburgh Post-Gazette*, January 20, 1982.
131. Jerry Buck, Associated Press, "'Blue and Gray' Keeps Director Busy," *Telegraph* [Nashua, NH], June 26, 1982.
132. "Travis McGee will air on ABC during the 1982–1983 Season," *Lewiston Daily Sun* [Maine], May 15, 1982.
133. McLaglen, telephone interview with author, August 23, 2010. See also Abraham Rabinovich, "Brooke Shields in Israel's 'Sahara,'" *Christian Science Monitor*, January 20, 1983, and Kristin McMurran, "Brooke Bobs Up in Israel," *People*, February 28, 1983: 29.
134. McMurran, "Brooke Bobs Up": 30–31. See also "McLaglen Signed to Direct 'Sahara,'" *Hollywood Reporter*, October 26, 1982.
135. Associated Press, "Lee Marvin Heads Up Another 'Dirty Dozen,'" *Spokesman-Review* [Spokane, WA], February 3, 1985.
136. McLaglen, interview with author, March 10, 2010, and telephone interview with author, August 23, 2010.
137. McLaglen, interviews with author, March 15, 2009, and March 10, 2010. See also Desmond Ryan, "'Return from the River Kwai' Called a Follow-up, Not a Sequel," *Philadelphia Inquirer*, May 29, 1988 and George Takei, *To the Stars* (New York: Pocket, 1994), 373.
138. McLaglen, interview with author, March 15, 2009. See also Pat H. Broeske, "A Man with No Name," *Los Angeles Times*, June 3, 1989, "Debbie Allen Awaits OK," *Daily News of Los Angeles*, September 4, 1989, and *Positif*, October 1991, 92–93.
139. Jeffrey Jolson-Colburn, "McLaglen Returns for 'Sextant,'" *Hollywood Reporter*, March 18, 1993.
140. Armstrong, "Looks Back," 83.
141. McLaglen, interview with author, March 10, 2010.
142. See Julia Nicholls, "Fans Attend Games in Comfort," *The Chronicle* [Centralia, WA], December 17, 2004.
143. McLaglen, telephone interviews with author on August 23 and October 13, 2010. Mary McLaglen is the co-author of a children's book about working in the film industry, *You Can be a Woman Movie Maker* (Marina del Rey, CA: Cascade Press, 2003). Josh McLaglen is the subject of a lengthy article by David Geffner titled "Born to Run (A Set)," which appeared in the Summer 2010 edition of *DGA Quarterly*, http://www.dgaquarterly.org/BACKISSUES/Summer2010/FeatureJoshMcLaglen.aspx (November 3, 2010).

Chapter 2

1. McLaglen, telephone interview with author, October 13, 2010.
2. See *Memo from David O. Selznick*, ed. Rudy Behlmer (New York: Viking Press, 1972), 337 and *American Film Institute Catalog: Feature Films, 1941–1950*, 2190–2191.
3. *Feature Films, 1941–1950*, 2192.
4. Ibid., 1817, 1423.
5. "Actress Veda Ann Borg Sues for Divorce," *Los Angeles Times*, February 26, 1957 (see chap.1, n. 29).
6. *Feature Films, 1941–1940*, 1817.
7. McLaglen, interview with author, March 9, 2010.
8. Landesman, *Wayne Filmography*, 83–84.
9. Fagen, *We're Glad*, 57.
10. 231.
11. Don Cusic, *Gene Autry: His Life and Career* (Jefferson, NC: McFarland, 2007), 114, 118.
12. McLaglen, interview with author (see chap.1, n. 31).
13. *The Making of The High and the Mighty* (see chap. 1, n. 75).
14. McLaglen, interview with author (see chap.1, n. 31).

15. *The Making of The High and the Mighty.*
16. Davis, *Life and Image*, 122–123.
17. *Feature Films, 1941–1950*, 90.
18. McLaglen, interview with author (see chap. 1, n. 31).
19. Robert W. Phillips, *Roy Rogers* (Jefferson, NC: McFarland, 1995), 38, 111.
20. See Weddle, *If They Move*, 127.
21. Roberts and Olson, *American*, 319.
22. McLaglen, interview with author, March 9, 2010.
23. Roberts and Olson, *American*, 319.
24. *Feature Films, 1941–1950*, 2079.
25. Ibid., 1275.
26. Roger Ruthart, "'The Rock Island Trail' Celebrated the coming of the Railroad," *Dispatch-Argus* [Quad Cities], June 21, 2004, http://qconline.com/archives/qco/display.php?id=199842&query=rockisland trailmcalester (June 23, 2010).
27. "'Torero' Made in Mexico on Seven-Week Schedule," *Los Angeles Times*, November 26, 1950.
28. Budd Boetticher, *When in Disgrace* (Santa Barbara, CA: Neville, 1985), 80–81.
29. Michael Wilmington, "Boetticher's Classic Restored," July 18, 1986.
30. Boetticher, *Disgrace*, 77.
31. O'Hara, *Herself*, 169.
32. Bill Levy, *John Ford: A Bio-Bibliography* (Westport, CT: Greenwood, 1998), 28.
33. Fagen, *We're Glad*, 104.
34. Munn, *Behind the Myth*, 120.
35. Michael Weldon, *The Psychotronic Video Guide* (New York: St. Marin's Griffin, 1996), 75.
36. SuzAnne Barabas and Gabor Barabas, *Gunsmoke: A Complete History and Analysis of the Legendary Broadcast Series* (Jefferson, NC: McFarland, 1990), 74–80. See also Joyner, "The Pro," *Westerners*, 68.
37. Barabas and Barabas, *Complete History*, 110–111. See also Wicking and Vahimagi, *American Vein*, 81.
38. Landesman, *Wayne Filmography*, 33–35.
39. See Roberts and Olson, *American*, 375–376, and Peter Roffman and Jim Purdy, "The Red Scare in Hollywood, HUAC and the End of an Era," in *Hollywood's America: Twentieth-Century America Through Film*, eds. Steven Mintz and Randy Roberts (Chichester, MA: Wiley-Blackwell, 2010), 179–186.
40. Martin, *Allied Artists*, ix. See also Walter Mirisch, *I Thought We Were Making Movies, Not History* (Madison: University of Wisconsin Press, 2008), 36–37 and Matthew Bernstein, *Walter Wanger, Hollywood Independent* (Minneapolis: University of Minnesota Press, 2000), 288.
41. Douglas Brode, *Shooting Stars of the Small Screen* (Austin: University of Texas Press, 2009), 231.
42. Bernstein, *Walter Wanger, Hollywood Independent*, 274–276, 288. See also Mirisch, *Making Movies*, 48–49.
43. Frank Richard Prassel, *The Great American Outlaw: A Legacy of Fact and Fiction* (Norman, OK: University of Oklahoma Press, 1996), 90–94.
44. Bernstein, *Wanger*, 274–276.
45. Thompson, *Wellman*, 243.
46. From *The Making of Island in the Sky*, a documentary that appears on Paramount's 2005 Special Collector's Edition DVD release of *Island in the Sky*.
47. Shepherd, Slatzer and Grayson, *Life and Times*, 191.
48. Bill Brubaker, *Stewards of the House: The Detective Fiction of Jonathan Latimer* (Bowling Green, OH: Bowling Green State University Popular Press, 1993), 21, 111–12
49. Arness, *Autobiography*, 129–130.
50. Roberts and Olson, *American*, 403–406
51. Ed Andreychuk, *Louis L'Amour on Film and Television* (Jefferson, NC: McFarland, 2010), 22–23.
52. Arness, *Autobiography*, 131–32.
53. *Life and Image* 174.
54. Fagen, *We're Glad*, 108.
55. From *The Making of The High and the Mighty*, Collector's Edition, DVD, 2005.
56. Robert Stack, *Straight Shooting* (New York: Macmillan, 1980), 162.
57. *Behind the Myth*, 159.
58. William Wellman, Jr., *The Man and His Wings* (Westport, CT: Praeger, 2006), 177.
59. Wellman, *Insanity*, 96 (see chap. 1, n. 52). Also McLaglen, interview with author (see chap. 1, n. 53).
60. Tag Gallagher, *John Ford: The Man and His Films* (Berkeley: University of California Press, 1986), 522.
61. Wellman, *Insanity*, 98–99.
62. Server, *Baby*, 258–259.
63. Ona L. Hill, *Raymond Burr: A Film, Radio and Television Biography* (Jefferson, NC: McFarland, 1994), 72.
64. Thompson, *Wellman*, 255. See also Landesman, *Wayne Filmography*, 42, Joanne Miller, *Best Places, Marin* (Seattle, Sasquatch Books, 2002), 104, and Brenda Scott Royce, *Lauren Bacall, A Bio-Bibliography* (Westport, CT: Greenwood, 1992), 67.
65. Aissa Wayne, *John Wayne, My Father* (New York: Random House, 1991), 33–34.

66. See Joyner, "The Pro," *Westerners*, 68 and Rothel, *Richard Boone*, 95.
67. Kenneth Turran, "A Good-Looking Bunch," *Los Angeles Times*, July 23, 2000.
68. "'An Exemplary Western,'" in *Cahiers du Cinema: The 1950s, Neo-realism, Hollywood, New Wave*, ed. Jim Hillier (Cambridge: Harvard University Press, 1985), 169–73.

Chapter 3

1. Andrew V. McLaglen, personal notes, shooting script for *Gun the Man Down*, 1956.
2. Andrew V. McLaglen, personal notes, shooting script for *The Abductors*, 1957. See also Philip K. Scheuer. "A Town Called Hollywood: 'Anything Goes' Transition Period Marks Film Making," *Los Angeles Times*, June 2, 1957.
3. See Chris Fujiwara, *The World and Its Double: The Life and Work of Otto Preminger* (New York: Faber and Faber, 2008), 43, and Kate Buford, *Burt Lancaster: An American Life* (New York: Knopf, 2000), 148.
4. *Stealing Lincoln's Body* (Cambridge: Harvard University Press, 2007), 87–88.
5. See Barabas and Barabas, *Complete History*, 110–111.
6. Ibid., 12. See also Kevin Thomas, "A Hard Ride to Top of Western Heap," *Los Angeles Times*, August 29, 1967.
7. Barabas and Barabas, *Complete History*, 191.
8. Roberts and Olson, *American*, 9.
9. Carey, *Company of Heroes*, 72.
10. "Actor John Carradine Dies; Starred in Classic Westerns," *Washington Post*, November 29, 1988.
11. Carey, *Company of Heroes*, 160.
12. For a thorough examination of Ford's friendship with Harry Carey, see Joseph McBride's *Searching for John Ford* (New York: St. Martin's, 2001), 98–118.
13. Davis, *Life and Image*, 144.
14. Rothel, *Richard Boone*, 95, 193, 228,
15. Wicking and Vahimagi, *American Vein*, 74.
16. James Stuart Olson, *Historical Dictionary of the 1950s* (Westport CT: Greenwood Radio, 2000), 121.
17. Rothel, *Richard Boone*, 101–102.
18. Joyner, "The Pro," *Westerners*, 71.
19. Scott Von Doviak, *Hick Flicks: The Rise and Fall of Redneck Cinema* (Jefferson, NC: McFarland, 2004), 133–34.
20. McLaglen, interview with author, March 9, 2010.
21. Everett Aaker, *Television Western Players of the Fifties* (Jefferson, NC: McFarland, 1997), 63.
22. See Brooks and Marsh, *Directory*, 797 and Les Brown, *Encyclopedia of Television* (Detroit: Gale, 1992), 321.
23. Andrew V. McLaglen, personal notes, shooting scripts for *The Lineup*, 1957.
24. Brooks and Marsh, *Directory*, 1072.
25. Michael Starr, *Hiding in Plain Sight: The Secret Life of Raymond Burr* (New York: Applause Theatre and Cinema Books, 2008), 88.
26. Brooks and Marsh, *Directory*, 590.
27. Patrick McGilligan, *Clint: The Life and the Legend* (New York: St. Martin's, 2002), 102.
28. "Victor M'Laglen, Screen Star, Dies" (see chap. 1, n. 73).
29. Brooks and Marsh, *Directory*, 637.

Chapter 4

1. Andrew V. McLaglen, personal notes, shooting script for *Freckles*, 1960.
2. Andrew V. McLaglen, personal notes, shooting script for *The Little Shepherd of Kingdom Come*, 1960.
3. Fred Bronson, *The Billboard Book of Number 1 Hits* (New York: Billboard Books, 2003), 27.
4. See introductory remarks to "Ed Faulkner—The Good Lieutenant," an interview in Joyner's *The Westerners*, 63.
5. O'Hara, *Herself*, 234 (see chap. 1, n. 39).
6. Munn, *Behind the Myth*, 245. See also Richard D. McGhee, *John Wayne: Actor, Artist, Hero* (Jefferson, NC: McFarland, 1990), 356.
7. See Davis, *Life and Image*, 247–250, and Richard L. Coe, "The State of Wayne," *Washington Post*, November 21, 1963.
8. Mae Tinee, "Wayne Stars with O'Hara in Western," *Chicago Tribune*, November 18, 1963.
9. Jay Robert Nash and Stanley Ralph Ross, eds., *The Motion Picture Guide* (Chicago: Cinebooks, 1985–1987), 1609.
10. Eliot, *Jimmy Stewart*, 356.
11. Gerard Molyneaux, *James Stewart: A Bio-Bibliography* (Westport, CT: Greenwood, 1992), 147.
12. Fishgall, *Pieces of Time*, 416.
13. *Motion Picture Guide*, 2541.
14. McLaglen, interview with author, March 15, 2009. See also John Boston, *Santa Clarita Valley* (San Francisco: Arcadia, 2009), 90, and Dave Smith, *Disney A to Z*, (New York: Hyperion, 1996), 338.
15. Smith, *Disney*, 338.

16. Elizabeth A. Brennan and Elizabeth C. Clarage, *Who's Who of Pulitzer Prize Winners* (Phoenix: Oryx Press, 1999), 224.
17. Andrew V. McLaglen, personal notes, shooting script for *The Way West*, 1966.
18. "The Way West' is Playing Citywide," July 19, 1967.
19. McLaglen, interview with author, March 10, 2010. See also Barabas and Barabas, *Complete History*, 119–121.
20. Andrew V. McLaglen, personal notes, shooting script for *The Ballad of Josie*, 1967.
21. McLaglen, telephone interview with author, October 13, 2010. See also David Kaufman, *Doris Day: The Untold Story of the Girl Next Door* New York: Virgin Books, 2008), 393.
22. Leo Sullivan, "Doris Day a Loser in the Old West," *Washington Post*, February 8, 1968.
23. Doris Day and A.E. Hotchner, *Doris Day: Her Own Story* (New York: Morrow, 1975), 220.
24. *The Western* (Woodstock, NY: Overlook Press, 1991), 301.
25. *Producer: A Memoir* (New York: Scribner, 2003), 161.
26. See Michelangelo Capua, *Yul Brynner: A Biography* (Jefferson, NC: McFarland, 2006), 94.
27. See Philip K. Scheuer "Bill Holden—His Heart's in Safariland," *Los Angeles Times*, March 17, 1968, and DeMar Teuscher and Dexter Ellis, "Chaff from the Legislative Mill," *Deseret News* [Salt Lake City], February 23, 1967.
28. Geoffrey Moorhouse, "War Film-Makers Take Italian Village," *Los Angeles Times*, August 1, 1967. See also Bob Thomas, *Golden Boy: The Untold Story of William Holden* (New York, St. Martin's, 1983), 161, and The American Film Institute, *The American Film Institute Catalog of Motion Pictures, Feature Films 1961–1970*, exec. ed. Richard P. Krafsur (New York: Bowker, 1976), 255.
29. McLaglen, interview with author, March 10, 2010.
30. Michelangelo Capua, *William Holden: A Biography* (Jefferson, NC: McFarland, 2010), 132–133.
31. Wolper, *Producer*, 164.
32. Fishgall, *Pieces of Times*, 314–315.
33. James D'Arc, *When Hollywood Came to Town* (Layton, UT: Gibbs Smith, 2010), 291.
34. Fishgall, *Pieces of Time*, 314.
35. For an interesting overview of Wayne's work on *The Green Berets* and director Mervyn LeRoy's uncredited contributions to the film, see Edward S. Feldman's memoir *Tell Me How You Love the Picture* (New York: St. Martin's, 2005), 88–91.
36. Roberts and Olson, *American*, 553.
37. From "Production Notes," *Hellfighters*, DVD, 1999.
38. *Popular Culture Review*, 13–14 (2003): 121–128.
39. Barabas and Barabas, *Complete History*, 528, 114–16, 90–91.
40. Gerald Pratley, *The Films of John Frankenheimer: Forty Years in Film* (Bethlehem, PA: Lehigh University Press, 1998), 1, and Stephen B. Armstrong, *Pictures About Extremes: The Films of John Frankenheimer* (Jefferson, NC: McFarland, 2008), 16–17.
41. *Lessons in Becoming Myself* (New York: Riverhead Books, 2007), 4.
42. Arness, *Autobiography*, 106.
43. Barabas and Barabas, *Complete History*, 208.
44. See R. Philip Loy, *Westerns and American Culture: 1930–1955* (Jefferson, NC: McFarland, 2001), 18.
45. McLaglen, interview with author, March 9, 2010.
46. Douglas B. Green, *Singing in the Saddle* (Nashville: Vanderbilt University Press, 2005), 83.
47. Susan King, "Ross' Western Grit," *Los Angeles Times*, June 30, 1991.
48. Brooks and marshal, *Directory*, 590. See also Rothel, *Richard Boone*, 193, 226 and Cyclops, "A Boone to the Whodunit Industry," *Life*, November 17, 1972: 23.
49. McLaglen, interview with author, October 13, 2010.
50. See Rothel, *Richard Boone*, 229.
51. Barabas and Barabas, *Complete History* 40–42.
52. Bill Ingram, *TV Party!* (Chicago: Bonus Books, 2002), 241–242
53. Richard McBrien. *Lives of the Saints: From Mary and Francis of Assisi to John XXIII and Mother Teresa* (San Francisco: Harper, 2001), 223.
54. Rothel, *Richard Boone*, 193
55. "Talman Gets 'Parry Mason' Role Back," *Los Angeles Times*, December 9, 1960.
56. Brooks and Marsh, *Directory*, 570.
57. See Hal Erickson, *Syndicated Television: The First Forty Years, 1947–1987* (Jefferson, NC: McFarland, 1989), 108.
58. See Nicholas Beck, *Budd Schulberg: A Bio-Bibliography* (Lanham, MD: Scarecrow, 2001), 154.
59. Brooks and Marsh, *Directory*, 786.
60. Wicking and Vahimagi, *American Vein*, 74.
61. Robert Vaughn, *A Fortunate Life* (New York: Thomas Dunne Books, 2008), 138.
62. David A. Jasen, *A Century of American Popular Music* (New York: Routledge, 2002), 135.
63. Brooks and Marsh, *Directory*, 1472–1473.
64. Ibid., 1479.

Chapter 5

1. A comprehensive filmography of Clothier's career can be found in George Stevens, Jr., ed., *Conversations with the Great Moviemakers of Hollywood's Golden Age* (New York: Knopf, 2006), 251–252.
2. Andreychuk, *L'Amour*, 107–108.
3. Dee Brown, *The American West* (New York: Scribner, 1994), 301–307.
4. Fagen, *We're Glad*, 193.
5. The statement from Nixon was delivered on August 3, 1970 in the Law Enforcement Assistance Administration at the Federal Office Building in Denver. See Mark Feeney, *Nixon at the Movies* (Chicago: University of Chicago Press, 2004), 85–86, David Hamilton Murdoch, *The American West: The Invention of a Myth* (Reno: University of Nevada Press, 2003), 110–111 and John S. Carroll, "Cult Leader is 'Guilty,' Nixon Says," *The Sun* [Baltimore], August 4, 1970. For a transcript, see "Nixon's Remarks on Manson and Statement in Washington," *New York Times*, August 4, 1970.
6. William F. Buckley, Washington Star Syndicate, "A Discussion of Mr. Nixon's Remark," *Victoria Advocate* [British Columbia], August 8, 1970.
7. David Bordwell, *The Way Hollywood Tells It: Story and Style in Modern Movies* (Berkeley: University of California Press, 2006), 56.
8. Andrew V. McLaglen, personal notes, shooting script for *Fools' Parade*, 1970.
9. Armstrong, "Looks Back," 82. See also Eliot, *Jimmy Stewart*, 377.
10. "Black Daubs on a Green Landscape," June 11, 1971: 20.
11. Tino Balio, ed., *The American Film Industry*, rev. ed. (Madison: University of Wisconsin Press, 1985), 546–547.
12. Andrew V. McLaglen, personal notes, shooting script for *Cahill, United States Marshal*, 1972–1973. Also Warga, "Real West" (see chap. 1, n. 104).
13. Stevens, *Conversations*, 251–252.
14. See Gene Siskel, "Mitchell," *Chicago Tribune*, August 26, 1975, and Steve Mitchell, "Poor Mitchell, Nobody Seems to Like Him," *Palm Beach Post*, August 31, 1975.
15. "Creating Contraptions is Not Mystery Science to Him," *Los Angeles Times*, November 28, 1998.
16. Garfield email (see chap.1, n. 111)
17. "The Last Hard Men," *Variety* (see chap. 1, n. 112).
18. From Lloyd's DVD commentary for *The Wild Geese* (see chap.1, n. 120). See also Robert Musel, UPI, "Financing $12 Million Burton Film" *The Hour* [Norwalk, CT], February 9, 1978.
19. Iredale, "Back in the Bush" (see chap. 1, n. 118).
20. Conlogue, "Black and White and Red All Over," November 15, 1978, and Mills, "The 'Africans': The Drums Are Beating," June 3, 1979.
21. Billy Watkins, *Apollo Moon Missions: The Unsung Heroes* (Lincoln: University of Nebraska Press, 2007), 105–116. See also "The Go-Go Astronauts," *Life*, December 5, 1969: 72–73.
22. Brooks and Marsh, *Directory*, 952.
23. Ibid., 100.
24. "Andrew McLaglen to Direct Joe Don Baker Starrer" (see chap. 1, n. 108).
25. See Cecil Smith, "Richard Boone, Have Microscope, Will Travel," *Los Angeles Times*, October 8, 1972, and William Hawes, *Filmed Television Drama, 1952–1958* (Jefferson, NC: McFarland, 2002), 106.
26. Brooks and Marsh, *Directory*, 952.
27. Ibid., 60.
28. Cecil Smith, "Jessica Walter: She's Striking a Blow for the Jane Does of TV," *Los Angeles Times*, December 22, 1974.
29. See Les Brown, *Encyclopedia*, 624–625, and Smith, *Disney A to Z*, 618.
30. "Saturday Night at the Movies," *Times-News* [Henderson, NC], May 29, 1975.
31. Cody Monk, *Legends of the Dallas Cowboys* (Champaign, IL: Sports Publishing, 2004), 35–45.
32. "Robert Forster in New Western," *Star Banner* [Ocala, FL], May 14, 1976.
33. Brooks and Marsh, *Directory*, 267.
34. Ibid., 457.

Chapter 6

1. Bob Thomas, "Macho Director" (see chap 1., n. 2)
2. "ffolkes' Zinger," April 21, 1980.
3. Lee Pfeiffer and Dave Worrall, *The Essential Bond: The Authorized Guide to the World of 007* (New York: HarperCollins, 2002), 91, 42–43.
4. Laura Kay Palmer, *Osgood and Anthony Perkins* (Jefferson, NC: McFarland, 1991), 333–334.
5. Weddle, *If They Move*, 512.
6. See Christopher Hicks, "A Good, Old-Fashioned Director," *Deseret News*, May 25, 1981.
7. See Sheridan Morley, *The Other Side of the Moon* (New York: Harper & Row, 1985), 264. Also Lloyd discusses

his contributions to *The Guns of Navarone* on his commentary for *The Wild Geese*, Thirtieth Anniversary Edition, DVD (see chap. 1, n. 119).

8. McLaglen, interview with author, March 15, 2009. Also McMurran, "Brooke Bobs Up": 29 (see chap. 1, n. 133).

9. Associated Press, "Brooke Shields Filming in Israel," *Daytona Beach Morning Journal*, January12, 1983.

10. McMurran, "Brooke Bobs Up": 29.

11. See "Return to the River Kwai," *Variety*, April 12–18, 1989, and Associated Press, "Flash!" *Newsday* [Long Island], July 11, 1997.

12. Brad Mengel, *Serial Vigilantes of Paperback Fiction* (Jefferson, NC: McFarland, 2009) 113–119.

13. McLaglen, interview with author, March 15, 2009, and Broeske, "No Name" (see chap. 1, n. 138).

14. John J. O'Connor, "TV: Tom Selleck Stars in a Western Romp," *New York Times*, September 28, 1982.

15. Buck, "Keeps Director Busy" (see chap. 1, n. 131).

16. Associated Press, "Lee Marvin," (see chap. 1, n. 135).

17. Howard Rosenberg, "Civil War Drama: CBS Rises Again?" *Los Angeles Times*, November 12, 1982.

18. Gerard Molyneaux, *Gregory Peck, A Bio-Bibliography* (Westport, CT: Greenwood, 1995), 193.

19. "Sam Rolfe, 69, Creator of 'U.N.C.L.E.' Series," *New York Times*, July 12, 1993.

20. Follett discusses his interactions with Perot on his website, *Ken Follett, Master Storyteller and Best-Selling Author*, http://www.ken-follett.com/bibliography/on_wings_of_eagles.html (December 1, 2010).

21. Buford, *Burt Lancaster*, 323. See also Ed Bark, "'On Wings of Eagles' is a Bumpy Flight," *Dallas Morning News*, May 18, 1986.

22. "Saturday Night at the Movies" (see chap. 5, n. 30) and Roberts and Olson, *American*, 569–570 (see chap. 1, n. 95).

23. Robert A. Baker and Michael T. Nietzel, *Private Eyes: One Hundred and One Knights* (Bowling Green, OH: Bowling Green University Popular Press, 1985), 61–63.

24. Buck, "Keeps Director Busy."

Appendix II

1. See Hilda Anderson, "An Island Retreat with an Ongoing Reason to Visit," *Seattle Post-Intelligencer*, March 9, 2000 and San Juan Community Theatre website, http://sjctheatre.org (December 3, 2010).

Bibliography

Aaker, Everett. *Television Western Players of the Fifties*. Jefferson, NC: McFarland, 1997.
Aldeman, Robert H., and George Walton. *The Devil's Brigade*. Philadelphia: Chilton, 1966.
The American Film Institute. *American Film Insti-tute (AFI) Catalog*. ProQuest. http://www.proquest.com/en-US/catalogs/databases/detail/american_film_inst.shtml.
_____. *The American Film Institute Catalog of Motion Pictures Produced in the United States, Feature Films, 1941–1950*. Exec. ed. Patricia King Hanson. 3 vols. Berkeley: University of California Press, 1997.
_____. *The American Film Institute Catalog of Motion Pictures, Feature Films 1961–1970*. Exec. ed. Richard P. Krafsur. 2 vols. New York: Bowker, 1976.
Andreychuk, Ed. *Louis L'Amour on Film and Television*. Jefferson, NC: McFarland, 2010.
Ansen, David. "Black Mischief." *Newsweek*, November 27, 1978.
Armstrong, Stephen B. "Andrew V. McLaglen Looks Back." *Classic Images*, April 2009.
_____. *Pictures About Extremes: The Films of John Frankenheimer*. Jefferson, NC: McFarland, 2008.
Arness, James, with James E. Wise, Jr. *James Arness: An Autobiography*. Jefferson, NC: McFarland, 2001.
Baker, Robert A., and Michael T. Nietzel. *Private Eyes: One Hundred and One Knights*. Bowling Green, OH: Bowling Green University Popular Press, 1985.
Balio, Tino, ed. *The American Film Industry*. Rev. ed. Madison: University of Wisconsin Press, 1985.
Barabas, SuzAnne, and Gabor Barabas. *Gunsmoke: A Complete History and Analysis of the Legendary Broadcast Series*. Jefferson, NC: McFarland, 1990.
Bazin, André. "'An Exemplary Western.'" In *Cahiers du Cinema: The 1950s, Neo-realism, Hollywood, New Wave*, edited by Jim Hillier. Cambridge: Harvard University Press, 1985.
Beck, Nicholas. *Budd Schulberg: A Bio-Bibliography*. Lanham, MD: Scarecrow, 2001.
Behlmer, Rudy, ed. *Memo from David O. Selznick*. New York: Viking Press, 1972.
Bernstein, Matthew. *Walter Wanger, Hollywood Independent*. Minneapolis: University of Minnesota Press, 2000.
Blair, Joan, and Clay Blair, Jr. *Return from the River Kwai*. New York: Simon & Schuster, 1979.
Boetticher, Budd. *When in Disgrace*. Santa Barbara, CA: Neville, 1985.
Bordwell, David. *The Way Hollywood Tells It: Story and Style in Modern Movies*. Berkeley, University of California Press, 2006.
Boston, John. *Santa Clarita Valley*. San Francisco: Arcadia, 2009.
Brennan, Elizabeth A., and Elizabeth C. Clarage. *Who's Who of Pulitzer Prize Winners*. Phoenix: Oryx Press, 1999.
Brode, Douglas. *Shooting Stars of the Small Screen*. Austin: University of Texas Press, 2009.
Bronson, Fred. *The Billboard Book of Number 1 Hits*. New York: Billboard Books, 2003.
Brooks, Tim, and Earle Marsh. *The Complete Directory to Prime Time Network and Cable TV Shows, 1946–Present*. 9th ed. New York: Ballantine, 2007.
Brown, Dee. *The American West*. New York: Scribner, 1994.
Brown, Les. *Encyclopedia of Television*. 3rd ed. Detroit: Gale, 1992.
Brubaker, Bill. *Stewards of the House: The Detective Fiction of Jonathan Latimer*. Bowling Green, OH: Bowling Green State University Popular Press, 1993.
Brundidge, Harry T. *Twinkle, Twinkle, Movie Star!* 1930. Reprint, New York: Garland, 1977.
Buford, Kate. *Burt Lancaster: An American Life*. New York: Knopf, 2000.
Burrows, Michael. *John Ford and Andrew V. McLaglen*. St. Austell, Cornwall: Primestyle, 1970.
Burstyn, Ellen. *Lessons in Becoming Myself*. New York: Riverhead Books, 2007.
Capua, Michelangelo. *William Holden: A Biography*. Jefferson, NC: McFarland, 2010.
_____. *Yul Brynner: A Biography*. Jefferson, NC: McFarland, 2006.

Carey, Harry, Jr. *Company of Heroes*. Metuchen, NJ: Scarecrow, 1994.
Clark, Donald, and Christopher P. Anderson. *John Wayne's The Alamo: The Making of the Epic Film*. Secaucus, NJ: Carol, 1995.
Coyne, Michael. *The Crowded Prairie*. New York: St. Martin's, 1998.
Craughwell, Thomas J. *Stealing Lincoln's Body*. Cambridge: Harvard University Press, 2007.
Cusic, Don. *Gene Autry: His Life and Career*. Jefferson, NC: McFarland, 2007.
Cyclops. "A Boone to the Whodunit Industry." *Life*, November 17, 1972.
D'Arc, James. *When Hollywood Came to Town*. Layton, UT: Gibbs Smith, 2010.
Davis, Ronald L. *Duke: The Life and Image of John Wayne*. Norman, OK: University of Oklahoma Press, 2003.
Day, Doris, and A.E. Hotchner. *Doris Day: Her Own Story*. New York: Morrow, 1975.
Dewey, Donald. *James Stewart: A Biography*. Kansas City: Turner, 1996.
Dixon, Wheeler W. *The "B" Directors: A Biographical Directory*. Metuchen, NJ: Scarecrow, 1985.
_____. "Andrew V. McLaglen: Last of the Hollywood Professionals." *Senses of Cinema*. http://archive.sensesofcinema.com/contents/09/50/andrew-v-mclaglen-interview.html (August 10, 2009).
Editors of *Time Out*. *Time Out Film Guide 2010*. London: Time Out Guides, 2009.
Eliot, Marc. *Jimmy Stewart: A Biography*. New York: Harmony, 2006.
Erickson, Hal. *Syndicated Television: The First Forty Years, 1947–1987*, Jefferson, NC: McFarland, 1989.
Fagen, Herb. *Duke, We're Glad We Knew You*. New York: Citadel, 1996.
_____. *The Encyclopedia of Westerns*. New York: Checkmark, 2003.
Feeney, Mark. *Nixon at the Movies*. Chicago: University of Chicago Press, 2004.
Feldman, Edward S., with Tom Barton. *Tell Me How You Love the Picture*. New York: St. Martin's, 2005.
Fishgall, Gary. *Pieces of Time*. New York: Scribner, 1997.
Follett, Ken. *Ken Follett, Master Storyteller and Best-Selling Author*. http://www.ken-follett.com/bibliography/on_wings_of_eagles.html.
Ford, Dan. *Pappy: The Life of John Ford*. Englewood Cliffs, NJ: Prentice Hall, 1979.
Fujiwara, Chris. *The World and Its Double: The Life and Work of Otto Preminger*. New York: Faber and Faber, 2008.
Gallagher, Tag. *John Ford: The Man and His Films*. Berkeley: University of California Press, 1986.
Garfield, Brian. *Western Films: A Complete Guide*. New York: Rawson, 1982.
Gebhart, Myrtle. "Hollywood Protects Itself against Kidnappers." *Los Angeles Times Magazine*. April 3, 1932.
Geffner, David. "Born to Run (A Set)." *DGA Quarterly* (Summer 2010): http://www.dgaquarterly.org/BACKISSUES/Summer2010/FeatureJoshMcLaglen.aspx (November 3, 2010).
Goodwin, Cliff. *Behaving Badly*. London: Virgin, 2002.
Green, Douglas B. *Singing in the Saddle*. Nashville: Vanderbilt University Press, 2005.
Hardy, Phil, ed. *The Western*. Updated ed. Woodstock, NY: Overlook, 1994.
Hatch, Robert, "Films: *Messidor, The Sea Wolves, History of the World, Part I*." *The Nation*, June 27, 1981.
Hawes, William. *Filmed Television Drama, 1952–1958*. Jefferson, NC: McFarland, 2002.
Heston, Charlton. *The Actor's Life: Journals, 1956–1976*. New York: E.P. Dutton, 1978.
Hill, Ona L. *Raymond Burr: A Film, Radio and Television Biography*. Jefferson, NC: McFarland, 1994.
Hoffman, Henryk. *"A" Western Filmmakers*. Jefferson, NC: McFarland, 2000.
Holland, Ted. *B Western Actors Encyclopedia*. Jefferson, NC: McFarland, 1989.
Hoppenstand, Gary. "Hollywood Cowboys and Confederates in Mexico." *Popular Culture Review* 13–14 (2003).
Ingram, Bill. *TV Party!* Chicago: Bonus Books, 2002.
Jameson, Richard T. "Seven Men from Now." In *The B List*, edited by David Sterritt and John Anderson. Cambridge: Da Capo, 2008.
Jasen, David A. *A Century of American Popular Music*. New York: Routledge, 2002.
Joyner, C. Courtney. *The Westerners*. Jefferson, NC: McFarland, 2009.
Kaufman, David. *Doris Day: The Untold Story of the Girl Next Door*. New York: Virgin, 2008.
Kelleher, Brian, and Diana Merrill. *The Perry Mason TV Show Book*. New York: St. Martin's, 1987.
Landesman, Fred. *The John Wayne Filmography*. Jefferson, NC: McFarland, 2004.
Levy, Bill. *John Ford: A Bio-Bibliography*. Westport, CT: Greenwood, 1998.
Loy, R. Philip. *Westerns and American Culture: 1930–1955*. Jefferson, NC: McFarland, 2001.
Lloyd, Euan, Roger Moore, Jonathan Sothcott, Andrew V. McLaglen. "Commentary." In *The Wild Geese*, DVD, 30th Anniversary Edition. Directed by Andrew V. McLaglen. 1978; Santa Monica: Victory Films, 2004.
The Making of Island in the Sky. In *Island in the Sky*, DVD, Special Collector's Edition. Directed by William A. Wellman. 1953; Hollywood: Paramount, 2005.
The Making of The High and the Mighty. In *The High and the Mighty*, DVD, Special Collector's Edition. Directed by William A. Wellman. 1954; Hollywood: Paramount, 2005.
The Making of The Quiet Man. In *The Quiet Man*, DVD, Collector's Edition. Written, produced and hosted by Leonard Maltin; no director's credit. 1992; Santa Monica: Artisan, 2002.
Martin, Len D. *The Republic Pictures Checklist*. Jefferson, NC: McFarland, 1998.
McBee, Susanna. "The Hullabaloo Is Old Hat to Hershey," *Life*, August 20, 1965.
McBride, Joseph. *Searching for John Ford*. New York: St. Martin's, 2001.

McBrien, Richard. *Lives of the Saints: From Mary and Francis of Assisi to John XXIII and Mother Teresa*. San Francisco: Harper, 2001.
McGhee, Richard D. *John Wayne: Actor, Artist, Hero*. Jefferson, NC: McFarland, 1990.
McGilligan, Patrick. *Clint: The Life and the Legend*. New York: St. Martin's, 2002.
McLaglen, Andrew V. "Director Commentary." In *Chisum*, DVD. Directed by Andrew V. McLaglen. 1970; Burbank: Warner Bros.,1998.
McLaglen, Mary, Lee Rathbone, et al. *You Can Be a Woman Movie Maker*. Marina del Rey, CA: Cascade Press, 2003.
McLaglen, Victor. *Express to Hollywood*. London: Jarrolds, 1934.
McMurran, Kristin. "Brooke Bobs Up in Israel." *People Weekly*, February 28, 1983.
Mengel, Brad. *Serial Vigilantes of Paperback Fiction*. Jefferson, NC: McFarland, 2009.
Miller, Joanne. *Best Places, Marin*. Seattle: Sasquatch Books, 2002.
Mirisch, Walter. *I Thought We Were Making Movies, Not History*. Madison: University of Wisconsin Press, 2008.
Molyneaux, Gerard. *Gregory Peck, A Bio-Bibliography*. Westport, CT: Greenwood, 1995.
_____. *James Stewart: A Bio-Bibliography*. Westport, CT: Greenwood, 1992.
Monk, Cody. *Legends of the Dallas Cowboys*. Champaign, IL: Sports Publishing, 2004.
Monush, Barry. *The Encyclopedia of Hollywood Film Actors*. New York: Applause Theatre and Cinema Books, 2003.
Moore, Roger, with Gareth Owens. *My Word Is My Bond: A Memoir*. New York: Collins, 2008.
Morley, Sheridan. *The Other Side of the Moon*. New York: Harper & Row, 1985.
Munn, Michael. *John Wayne: The Man Behind the Myth*. New York: New American Library, 2004.
_____. *Charlton Heston*. New York: Robson, 1986.
Murdoch, David Hamilton. *The American West: The Invention of a Myth*. Reno: University of Nevada Press, 2003.
Nash, Jay Robert, and Stanley Ralph, eds. *The Motion Picture Guide*. 12 vols. Chicago: Cinebooks, 1985–1987.
O'Hara, Maureen, with John Nicoletti. *'Tis Herself: A Memoir*. New York: Simon & Schuster, 2004.
Okuda, Ted. *The Monogram Checklist: The Films of Monogram Pictures Corporation, 1931–1952*. Jefferson, NC: McFarland, 1987.
Olson, James Stuart. *Historical Dictionary of the 1950s*. Westport CT: Greenwood, 2000.
Palmer, Laura Kay. *Osgood and Anthony Perkins*. Jefferson, NC: McFarland, 1991.
Parish, James Robert, and Michael R. Pitts. *The Great Western Pictures II*. Metuchen, NJ: Scarecrow, 1988.
Pfeiffer, Lee, and Dave Worrall. *The Essential Bond: The Authorized Guide to the World of 007*. New York: HarperCollins, 2002.
Phillips, Robert W. *Roy Rogers*. Jefferson, NC: McFarland, 1995.
Pickard, Roy. *Jimmy Stewart: A Life in Film*. New York: St. Martin's, 1992.
Pilkington, William T., and Don Graham. *Western Movies*. Albuquerque: University of New Mexico Press, 1979.
Prassel, Frank Richard. *The Great American Outlaw: A Legacy of Fact and Fiction*. Norman: University of Oklahoma Press, 1996.
Pratley, Gerald. *The Films of John Frankenheimer: Forty Years in Film*. Bethlehem, PA: Lehigh University Press, 1998.
"Production Notes." In *Hellfighters*, DVD. Directed by Andrew V. McLaglen. 1968; Universal City: Universal, 1999.
Roberts, Jerry. *Robert Mitchum: A Bio-Biography*. Westport, CT: Greenwood, 1992.
Roberts, Randy, and James Stuart Olson. *John Wayne: American*. New York: Free Press, 1995.
Roffman, Peter, and Jim Purdy, "The Red Scare in Hollywood, HUAC and the End of an Era." In *Hollywood's America: Twentieth-Century America Through Film*, edited by Steven Mintz and Randy W. Roberts. Chichester, MA: Wiley-Blackwell, 2010.
Rothel, David. *Richard Boone: A Knight Without Armor in a Savage Land*. Madison, NC: Empire, 2000.
Royce, Brenda Scott. *Lauren Bacall, A Bio-Bibliography*. Westport, CT: Greenwood, 1992.
_____. *Rock Hudson: A Bio-Bibliography*. Westport, CT: Greenwood, 1995.
Schickel, Richard. "Black Daubs on a Green Landscape." *Life*, June 11, 1972.
Schoell, William. *Martini Man: The Life of Dean Martin*. Dallas: Taylor, 1999.
Server, Lee. *Robert Mitchum: 'Baby, I Don't Care.'* New York: St. Martin's, 2001.
Shepherd, Donald, Robert Slatzer and Dave Grayson. *Duke: The Life and Times of John Wayne* New York: Citadel, 2002.
Simpson, Paul. *The Rough Guide to Westerns*. New York: Rough Guides, 2006.
Smith, Dave. *Disney A to Z: The Official Encyclopedia*. New York: Hyperion, 1996.
Spoto, Donald. *Laurence Olivier: A Biography*. New York: Cooper Square Press, 2001.
Staff. "Cinema: Dry Well." *Time*. February 21, 1969.
Staff. "The Go-Go Astronauts." *Life*, December 5, 1969.
Stack, Robert, with Mark Evans. *Straight Shooting*. New York: Macmillan, 1980.
Starr, Michael. *Hiding in Plain Sight: The Secret Life of Raymond Burr*. New York: Applause Theatre and Cinema Books, 2008.
Stevens, George, Jr., ed. *Conversations with the Great Moviemakers of Hollywood's Golden Age*. New York: Knopf, 2006.
Takei, George. *To the Stars*. New York: Pocket, 1994.
Terrace, Vincent. *The Complete Encyclopedia of Television Programs, 1947–1979*. 2nd ed., rev. 2 vols. South Brunswick, NJ: A.S. Barnes, 1979.

_____. *Experimental Television, Test Films, Pilots and Trial Series, 1925 through 1995*. Jefferson, NC: McFarland, 1997.
_____. *Television Characters and Story Facts*. Jefferson, NC: McFarland, 1993.
Thomas, Bob. *Golden Boy: The Untold Story of William Holden*. New York: St. Martin's, 1983.
Thomas, Tony. *The Films of Kirk Douglas*. Secaucus, NJ: Citadel Press, 1991.
Thompson, Frank T. *William A. Wellman*. Metuchen, NJ: Scarecrow, 1983.
Ungermann-Marshall, Yana. *La Cañada*. San Francisco: Arcadia, 2006.
Vaughn, Robert. *A Fortunate Life*. New York: Thomas Dunne Books, 2008.
Von Doviak, Scott. *Hick Flicks: The Rise and Fall of Redneck Cinema*. Jefferson, NC: McFarland, 2004.
Walsh, Moira. "Near Misses." *American*, October 2, 1971.
Watkins, Billy. *Apollo Moon Missions: The Unsung Heroes*. Lincoln: University of Nebraska Press, 2007.
Wayne, Aissa. *John Wayne, My Father*. New York: Random House, 1991.
Weddle, David. *If They Move ... Kill 'em!* New York: Grove, 2001.
Weldon, Michael. *The Psychotronic Video Guide*. New York: St. Marin's Griffin, 1996.
Wellman, William A. *A Short Time for Insanity*. New York: Hawthorn, 1974.
Wellman, William, Jr. *The Man and His Wings*. Westport, CT: Praeger, 2006.
West, Richard. *Television Westerns: Major and Minor Series, 1946–1978*. Jefferson, NC: McFarland, 1987.
Wicking, Christopher, and Tise Vahimagi. *The American Vein, Directors and Directions in Television*. New York: E.P. Dutton, 1979.
Wills, Garry. *John Wayne's America: The Politics of Celebrity*. New York: Simon & Schuster, 1997.
Wolper, David L., with David Fisher. *Producer: A Memoir*. New York, Scribner, 2003.
Wood, Amy Louise. *Lynching and Spectacle: Witnessing Racial Violence in America*. Chapel Hill: University of North Carolina Press, 2009.

Index

Page numbers in ***bold italics*** indicate illustrations.

Aaker, Lee 57
Abbott, Bruce 241
ABC (television network) 22, 24, 192, 194, 216, 219, 243, 244
ABC Circle Films 216
The Abductors (film) 4, 6, 14, 32, 69, *73*–74, 93, 100
"Abe Blocker" (*Gunsmoke*) 164–165
Abel, Walter 53
Abney, William 224
Abraham, F. Murray 237
Academy Awards 28
Acosta, Rodolfo 44, 57, 94, 125
Adair, Paul N. "Red" 152
Adams, Dorothy 75
Adams, Lillian 117
Adams, Mary 97
Addinsell, Richard 229
Adlar Productions 237
Adler, Jay 99
Adler, Robert 164
Adventures of Red Ryder (serial) 166
Agar, John 41, 42, 152, 193
Aguilar, Tony 152
Ahn, Philip 116
Ahuet, Julio 242
Aidman, Charles 89, 101, 115, 218
Air Transport Command 55
Akins, Claude 92, 145
The Alamo (film) 133, 149, 195
Alaniz, Rico 112
"Alaska" (*Have Gun, Will Travel*) 109
Albertson, Jack 94
Albertson, Mabel 112, 159
Albright, Lola 141
Alcade, Mario 108
Alcaide, Chris 81, 98, 123, 126, 187

Aldeman, Robert H. 145, 146
Alderman, John 190
Alderson, John 104, 212, 221
Aldon, Mari 122
Aldrich, Robert 7, 25, 147, 240
Aley, Albert 100, 102, 106, 109, 111
Alford, Philip 134
Algar, James 219, 220
Alice Doesn't Live Here Anymore (film) 161
Alland, William 137
Allen, Corey 125
Allen, Fred 34, 35
Allen, Patrick 212, 229
Allen, Valerie 162
Allied Artists 51, 52, 53, 209, 215
Allison, Jean 98
Allman, Sheldon 127
Altman, Robert 201
Alton, John 31
Alton, Kenneth 95
Alzamora, Armand 202
American Masters (television series) 247
Ames, Allyson 171
Amrani, Gabi 233
Amsterdam, Morey 106
Amy Prentiss (television series) 20, 217, ***219***
Andersen, Jurgen 229
Anderson, Bob 155
Anderson, Donna 172, 191
Anderson, Guy 53
Anderson, James 159
Anderson, John 101, 105, 221
Anderson, Pat 223
Anderson, Robert 110
Anderson, Warner 118
Andre, Charles 32
Andrews, Dana 145
Angel and the Badman

(film) 3, 9, 37–39, 62
Ankrum, Morris 52, 102, 121, 125
Anna-Lisa 155, 190
Annie Oakley (television series) 140
Antonio, Lou 174
The Apache Kid (film) 166
Apache Rose (film) 3, 39–41, 53
Apartheid 22
Apick, Mary 242
Apone, John 89
Applegate, Royce D. 241
Arabian Sea 24
Archard, Bernard 229
Archer, Anne 221
Argosy Pictures 45
Arizona Mission see *Gun the Man Down*
Armatrading, Joan 212
Armendariz, Pedro, Jr. 193, 221, 242, 243
Arms, Russell 157, 179, 189
Armstrong, Lyle 241
Armstrong, R.G. 100, 159, 166, 189, 238
Armstrong, Robert 103
Army Air Corps 36
Arness, James 11, 12, 14, ***16***, 48, 49, ***50***, 53, 57, ***58***, 59, 69, ***70***, 71, 75, 77
Arnette, Jeannetta 238
Arngrim, Stefan 141
Arnold, Phil 121
Arnold, Sean 224
Around the World in Eighty Days (book) 175
Arrowhead (film) 49
Arthur, Art 31
Arthur, Robert 134, 136, 150, 152, 196
Artisan Home Entertainment 246
Ashby, John 208

Ashford Castle Hotel 11
Ashley, Edward 8, ***30***, 31
Ashley, Joel 113
Askew, Luke 145
Associated Artists 52
Associated Producers 128, 129
Asther, Nils 31
Atterbury, Malcom 105, 125
Atwater, Barry 98
Aubuchon, Jacques 109, 173
Audrey, Christie 143
Austin, William 46, 51
Austria 26, 227
Autry, Gene 8, 35, ***36***
Avatar (film) 28
Avedon, Doe 59
Avery, Phyllis 181
Avila, Cynthia 216
Axton, Hoyt 208
The Ayatollah's Widow (book) 237, 238
Ayer, Eleanor 125

Bacall, Lauren 65, ***66***
Bacharach, Burt 202
Back to Bataan (film) 153
Bacon, Irving 51
"Bad Sheriff" (*Gunsmoke*) 157
"The Badge" (*Gunsmoke*) 156
Baer, Buddy 94
Baer, Parley 182
Baiotto, James 126, 168, 188, 189
Baker, Buddy 220
Baker, Diane 241
Baker, George 224
Baker, Glyn 212
Balinda, Carla 118
"The Ballad of John Chisum" (song) 193
The Ballad of Josie (film) 4, 17, 46, 77, 86, 128,

265

134, 143–145, 155, 164, 176, 177, 178, 234, 235
"The Ballad of Josie" (song) 143
"The Ballad of Paladin" (song) 102
Balsam, Martin 208
Banacek (television series) 20, **21**, 193, 216, 217, 244
Bandolero! (film) 4, 17, 19, 35, 43, 52, 77, 86, 93, 105, 111, 128, 147, **148**–150, 155, 163, 164, 166, 177, 194, 201, 204, 208, 218, 234, 237
Banjo Hackett (television pilot) 4, 21, 43, 221–222, 223
Banjo Hackett: Roamin' Free see *Banjo Hackett*
"Bank Baby" (*Gunsmoke*) 174
Bank, Douglas 113
Baptiste, Thomas 212
Barcroft, Roy 14, 34, 35, 43, 93, 100, 110, 111, 127, 128, 129, 141, 148, 156, 157, 173, 175, 180, 187, 188–189
Bardette, Trevor 85, 115, 155, 174, 176
Barnes, Joanna 185
Barnes, Rayford 14, 57, 59, 104, 105, 134, 157, 161, 162, 169, 176, 179, 187, 205, 207, 208
Barnes, Walter 205
Barrat, Robert H. 34
Barrett, James Lee 16, 19, 111, 134, 148, 149, 152, 199, 200, 201, 202, 204, 205, 248
Barrier, Michael 163
Barry, Donald "Red" 67, 104, 148, 165, 166
Barry, John 225
Barry, Patricia 156
Barrymore, Lionel 29
Bartell, Harry 100, 159
Bartell, Richard 159
Bartlett, Bennie 47, **48**
Barton, Anne 108
Barton, Joan 37
Barzell, Wolfe 177
Bass, Todd 208
Basserman, Albert 29
Bassett, Joseph "Joe" 94, 165
"The Bassops" (*Gunsmoke*) 170
Bat Masterson (television series) 140
Bates, Jeanne 107, 121, 125
Batjac Productions 3, 13, 15, 19, 39, 65, 69, 71, 131, 134, 152, 193, 194, 205, 240, 246
"The Batjac Story: Part 1" 246
Baton Rouge, Louisiana 19
Battista, Lloyd 193
Battle, John Tucker 105

Battle of Little Big Horn 52, 110
Baxer, Alan 159
Baxley, Barbara 100, 122
Baxter, Alan 168, 193
Baxter, Anne 199
Baylor, Hal 50, 53, 80, 101, 119, 171, 185, 217
Bazin, André 68
BBC TV 245
"Bearbait" (*Have Gun, Will Travel*) 176
Beatty, Clyde 61
Beaudine, William 47
Beaumont, Hugh 46
Becker, Ken 127, 159
Beckman, Henry 163
Beddoe, Don 97, 116, 177
Bedi, Kabir 242
Beery, Noah, Jr. 169
Bel Air Country Club 16
Belford, Christine 217
Bell, Dennis 242
Bell, James 118
Bellamy, Ralph 221
Beller, Kathleen 241
"Ben Jalisco" (*Have Gun, Will Travel*) 179
"Ben Tolliver's Stud" (*Gunsmoke*) 156–157
Bend, Oregon 17, 91, 173, 181
Bender, Russ 177, 181, 189
Benedict, Jay 239
Benedict, Val 99
Benet, Vicki 182
Bennett, Constance 32, **33**
Bennett, Joan 52
Bennett, Marjorie 118
Benson, Hugh 241
Benson, Martin 229
Beradino, John 67
Berard, Roxanne 112
Berardino, John 107
Bercovici, Eric 220
Berger, Fred 84, 91
Berlin 229
Bermuda Triangle 223
Bernard, Ralph 185
Berneis, Peter 226
Bernstein, Elmer 205
Best, James 95, 134, 166
Bettger, Lyle 171
Bezzerides, A.I. 63
Bice, Robert 96, 170
Biery, Edward A. 191, 218
Big Bear, California 111
The Big Clock (film) 57
Big Hand for the Little Lady (film) 198
Big Jake (film) 194
Big Jim McLain (film) 11, 39, **50**–51, 57
"Big Tom" (*Gunsmoke*) 87–88
Billy the Kid in Texas (film) 166
Binns, Edward 82, 97
Birch, Paul 103
"The Bird of Time" (*Have Gun, Will Travel*) 184

"Birds of a Feather" (*Have Gun, Will Travel*) 100
Biroc, Joseph 205, 207
Bishop, Julie 41, 59
Bissell, Whit 97, 125, 186
"Bitter Wine" (*Have Gun, Will Travel*) 99
Black, Don 205
Black Fox Military Institute 6
"The Black Handkerchief" (*Have Gun, Will Travel*) 113
Black Pearl Productions 220
The Black Watch (film) 6
Blackman, Honor 202
Blackmer, Sidney 59
"The Blacksmith" (*Gunsmoke*) 155
Blair, Clay, Jr. 26, 235, 236
Blair, Joan 26, 235, 236
Blaise, Alexandre 235
Blake, Amanda 75
Blake, Larry 84, 109, 111, 137, 171, 172
Blake, Robert "Bobby" 34, 35, 37, 184, 185
Blakeney, Olive 34
Blangsted, Folmar 148, 150
Blazing Saddles (film) 198
Blecha, Norbert 237
Blood Alley (film) 13, 65–**66**, 72, 77
"Bloody Hands" (*Gunsmoke*) 79
Bloom, Harold Jack 110, 218, 220
Bloomfield, Robert 123
The Blue & The Gray (miniseries) 24, 84, 101, 131, 190, 224, 241–242
"Blue Horse" (*Gunsmoke*) 84–85
The Blue Max (film) 233
"The Bluegrass Special" (*Wonderful World of Disney*) 219–220
Boarding Party: The Last Action of the Calcutta Light Horse (book) 229, 230
Bob Nolan and the Sons of the Pioneers 40
Bochner, Lloyd 191
Boer War 6
Boetticher, Oscar "Budd" 10, 13, 42, 43, 44, 45, 67, 68, 248
Bogdanovich, Peter 247
Bohem, Endre 78, 123, 189
Bolder, Cal 161
Bolding, Bonnie 104
Bonar, Ivan 185
Bond, Ward 12, 34, 35, 45, 48, 57, **58**, 192
Bondi, Beulah 63
Bonnie and Clyde (film) 202
Bookholane, Fats 212
Books, Donna 174
Boone, Peter 183

Boone, Richard 14, 20, **91**, 111, 173, 218
Booth, Adrian 37, 43
Booth, John 215
Booth, Karin 121
Borden, Lynn 223
Borg, Veda Ann 3, 8, 31, 32, 50, 51
Borgnine, Ernest 25, 239
Borodin, A. 212
"The Bostonian" (*Have Gun, Will Travel*) 98–99
Bottoms, Timothy 235
Bouchey, Willis 93
Boulle, Pierre 236
Bourneuf, Philip 75
Bowen, Dennis 223
The Bowery Boys 47, 48
Bowery Leathernecks see *Here Come the Marines*
Bowser, Kenneth 247
Boxleitner, Bruce 216
Boyd, Benjamin 74
Boyett, William 113, 173
Bracho, Diana 242
Bracken, Richard 243
Brackettville, Texas 149
Bradford, Lane 82, 88, 108, 134, 163, 164, 173
Bradford, Marshall 48
Bradley, Bart 102
Brady, Ben 116, 117, 120, 121, 122, 123
Brady, Buff 107
Brand, Neville 205
Brandon, Henry 96, 158
Breakthrough (film) 4, 23–24, 64, 76, 147, 198, 226–229, **228**, 231, 240
Breanner, Gordon D. 220
Breck, Peter 104
Brenlin, George 82, 186
Brennan, Walter 34
Brennan, Walter, Jr. 94
Bretherton, David 199
Brian, David 59, 137
Brick, Peter 167
Bricusse, Leslie 229
"The Bride" (*Have Gun, Will Travel*) 93
The Bridge on the River Kwai (film) 236, 237
The Bridge Over the River Kwai (book) 236
Bridges, Lloyd 24, 215, 241
Briggs, Charles 168
Brinegar, Paul 123
Bring Me the Head of Alfredo Garcia (film) 212
Brinkley, Don 94, 95, 96
Brocco, Peter 93
Broderick, Helen 31
Brodie, Lea 224
Brogan, Ron 115
Bromfield, John 61
Bronson, Charles 14, 92, 103, 179, 186
Bronson, Lillian 123, 177, 188
Brook, Faith 224, 229
Brooke, Walter 215, 241
Brookholane, Fats 212

Brooks, Barry 123
Brooks, Foster 163
Brooks, Geraldine 117
Brooks, Mel 198
"Brotherhood" (*Have Gun, Will Travel*) 186
Brothers, Jamie 183
"The Brothers" (*Have Gun, Will Travel*) 180
Broughton, Bruce 241
Brown, Harry 41
Brown, James 41
Brown, Larry 208
Brown, Lew 86, 89, 182
Brown, Tom 105
Brown, Wally 119, 122
Browning, Tod 6
Brubaker, Robert 83, 156, 164
Bruce, Virginia 8, **30**, 31
Bruce Lansbury Productions 221, 223
Brunner, Robert F. 139
Bryan, Brandy 123
Bryant, William 165, 177, 193
Bryon, Carol 168
Buchanan, Edgar 46, 47, 132, 160
Buchanan Rides Alone (film) 68
Bucholz, Horst 232
Buck, Connie 86
Buckley, Hal 217
Budd, Roy 212, 229, 231
Budd Boetticher: A Man Can Do That (documentary) 246
Buena Vista Distribution Co. 141
Bullet 41
Bullfighter and the Lady (film) 10, 11, 39, 43, 44–45
Bumiller, William 242
Burbridge, Betty 37
Burgade (discarded film title) 211
"The Buried People" (*Gunslinger*) 188–189
"The Burning Tree" (*Have Gun, Will Travel*) 186
Burk, Jim 193, 197
Burke, Paul 127
Burke, Robert 57
Burke, Walter 88
Burma Railway 236
Burns, Michael 192
Burr, Raymond 120
Burrell, Jan 113
Burrows, Michael 1
Burton, Richard 1, 22, 23, 24, 212, 214, 226, 227
Burton, Robert 79
Busch, Paul 145
Butts, Dale 35
Byrnes, Jim 222, 238

Cabal, Robert 105
Cabot, Bruce 15, 37, 43, 132, 133, 150, 152, 193
Cabot, Susan 98, 110

Cacavas, John 216
Cahill, Barry 92, 93, 96, 163
Cahill, United States Marshal (film) 1, 4, 19, 22, 77, 90, 104, 107, 125, 155, 171, 193, 205–207, **206**
Cahn, Dann 221
Cahoon, Richard 121, 188
Caillou, Alan 113, 137, 150
Cain, Arthur 200
Caine, Howard 88
Cairncross, William O. 223
Calcutta Light Horse (CLH) 230
Calder, King 101
Calhoun, Rory 241
Calihan, William, Jr. 52, 53
The Call of the Road (film) 5
Callaghan, Duke 209, 220
Callahan, James 215
Calvelli, James 118, 119
Camacho, Corrine 219
Camargo, Mexico 58
Camp Pendleton 41, 190
Camp W.G. Williams 146
Campbell, Lindsay 224
Campbell, William 13, **15**, 59, **60**, 71, 72, 218
Campos, Rafael 112
Canino, Jim 119
Cannon, Diane 103
Cannon, Kathy 200
Cannon Films 24
Cannon Group 232
Capone, Joe 238
Cara Entertainment 245
"Caravan" (*Have Gun, Will Travel*) 186–187
Cardan, Carlon 242
Carey, Harry 37, 86, 181
Carey, Harry, Jr. 14, 53, 69, **70**, 71, 77, 85, 86, 103, 104, 112, 116, 118, 126, 127, 134, 137, 141, 143, 145, 148, 152, 157, 163, 164, 168, 173, 175, 179, 181, 187, 190, 196–197, 202, 205, 207, 238, 245, 246
Carey, Olive 180, 181
Carey, Phillip 218
Carillo, Daniel 26–27, 237, 238
Carl, Richard 200
Carl Curtis School 6
Carleton, Claire 118
Carlson, Richard 191
Carlson, Karen 242
Carlsson, Erika 242
Carneol, Jess 111
Carney, Daniel 212, 214
Carney, Thom 111
Carol, Jack 119
Carpinteria, California 6, 7, 113, 169, 222
Carr, Marian 61

Carradine, John 85, 102, 215
Carricart, Robert 180
Carroll, Janice 241
Carruthers, Steve 122
Carson, Robert 123
Carter, Conlan 156, 158, 169, 190
Cartwright, William 145
Caruso, Anthony 92, 108, 115, 156, 159, 168, 172, 179
Carver, Mary 89
Case, Allen 107, 109, 171
"The Case of the Clumsy Clown" (*Perry Mason*) 188
"The Case of the Deadly Double" (*Perry Mason*) 120
"The Case of the Empty Tin" (*Perry Mason*) 121
"The Case of the Gilded Lily" (*Perry Mason*) 122
"The Case of the Screaming Woman" (*Perry Mason*) 121
"The Case of the Shattered Dream" (*Perry Mason*) 123
"The Case of the Terrified Typist" (*Perry Mason*) 63, 122–123
Cass, Dave 172, 222
Cass County Boys 35
Cassell, Wally 41, 53
Castiglioni, Iphigenie 180
Cat Ballou (film) 198
Catch-22 (film) 201
Cates School 6, 7, 113, 169, 222
Catton, Bruce 241
CBS Radio 94
CBS Television 1, 4, 11, 14, 15, 16, 17, 20, 21, 22, 24, 49, 59, 69, 71, 75, 86, 91, 118, 120, 123, 126, 128, 144, 158, 173, 187, 188, 207, 208, 215, 219, 222, 238, 239, 241, 243
Cedar, Jon 215
Central Airport (film) 11
Cezon, Connie 122
Challee, William 160
Challenger, Rudy 217
Chama, Syndey 212
Chambers, Phil 115, 164
Chambliss, Woodrow 95
"Champagne Safari" (*Have Gun, Will Travel*) 114
Champion **36**
Champion, John C. 48
Chan, George 65
Chan, W.T. 65
Chandler, George 59, 197
Chandler, Lane 112, 114, 118, 157, 159, 164, 168, 173, 179, 189
Chaney, Lon, Jr. 108, 124
Chang, Jane 111
"Change of Heart" (*Gunsmoke*) 84

Chapter Two (play) 248
Chase, Borden 191
"Cheap Labor" (*Gunsmoke*) 79
Chekhov, Anton 27, 248
Chermak, Cy 191, 216, 219
"Cherry Red" (*Gunsmoke*) 90–91
Chester Goode **16**, 155
Chevalier, Maurice 139, 141
Cheyenne (television series) 138
Cheyenne Autumn (film) 85
Cheyenne Social Club (film) 198
"Chicken" (*Gunsmoke*) 172–173
Chief White Horse 116
Chiles, Linden 166, 217
Chisum (film) 1, 4, 19, **20**, 43, 43, 47, 90, 93, 111, 114, 163, 166, 167, 168, 173, 178, 193–196, 207, 208, 212, 232, 234, 245
"Chisum and the Lincoln County Cattle War" (story) 193
"Cholera" (*Gunsmoke*) 77
Christensen, Carol 128
Christie, Andrey 143
Christine, Virginia 173
Christy, Ken 118
Chulack, Fred A. 143, 208, 209, 241
Chung, Byron 223
Churubusco-Azteca Studios 57
Ciannelli, Eduardo 99
Cinema Center Films 202
Cinema Seven Productions Ltd. 224
CinemaScope 61, 63
Cisar, George 109
Claman, Julian 91, 92, 93, 93, 94, 95, 96, 97, 98, 99, 100, 101, 102, 106
Clark, Dort 200
Clark, Ellen 115
Clark, Marian 84, 87, 88, 89, 156, 161
Clark, Walter Van Tilburg 13, 63
Clarke, Angela 163
Clarke, Gage 78, 101, 162
Cleave, Van 168, 182
Clements, Calvin, Jr. 220
Cline, Kathy 61
Close, John 88, 109
Clothier, William H. 15, 16, 17, 53, 55, 59, 61, 63, 64, 65, 67, 69, 71, 72, 132, 137, 141, 143, 145, 148, 149, 150, 152, 193, 194, 207, 234, 245
Clute, Sidney 208
Clyde, Jeremy 224
Clyde Beatty Circus 63
Coates, Phyllis 164, 191
Cobb, Lee J. 191, 192
Coburn, James 21, 22, 209, **210**, 212, 227

Coby, Fred 169
Code R 22, 222–223
"Cody's Code" (*Gunsmoke*) 159–160
Coe, Peter 41, 48, 94
Colbert, Claudette 8, *9*, 29
Cole, Joe 212
Coleman, Pat 119
Coley, Thomas 87
Collier, Don 171, 192
Collier, Marian 121, 191
Collins, Gary 223
Collins, Lewis D. 46, 167
Collins, Patrick 242
Collins, Ray 120
Colmans, Edward 112
Colon, Miriam 186
"The Colonel and the Lady" (*Have Gun, Will Travel*) 95
The Colorado Kid (film) 166
Columbia 202, 235
Columbia Pictures Television 221, 223, 238, 241
Columbo (television series) 216
"Comanche" (*Have Gun, Will Travel*) 110
Comanche Station (film) 68
The Comancheros (film) 152
Combs, Gary 208
comic Westerns 15, 17, *18*, 19, 39, 133, 198
"Coming of the Tiger" (*Have Gun, Will Travel*) 182
Commander Films Corporation 48
Conde, Antonio Diaz 55
Condon, David 47, *48*
Cong, Ireland 11, 24
Connelly, Chris 172, 190
Connors, Chuck 221
Connors, Mike "Touch" 53, 76, 93
Conrad, Charles, Jr. 215
Conrad, William 181
Conreid, Hans 50
Constance Bennett Productions, Inc. 32
Constant, Yvonne 139
Contreras, Roberto 94
Conway, Russ 94, 127, 189
Coogan, Jackie 205
Coogan, Richard 168
Cook, Elisha, Jr. 87
Cook, Fielder 198
Cook, Fredric 241
Cook, Perry 90, 105, 109, 112, 162, 176
Cook, Whitfield 114
Cool Million (television) 216
Coolidge, Philip 110, 160, 180
Cooney, Ray 249
Cooper, Ben 197
Cooper, Jeanne 185
Cooper, Merian C. 45
Cooper, Olive 35

Copelan, Jodie 129
Copper Sky (film) 49
Corbett, Glenn 134, 173, 193, 221
Corbin, Barry 243
Cordova, Linda 184
Corey, Jeff 43, 212, 221
Corrie, William 162
Cortez, Stanley 29
Costa, Don 143
Coswick, Harry 93, 94, 102, 103, 104, 105, 106, 107, 108, 109, 110,
Cotten, Joseph 8, *9*, 29
"Cow Doctor" (*Gunsmoke*) 75
Coward, Noël 248
The Cowboys (film) 207
Craft, Charles 37
Craig, James 52, 100
Craig, May 45
Craig, Robert B. 238
Crane, Norma 97, 107
Crawford, Diane 109
Crawford, John "Johnny" 86, 97, 161
Crenna, Richard 25, 242
Crenna, Richard A. 242
Cromwell, John 29
"Crooked Mile" (*Gunsmoke*) 172
Crosby, Floyd 128, 129
Cross, Ben 237
Cross, Dennis 102
Cross of Iron (film) 76, 227, *228*, 229
Crothers, Joel 176
"Crowbait Bob" (*Gunsmoke*) 89
Crowe, Eileen 45
Crutcher, Jack 47
Crutchfield, Les 77, 83, 85, 86, 88, 89, 90, 165, 169, 171, 172
Culver, Howard 81, 87
Cummings, Dale 110
Cumnock School 7
Curran, William Brian 241
Curry, Mason 127
Curtis, Jack 177
Curtis, Keene 215
Curtis, Ken 82, 84, 89, 90, 112, 114, 128, 129, 155, 165, 168, 169, 174, 175, 178, 183, 188
Curtiz, Michael 152
Custer, Gen. George Armstrong 110, 52
Cutherbertson, Allan 229
Cutts, John 215

"Daddy-O" (*Gunsmoke*) 80
Dakota (film) 3, 8, *34*–35, 77, 93, 184, 207
Dale, Fred 101
Dallas Cowboys 222
Dalton, Audrey 165
Daly, Elizabeth 247
Damante, Susan 217
Damon, Les 185

"Dance of Death" (song) 212
Dano, Royal 152, 171, 172, 175, 188
Dante, Floyd 143
Dante, Michael 235
Dante, Ronnie 143
D'Antonio, Carmen 186
Darfler, Gene 168
Darro, Frankie 98, 122
David, Hal 202
David, Kristina 238
David, Mack 141
Davidson, Ben 223
Davidson, I.B. 5
Davies, Jack 224, 226
Davis, Bob 190
Davis, H.L. 220
Davis, Jim 185, 220
Davis, Susan 115
Davis, Vance 205
Dawson, Ralph 53, 57, 59
Dawson, Richard 145
Day, Doris 17, 134, 143, 144, 145
Day, John 119
Day, Larraine 59
Day, Lynda *see* Lynda Day George
D-Day June 6, 1944 (documentary) 146
Deacon, Richard 77
The Deadly Companions (film) 76
Dean, Felicity 237
De Anda, Miguel 175
Death of a Salesman (play) 4, 249
DeBenedictis, Dick 217
De Carlo, Yvonne 132
Decision at Sundown (film) 68
De Corsia, Ted 96
Deering, Olive 121
DeGualle, Gen. Charles 33
DeHaven, Gloria 221
Dehner, John 37, 80, 94, 156
De Kova, Frank 78, 85
Delegall, Bob 242
Delevanti, Cyril 76, 80, 115
Dell, Myrna 47, *48*
Della, Jay 166
Della Street 120
Dellar, Melvin A. 62
Dells, Dorothy 114, 183
Del Ray, Pilar 108
Del Valle, Jaime 118, 119
De Marco, Tony 183
DeMario, Donna 40
De Mario, Tony 53
De Marney, Terrence 113
De Metz, Danielle 112
DeMille, C.B. 62
Dennis, John 241
Dennis, Nick 97
Dennis, Robert C. 122, 187
Denny, Reginald 52
Dentith, Edward 229
Denys, Crispin 239
DePierto, Joe 249
DeSales, Francis 184

De Santis, Joe 98
"Deserter's Patrol" (*Rawhide*) 190–191
Desilu 118
"The Desperate World of Jane Doe" (*Amy Prentiss*) 219
Destry Rides Again (film) 198
Detroit 28, 233
Deuel, Geoffrey 193
De Villiers, Gérard 26, 237, 238
The Devil's Brigade (book) 145, 146
The Devil's Brigade (film) 1, 4, 17, 42, 86, 92, 114, 128, 145–148, **146**, 161, 163, 166, 215, 218, 229, 231
Devine, Andy 53, 143
De Vol, Frank 132, 143
Devon, Richard 127, 168
De Walt, Adeline 102
Dewhurst, Colleen 241
Dexter, Alan 122, 165
Dexter, Brad 102
Dexter, Maury 129
Diaz, Rudy 148
Dickinson, Angie 14, 69, 71, 78, 93
Dimas, Ray 197
The Dirty Dozen (film) 7, 25, 147, 148, 240
The Dirty Dozen: Next Mission (telefilm) 4, 25, 42, 147, 166, 220, **239**–240
The Dirty Dozen: The Deadly Mission (telefilm) 240
The Dirty Dozen: The Fatal Mission (telefilm) 240
Disney, Walt 139
Disney Studio 17, 140
Disneyland (television series) 219
Divine Secrets of the Ya-Ya Sisterhood (film) 28
Dix, Robert 130, 131, 159, 189
Dixon, Ivan 176
Dixon, Lee 37
Dmytryk, Edward 153
"The Do-Badder" (*Gunsmoke*) 159
Dobe and a Company of Heroes (documentary) 246
Dobkin, Lawrence 79, 92, 117, 185
Dobson, Tamara 216
Doc Adams 75
Dodd, Barbara 81
Dodge, David 55
Dodge City **16**, 75
Dodgeball (film) 28
Domasin, Larry 137
Domenzain, Elia 242
Don Baker, Joe 208, 209
Donahue, Elinor 186
Donahue, Jerry 212

Donahue, Marc 212
Doner, Jack 185
Donlevy, Brian 125
Donlon, Dolores 180
Donner Lake 55
Donner, Robert 193, 196, 200, 202, 209, 220
Donno, Eddy 194
Donovan's Reef (film) 133
Doohan, James 163
Doolittle, John 242
Doran, Ann 59
Double Indemnity (film) 158
Doucette, John 81, 100, 196
Doud, Gil 76, 78, 79
Douglas, Burt 171
Douglas, Kirk 17, 141, 143, 245
Douglas, Sam 239
Dove, Walter 200
Dowling, Doris 111
Doyle, David 241
Doyle, Martin 242
Dozier, Robert 117, 180
Dragnet (television series) 118
Drake, Christian 91
Drake, James 169
Drake, Kenn 81
Drake, Marcia 103
Drake, Tom 191, 218
Draper, Jack 44, 55
The Dreadful Lemon Sky (book) 244
"The Dreamers" (*Gunsmoke*) 162
Drier, Moosie 222
Driscoll, Robert 125
Drury, James 84, 107, 191, 192
Dryenforth, Harold 122
Dubbins, Don 169
"Duel at Florence" 103–104
Duffy, Julia 241
Dugan, Jim 53
Duggan, Andrew 79
Duggan, Bob 189
Duke, John 103, 163
The Duke & The General (documentary) 245
Dumbrille, Douglas 55
Dun, Ralph 31
Duncan, Craig 109, 159
Duncan, Pamela 67, 126
Duncan, Robert 186
Duncan, Wanda 43
Dunham, By 67, 71, 129
Dunkel, John 75, 78, 125, 159, 164, 169, 172, 188
Dunlap, Paul 48, 50, 52
Dunne, Dominique 238
Dupar, Edwin 61
Dupre, Anne 32
Dupre, Paul 32
Durango, Mexico 194, 207, 245
Durney, Dennis 238
Duthie, Michael J. 232
Dwan, Allan 1, 41, 190
Dynamite Man from Glory Jail see *Fools' Parade*
Dyrenforth, Harold 122
Earl, Clifford 229
East, Stewart 109, 110, 114, 116, 179, 180, 184, 185
East, Stuart see East, Stewart
Eastwood, Clint 5, 14, 123, **124**, 246
"Easy Come" (*Gunsmoke*) 168
Ebsen, Buddy 180
Eckstein, George 243
Eden, Chana 188
Edens, Alric 219
Edgar Scherick Productions 242
Edmiston, Walker 178
Edmondson, Patricia 235
Edwards, John 200
Edwards, Sam 168
Edwards, Vince 145
Efraim, R. Ben 207
Eggers, Fred 100, 119
Eisenmann, Ike 221, 223
Ekberg, Anita 65, 71, 72
El Toro Marine Air Station 41
Elam, Jack 82, 86, 137, 141
Elan, Joan 122, 181
Elboym, Yehuda 233
Eldridge, John 128
Electronic Data Systems (EDS) 242, 243
"Ella West" (*Have Gun, Will Travel*) 97
Elliot, Ross 87
Elliott, Denholm 235
Elliott, Jack 40
Elliott, Ross 90
Elliott, Sam 24, **26**, 238, 243
Elman, Josef 120
Emhardt, Robert 181
Emmett, Michael 69, 76
Emory, Richard 48
Emperor Maximilian 153, 154, 198
The Empty Copper Sea (book) 24, 243, 244
Encore Westerns 247
Engel, Roy 159
English, Richard 50, 51
"The Englishman" (*Have Gun, Will Travel*) 96
Engstrom, Jean 183
Engstrom, Jena 175, 189
Ensenada, Mexico 43
The Epic of Josie (discarded film title) 144
Erdman, Richard 122
Erickson, Leif 223
Ericson, Devon 220
Erwin, Lee 94
Erwin, William 100, 106
Espinoza, José Angel 202, 221
Espinoza, Robert 42
Essex Enterprises Ltd. (production company) 20, 207
Estabrook, Howard 34
Esther, Ruth & Jennifer (book) 224
Europex (distributor) 238
Evans, Dale 40, 41
Evans, Evans 158
Evans, Linda 208, 218
Evans, Richard 88
Evans, Gene 238, 243
"The Eve of St. Elmo" (*Have Gun, Will Travel*) 187
Everglades (television series) 178, 189
Evern, Carole 114
Evers, Jason 218, 223
"Executioner" (*Gunsmoke*) 78
The Exorcist (film) 161
"Ex-Urbanites" (*Gunsmoke*) 89–90
The Eye of the Needle (book) 243
Eye of the Widow (film) 4, 26–27, 222, 237–238

"The F.U." (*Gunsmoke*) 82
Fabregat, Enrique 55
A Face in the Crowd (film) 189
"Face of a Shadow" (*Have Gun, Will Travel*) 187
Fadden, Tom 51
Fairbanks, Douglas, Jr. 7, 23
Fairhaven 3, 6
Faith, Dolores 186
"False Front" (*Gunsmoke*) 165
Fancher, Hampton 113, 116
The Fantastic Journey (television series) 22, 193, 215, 223
Farnsworth, Richard 243
Farrady & Company (television series) 216
Farrell, Richard W. 120
Farrell, Sharon 166
Farrow, John 3, 11, 12, 55, 57, 202
"The Fatal Flaw" (*Have Gun, Will Travel*) 175
Faulkner, Barbara 215
Faulkner, Edward "Ed" 14, 15, 82, 89, 103, 104, 109, 113, 117, 125, 126, **130**, 132, 134, 143, 150, 152, 165, 168, 178, 180, 181, 189, 190, 191, 193, 202, 215, 220, 221
Faure, John D. 29
Faust, Lous 37
Fawcett, William 92
"Fawn" (*Gunsmoke*) 83
Fayetteville, Arkansas 24
Feitelson, Benjamin 237
Felix Leitner 225
Fellini, Federico 63
Fellows, Arthur 29
Fellows, Eleanor 13
Fellows, Robert "Bob" 11, 12, 13, 50, 53, 55, 56, 59, 61, 62, 63
Fenady, Andrew J. 193, 194
Fennelly, Parker 101
Fenton, Frank 53
Ferguson, Frank 176
Fernandez, Abel 94, 96
Ferrer, Mel 237
Fessier, Michael 95
Festus Haggens 155, 165, 169, 174
ffolkes (film) 4, 24, 27, 224–226, 232
Fickett, Mary 178
Fieberling, Hal 41
Field, Sally 17, 141, **142**
Fields, Gracie 32
"The Fifth Bullet" (*Have Gun, Will Travel*) 183
The Fighting Kentuckian (film) 39, 207
The Films of Budd Boetticher (DVD set) 246
Finaly, Frank 212
Fink, Harry Julian 107, 108, 174, 179, 183, 184, 205
Fink, Rita M. 107, 205
Finn, Mickey 104
1st Special Service Force 146
Fisher, Shug 159, 161, 162, 168, 169, 171, 179, 181, 183, 186, 220
Fisher, Steve 93
FitzSimons, Charles 45
Fix, Paul 13, 34, 35, 37, 53, 57, 59, 61, 63, 65, 71, 72, 77, 134, 143, 152, 172, 186, 202, 205, 207
"The Fleet Queen Case" (*The Lineup*) 118
Fleischman, A.B. 65
Fleming, Eric 123, **124**
Fletcher, Bill 145
"Flight of the Wild Geese" (song) 212
Flippen, Jay C. 150
Flynn, Joe 82
"Fogg Bound" (*Have Gun, Will Travel*) 175
Follett, Ken 25, 242, 243
Fong, Benson 116, 121
Fools' Parade (book) 4, 19, 199
Fools' Parade (film) 19, 81, 111, 131, 155, 193, **199**–202, 218, 220
Foran, Dick 166
Ford, Barbara 8
Ford, Constance 76, 98, 120
Ford, Francis 45
Ford, Frederick 98
Ford, Glenn 55, **56**
Ford, John 1, 3, 5, 6, 7, 8, 10, 11, 12, 15, 29, 44, 45, 46, 47, 59, 133, 181, 186, 187, 202, 205, 214, 245, 247
Ford, Patrick 8
Ford, Terence 237
Foreman, Carl 34, 213
Forrest, Michael 104

Forrest, Steve 233
Forrest, William 119
Forster, Robert 222
Forsyth, Rosemary 134, 192
Fort Apache (film) 207
Fort Vengeance (film) 52–53
Fortier, Robert 165, 171
Foster, Barry 212
Foster, Carey 191
Foster, Donald 99
Foster, Irene 150
Foster, Preston 188
Fowley, Douglas 42, 51, 59
Fox, Craig 89
Fox, Edward 235
Fox, John, Jr. 129
Foy Willing & The Riders of the Purple Sage 37
"Fragile" (*Have Gun, Will Travel*) 113
France 26
France Conquest to Liberation (documentary) 146
Francis, Al 221, 241
Francis, Anne 126, 221
Franken, Steve 242
Frankenheimer, John 158
Franklin, Carl 223
Franklin, Jerry 188
Franz, Arthur 41, 91
Fraser, Elizabeth 143
Fraser, Ronald 212
Freckles (book) 128, 129
Freckles (film) 4, 14, 35, 43, 82, 84, 93, 106, 128–129, 131, 176
Fredericks, Charles 162, 165
Free French Forces 33
Freed, Bert 82
Freedle, Sam C. 69
Freeman, Joan 164
Freiberger, Fred 125, 126
French, Valerie 114
The French Connection (film) 201
Friday Harbor, Washington 4, 5, 2, 22, 27, 224, 248
Friedgen, Bud 238, 241
Friedhofer, Hugo 57
Friedkin, William 161, 201
Fritch, Hanson 32
Frontiere, Dominic 193
Frost, Fran 111
Frost, Terry 40
Ft. Smith, Arkansas 24
Fudge, Alan 242
Fuentes, Miguel Angel 242
Fuhrman, Ben 238
Fuji 116, 182
Fuller, Barbra 43
Fuller, Clem 87, 88, 90
Fuller, Robert 192
Fuller, Sam 51
Funny Money (play) 249
Furillo, Bud 166

Gabriel, Roman 152
Gail, Scanlon 238
Gainey, M.C. 241
Galindo, Nacho 42
Galloway, Don 137, 192
"The Gallows" (*Gunsmoke*) 160–161
Gallup, New Mexico 91
Galway, Ireland 24
Gammell, Robin 241
Gampu, Ken 212
Gann, Ernest 53, 55, 59, 61
Gannon, Kim 37
Gardner, Don 121
Gardner, Earle Stanley 120
Garfield, Brian 21, 22, 209, 211
Garfunkel, David 232
Gargan, Jack 120, 121, 122
Garland, Beverly 167
Garland, Gregory 242
Garmes, Lee 29, 32
Garriguenc, Rene 87, 90, 115, 160, 176, 177, 178, 180, 186, 187
Gates, Nancy 162
Gatlin, Jerry 184
Gautier, Dick 217
Gavin, James 97
Gaye, Gregory 32
Gaye, Lisa 97
Gayle, Monica 216
Gaylord, Bill 242
Gaynor, Jock 189
Gebert, Gordon 77
Geer, Lennie 98
Geer, Will 148
Gehring, Ted 223
Geller, Bruce 104, 108
George, Christopher 193
George, Lynda Day 193, 216
Geraghty, Gerald 39
Gerard, Merwin 166, 223
German Wehrmacht 198, 227
Germany 227
Gerry, Toni 121
Gerstad, Harry 128
Gerstle, Frank 111
Getchell, Sumner 53
Ghandi, Rusi 229
Giambalvo, Louis 242
Gibbons, Robert 177
Gidley, Cass 53
"The Gift of Cochise" (short story) 57, 59
Gillis, Michael 246
Gilman, Sam 102
Gilroy, Frank 104
Gim, H.W. 133
The Girl in the Plain Brown Wrapper (book) 244
"Les Girls" (*Have Gun, Will Travel*) 111–112
Gist, Robert 115, 125, 182
Gittens, George 125
Glass, Ned 89, 94
Glass, Paul 73
Gleason, James 220
Gleason, Regina 181
Glen, John 212, 229
Glen Canyon National Recreation Area 149
Globus, Yoram 24, 232
Glouner, Richard C. 216
Glover, Charles 208
Go West (film) 198
Goa, India 24
Goddar, John 118
Golan, Menahem 24, 232, 233, 234
Gold, Samuel "Sam" 80, 81, 84, 92, 93, 94, 95, 96, 97, 99, 100, 101, 102, 103, 104, 105, 106, 107, 108, 109, 111, 112, 113, 114, 115, 116, 117, 175, 176, 179, 180, 181, 182, 183, 184, 185, 186, 187
Golden Oak Ranch 140
"The Golden Toad" (*Have Gun, Will Travel*) 113–114
Goldfinger (film) 225
Goldin, Pat 118
Goldsmith, Jerry 148, 151, 155, 174, 209
Goldwyn Studio 61, 131
Gómez, Antonio 44
Gomez, Luis 98
Gonzales, Pedro, Jr. 133
Gonzalez, Pedro Gonzalez 59, 61, 69, 71, 72, 150, 168, 193,
"Good Love" (song) 67
Gorcey, Bernard 47
Gorcey, Leo 47, **48**
Gordon, Bruce 93
Gordon, Don 218
Gordon, Leo 92, 57
Gorman, Eric 45
Gorshin, Frank 110
Gottlieb, Robert 116
Gould, Berni 98
Grace, Martin 212
The Graduate (film) 172
Graham, Fred 37, 81, 102
Graham, Richard 235
Grainger, Edmund 41
Granger, Michael 52, 95
Granger, Stewart 212, 214
Grant, Cary 7, 23
Grant, Harvey 79
Grant, James Edward 9, 10, 12, 15, 37, 39, 41, 43, 44, 50, 57, 59, 61, 62, 63, 132, 133
Grant, Stephen 37
The Grapes of Wrath (film) 85
Gravage, Robert "Bob" 137, 152, 159, 160, 163, 172, 202
Gravers, Steve 106
Graves, Peter 143
Gray, Bonnie 104
Gray, Charles 115, 170, 188
Gray, Coleen 179
Gray, Louis 36
Gray, Charles 104
The Great Escape (film) 148
"The Great Mojave Chase" (*Have Gun, Will Travel*) 92
Great War *see* World War I
The Greatest Show on Earth (film) 62
Greece 26
Green, Dorothy 156
Green, Gilbert 190
Green, Mike 88
Green, Ronald 107
The Green Berets (film) 152, 153
Greene, Joe 127
Greenleaf, Raymond 119
Greer, Dabbs 81, 82, 87, 156, 161, 162, 163, 164
Greer, Jane 238
Gregg, Virginia 164
Greig, Robert 31
Grey, Duane 94, 100, 111, 124, 186
Grey, Harry 31
Grey, Richard 122
Grey, Virginia 44
Griem, Helmut 226
Griffith, James 51, 170, 184
Griffith, Kenneth 212, 229, 231
Grimes, Gary 205
"Groat's Grudge" (*Gunsmoke*) 87
Gross, Robert 7
Gross, Roland 124, 125, 126
Grossinger, Fred 85
Groves, Herman 181
Grubb, Davis 199, 200, 201
Gruber, Frank 71, 72
Grunenwaldt, Luce 237
Grunfield, Svea 113
Guerillas of the Underground see *Paris–Underground*
Guillermin, John 24, 233
Guillofoyle, Paul 156
Gulager, Clu 109
Gulf of Thailand 236
Gulick, William 127
Gun Down (novel) 21, 209, 211
Gun the Man Down (film) 4, 14, 69–71, **70**, 78, 86, 88, 131, 157, 168, 194, 198
Gunga Din (film) 7, 23
Gunga Din (planned remake) 23, 24
The Guns of Navarone (film) 214, 231
Gunslinger (television series) 41, 49, 188
Gunsmoke (radio) 49, 77, 181
Gunsmoke (television series) 1, 4, 11, 14, **16**, 41, 49, 59, 69, 71, 75–91, 101, 111, 155–173, 174, 178, 189, 208, 215, 218, 222
Gurfinkel, David 232
Guthrie, A.B., Jr. 141, 143

Hackford, Taylor 246
Hadley, Nancy 105

Hadley, Reed 51
Hageman, Richard 37
Hagen, Kevin 101, 114, 134, 161, 167, 169, 184
Hagen, Michael 105
Hagerthy, Ron 126
Haggard, Merle 193
Haggerty, Don 46, 109, 125
Hahn, Paul 100, 107
Hairston, Jester 124, 185
Hajeno Productions 243
Hale, Barbara 120
Hale, Barnaby 190
Hale, Barney 190
Hale, Betsy 171
Hale, Jonathan 34, 51
Hale, Monte 37, 84, 85
Hall, Bobby 107
Hall, Huntz 47, **48**
Halloran, John 37
Hambleton, Duffy 208
Hamel, William R. 48
Hamilton, Big John **18**, 76, 133
Hamilton, Joseph 115
Hamilton, Murray 98, 120, 216
Hamlisch, Marvin 202
Hammond, John 241
"The Hanging Cross" (*Have Gun, Will Travel*) 96–97
"The Hanging of Roy Carter" (*Have Gun, Will Travel*) 103
Hanley, Tom 170
Hannemann, Walter 51, 52
Hansen, Joachim 226
"The Happy Janitor Case" (*The Lineup*) 119
Harari, Clement 139
Hardin, Jerry 208, 239
Hardman, Ric 137, 138
Harens, Dean 104
Harold Hecht Corp. 141
"The Harpe's Blood" (*Gunsmoke*) 158
Harper, David 241
Harper, Paul 241
Harper, Rand 88
Harris, Julius 241
Harris, Phil 59
Harris, Richard 1, 22, 23, 24, 212, 214
Harris, Richard A. 216
Harris, Robert H. 75, 78, 100
Harrison, Jan 90
Harrison, Peggy 3, 8
Hart, Bill 184
Hartman, David 143
Hartman, Lisa 216
Hartman, Paul 180
Hartunian, Richard 99
Hartwig, Wolf C. 23, 226, 227
Harvey, Alex 241
Harvey, Marilyn 164
Harvey, Richard 239
Hashim, Edmund 150
Hass, Hugo 34
Hatari (film) 153

Hatch, Wilbur 160
"The Hatchet Man" (*Have Gun, Will Travel*) 116–117
Hatton, Raymond 88
"The Haunted Trees" (*Have Gun, Will Travel*) 111
Hauser, Robert 218
Have Gun, Will Travel (radio) 94
Have Gun, Will Travel (television series) 1, 4, 14, 16, 20, 32, 35, 37, 41, 68, 69, 74, 81, 84, **91**–118, 126, 128, 129, 138, 157, 173–187, 189, 190, 192, 215, 220, 238, 243, 244
"Havin' Myself a Fine Time" (song) 196
Hawaii 11, 26, 50, 51
Hawks, Howard 153, 194
Haworth, Joe 89, 160
Hayden, Sterling 11, 24, 48, 51, 241, 242
Hayes, Ron 163, 189
Haymes, Dick 218
Hayward, Chuck 82, 174
Hazard, Lawrence 34
Haze, Stan 221
"A Head of Hair" (*Have Gun, Will Travel*) 174
Healey, Myron 51, 161, 163, 186, 189
Heaton, Tom 148
Hec Ramsey (television series) 20, 160, 193, 216, 217, 218
Hecht, Harold 17, 141
Hecht, Ted 42
Hedison, David 224, 225
Heffley, Wayne 102
Heggen, Thomas 248
"Helen of Abajinian" (*Have Gun, Will Travel*) 97
Hellfighters (film) 4, 17–18, 24, 92, 111, 128, 141, 150–152, **151**, 168, 172, 178, 192, 207, 244
Hellgate (film) 11, 48–50, 123, 242
Helmore, Tom 96
Helton, Percy 161
Henderson, Doug 188
Hendry, Len 125
Hendry, Marsh 139
Hendry, Wayland M. 29
Henry, Carol 112
Henry, Gregg 241
Herbert, Percy 212, 229
Here Come the Marines (film) 11, 47–**48**
Herman, Leonard W. 42
Herrera, David 209
Herrmann, Bernard 91, 157
Hershey, Barbara 209
Herzberg, Paul 239
Heston, Charlton 21, 209, 211, 212
Hey Boy 91, 117, 173, 174, 191

Hey Girl 117, 174
Hickman, Darryl 53, 85
Hickman, George 124
Hicks, Chuck 202
Higgin, Michael 166, 171
"High Adventure" (*Code R*) 222–223
The High and the Mighty (book) 59, 61
The High and the Mighty (film) 1, 3, 12, 13, 59–61, **60**, 72, 77, 160, 168, 194, 221
"The High Graders" (*Have Gun, Will Travel*) 98
"High Wire" (*Have Gun, Will Travel*) 94
Highroad Productions 213
Hilary, Jennifer 224
Hildebrandt, Jeff 247
Hildyard, Jack 212
Hiler, Tom 220
Hill, Hallene 119
Hill, Rich 237
Hillarie, Marcel 139
Hillias, Peg 77, 96
"Hinka Do" (*Gunsmoke*) 88
Hinkle, Robert 76, 163
Hinn, Michael 78, 102, 103
Hitchcock, Alfred 24
Hite, Kathleen 81, 158, 160, 161, 167, 170
Hitler, Adolf 23, 227, 229, 240
Hoagland, Charles 220
"Hobson's Choice" (*Have Gun, Will Travel*) 182
Hoch, Winston C. 45
Hodgins, Earle 80, 92, 97, 107, 108, 126, 163, 166
Hoffman, Dustin 172
Hoffman, Steve 208
Hoffmann, Robert 229
Hofmann, Susanna 237
Holden, James 41
Holden, William 17, 145, **146**–147
Holdridge, Lee 223
Hole, Jonathan 92
Holland, Bert 121
Holland, Jack 98
Holland, John 181
Holliman, Earl 126
Holloran, John 46
Holloway, Sterling 35
The Hollywood Greats: John Wayne 245
Holm, Celeste 220
Holman, Rex 155
Holt, Patrick 229
"Homecoming" (*Have Gun, Will Travel*) 110–111
Homer 185
Hondo (film) 3, 12, 39, 57–59, **58**, 77, 133, 194
Hondo (television series) 194
"Honeycomb" (song) 131
Hong, James 182
Hopkins, Bob 88, 106, 112, 117

Hopkins, John 179
Hopper, Hedda 121
Hopper, William D. 13, 59, 63, **64**, 120, 121
Horne, Victoria 31
"Horse Deal" (*Gunsmoke*) 85–86
Horton, Michael 241
Horton, Robert 192
Horvath, Charles 103
Horwitz, Howie 217
Hotel de Paree 14, 41, 81, 126–127
Hough, Stanley 148, 152
House Un-American Activities Committee 50, 51
Houston, Donald 229
Houston, Glyn 229
Houston Astrodome 216
Houston Astros 216
How the West Was Won (film) 144
Howard, John 59
Howard, Susan 223
Howard, Trevor 229
Howat, Clark 120
Howlin, Olin 40
Hoyt, Clegg 87
Hoyt, John 116, 184
Hubbard, John 44, 50
Huckabee, Cooper 216, 241
Huddleston, David 200, 202
Huddleston, Floyd 143
Hudgins, Ken 163
Hudson, John 169
Hudson, Rock 18, 19, 152
Huffaker, Clair 150, 152
Hughes, Bill 165
Hunt, Allan 168
Hunt, Helen 219
Hunt, Jimmy 43
"The Hunt" (*Have Gun, Will Travel*) 181
"Hunt the Man Down" (*Have Gun, Will Travel*) 107
Hunter, Ian McLellan 241
Hunter, Tab 13, 63
Hurst, Paul 37
Hurt, Mary Beth 222
Hutchins, Linda 165
Hutchinson, Josephine 121
Hutton, Brian 118
Hutton, Jim 150, 152
Hyer, Martha 46
Hyland, Dick Irving 31
Hyland, Jim 111
Hylton, Jane 212

I Married a Communist (film) 51
Imi, Tony 224, 226, 229
Immel, Jerrold 222, 238, 243
"In an Evil Time" (*Have Gun, Will Travel*) 102–103
Inchon (film) 23
"Incident at Borrasca

Bend" (*Have Gun, Will Travel*) 108–109
"Incident of Fear in the Streets" (*Rawhide*) 125
"Incident of the Dry Drive" (*Rawhide*) 125–126
"Incident of the Power and the Plow" (*Rawhide*) 125, 218
"Incident of the Shambling Man" (*Rawhide*) 74, 100, 126
"Incident on the Edge of Madness" (*Rawhide*) 123–125
"Indian Ford" (*Gunsmoke*) 159
Indio, California 16
The Informer (film) 3, 5, 7
Ingalls, Don 105, 178, 183, 184, 187, 191
Ingram, Jean 157
Ingster, Boris 32
Inness, Jean 126
"Invasion" (*Have Gun, Will Travel*) 182–183
Iranian Revolution 25, 243
Ireland, David 220
Irish, Tom 57
Ironside (television series) 219
Irwin, Charles 52
Ishimoto, Dale 180
Island in the Sky (book) 53, 55, 61
Island in the Sky (film) 11, 53–55, **54**, 61, 72, 77, 86, 105, 194
Ivano, Paul 190–191
Ivins, Perry 84, 100

Jacks, Robert L. 148, 152
Jackson, Eugene, Jr. 134
Jacobs, Jack 99, 115, 127
Jaeckel, Richard 25, 41, 42, 145, 166, 184, 193, 239
James, Kyle 48
James, Robert 118
James Bond 225, 226
"Japanese Theme" (song) 235
Jarmyn, Jill 118, 119
Jasmin, Paul 101
Jason, Harvey 219
Jason, Peter 241
"Jayhawkers" (*Gunsmoke*) 81
Jaynes, Enid 187
"Jealousy" (*Gunsmoke*) 81
Jenkins, Dal 184
Jenks, Frank 120
"Jenny" (*Gunsmoke*) 163
"Jenny" (*Have Gun, Will Travel*) 115
Jensen, Marlowe 89
Jerusalem 233
"Jesse" (*Gunsmoke*) 82
Jochim, Anthony 121
John Ford and Andrew V. McLaglen (book) 1
John Ford/ John Wayne: The Filmmaker and The Legend (documentary) 247
John Wayne and "Chisum" (documentary) 245
Johnson, Arch 161
Johnson, Ben 46, 47, 137, 152, 167, 174, 179, 183, 193, 202, 238
Johnson, Chal 164
Johnson, Chubby 168, 173
Johnson, Russell 79
Johnston, Edmund 103
Johnston, John Dennis 241
Johnstone, Iain 245
"Joie de Vivre" (song) 139
Jollye, I. Standford 46
Jones, Davy 220
Jones, Dean 139
Jones, Gordon 50, 53, 127
Jones, J.J. 215
Jones, Jennifer 8, **9**, 29, 31
Jones, L.Q. 221
Jones, Miranda 107, 164, 190
Jones-Moreland, Betsy 177
Jordan, James Carroll 241
Jory, Victor 126
Joseph, Al 82, 85, 86, 87, 88, 89, 90, 98, 155, 156, 157, 158, 161, 163, 164, 165, 166, 167, 168, 169, 170
Joslin, Warren 186
Joslyn, Allyn 53, 175
The Joy of Ireland (documentary) 246
Joyce, Jimmy 218
Joyce, Patricia 170
Joyce, Stephen 126
Judean Hills, Israel 233
"Juliet" (*Have Gun, Will Travel*) 107
Jullien, Yvan 237
Jung, Allen 116
Junge, Kellogg, Jr. 120
Jurado, Katy 44
Jurgens, Curt 24, 226

Kahler, Wolf 229, 239
Kane, Joel 98, 116
Kane, Joseph 34, 43, 93
Kane, Michael 239
"Kangaroo" (*Gunsmoke*) 86
Kani, John 212
Kansas Pacific (film) 51–52, 53, 242
Kaper, Bronislau 141
Karnes, Robert 79, 83, 88, 92, 105, 107, 126, 177
Karpf, Elinor 219
Karpf, Steven 219
Kastner, Elliott 224
Katzin, Lee H. 240
Katzman, Leonard 223
Kay, Edward J. 42
Kaye, Stubby 141
Keach, Stacy 24, 241
Keaton, Buster 198
Keefer, Don 92, 105, 157, 167
Keep, Michael 141, 163, 173, 186
Kehr, Dave 246
Keith, Brian 76, 137, 139, 202
Keith, Sherwood 117
Keller, Harry 37
Kellermann, Barbara 229
Kelley, DeForest 185
Kellin, Mike 105, 177, 200
Kelly, Gene 198
Kelly, Jack 81
Kelly, John 202
Kelly, Nancy 216
Kelly, Paul 59
Kemmerling, Warren 158
Kemp, Dan 205
Kennally, James 74
Kennedy, Burt 13, 14, 67, 68, 69, 71, 72, 76, 152, 194, 198
Kennedy, Douglas 90, 91, 116
Kennedy, George 130, 131, 134, 143, 148, 155, 157, 172, 174, 175, 176, 178, 187, 188, 199, 201, 205, 207, 246
Kennedy, Jayne 218
Kennedy Space Center 215
Kent, Walter 37
Kern, Robert James 190, 191
Kerwin, Brian 241
Ketchum, Cliff 82, 91, 173
Keymas, George 168
Keys, Robert "Bob" 50, 51, 53, 59, 78, 71
Khartoum (film) 17
Khashoggi, Nabila 237
"Kick Me" 78
Killer Shark (film) 10, 42–43
"Killer's Widow" (*Have Gun, Will Travel*) 100
Kilroy, Mathias 224
Kim, Joy 59, 65
King, Brett 165
King, Chris 185
King, Wright 97, 164, 169, 177, 180
Kingsford, Guy 52
Kinskey, Leonid 181
Kinsolving, Lee 110, 172
Kirk, Tommy 75
Kirkpatrick, Jess 76, 95
"Kisses Sweeter than Wine" (song) 131
Kitaro 25
"The Kite" (*Gunsmoke*) 170–171
"Kitty Shot" (*Gunsmoke*) 157
"Kitty's Outlaw" (*Gunsmoke*) 81
Klemperer, Werner 113, 177
Kline, James 105
Klingler, Christina 237
Knapp, Robert 159
Kneubuhl, John 183
Knight, Don 202, 217, 223
"A Knight to Remember" (*Have Gun, Will Travel*) 180
Knoth, Fred 152
Knowles, Patric 114, 141, 145, 172, 175, 193
Knudsen, Peggy 122
Kobe, Gail 173
Kolb, Ken 94, 98, 99, 101
Korean War 23
Kosleck, Martin 217
Kowal, Mitchell 97, 117
Krasner, Milton 143
Kreuger, Kurt 32
Krim, Arthur 17
Kroeger, Berry 65, 71, 121
Krueger, Kurt 123
Kruger, Hardy 212, 214
Krugman, Lou 114
Kruschen, Jack 132, 221

L'Amour, Louis 12, 24, 57, 59, 238
La Cañada, California 3, 6, 7
Lacey, Ronald 232
Lada, Edmund, Jr. 217
Ladd, David 212
"The Lady" (*Have Gun, Will Travel*) 105
The Lady from Shanghai (film) 158
"The Lady Killer" (*Gunsmoke*) 90
Laird, Jack 98, 127, 175
Lake, Janet 179
Lake Michigan 74
Lake Powell 149
Lambert, Douglas 182
Lambert, Jack 84, 117, 128, 129, 157, 165, 168
Lambert, Paul 78
Lamberti, Mark 245
Lamberti Productions Corp. 245
Lancaster, Burt 25, 26, 242
Landers, Harry 96, 117
Landham, Sonny 239
Landon, Tom 118
Landry, Karen 242
Lane, Allan 156, 158
Lane, Richard 35
Lang, Charles 42
Lang, Jennings 52
Lang, Perry 232
Langan, Glenn 193
Lange, Arthur 50, 61
Langley, Victor 229
Langton, Paul 120
Lanigan's Rabbi (television series) 216
Lanning, Reggie 35, 41
Lansbury, Bruce 221, 223
Larch, John 67, 103, 158
Laredo (television series) 138
Larence, Tom 208
La Roche, Mary 167
Larsen, Keith 52
Larson, Charles 126
LaSalle, Martin 242
LaShelle, Joseph 73, 74
The Last Hard Men (film) 4, 21–22, **23**, 138, 155,

164, 193, 208, 209–212, **210**, 220, 237
"The Last Laugh" (*Have Gun, Will Travel*) 98
Lathrop, Philip 124, 125
Latimer, Jonathan 55, 57
Lau, Wesley 87, 110, 155
Laughton, Charles 201
Launder, S. John 101
Laura (film) 74
Laurenz, John 40
Lauter, Harry 88, 90, 118, 156, 175
Lava, William 116, 179
Lawless, Kevin 45
Lawman (television series) 138
Lawrence, Fanya 103
Lea, Jennifer 118
Leach, Britt 221
Leachman, Cloris 75
Lean, David 236, 237
Leary, Nolan 37, 116
Leasor, James 229
Leavitt, Sam 217, 222, 223
"The Ledge" (*Have Gun, Will Travel*) 116
Lee, Ann 119
Lee, Guy 197
Lee, Harper 249
Lee, John 224
Lee, Ruta 121, 163
Leeds, Peter 115
Leeds, Robert 220
Leekley, John 241
"The Legacy" (*Have Gun, Will Travel*) 175
"Legal Revenge" (*Gunsmoke*) 75
Leigh, Janet 216
Leisure Time (production company) 235
LeMat, Paul 242
Lemus, Conchita 40
Lenard, Kay 111
Lend Me a Tenor (play) 249
Lenz, Rick 218
LePicard, Marcel 47
Leslie, Bethel 161
Leslie, Joan 48
Leslie, Vana 179
Lester, Seeleg 121, 123, 188
"Let the Chips Fall Where They May" (song) 71
Levy, Melvin 106
Lewis, Geoffrey 238, 243
Lewis, Harrison 182
Lewis, Michael J. 224, 225
"Liar from Blackhawk" (*Gunsmoke*) 80–81
The Lieutenant (television series) 92, 178, 190
Ligarde, Sebastian 242
Lighter, Sacha 237
Lilburn, James 45
Lincoln, Abraham 14, **73**, 74, 241
Lincoln County War 19
Lind, Kevan Ross 237
Lindemann, Mitch 141
Lindgren, Orely 46
Lindon, Lionel 191

Lindsay, Mark 202
The Lineup (television series) 14, 118–120
Link, John F. 216
Link, Michael 215
Litel, John 179
Little, Herbert, Jr. 123
Little Big Horn (film) 49
"Little Bit Different" (song) 37
"The Little Hero Case" (*The Lineup*) 119–120
The Little Shepherd of Kingdom Come (book) 129
The Little Shepherd of Kingdom Come (film) 4, 14, 43, 89, 106, 128, 129–131, **130**, 136, 155, 165, 173, 178, 190, 232
"The Little Shepherd of Kingdom Come" (song) 129
Little Sky, Dawn 158, 159, 186
Little Sky, Eddie 105, 115, 141, 158, 222
Liu, Dan 50
Live and Let Die (film) 225
Livingston, Robert 34
Lloyd, Euan 22, 193, 212, 213, 214, 229, 231
Lloyd, Rosalind 212
Lloyd, Suzanne 85
The Lock and the Key (book) 71, 72
Lockhart, June 96, 101
Lockheed Corporation 3, 7, 9, 33
Lockwood, Alexander 100
Lockwood, Gary 190
Loeb, Lee 31
Loewitsch, Klaus 226
The Log of the Black Pearl (television pilot) 4, 20, 173, 178, 220–221, 243
Logan, Joshua 248
Lola Montes (film) 63
London, Dirk 89
London, Tom 37
London 22, 214, 233
Lone Pine, California 7, 67, 91, 173
Lone Ranger 52
Long, Ed 191
Long, Richard 99
"Long Hours, Short Pay" (*Gunsmoke*) 158
"The Long Hunt" (*Have Gun, Will Travel*) 108
"Long, Long Trail" (*Gunsmoke*) 158–159
"The Long Night" (*Have Gun, Will Travel*) 95
"Long Way Home" (*Have Gun, Will Travel*) 176–177
Longdon, Terence 229
Loo, Richard 196
Lopez, Perry 132, 137, 148, 177
Lord, Barbara 159

Lord, Jack 91
Lorimar 229
Lormer, Jon 101
Los Angeles 13, 22
Los Padres National Forest 222
Lost in Yonkers (play) 249
The Lost Patrol 7, 63
Louis L'Amour's The Shadow Riders 4, 24, **26**, 59, 86, 149, 164, 172, 189, 238–239
Love, Honor and Goodbye (film) 3, 8, **30**, 31–32, 46
"Love of a Bad Woman" (*Have Gun, Will Trave*) 117
"Lover Boy" (*Gunsmoke*) 168
Lovering, Otho 17, 46, 132, 134, 141, 143
"Love's Young Dream" (*Have Gun, Will Travel*) 174
Lovsky, Celia 103
Lowery, Robert 126, 132, 143, 164
Lu, Lisa 116, 117
Luciano, Michael 79, 80, 95, 96, 97, 98, 99, 99
Lucking, William 241
Ludwig, Edward 50, 51
Ludwig, Jerry 220
Ludwig, Ken 249
Luez, Laurette 42
Lund, Art 165
Lundy, Ken 35
Lupton, John 157
Lydon, James 53
Lynch, Kenneth "Ken" 106, 119, 157
Lyndon, Barré 129
Lynn, Diana 55, 63, 64
Lynn, Emmett 61
Lynn, Rita 99
Lynn, Teri 222
Lyon, Therese 31
Lyons, Gene 176

MacDonald, Francis 91
MacDonald, Ian 107
MacDonald, John D. 24, 243, 244
MacDonald, Kenneth R. 122
Macdonald, Philip 61, 63, 122
Macdonnell, Norman 49, 75, 77, 78, 79, 80, 81, 82, 83, 84, 85, 86, 87, 88, 89, 90, 143, 144, 155, 156, 157, 158, 159, 160, 161, 162, 163, 164, 165, 166, 167, 168, 169, 170, 171, 172, 173
MacDowell, Fred 61, 63, 65
MacGowran, Jack 45
MacLane, Barton 51
MacLeod, Murray 205
Macnee, Patrick 229, 237

MacRae, Elizabeth 165, 169, 171
Macready, George **73**
Madame Pimpernel see *Paris-Underground*
Maddow, Ben 141
Madigan, Amy 243
Madigan (television series) 216
Madison, Guy 29
Madrid, Joe 186
"Maggie O'Bannion" (*Have Gun, Will Travel*) 109
The Magical World of Disney (television series) 219
The Magnificent Seven (film) 146
Maguire, Fred 127
Mahan, Larry 216
Main, George 166
Major Dundee (film) 212
The Making of Island in the Sky (documentary) 246
The Making of McLintock! (documentary) 246
The Making of The High and the Mighty (documentary) 246
The Making of 'The Quiet Man' (documentary) 245
Malis, Cy 104, 108, 122, 123
Malko Linge 26, 222, 237–238
Mallinson, Rory 48
Maloney, James 82
Maltby, Richard, Jr. 196
Maltin, Leonard 245
Malvern, Paul 43
The Man from U.N.C.L.E. (television series) 242
"A Man Gets to Thinkin'" (song) 205
Man in the Vault (film) 3, 13, **15**, 69, 71–72, 74, 77, 93, 97, 121, 131, 160, 168, 194, 218
The Man Who Shot Liberty Valance (film) 85
"The Man Who Struck Moonshine" (*Have Gun, Will Travel*) 181
"The Man Who Wouldn't Talk" (*Have Gun, Will Travel*) 103
The Man with the Golden Gun (film) 225
Manley, David 168
Mann, Delbert 74
Mann, Jack 81
Mannuzzi, Armando 232
Manson, Jean 217
Manza, Ralph 217
Maples, Terence 100
Mara, Adele 41, 43
Marcuse, Theodore "Ted" 91, 93, 94, 108, 123
Margulies, William 92, 93, 94, 95, 96, 97, 98, 99, 100

Marin County, California 65
Marion, Charles R. 47, **48**
Marion, Paul 52
Mark VII (production company) 218, 220, 221
"The Mark of Cain" (*Have Gun, Will Travel*) 180–181
Marker, Harry 55
Markland, Ted 109
Marley, John 191
Marlowe, Lucy 84
Marlowe, Nora 118
Marlowe, Scott 103
Marly, Florence 115
Marno, Marc 182
Marshal, George 198
Marshall, Alan 122, 124
Marshall, Gloria 79
Marshall, Joan 100, 161
Marshall, Marion 109, 123
Marshall, Mike 237
Marshall, Shary 165
Marta, Jack 34, 40, 43
Martell, Arlene 217
Martin, Dean 19, 52, 148, 149, 150, 164, 202, **203**, 204
Martin, Eugene 190
Martin, Ian Kennedy 207
Martin, Jared 223
Martin, Kiel 221
Martin, Lewis 111, 117, 183
Martin, Pepper 205
Martin, Strother 14, 15, 19, 81, 93, 94, 126, 132, 134, 159, 164, 169, 199
Marty (film) 74
Marvin, Lee 25, 67, 147, 239
M*A*S*H (film) 201
Mason, James 224
Mason, LeRoy 40
Massen, Osa 123
Matheson, Murray 217
Mathews, Carole 120
Matt Dillon 11, 14, **16**, 49, 75, 77, 181, 208
"A Matter of Ethics" (*Have Gun, Will Travel*) 93
Matthews, George 184
Matthews, Junius 103
Maverick Pictures 229
Maxey, Paul 47, **48**
Maxwell, Lester 184
May, Natalie 238
"May Blossoms" (*Gunsmoke*) 170
Mayer, Ken 93, 100, 104
Mayersberg, Paul 235
Mayo, Jacqueline 101
Mazurki, Mike 13, 34, 35, 65, 71, 72, 97, 174
McAlester, Oklahoma 43
McCarey, Leo 51, 198
McCargo, Marian 152
McClory, Sean 45, 53, 55, 61, **62**, 63, 105, 148
McCloud (television series) 216

McClure, Doug 134, 191, 192
McCormack, Patricia 242
McCorry, Tom 223
McCoy (television series) 216
McDaniel, Hattie 29
McDonald, Francis J. 103
McDonald, Fred 35, 158
McDowall, Roddy 42
McGough, Johnny 76
McGreevey, Michael 141
McGuire, John 41
McIntire, Holly 169
McIntire, John 192
McIntire, Tim 134
McKee, John R. 220, 245, 246
McLaglen, Andrew V. 5–28
McLaglen, Andrew V., Jr. 4, 8
McLaglen, Enid 3, 5
McLaglen, Josh 4, 14, 24, 25, 28, 232, 239
McLaglen, Mary 4, 14, 22, 28
McLaglen, Sharon 3, 8, 17
McLaglen, Sheila (McLaglen's sister) 3, 5, 7
McLaglen, Sheila Greenan (McLaglen's wife) 4, 25, 235, 237
McLaglen, Victor 3, 4, **6**, 7, 8, 11, **12**, 14, 23, **30**, 31, 32, 45, 46, 69, **73**, 74, 100, 126, 201, 212
McLeod, Catherine 167
McLiam, John 164
McLintock! (film) 1, 4, 15–16, 17, **18**, 19, 39, 43, 46, 47, 81, 83, 92, 128, 131–134, **132**, 136, 141, 144, 160, 164, 165, 166, 177, 178, 194, 195, 198, 207, 211, 218, 221, 237, 246
McMahan, Whitney 152
McMillan and Wife (television series) 216
McMullan, James 134, 215
McMyler, Pamela "Pam" **20**, 193, **196**, 197
McQuade, Arlene 175
McQueen, Red 50
McRae, Ellen 161
McShane, Ian 223
McVey, Patrick 185
Meadow, Herb 91, 92, 185, 186
Medina, Patricia 55, **56**, 105, 108
Medwin, Michael 229
Megowan, Don 69, 88, 101, 105, 111, 164, 189
Meiklejohn, Linda 143
Mell, Joseph 157
Mellinger, Max 186
Merchant, Cathy 162
The Merchant of Venice (play) 90
Meredith, Don 221, 222

Meredith, Judi 126, 176, 202, **203**
Meriwether, Lee 152. **154**
Merrill, Gary 125
Merriman, Paul 200
Meston, John 49, 75, 76, 77, 78, 79, 80, 81, 82, 83, 84, 85, 86, 87, 88, 89, 90, 155, 156, 157, 158, 159, 160, 161, 162, 163, 164, 165, 166, 168, 169, 170, 171, 172, 173
Metcalfe, Burt 111
Metrano, Arthur 219
Metro, George 200
Metzler, Jim 242
Mexico City, Mexico 57, 243
Meyer, Emile 69, **70**, 71
Meyer, Otto W. 85, 86, 87, 88, 90, 91, 121, 122, 155, 156, 157, 158, 159, 160, 161, 162, 163, 164, 168, 169, 170, 171, 172, 173, 176
Meyler, Fintan 87
MGM/UA Television 240
Michaelian, Katharyn 223
Michaelian, Michael 223
"Mickey Spillane's 'Velda'" (song) 61
Middleton, Polly 218
"Miguel's Daughter" (*Gunsmoke*) 87
"The Mike Hammer Theme" (song) 61
Mikell, George 229
Mikler, Michael "Mike" 156, 165
Miles, Vera 150, 192, 243, 244
Milford, John 176
Miller, Arthur 249
Miller, Ernest W. 48
Miller, Eve 51
Miller, Kenny 130
Miller, Pete 200
Miller, Ron 139
Mills, Edwin 117
Mills, John 233
Mills, Juliet 137
Mills, Mort 83
Milton, Gerald 94, 182
Mimieux, Yvette 139, **140**
Mims, William "Bill" 110, 114
Minardos, Nico 98
Minn, Michael 85
Miranda, Raul 242
Mirisch, Walter 46, 52
Mirpuri, Lolita 235
The Misadventures of Merlin Jones (film) 140
"The Misguided Father" (*Have Gun, Will Travel*) 116
Miss Kitty 75, 162
"The Missing Crime Case" (*The Lineup*) 118
"The Missing Russian Hill Matron" (*The Lineup*) 119

"The Mistake" (*Gunsmoke*) 76
Mr. Garlund (television series) 173–174
Mister Roberts (play) 248
Mitchell, Cameron 219
Mitchell, Carlyle 73, 98, 120
Mitchell, Dallas 87, 112, 114, 168
Mitchell, George 104
Mitchell, Gwenn 219
Mitchell, Steve 67, 92
Mitchell (film) 4, 20–21, 104, 143, 207–209, 218
"Mitchell" (song) 208
Mitchum, Christopher 209
Mitchum, John 71, 93, 141, 148, 166, 181, 193
Mitchum, Julie 59
Mitchum, Robert 13, 17, 24, 63, **64**, 65, 66, 141, 143, 201, 226, 227
Mitla, Mexico 57
Mobley, Mary Ann 223
Moede, Titus 182
Moffett, Hal 165
Mohawk Valley, Oregon 16
The Monkeys (book) 139
Monkeys, Go Home! (film) 4, 17, 46, 86, 93, 139, 173, 192, **196**–199
The Monkey's Uncle (film) 140
Monogram Distributing Corp. 43, 47
Monogram Pictures Corp. 10, 46, 52
Monogram Productions Corp. 47
Monogram Productions, Inc. 42
Monro, Matt 229
Monsour, Nyra 97
"Monster Mash" (song) 191
Montalban, Ricardo 191
Montana, Monte, Jr. 163
Monte Alban 57
Montell, Lisa 112
Montenegro, Hugo 152
Monument Valley 9
"Moo Moo Raid" (*Gunsmoke*) 88–89
Moon, Sun Myung 23
Mooney, Hal 218
Moore, Clayton 51, 52
Moore, Dick 42
Moore, Jacqueline 31
Moore, Joanna 91, 122
Moore, Mary Tyler 222
Moore, Norma 98
Moore, Roger 1, 22, 23, 24, 212, 214, 224, 225, 226, 229, **231**
Moorehead, Agnes 29
"The Moor's Revenge" (*The Lineup*) 106
Mor-Film Fare, Inc. 215
Morales, Esai 242
Morawcck, Lucien 114, 127, 177, 182, 186

Moreno, Rita 52
Morey, Edward, Jr. 51, 52
Morgan, Harry 218
Morgan, Red 101, 122
Morgan, Tim 196
Morgan, Tommy 171
Morin, Alberto 193
Morison, Patricia 106
Morley, John 73
Moross, Jerome 157, 176
Morricone, Ennio 232, 234
Morris, Ben 100
Morris, Frances 119
Morris, Gary 141
Morris, Jeff 221
Morrison, Robert E. 13, 14, 67, 68, 69, 71
Morrow, Byron 217
Morrow, Patricia 191
Morrow, Susan 79
Motion Picture Academy 59
Motion Picture Association of America 202
Moundsville, West Virginia 19, 201
Mount Bachelor 17
Mt. Rainier, Washington 64
MTM Enterprises 222
MTM Productions 222
Muir, Gavin 73
Muldaur, Diana 196
Mulhall, Jack 118
Mullally, Don 116
Mulqueen, Kathleen 119
Munday, Mary 183
Munson, Ona 34
Murder at the World Series (telefilm) 4, 22, 216
"Murder Warrant" (*Gunsmoke*) 83–84
Murdock, George 218
Murdock, Jim 123
Murkison, Harvey 216
Murphy, Bill 41
Murphy, William 84
Murray, Don 219
Murray, Jack 45, 50
Murray, Jan 221
Murray, Mark 169
Musuraca, Nick 118, 119
"My Brother's Keeper" (*Have Gun, Will Travel*) 177
My Son John (film) 51
Myers, Dick 127
Mystery Science Theater 3000 (television series) 209

Nagamori, Masato 235
Nagel, Conrad 162
Nakadai, Tatsuya 235
Nakamura, Henry 65
"The Naked Gun" (*Have Gun, Will Travel*) 114, 174
Napier, Alan 50
Napier, Charles 241
NASA 215

National Film Network 246
National Football League (NFL) 28, 222
National General Pictures 205
Natwick, Mildred 45
Nazarro, Ray 44, 51
NBC (television network) 20, 21, 22, 25, 41, 92, 190, 191, 192, 216, 218, 219, 220, 221, 222, 223, 240, 242
The NBC Mystery Movie (television series) 4, 20, 216–**219**
Needham, Harold "Hal" 15, 111, 112, 114, 115, 116, 133, 167, 174, 180, 184, 186, 190, 196
Nelson, Billy 119
Nelson, Burt 93
Nelson, Dick 192, 196
Nelson, Ed 83, 87, 111, 113, 125, 162, 177
Nelson, Gene 84, 86, 108, 126, 156
The Nerd (play) 249
Neuman, Sam 120, 188
Neumann, Dorothy 160, 162
Neumann, Harry 46, 51, 52
Neustaedtl, Elvira 237
"Never Help the Devil" (*Have Gun, Will Travel*) 117
Nevil, Steve 241
Nevins, Frank J. 43
New Mexico Territory 194, 195
New York Film Festival 68
Newman, Emil 50, 53, 57, 61
Newman, John 171
Newman, Melissa 152
Newport Beach, California 24
Newton, John 159
Newton, Mary 119
Newton, Robert 59
Ney, Richard 127
Nichols, Mike 172, 201
Nickolaus, John M., Jr. 125, 126, 188
The Night of the Hunter (book) 201
The Night of the Hunter (film) 178, 201
Niven, David 24, 214, 229, **231**
Nixon, Richard **20**, 195
"No Hands" (*Gunsmoke*) 169–170
"No Visitors" (*Have Gun, Will Travel*) 95–96
Nobles, Verne 238
Noel, Chantal 107
Nogales, Arizona 15, 211
Nolan, Jeanette 126, 174
Nolan, Jim 119
Nolan, Kathy 119

Nolan, Lloyd 53
Noonan, Sheila 80
Noriega, Eduardo 55
Norris, Edward 42
North, Alex 145
North, Sheree 168
Norwick, Natalie 178
"Now That April's Here" (*Gunsmoke*) 174
Ntshona, Winston 212
Nuell, Faye 95
Nugent, Frank S. 45, 46
"The #17643 Case" (*The Lineup*) 119
Nusser, James 79, 159, 160, 163, 166, 168, 169, 170, 171, 205, 207
Nuth, Jonathan 224
Nuyen, France 196
Nye, Louis 191

Oak Ridge Cemetery 74
Oakland, Simon 87, 102
Oakland Athletics 216
Oates, Warren 24, 101, 134, 155, 159, 170, 241
Oaxaca, Mexico 57
Ober, Philip 121
O'Brian, Hugh 216
O'Brien, Clay 205
O'Brien, Kenneth 221
O'Brien, Pat 61
O'Brien, Philip 224
O'Connell, Arthur 192
O'Connell, William 190
O'Connor, Carroll 145
O'Dea, Joseph 45
The Odd Couple (play) 249
"Odd Man Out" (*Gunsmoke*) 86–87
Odin, Susan 46
Odney, Doug 119
O'Donnell, Gene 76
O'Donnell, Paddy 45
Odyssey (poem) 185
"The Odyssey of Jubal Tanner" (*Gunsmoke*) 167
L'Oeil de la Veuve see *Eye of the Widow*
Offenbach, Jacques 47
O'Flynn, Damian 119
Oh, Soon-Talk 196
O'Hara, Maureen 11, **12**, 16, 45, 76, **132**, 133, 134, 137, 139, 245, 246
O'Hara, Shirley 89, 110, 130, 134, 143, 177, 221
"The O'Hare Story" (*Have Gun, Will Travel*) 74, 99–100
O'Herlihy, Dan 221
O'Herlihy, Gavan 239
Ojeda, Manuel 242
Okazaki, Bob 182
"Old Dan" (*Gunsmoke*) 160
Old Tucson, Arizona 15, 211
O'Leary, John 221
Oliver, Stephen 223
Olkewicz, Walter 241, 243
O'Loughlin, Gerald S. 216, 241

Olsen, Merlin 197, 202, 208
Olsen, Merritt 248
Olsen, Phil 197
Olson, Nancy 50
O'Malley, J. Pat 162
On Golden Pond (play) 249
On the Waterfront (film) 189
On Wings of Eagles (book) 242, 243
On Wings of Eagles (miniseries) 4, 25–26, 224, 238, 242–243
"Once a Haggen" (*Gunsmoke*) 169
100 Years of John Wayne (documentary) 247
One More Train to Rob (film) 4, 19, 20, 72, 86, 93, 173, 192, 193, **196**–199, 217
Ophuls, Max 63
Opp, Peter 120
O'Reilly, Cyril 242
Orlebeck, Les 40
Orloff, Arthur 118
Orr, Owen 238
Osborne, Bud 115
Osborne, Frances 97
Osmond, Cliff 186
Osterhage, Jeffrey **26**, 238
Othello (play) 106
"The Other Half" (*Gunsmoke*) 172
O'Toole, Ollie 159, 160, 162, 167, 170, 172, 182
Our Gang 184
Out California Way (film) 36–37, 85, 93, 184
"The Outlaw" (*Have Gun, Will Travel*) 92
Over the River and Through the Woods (play) 249
Overlander, Web 45
Overton, Frank 191
The Ox-Bow Incident (book) 13
The Ox-Bow Incident (film) 13

Padilla, Ruben 44
Page, Geraldine 12, 24, 57, 59, 241
Page, Joy 44
Paiva, Nestor 187
Paladin **91**, 94, 173, 174, 244
Paliotti, Michael 239
Pall, Gloria 99
Palladium-Rapid (production company) 226
Palmer, Gene 192
Palmer, Gregg 88, 113, 116, 164, 167, 171, 177, 193, 241
"Pancho" (*Have Gun, Will Travel*) 112
"Pandora's Box" (*Have Gun, Will Travel*) 183

Paramount Home Video 246
Paris-Underground (film) 3, 8, 32–*33*
Parish, Geoff 98
Parker, Earl 105, 119
Parker, Warren 92
Parks, Michael 24, 209, 216, 222, 224, 225, 226
Parnell, Emory 52
Parnell, Jim 92
Parrish, Julie 172
Parsons, Lydsley 42
Pascal, Milton 98
Pat Garrett and Billy the Kid (film) 212
Pate, Michael 12, 57, 59, 83, 84, 94, 125, 132, 179, 181
Patnel Productions 37, 39, 62
Patten, Luana 130
Patterson, Hank 83, 89, 102, 103, 104, 113, 122, 155, 157, 171, 181
Patterson, Herbert 116, 174
Paul, Byron 140
Paul Drake 64, 120
Paull, Morgan 200, 205, 208, 209, 215
Paxton, Richard 48
Payne, Brad 82
Peabody, Dick 164
Peck, Ed 163
Peck, Gregory 24, 214, 229, **231**, 241, 242
Peck, Steven 128
Peckinpah, Sam 22, 24, 75, 76, 79, 97, 99, 212, 227, **228**, 229
Pegasus Group (production company) 238
Penbar Productions 199, 202
"Penelope" (*Have Gun, Will Travel*) 185
Penn, Christopher 235
Pennell, Larry 110
Peppard, George 19, 20, *21*, **196**, 199, 217
Perez, Ismael 44
Perkins, Anthony 24, 224, 225
Perot, H. Ross 25, 26, 242, 243
Perreau, Gigi 173
Perrin, Vic 79, 92, 94, 171
Perry, Elizabeth 221
Perry, Jack 101
Perry, Joseph "Joe" 113, 161
Perry Mason (television series) 1, 4, 14, 57, 63, 64, 69, **120**–123, 128, 177, 188
Peters, Lauri 170
Peters, Vicky 208
Petlock, John 241
Petrie, George O. 241
Peyser, Penny 241
Philippines 26, 237
Philips, William T. 222
Phillips, Arthur 31

Phillips, Barney 83, 115
Phillips, Frank 127, 166, 167, 168, 169, 170, 171, 172, 173, 174, 175, 176, 177, 178, 179, 180, 181, 182, 183, 184, 185, 186, 187
Phillips, John 67
Phillips, Robert 208
Phipps, William 87, 162
"Phoebe" (*Gunsmoke*) 164
Piccaro, Steven 185
Pickard, John 48, 165, 173, 193
Pickens, Slim 169, 221
Pickett, Bobby 191
Pickford, Jack 131
Pickup on South Street (film) 51
Pierce, Sally 4, 14, 22
Pierson, Carl 129
Pierson, Frank R. 112, 113, 114, 174, 175, 176, 177, 178, 179, 180, 181, 182, 183
Pittack, Robert 166
"A Place for Abel Hix" (*Have Gun, Will Travel*) 183–184
Plante, Edward 222
Platt, Edward 107
Plaza, Mexico 44
Plaza Suite (play) 249
"The Pledge" (*Have Gun, Will Travel*) 115
Plummer, Dorothy 242
Plunder of the Sun (film) 11, 55–57, **56**, 105
Polk, Gordon 113
Pollis, Eunice 170
Pollock, Dee 188
Poole, Roy 218
"Poor Pearl" (*Gunsmoke*) 76
"The Posse" (*Have Gun, Will Travel*) 112, 157
Potts, Cliff 232
Poulton, Raymond 226
Powers, Stefanie 132, 246
Powers, Tom 37
"Prairie Wolfer" (*Gunsmoke*) 169
"Praise God, From Whom All Blessings Flow" (song) 136
Pratt, Judson 80, 102
"The Precious Moments" (song) 229
"The Predators" (*Have Gun, Will Travel*) 184–185
Prelude to War (documentary) 146
Preminger, Otto 74
Pressman, Lawrence 242
Price, Stephen 191
Price, Vincent 106
Priest, Pat 47
"Primer for Pioneers" (*Everglades*) 189
Prince, Robert 223

Prine, Andrew 145, 148, 162, 163, 165, 168, 193, 218, 219
"The Prisoner" (*Gunsmoke*) 162–163
Private Lives (play) 248
"The Prize Fight Story" (*Have Gun, Will Travel*) 101
Producer (book) 146
Production Code 202
Professional Films 245
"The Promoter" (*Gunsmoke*) 171
"The Prophet" (*Have Gun, Will Travel*) 114–115
"The Protégé" (*Have Gun, Will Travel*) 104
"The Proud and the Angry" (*The Lieutenant*) 190
Pryor, Ainslie 81
Psycho (film) 24
"Pucket's New Year" (*Gunsmoke*) 77
Purcell, Gertrude 32
Purdy, Stan 61
Pyle, Denver 14, 76, 77, 81, 95, 99, 106, 120, 127, 134, 148, 165, 167, 169, 191, 202, 205, 207

Quade, John 209
Qualen, John 59
Quantrill, William Clarke 52, 149
Quayle, Anthony 214
"The Quest for Asa Janin" (*Gunsmoke*) 167–168
The Quiet Man 1, 3, 10, 11, *12*, 15, 24, 29, 32, 45–46, 105, 133, 134, 245, 246
"The Quiet Man" (short story) 46
Quincy, M.E. (television series) 216
Quinn, Anthony 214
Quinn, Teddy 143
Quint Asper 155
"Quint Asper Comes Home" (*Gunsmoke*) 163
"Quint-Cident" (*Gunsmoke*) 167
Quo, Beulah 182

R.L. Lippert Pictures 50
Rabjohn, Richard 223
"The Race" (*Have Gun, Will Travel*) 179
"Rafer's Theme" (song) 212
Raine, Jack 122
Raines, Steve 82, 123
Ralston, Vera Hruba *34*, 35
Ramirez, Dario 44
Ramon Alvarez 242
Rank Film Distributors 237
Rankin, Gilman "Gil" 114, 119, 123, 161, 166
The Rare Breed (film) 4,

16–17, 82, 128, 134, 137–139, **138**, 163, 167, 177, 194, 234, 235
Rasulala, Thalmus 209
Ratoff, Gregory 8, 32
Rawhide (television series) 4, 14, 32, 41, 49, 69, 74, 100, 123–126, **124**, 128, 138, 178, 189, 218
Rawley, James 156
Ray, Don 189
Ray, Oscar 32
Raybould, Harry 164
Raymond, Guy 143, 158
Raynor, Grace 103
Raynor, Lynn 242
Rea, Peggy 95, 109, 168
Reagan, Ronald 245
Reagan, Tony 118
Real Steel (film) 28
"The Reasonable Man" (*Have Gun, Will Travel*) 97–98
Reda, Lou 241
Redd, Veronica 241
Redman, Frank 120, 121, 122, 123, 188
Redmond, Liam 162
Reed, Carol 62
Reed, Marshall 37, 164
Reed, Ralph 107, 124, 176
Reed, Richard 187
Reed, Susanne 223
Reed, Walter 67
Reese, Tom 174
Reeves, Richard 88, 159
Reflections on the Civil War (book) 241
Regal Films, Inc. 73
Regehr, Duncan 241
Reindel, Carl 168
"Renegade White" (*Gunsmoke*) 81
"The Renegades" (*Gunsmoke*) 165–166
Rennick, Nancy 189
Rennie, Michael 145
Republic Pictures 3, 8, 9, 10, 29, 30, 31, 32, 34, 35, 36, 37, 38, 39, 41, 42, 43, 44, 45, 46, 47, 53, 94, 166
Resner, Lawrence 119
Return from the River Kwai (book) 26, 235, 236
Return from the River Kwai (film) 4, 26, 147, 229, 232, 235–237
"The Return of Dr. Thackeray" (*Have Gun, Will Travel*) 101–102
"The Return of Roy Carter" (*Have Gun, Will Travel*) 109–110
"The Return of the Lady" (*Have Gun, Will Travel*) 108
"Return to Fort Benjamin" (*Have Gun, Will Travel*) 115–116
"The Revenger" (*Have Gun, Will Travel*) 179

Reynolds, Burt 14, 111, 155, 163
Rhapsody Films 246
Rhodes, Jordan 241
Rhodesia 22
Rhue, Madlyn 107
Rhys-Davies, John 232
Rich, Charlie 205
Rich, Dick 89, 111, 117
Rich, Irene 37
Richard, Darryl 127
Richardson, Ashley 237
Richardson, George 105
Richmond (producton company) 212
Ricker, Bruce 246
Ride a Violent Mile (film) 49
Ride Lonesome (film) 68
Ride the High Country(film) 76
Rigaud, George 32
Riley, Robin 107
Ring of Fear (film) 12, 39, 61–63, **62**, 105, 168
Rio Grande (film) 47, 133
Rio Lobo (film) 194
Rios, Lalo 158
Ritchie, Clint 148
Rivero, Jorge 209
Rivero, Julian 42
Riverton, Utah 146
RKO 13, 72
Road, Mike 223
"The Road" (*Have Gun, Will Travel*) 176
"The Road to Wickenberg" (*Have Gun, Will Travel*) 104
Roberson, Chuck 15, 67, 90, 132, 164, 175, 178, 179
Roberts, Arthur 43
Roberts, Lynne 35
Roberts, Roy 159, 173, 182
Roberts, Stephen "Steve" 108, 176
Roberts, William 145, 146, 196
Robertson, Cliff 145
Robin Crusoe, U.S.N. (film) 140
Robinson, Bartlett 77, 85
Robinson, Charles 134
Rock Island Trail (film) 10, 43
"Rocket to Oblivion" (*Banacek*) 217–218
Rockwell, Robert 83
Roddenberry, Gene 92, 96, 97, 103, 104, 107, 109, 111, 112, 113, 190, 191
Rodgers, Jimmie **130**, 131
Rodriguez, Alberto 242
Roehn, Franz 117
Rogell, Albert S. 31
Rogers, Joy 242
Rogers, Roy 8, **40**, 41
Rogers, Stephen 215
Rogers, Wayne 159
Roistang, Hubert 237
Roland, Gilbert 44, 45
Rolfe, Samuel "Sam" 91, 92, 93, 95, 96, 101, 102, 103, 104, 105, 106, 107, 108, 109, 110, 111, 112, 113, 114, 115, 126, 127, 242, 243
Roman, Ric 88, 107
Roman Vengeance (book) 237, 238
Roomer, Charles 55
Rooney, Wallace 164, 165, 168
Roope, Fay 82, 83, 109, 122, 124
Roope, Ray 100
Rorke, Hayden 46
Rose, Reginald 22, 212, 248, 229, 231
Rosenman, Leonard 150
Rosenthal, Laurence 221, 242
Ross, Katharine 24, 134, 150, **151**, 172, 238, 243, 244
Ross, Ralph 217
Ross, Ricco 239
Ross, Robert C. 80
Rothwell, Robert 218
Rounds, David 241
Roy, William 43
The Roy Rogers Show (television series) 41
Royce (television pilot) 21, 222
The Rubaiyat of Omar Khayyam (poem) 184
Ruben, Albert 186
Rubin, Mann 218
Rubine, Irving 102
Rudley, Herbert 100
Ruggles of Red Gap (film) 198
Rule, Janice 91
Rumors (play) 4, 249
Rumsey, Bert 76, 77, 79, 81
Rundle, Robbie 223
Ruskin, Joseph 160
Russek, Marcos 242
Russell, Don 159
Russell, Gail 37, **38**, 67
Russell, Kurt 19, 199, 218
Rust, Richard 86, 116, 156, 176, 190
Ryan, Michael 190
Ryan, Richard 121
Ryan, Tim 47
Rydell, Mark 246

Saber, David 79
The Sacketts (miniseries) 239
Sahara (film) 4, 24–25, 164, 220, 232–235, 234, 237
St. Elmo 187
Salinger, Diane 242
Salmi, Albert 202, 218
Salsedo, Frank 223
"Saludos" (*Gunsmoke*) 86
San Bernardino National Forest 129, 131
San Fernando Valley 144
San Francisco Bay 65
San Juan Community Theatre 4, 27, 248
San Juan Islands 5, 22, 248
Sande, Walter 188
Sanders, Dennis 106
Sanders, Hugh 160
Sanders, Terry 106
Sandor, Steve 196, 219
Sands, Lee 116
Sands of Iwo Jima (film) 3, **10**, 39,, 41–42, 133, 190
Sanford, Ralph 35
Santa Barbara County, California 222
Sant'Elia Fiume Rapido 146
Sargent, Joe (actor) 84
Sargent, Joseph (director) 226
Sauli, Joshua 237
Savage, Paul 127, 167
Sawyer, Connie 141
Saxe, Carl 101
Saxon, John 208
Saxon, Rolf 239
"Say Uncle" (*Gunsmoke*) 156
Sayyad, Parviz 242
"Scar Tissue" (*Hec Ramsey*) 218
Schaefer, Armand 35
Schallert, William 59, 95, 161
Scharf, Walter 34
Schifrin, Lalo 235, 237
Schiller, Wilton 98
Schmitt, Joe W. 215
Schoengarth, Russell F. 137
Schofield, Annabel 237
Schrager, Rudy 172
Schreyer, John 215
Schulberg, Budd 189
Schulberg, Stuart 189
Schwartz, Howard 102, 103, 104, 105, 111,
Schweikle, Tony 246
Scorcese, Martin 161, 247
"The Scorched Feather" (*Have Gun, Will Travel*) 107–108
Scott, Jacqueline 102, 106, 113
Scott, Morton 40
Scott, Nathan G. 37, 117, 185
Scott, Pippa 159, 177
Scott, Randolph 67, 68
Scott, Timothy 143
The Sea Wolves (film) 4, 24, 147, 229–232, **231**, 248, 242
The Sea Wolves: The Last Charge of the Calcutta Light Horse see *The Sea Wolves*
The Searchers (film) 86, 181
Seattle, Washington 28
Seay, James E. 71
Sebastian, Julio 42

Secret Service see *The Abductors*
Sedalia Trail 123
Seel, Charles 158, 197
Seelus, Achim 226
Seid, Art 123
Selander, Lesley 36, 52, 53
Selby, Sarah 170, 171
Seldes, Marian 93, 121
Selective Service System 8
Self, Edwin 222
Self, William 41
Selk, George 82, 83, 87, 90, 167
Selleck, Tom 24, **26**, 238, 246
Seltzer, Walter 209
Selzer, Milton 182
Selznick, David O. 3, 8, 29, 31
Selznick International Pictures 29
Sendrey, Albert 51
Senekal, Taks 212
Sentry, Frank 116, 158
The Serendipity Singers 141
Sergeant Steiner see *Breakthrough*
Sergel, Christopher 249
Seven, Johnny 216, 219
Seven Angry Men (film) 49
Seven Men from Now (film) 13–14, 43, 67–68, 72, 240
"Seven Men from Now" (song) 67
Sevilla, Alfred 242
The Sextant (proposed film project) 27
The Shadow Riders see *Louis L'Amour's The Shadow Riders*
Shahan, Rocky 77, 94, 123
Shakespeare 90, 106, 134
Shane (film) 59
Shannon, Harry 51, 91, 102
Shannon, Richard 99, 106, 109, 116, 160, 164
Sharp, Alex 100, 158
Sharp, Margaret 245
Sharpe, Karen 13, 59, 71, 72
Shaw, Anthony Pullen 224
Shaw, Lou 182
Shaw, Peggy 182
Shaw, William 107, 110
Shawlee, John 196
She Wore a Yellow Ribbon (film) 47
Sheets, Bud 118, 119
The Sheik (film) 234
Shelton, William R. 215
Shenandoah (film) 1, 4, 5, 16, 17, 19, 21, 24, 77, 81, 82, 86, 95, 101, 104, 111, 128, 131, 134–137, **135**, 139, 155, 166, 172, 173, 178, 191, 192, 201, 204, 215, 229, 237
Shenandoah (play) 4, 27, 248
Sheppard, Morgan 229
Sherman, George 194

Sherman, Harry R. 239
Sherman, Lennie 119
Sherman, Orville 160, 168, 169
Sherman, Richard M. 139
Sherman, Robert B. 139
Shiber, Etta 32
Shields, Arthur 45, 121
Shields, Brooke 24, 232, **234**
Shiloah, Yossef 233
Shimada, Teru 182
Shipman, Barry 37
Shipp, Mary 121
Shire, David 196
Shirley, Mercedes 95, 159
Sholdar, Mickey 170
"Shooting Stopover" (*Gunsmoke*) 156
The Shootist (film) 207
"Shootout at Hog Tooth" (*Have Gun, Will Travel*) 185
Shor, Dan 241
Shores, Richard 171
"Show of Force" (*Have Gun, Will Travel*) 94–95
Shue, Larry 249
Sibly, Jennifer 242
Sickner, William 42
"The Siege" (*Have Gun, Will Travel*) 177
"Silent Death, Secret Death" (*Have Gun, Will Travel*) 181–182
Siliphant, Sterling 243
Silke, James R. 232
Silo, Jon 175
Silva, Henry 192
Silver, Rick 179, 180
"The Silver Lady" (*Wagon Train*) 192
Silverman, Stanley H. 101
Silverstein, Ellis 198
Simcox, Tom 134, 190, 191
Simms, Jay 108, 113, 174, 186, 177, 187, 190
Simon, Neil 248, 249
Simon, Robert F. 79, 95
Simons, Col. Arthur 26, 238, 242
Simpson, Mickey 109
Simpson, Robert L. 152, 193, 196, 199, 202, 205
Sims, Warwick 241
"Sin Ella" (song) 55
Since You Went Away (film) 3, 8, **9**, 29–31
Since You Went Away: Letters to a Soldier from his Wife (book) 29, 31
"The Singer" (*Have Gun, Will Travel*) 99
singing cowboys 37, 40, 94
Singleton, Doris 164
"Sins of the Father" (*Gunsmoke*) 78
Sioux City Sue (film) 35–36
Siroloa, Joseph 168
Sitting Bull 52
Skiles, Martin 46
Skinner, Frank 134

Slate, Jeremy 145, 160, 161, 215
Slater, Barney 205
Slattery, Richard X. 170
Slocum, George 42
"Small Water" (*Gunsmoke*) 155
"Smile of a Dragon" (*The Virginian*) 191–192
Smith, Ebbe Roe 241
Smith, Hal 92
Smith, Jim B. 208
Smith, John 59, 77
Smith, K.L. 103, 165, 168
Smith, Kent 95, 166
Smith, P.L. 187
Smith, Paul 237
Smith, Wingate 10, 11
Smokey and the Bandit (film) 111
The Snoop Sisters (television series) 216
Snyder, William 139
Soble, Ron 193
Sofaer, Abraham 97, 120, 159, 193
Sokoloff, Vladimir 32, 97
"Soledad Crossing" (*Have Gun, Will Travel*) 178
"The Solid Gold Patrol" (*Have Gun, Will Travel*) 105
Somers, Brett 187
Somerville, Karen 223
"something big" (film) 4, 19, 47, 72, 77, 86, 111, 163, 164, 167, 178, 193, 201, 202–205, **203**, 218, 220
"Something to Live For" (*Have Gun, Will Travel*) 105–106
Sommerfield, Diane 241
Sondergaard, Quentin 115
Sonora, California 16
"The Sons of Aaron Murdock" (*Have Gun, Will Travel*) 110
Sony 246
Soo Yong, Madame 50
Sorenson, Paul 112, 118
Sorrentino, John 119
Soulé, Olan 101, 115, 125, 174, 182
The Sound of Music (film) 227
South Africa 6, 22, 214
Southcott, Fleet 75, 76, 77, 78, 79, 80, 81, 82, 83, 84, 85, 86, 87, 88, 89, 90, 91, 100, 101, 102, 103, 104, 112, 155, 156, 157, 158, 159, 160, 161, 162, 163, 164, 165, 189
Space, Arthur 47
Spain, Fay 73, 94, 188
Spain 26
Spalding, Harry 128, 129
Sparks, Robert 183, 184, 185, 186, 187
"Speak Me Fair" (*Gunsmoke*) 90

Special Operations Executive (SOE) 230
Spencer, Glenn 40
Spencer, Steven 242
Spencer, Tim 40
Spiegel, Sam 236–237
Spillane, Mickey 61
Springfield, Illinois 74
Spurrier, Paul 212
Spy Guise Video 245
The Spy Who Loved Me (film) 225
Stack, Robert 44, 59, **60**
Stafford, Dan 158, 166, 178, 189
Stafford, Hanley 47
Stagecoach (film) 85
Standing, John 229
Stang, Jack 61
Stanier, John 239
Stanley, Helene 112
Stanmore Productions 199, 202
Star Trek (television series) 92, 190
Star Wars (film) 22
Stark, Graham 229
Stark, Sheldon 220
Stark, William 220
Stars' War: The Flight of the Wild Geese (documentary) 245
Starz! Encore Entertainment 247
"The Statue of San Sebastian" (*Have Gun, Will Travel*) 102
Stauffer, Jack 223
Steadman, Robert 242
Steele, Mike 108
Steele, Robert "Bob" 15, 53, 98, 125, 132, 133, 134, 165, 166, 173, 202
Steele, Tom 107
Stehli, Edgar 77
Steiger, Rod 24, 226, 227
Steinberg, Betty 73
Steiner, Fred 88, 89, 158, 161, 168, 173, 175, 181, 218
Steiner, Max 29, 31
Stenger, Dick 121
Sterling, Jan 59
Sterlini, John 242
Stern, Tom 145, 241
Sterrett, Charles 90
Stevens, Craig 29
Stevens, George 7
Stevens, Leith 87, 156, 159
Stevens, Morton 221
Stevens, Naomi 97
Stevens, Onslow 83, 94
Stevens, Warren 96, 121, 187
Stevens, William 103
Stevenson, Keith 229
Stevenson, Robert (director) 51, 95
Stevenson, Robert J. (actor) 160, 161, 166, 183
Stevlingson, Ed 118
Stewart, David J. 177

Stewart, James 1, 5, 16, 17, 19, 134, **135**, 136, 137, **138**, 139, 148, 149, 199, 201, 202, 246
Stewart, Nicodemus 34
Stewart, Peggy 83, 92, 141, 159, 171, 180
Stockwell, Guy 125
Stoehr, Suzann 200
"Stolen Horses" (*Gunsmoke*) 157–158
Stone, Christopher 241
Stone, George E. 101, 120
Stone, Harold J. 80, 93, 97, 208
Stone, James 122
Stone, Milburn 75
Stone, Stan 208
Storey, Ruth 96
The Story of G.I. Joe (film) 65
Stossel, Ludwig 123
Stout, Archie J. 37, 50, 53, 57, 59
Stowaway to the Moon (telefilm) 4, 20, 85, 161, 178, 215–216
Stowaway to the Moon: The Camelot Odyssey (book) 215
Strachan, Alan 224, 235, 239, 242
La Strada (film) 63
Stradling, Harry, Jr. 199, 202, 208
Strange, Glenn 159, 162, 163, 164, 166, 169, 170, 171
"Strange Vendetta" (*Have Gun, Will Travel*) 93–94
Stratton, Gil, Jr. 47, 48
Stratton-Porter, Gene 128, 129
Straw Dogs (film) 212
Strenge, Walter 192
Strickland, Amzie 125
Strong, Robert 75
Stroud, Don 143
Strudwick, Shepherd 115
Stuart, Wendy 83
Sturges, John 146
Sturlin, Ross 186
Stuthman, Fred 241
Styner, Jerry 208
Sullivan, Bill 208
Sullivan, Francis L. 55
Sullivan, Liam 78
Sully, Frank 42
Summer, Jerry 187
"The Summons" (*Gunsmoke*) 161–162
"Sundance and the Blood Money" (*Hotel de Paree*) 127
"Sundance and the Greenhorn Trader" (*Hotel de Paree*) 127
"Sundance and the Long Trek" (*Hotel de Paree*) 127
Sundberg, Clinton 96
Sundrey, Irma 178

Support Your Local Sheriff (film) 198
Sutherland, Edward 67, 71
Sutherland, Everett 112, 113, 114, 115, 117, 118, 174, 175, 177, 178, 180, 181, 182, 183, 185, 186, 187
Sutorius, James 242
Suymonds, Robert 241
Swain, Jack 189
Swan, Robert 224
Swan, William 97
Swanton, Harold 143
Sweet, Tom 184
Swegles, Lewis 74
Swenson, Karl 102, 109
Swenson, Karly 177
Switzer, Carl 53, 59, 63
Swoger, Harry 156

Taeger, Ralph 194
"The Taffeta Mayor" (*Have Gun, Will Travel*) 106–107
Taft Entertainment 242
Tait, Don 196
Takahashi, Esushi 235
Takei, George 235
The Taking of Pelham One Two Three (film) 226
Talbot, Gloria 159
The Tall T (film) 68
Talman, William 120, 143, 176, 177, 188
Talton, Alix 96
Tamburro, Charles 208
Tamimi, Sargon 235
The Taming of the Shrew (play) 134
Tannen, Charles 104
Tansman, Alexandre 32
Tapscott, Mark 107
Tarantino, Quentin 246
"Target" (*Gunsmoke*) 85
Tate, Nick 235
Tayback, Victor 127
Taylor, Buck 185, 191
Taylor, Dub 148, 154
Taylor, Eric 50
Taylor, Robert 161
Teague, Marshall 238, 243
Teal, Ray 193
Tegland, Archie L. 117, 183
television Westerns 1, 41, 205
Temple, Shirley 8, **9**, 29
Tenafly (television series) 216
"The Tender Gun" (*Have Gun, Will Travel*) 174–175
Terrell, Steven 80, 93
Terry, Tex 40, 107
Tesler, Jack 176
Tetrick, Bob 103
Tetzel, Joan 81
Thacher, Russell 209
Thackeray, Bud 37
Thatcher, Margaret 234
Thayer, Lorna 114, 115, 128, 174, 183
Thayler, Carl 73

"There Was Never a Horse" (*Gunsmoke*) 84
Thinnes, Roy 165
Thirteen/WNET (television station) 247
Thomas, Jerome B. 190
Thomas, Jerry 47
Thomas, Peter 226
Thomas, Scott 223
Thomas, Steve 126
Thomason, Harry 241
Thompson, Ernest 249
Thompson, Hilarie 218
Thompson, J. Lee 231
Thompson, Robert E. 115, 162, 175, 176, 179, 180, 182, 185
Thompson, Russ 188
Thompson, Stuart 105, 106, 107, 108, 109, 110, 118
Thordsen, Kelly 191
Thorsen, Russ 96
"Three Bells to Perdido" (*Have Gun, Will Travel*) 91–92
3-D 58–59
3 Godfathers (film) 86, 207
"The Three Million Dollar Piracy" (*Banacek*) **21**, 217
"Three Sons" (*Have Gun, Will Travel*) 101
Thunderbirds (film) 11
Thurston, Carol 92, 125
Tiomkin, Dimitri 59, 61
Tischler, Stanford 189
Titanic (film) 28
To Kill a Mockingbird (play) 249
"To Take Up Serpents" (*The Lieutenant*) 190–191
Tobey, Kenneth 61, 169, 188
Tokyo 22
Toluca, Mexico 243
Tombragel, Maurice 139, 140
Tombstone, Arizona 15
Tommy Dorsey Band 169
Tompkins, Bee 166
Tong, Kam 91, 117, 191, 192
Tonge, Philip 63
Toomey, Regis 53
Torn, Rip 190, 241
Torres, Gabriel 220
Torrey, Roger 170
"Tour of Duty" (*The Lieutenant*) 191
The Towering Inferno (film) 233
Towers, Constance 242
Townes, Harry 98
Townsley, Herman 152
The Track of the Cat (book) 13, 63
Track of the Cat (film) 13, 63–65, **64**, 65, 72, 194
Tracy, Spencer 61
"Trail of Danger" (*Wonderful World of Disney*) 219, 220

The Train Robbers (film) 194
Trapeze (film) 62–63
"The Trappers" (*Gunsmoke*) 164
Travis McGee 244
Travis McGee (television pilot) 24, 172, 192, 243–244
"The Treasure" (*Have Gun, Will Travel*) 185–186, 220
Trent, Russell 126
Trevey, Ken 221
Trevor, Claire 59
Triesault, Ivan 123
Trigger 41
Tripp, Paul 183
Triston and Isolde 22
Trivers, Barry 181
Troupe, Tom 145
Truax, Louise 120
Truckee, California 55
Trueblood, Guerdon 21, 209, 211
Trumbull, Brad 111
Tucker, Forrest 41, 42, 43, 193
Tucson, Arizona 15, 133, 211
Tully, Tom 118
Turley, Jack 217
Turner, Moira 158
Turner Classic Movies 246
Twelve Angry Men (play) 248
Twentieth Century–Fox 17, 18, 19, 21, 74, 129, 131, 133, 148, 150, 152, 154, 209, 212
"Twenty-Four Hours at North Fork" (*Have Gun, Will Travel*) 102
"The Twins" (*Have Gun, Will Travel*) 117–118
"Two of a Kind" (*Gunsmoke*) 166
Two Rode Together (film) 149, 181

UCLA Film and Television Archive 44, 68
Ullman, Dan 46, 51, 52
Umeki, Miyoshi 191
"Uncle Oliver" (*Gunsmoke*) 80
Uncle Vanya (play) 248
The Undefeated (film) 1, 4, 5, 18–19, 47, 77, 86, 90, 111, 128, 147, 149, 152–**154**, 163, 171, 178, 198, 201, 204, 215, 238, 243
"The Uneasy Grave" (*Have Gun, Will Travel*) 177–178
"The Unforgiven" (*Have Gun, Will Travel*) 113
Unger, Kurt 26, 235, 237
The Unholy Three (film) 6
Unification Church 23
United Artists 17, 31, 71, 134, 143, 148, 189, 232

Universal City 144
Universal Pictures 16, 17, 134, 137, 139, 143, 144, 145, 150, 152, 196, 199, 226
Universal Television 20
University of Virginia 3, 7
"Unwanted Deputy" (*Gunsmoke*) 89
Urecal, Minerva 40
"Us Haggens" (*Gunsmoke*) 165
U.S. Civil War 52, 131, 136, 188, 192, 241
Utah National Guard 146

Vadis, Dan 205
Valderon, Pierre 235
Valentine, Karen 216
Valentine, Nancy 114
Valentino, Rudolph 233
Vallin, Rick "Ric" 42, 100
Van Cleef, Lee 185, 187
Vandis, Tito 217
Van Dyke, Jerry 132
Van Enger, Richard L. 31, 41, 44
Vanguard Films, Inc. 29
Van Husen, Dan 229
Van Patten, Dick 125, 218
Van Patten, Joyce 202, **203**, 219
Van Scoyk, Robert 217
Van Zandt, Julie 78
Varela, Nina 88
Vari, John 163
Various Entertainment Trading Co. 212, 245
Vars, Henry 67, 71, 128, 129, 199
Vaughn, Robert 190, 241
Vendell, Veronique 226
Ventura, California 244
Ventura Harbor 244
Veracruz, Mexico 57
Verne, Jules 175
Vernon, John 196, 241
Victor, David 123
Victory Films 212
Vidor, Leslie 75, 76, 77, 78, 79, 80, 82, 83, 84, 92, 98, 101
Vienna 229
Viet Cong 153
"The Vigil" (*Have Gun, Will Travel*) 178
Vignon, Jean-Paul 145
Villareal, Julio 55
Vincent, June 94, 95
Vincent, Michael 152
Vincent, Russ 40
Vincent, Virginia 123
The Virginian (television series) 41, 191–192
Vittes, Louis 78, 188, 189
Voldstad, John 241
von Beltz, Brad 109, 115
von Homburg, Wilhelm 171
Von Zerneck, Peter 241

"The Vortex" (*The Fantastic Journey*) 223
Vye, Murvyn 96

"The Wager" (*Have Gun, Will Travel*) 106
Wages, David 221
Wagner, Max 122
"Wagon Girls" (*Gunsmoke*) 161
Wagon Master (film) 47, 86
Wagon Train (television series) 41
Wahl, Ken 239
Wake of the Red Witch (film) 13
Walberg, Garry 166
Wald, Marvin 99
Waldis, Otto 121, 177
Walker, Robert 29, 31
Walker, Scott 205
Wallace, Art 191
Wallace, George 168
Wallace, Helen 35
Wallace, Irving 105
Walsh, Maurice 45, 46
Walt Disney (television series) 219
Walt Disney Presents (television series) 219
Walt Disney Productions 139, 219
Walt Disney's Wonderful World of Color (television series) 219
Walter, Jessica 20, **219**
Walters, Nancy 160
Walton, Col. George 145, 146
Wander, Ray 73
Wandsworth Common 3, 5
Wang, Gene 121, 122
Wanger, Walter 51, 52, 53
"The War Called Peace" (*The Lieutenant*) 190
The War Wagon (film) 152
"The Warden" (*Gunsmoke*) 171–172
Ware, Midge 188
Warner Bros. 51, 55, 57, 59, 61, 63, 65, 66, 68, 196, 207, 245
Warner Bros. Television 22, 243
Warren, Charles Marquis 11, 48, 49, 75, 76, 77, 78, 123, 125, 126, 188
Warren, Jennifer 221
Warren, Sonia 118
Warren, Steve 158, 177
Waters, James 99
Watkin, Pierre 34, 35, 120
Watson, Jack 145, 212, 224, 229, 231
Watson, Morey 229
Watts, Robert 217
The Way West (film) 4, 17, 46, 64, 82, 83, 86, 93, 114, 128, 141–143, **142**
The Way West (book) 141, 143
Wayland, Len 241

Wayne, Aissa 65, 132
Wayne, John 1, 3, 5, 8, 9, **10**, 11, **12**, 13, 15, 17, **18**, 19, **20**, 24, **34**, 35, 37, **38**, 39, 41, 42, 44, 45, **50**, 51, 53, **54**, 55, 57, **58**, 59, **60**, 61, 62, 65, **66**, 67, 72, 77, 90, **132**, 133, 134, 150, **151**, 152, 153, **154**, 193, 194, 195, 196. 205, **206**, 207, 240, 246, 247
Wayne, Michael A. 15, 19, 131, 133, 205
Wayne, Patrick 132, 133, 134
Wayne-Fellows Productions 3, 11, 39, 50, 51, 53, **54**, 55, 57, 59, 61, 63, 72, 105, 160, 168, 194
"We Almost Lost Hawaii to the Reds" (article) 51
Weatherwax, Paul 127
Weaver, Dennis **16**, 155
Weaver, Doodles 185, 221
Webb, Jack 118
Webb, Richard 41
Webb, Roy 31, 63, 65
Webber, Peggy 79
Wee Willie Winkie (film) 7
Welch, Raquel **148**, 167
Weldon, Johan 99
Welles, Mel 104
Welles, Orson 158
Wellman, Maggie 216, 241, 242, 243
Wellman, Michael 59, 246
Wellman, William A. 1, 3, 11, 13, 53, 55, 59, 61, 62, 63, 64, 65, **66**, 84, 86, 194, 202, 242
Wellman, William "Bill," Jr. 84, 112, 114, 117, 160, 161, 182, 241, 242
Wells, Terry 212
Wendell, Bruce 126
Wendell, Howard 169
Werle, Barbara 137
West, Martin 128, 176, 183
West Los Angeles 3
West Virginia State Penitentiary 201
Westbook, John 224
Westcoatt, Rusty 103
Western, Johnny 101, 102
Weston, Brad 115, 177
Westward the Women (film) 161
Wexler, Paul 78, 80
What Ever Happened to Baby Jane? (film) 7
What Price Glory? (film) 6
"What the Whiskey Drummer Heard" (*Gunsmoke*) 79
"When Love is Young" (song) 129, 131
White, Carol 202
White, Christine 100, 104
White, David 114
White, Edward J. 39
White, Larry 241

White, William 190
Whitman, Chris 162
Whitman, Gayne 50
Whitman, Jack 238, 243
Whitman, Stuart 67, 77, 98
Whitney, Cece 162
Whitney, Peter 78, 86, 98, 158, 175
Whittlesey House (publisher) 31
"Who Lives by the Sword" (*Gunsmoke*) 80
Whyte, Patrick 52
Widmark, Richard 17, 141, 143
Wiensko, Bob 89
Wightman, Robert 242
Wilcox, Frank 121
Wilcox, Larry 209, 220, 239
Wilcoxon, Henry 221
The Wild Bunch (film) 76, 212
The Wild Geese (book) 212, 214
The Wild Geese (film) 4, 5, 22–23, 24, **25**, 26–27, 43, 147, 193, 212–215, 225, 231, 237, 238, 245, 248
Wild Stallion (film) 11, 46–47, 167
Wilder, Billy 158
Wilder, Margaret Buell 29, 31
Wilk, Eileen 114
Wilke, Robert 48, 69, 71, 86, 88, 89, 98, 107, 114, 115–116, 170
Willard, Ellen 184
William Morrow (publisher) 243
Williams, Adam 98, 159
Williams, Brook 212
Williams, Elmo 48
Williams, Johnny 137
Williams, Pat 215
Williamson, Tony 226
Williford, Ray 188
Willingham, Noble 241
Willock, Dave 168
Wills, Chill 15, 43, 130, 131, 132, 164, 165, 218
Wilson, Anthony 182, 191, 217
Wilson, G.K. 139
Wilson, Lambert 232
Wilson, Terry 192
Wincelberg, Shimon 102, 105, 108, 112, 113, 114, 115, 116, 175, 176, 178, 180, 185
"Winchester Quarantine" (*Have Gun, Will Travel*) 92–93
Windom, William 165, 199, 220
Windsor, Marie 125, 196, 205, 207
Winfield, Paul 241
Wings (film) 11

The Wings of Eagles (film) 133, 181
Winitsky, Alex 226
Winters, Roland 42
Wiseman, Joseph 216
"With a Smile" (*Gunsmoke*) 166
Withers, Grant 34, 35, 43, 77, 92, 96, 101, 122
Witney, Michael 141
Witney, William 39
Wolger, Ken 205
Wolper, David L. 145, 146, 147
Wolper Pictures, Ltd. 145
The Wonderful World of Disney (television series) 22, 219–220
Wood, Allen 177
Wood, David 224
Wood, Lynn Teri 222
Woodell, Barbara 46
Woods, Craig 37
Woods, Harry 80
Woodson, William 187
Woodward, Bob 185
Wooley, Sheb 48, 123
Woolley, Monty 29
Wooster, Arthur 235, 237
Worden, Hank 15, 37, 193
Woringer, Bernard 139, **140**
World War I 5, 11
World War II 8, 9, 24, 26, 31, 51, 55, 214, 227, **231**, 236
Wright, Ben 87, 109, 122, 161, 165, 166, 176, 177
Wright, Howard 165
Wright, Teresa 63
Wyenn, Than 81, 102
Wyler, Gretchen 145
Wynant, H.M. 159
Wynn, Keenan 29

Yamaji, Setsuko 182
Yang, C.K. 196
A Yankee Dared: A Romance of Our Railroads (novel) 43
Yates, Herbert J. 8, 35, **38**
York, Elizabeth 87, 109, 110
Young, Buck 97, 127, 157, 161, 208
Young, Carleton G. 120, 122
Young, David 221
Young, Richard 221, 237
Young, Tony 188
Young, Victor 41, 44, 45
Young Eagles (film) 11
Yule, Ian 212
"The Yuma Treasure" (*Have Gun, Will Travel*) 96
Yung, Victor Sen 119

Zacha, W.T. 223
Zinnemann, David 17
Zinnemann, Fred 17
Zorro (television series) 140
Zuckert, William 163
Zuniga, Albert J. 217